DICKSON COUNTY TENNESSEE

County and Circuit Court Minutes, 1816–1828

and

Witness Docket

Abstracted by

Carol Wells

HERITAGE BOOKS
2014

HERITAGE BOOKS
AN IMPRINT OF HERITAGE BOOKS, INC.

Books, CDs, and more—Worldwide

For our listing of thousands of titles see our website at
www.HeritageBooks.com

Published 2014 by
HERITAGE BOOKS, INC.
Publishing Division
5810 Ruatan Street
Berwyn Heights, Md. 20740

Copyright © 1993 Carol Wells

All rights reserved. No part of this book may be reproduced or transmitted in any form or by any means, electronic or mechanical, including photocopying, recording or by any information storage and retrieval system without written permission from the author, except for the inclusion of brief quotations in a review.

International Standard Book Numbers
Paperbound: 978-1-55613-835-5
Clothbound: 978-0-7884-9041-5

TABLE OF CONTENTS

FOREWORD v

COURT MINUTES
    March 1816 1
    September 1816 4
    March 1817 8
    September 1817 10
    February 1818 13
    August 1818 14
    February 1819 19
    August 1819 23
    March 1820 27
    September 1820 31
    March 1821 35
    September 1821 41
    March 1822 46
    October 1823 50
    January 1824 59
    April 1824 67
    July 1824 75
    October 1824 79
    January 1825 84
    April 1825 90
    July 1825 96
    October 1825 103
    January 1826 108
    April 1826 115
    July 1826 121
    October 1826 127
    January 1827 134
    April 1827 141
    July 1827 150
    October 1827 157
    January 1828 164
    April 1828 171
    July 1828 177

WITNESS DOCKET 187

INDEX 199

FOREWORD

The County and Circuit Court Minutes abstracted in this book are new to family historians. So untouched for the last 170 years that the pages have never been numbered, these minutes open to us new insights on life in Dickson County in the early 1800s. Questions about family relationships may be answered by paternity suits; relatives may be found when orphans are given guardians or impoverished folk are provided with care-givers. Neighbors are named when road hands are listed. Bond securities reveal meaningful names.

These minutes were transcribed from microfilm. Every name written in the original minutes is in this book. Since the Justices of the Peace who wrote so long ago used their own spelling and handwriting, today's reader must use imagination when searching the index to allow for misinterpretations. An uncrossed letter t may look like the letter l. Hastily-written u and n look alike. R and s can be confused. Middle initials have a likelihood of being wrong. Example: the surname Crow may really be Cross; Bosley may be Boxley; Gilmore, Gilman, and so forth. Consult the original when in doubt.

Paragraphs of conventional wording describing the proving of deeds of conveyance now appear as a single line giving names of vendor, vendee, and witnesses. Similarly, a paper of writing purporting to be the last will and testament is shortened to the single word Will. And so forth with other documents.

Please read the entire page on which a name appears. Having made the arduous trip to Charlotte for the Court session, our ancestors often transacted more than one item of business.

Carol Wells

MARCH 1816

At a Circuit Court begun and held for the County of Dickson, State of Tennessee at the Courthouse in Town of Charlotte on the first Monday in March, fourth day of said month, Year of Our Lord one thousand Eight hundred and Sixteen, the 40 year of our Independance of the United States of America.
Present the Honorable Nathaniel W Williams Esquire Judge

After Proclamation duly made the Sheriff of this County made return of the Venire Facias to him directed from Worshipfull county court of Pleas and quarter Sessions, that he had summoned the following to serve as Jurors at this Term. Mathew Crumpler, James Douglass, Francis S Ellis, Chris^r Robertson, Andrew Moody, John Crague, Thomas Simmons, Clabourne Harris, Lewis Ragan, David Shropshire, Wm Goodwin, Thomas Bullian, Jeremiah Pearsall, Wm Parker, John May, David Hogan, David Curry, George Powel, Thomas Napier, Nehemiah Hardy, Thomas Mitchell, Pleasant Crews, Charles Teal, Jno Mitchell, Robert Weakly, Benjn Williams

p.2 Of whom grand Jury David Hogan Foreman, James Douglass, Jno Mitchell, Mathew Crumpler, George Powel, Thomas Simmons, Lewis Ragan, David Shropshire, Thos Mitchell, Thomas Napier, Robert Weakley, David Curry, Nehemiah Hardy. William Adams, a constable sworn to attend them

Ordered Christopher Robertson be discharged from further attendance at this term. Francis S Ellis discharged from further attendance at this term
Court adjourned untill to Morrow Morning 9 Oclock

p.3 Tuesday Morning 5th March 1816 Present Nathaniel W Williams Esquire, Judge.

State vs Elias W Napier. Rape. Appeared Elias W Napier late of Dickson County indicted for a rape on Body Rachel Wells, pleads not guilty. Continued

State vs Charles Williams. Indictment. Returned to consider of further Presentment

p.4 State vs Acles Strowd. Grand Jury Indictment ag^t Acles Strownd(sic) returned to consider of further Presentment.

State vs Joseph Hamilton. Grand Jury Indictment against Joseph Hamilton returned to consider of further Presentment

State vs Alby Harris. Grand Jury Bill of Indictment against Alby Harris returned to consider of further presentment

MARCH 1816

Sterling Brewer vs Montgomery Bell. Parties by attorneys. Jury Andrew Moody, Jn⁰ Craig, William Goodwin, Thoˢ Bullian, p.5 William Parker, Jn⁰ May, Benjⁿ Williams, Samuel Sparks, William Tatom, John McAdoo, Jesse May, Edmond Howard. Court Adjourned untill to morrow morning 9 oclock.

Wednesday morning March 6th 1816. Present the Honorable Nathaniel W Williams Esquire Judge

State vs Elias W Napier. Defendant appeared in open Court. Cause continued untill next term

Sterling Brewer vs Montgomery Bell. Parties by attʸˢ. Jury p.6 Andrew Moody, Jn⁰ Craig, Wᵐ Goodwin, Thomas Bullian, Wᵐ Parker, Jn⁰ May, Benjⁿ Williams, Samˡ Sparks, Wᵐ Tatom, John McAdoo, Jesse May, Edmund Howard who find in favour of Plᵗᶠ and assess his damages to 491 dollars 51 1/3 cents. Cause adjourned to next Superior Court of Errors

Samuel Vance vs Thomas Napier. Debt. Parties by attʸˢ. Jury Robert Mason, Jesse Russell, Wᵐ Edward, Aaron Vanhook, John Choate, Eleazor Smith, Hodge Adams, Daniel Leach, Jn⁰ Kelly, Wᵐ Morrisett, Daniel Coldman, Benjⁿ Clark, who find for plᵗᶠ his debt 570 Dollars 65½ cts also 26 Dollars 39 cents damage sustained by detention of debt from time it became due to 4 October 1815 p.7 besides his costs. Plᵗᶠ to recover agᵗ defᵗ, also agᵗ Henry A Napier & George F Napier his security 575 Dollars 65½ cts the debt in the declaration mentioned as also 26 Dollars 39 cts damage afˢᵈ as also 12½ cts interest

State vs Elias W Napier. Recognizance nine thousand dollars, to appear and answer indictment for rape on Rachel Wells

p.8 State vs Elias W Napier. Appearance bond of Montgomery Bell, Richᵈ C Napier, Danˡ H Williams, Joseph Williams, Thoˢ Simpson, David Hogan, Ge⁰ Hays, Francis Ellis, John C Read, & Nehemiah Scott, condition Elias W Napier personally appear before Judge first Tuesday after first Monday in September

p.9 State vs Charles Williams. Chaˢ Williams late of Dickson indictment larceny, plead not guilty. Jury Robᵗ Mason, Jesse Russell, William Edwards, Aaron Vanhook, Jn⁰ Choate, Eleazor Smith, Hodge Adams, Daniel Leech, John Kelly, Wᵐ Morrisett, Daniel Coldman, Benjamin Clark who find Defendant guilty

State vs Charles Williams. On Motion, ordered a new trial be had at next term

p.10 State vs Charles Williams. Appearance bond Acles Strowd

MARCH 1816

& William Allen, 250 Dollars each, condition they personally appear to give evidence behalf the State ag^t Chas Williams

State vs Charles Williams. Appearance bond 500 Dollars

p.11 State vs William Ward. A.B. Indictment.

p.12 Benjamin Andrews vs Elias W Napier. Cause is referred to award of Sterling Brewer which is to be judgment of Court

Robert Thompson vs Jacob Garrison. Cause is adjourned to the Superior Court of Errors

Jemimah Gower vs Elish Gower. Petition for divorce. Order copy of petition issue to defendant in Davidson County

p.13 United States vs James Walker. Order U.S. have judgment against Walker 67 Dollars 20 c^{ts} debt, damage 6 Doll^s 36 c^{ts}

United States vs James Walker. Order U.S. have judgment ag^t
p.14   Walker 99 Dollars 36 c^{ts} debt, damage 3 Doll^s 36 c^{ts}

State vs Joseph Hamilton. Larceny. Pleads not guilty. Jury Andrew Moody, Jno Craig, Wm Goodwin, p.15 Thomas Bullian, John May, Benjamin Williams, Pleasant Cruise, David McAdoo, Jehugh Stewart, John Lauber(?), Wm Stands, Wm Adams who find defendant guilty. Def^t by attorney moves judgm^t be arrested.

State vs Joseph Hamilton. Bond, Robt Weakley & Wilson Blount
p.16   condition Joseph Hamilton personally appear Sept Term

State vs Joseph Hamilton. Appearance bond one thousand doll^s

p.17 Thomas W Frazier vs Edward Williams. Parties by att^{ys}. Cause adjourned to Circuit Court of Montgomery County
Court adjourned untill to morrow morning 9 OClock

Thursday morning March 7th 1816   Present the Honorable Nathaniel W Williams, Esquire, Judge

p.18   Deed of conveyance Howel Adams to Jesse Strowd 150 acres on Turn Bull Creek proven by David Hogan & John Craig

State vs Acles Strowd.   Bond of Acles Stroud, one thousand dollars, condition his personal appearance September Court

p.19 State vs Acles Strowd. Jesse Strowd and Thomas Johnson bond, condition Acles Strowd make personal appearance Court

SEPTEMBER 1816

p.20 State vs Wilson Blount. Appearance bond 1,000 dollars

State vs Wilson Blount.   Francis S Ellis and Robert Weakley
p.21   bond, 500 dollars each, condition Wilson Blount personally appear September Court
Court adjourned untill Court in Course.   Nath W Williams

p.22   Circuit Court, Dickson County, in town of Charlotte, first Monday September 1816. Present the Honorable Bennett Searcy, Esquire, Judge

Jury Wm Terner, Andrew Caldwell, Edward Lucas, Henry Harden, Moses Parker, Michael Robertson, Esaph Parker, Aquilla Mc-Crackin, Wm Drainess(?), Nathan Nall, Alexander Chisenchall, James McKee, James Robertson, Alexander Dickson, Robt West, Daniel Williams, Jeremiah Pearsall, Charles Thompson, Thomas Kee, John Young, John H Humphreys, John Jourdon

p.23 Grand Jury Jere^h Pearsall, John Young, Thos Kee, Alex^r Chisenchall, James Robertson, Chas Thompson, Alexander Dickson, James McKee, John Jourdon, Daniel William, Michael Robertson, Andrew Caldwell, John H Humphreys
William Adams, constable, sworn to attend the Grand Jury

Juror Henry Harden discharged from further attendance. Juror Wm Turner discharged from further attendance this Term

Three deeds from Little Berry Matlock to Reuben Chambers ten acres each, lying on Harrisons Creek that emties into Duck River proven by Andrew Moody and Hardy Chambers

p.24   Deed Little Berry Matlock to Reuben Chamber 20 acres Harrisons Creek proven by Andrew Moody and Hardy Chambers

Deed John Larkins Senr to Richard C Napier 3 tracts on four mile fork of Jones Creek acknowledged in open court

Deed John Larkins Senr to Richard C Napier 28 acres 70 poles on Four mile fork of Jones Creek ack^d in open court

Robert P Dunlap Esqr admitted as an attorney at Law to practice at this Court
Court adjourned untill to morrow morning nine OClock

p.25 Tuesday morning September 3rd 1816. Present the Honble

SEPTEMBER 1816

Bennett Searcy Esquire Judge

State vs Elias W Napier. Solicitor general to prosecute no further; defendant to recover ag^t State the cost of s^d suit

State vs Nancy Coldman. Solomnly called to give evidence on behalf the State against Elias W Napier, came not. State to recover 125 Dollars against defendant

State vs Rachel Wills. Solicitor general on part of State, deft solomnly called to give evidence behalf State agt Elias W Napier came not. State to recover against defendant Rachel p. 26   Wells one hundred twenty five Dollars

State vs Charles Williams. Solomnly called, came not. Recognizance forfeited

State vs Joseph Hamilton. Solemnly called, came not. Recognizance forfeited

p.27   State vs Wilson Blount and Robert Weakley. Solomnly called to bring Joseph Hamilton in Court, but came not. Recognizance of said Defendants forfeited

State vs Wilson Blount. Solomnly called, came not. Recognizance forfeited.

State vs Francis S Ellis and Robert Weakley. Solomnly called to bring Wilson Blount, came not p.28 Recognizance forfeited

State vs Acles Straud. After Proclamation duly made, defendant came not. Recognizance forfeited.

State vs Thomas Johnson, Jesse Straud. Def^{ts} solomnly called to bring Acles Straud, came not. Recognizance forfeited.

p.29   Raworth & Beddle vs Benjamin M Pryor & his securities. Parties by att^{ys}. Agreeable to Order of September Term 1815, suit referred to award of Jesse S Ross, Francis S Ellis, and Christopher Robertson, who find for plaintiff 898 Dollars 10 2/3 cts. Pl^{tfs} have recovered 387 Dollars 27 c^{ts}. Therefore pl^{tfs} to recover against def^t & John Barnard, Joseph Wingate & John Read his securities 410 Doll^s 83 2/3 c^{ts} and interest thereon from 9 September 1815 as also costs of their suit

State vs Aaron Fletcher. The Clerk of Stewart County to send a more compleat record of this suit

p.30   Frances Schmidt vs Edward Teal admr. Parties by attys. Jury Marble Stone, John Capling, Tandy Russell, Elias Abney,

SEPTEMBER 1816

Nathan Norman, Isaac Johnson, Robert Weakley, Cary Wiggins, John Hall, John May, Elisha Simmons, Nathan Kell who do find for plaintiff twenty Dollars ninety five cents

State vs Acles Straud. Forfeiture of def^t and his securities Thomas Johnson & Jesse Straud be remited on payment of debt

p.31 State vs Wilson Blount. Forfeiture of deft & securities Francis S Ellis and Robert Weakley be remitted on payment of the cost. Blount and Jesse Blount pay cost of his securities

State vs William Ward. AB. Defendant pled Guilty. Fined 10 Dollars and cost of suit

State vs Acles Straud. Appearance bond 1000 Dollars

p.--. State vs Acles Straud. Bond of Wm Adams & John Johnson for appearance of Acles Straud at March Court

State vs Aaron Fletcher. Appearance bond of John Scott and Philip Hornbarger; said Scott's and Hornbarger's appearance p.--. at March Court on behalf State against Aaron Fletcher

State vs Wilson Blount. Appearance bond of Wilson Blount to answer State on a bill of Indictment at March Court

p.--. State vs Wilson Blount. Bond of Jiles Jones & Nathan Norman, condition Wilson Blount appear at March Court

Deed Michael Molton to Thomas Ellis 316 acres ackd
Deed Edward Pearsall to William Balthrop 260 acres ackd
Deed Hardy Valentine to John Hunter 103 acres ackd
Court Adjourned untill to morrow morning nine OClock

                                       B Searcy

p.--. Wednesday morning September 4th 1816. Present the Honorable Bennett Searcy Esquire Judge

State vs Aaron Fletcher. Ordered Aaron Fletcher be taken into custody of Sheriff. The gaol of this County insufficient for safekeeping of prisoners, Order sd Aaron be remanded to Robertson County gaol, unless Aaron give security in sum 600 Dollars. Bond of Aaron Fletcher to appear at March Court

p.--. Willie Barrow Lessee vs William McClure and James McMurtry. Parties by att^{ys}. Jury Jeremiah Pearsall, Jno Young, Alex^r Chizanhall, Ja^s Robertson, Chas Thompson, Alex^r Dickson, Jno Jourdan, Daniel Williams, Michael Robertson, Andrew Calwell, Nathan Nall, Roser Brown who are permitted disperse

SEPTEMBER 1816

untill to morrow.
Court adjourns untill to morrow morning nine OClock

B Searcy

p.--. Thursday morning September 5th 1816 Present the Honorable Bennett Searcy Esquire Judge

Willie Barrow Lessee vs William McClure and James McMurtry. Ejectment. [Jury above, except Calwell now spelled Caldwell] Find def^t guilty of trespass of ejectment as pl^{tf} alledged; assess pl^{tf}'s damage to one Cent. Pl^{tf} to recover his term yet to come in the premises together with his cost of suit

p.--. Willie Barrow Lessee vs William McClure and James McMurtry. Motion for new trial. Defendants by attorneys
Court adjourned untill tomorrow morning nine OClock

B Searcy

p.--. Fryday morning September 6th 1816. Present the Honorable Bennett Searcy Esquire Judge

Henry Jones vs Montgomery Bell. Parties by att^{ys}. Jury Jeremiah Pearsall, John Young, Alexander Chezanhall, Ja^s Robertson, Charles Thompson, Alexander Dickson, John Jourdan, Danl Williams, Michael Robertson, Andrew Caldwell, Nathan Nall, Thomas Hay who find for pl^{tf}, assess his damage to 595 Doll^s 55 cents. Pl^{tf} to recover besides his cost of suit

p.--. Francis Schmtts vs Edward Teal admr. Motion for a new trial. Ordered Defendants motion be for naught.

Jemima Gower vs Elisha Gower. Petition for Divorce. Pl^{tf} by her attorney. Defendant came not. Return next Term

Joseph Kimbell vs William P Hardon. Return next Term

p.--. Willie Barrow lessee vs Robert Wilson. Ejectment. Def^t confesses guilt as in pl^{tfs} declaration. Pl^{tf} to recover his term yet to come and one half of court costs & attendance of witnesses except Abraham Estes which pl^{tf}'s lessee pays, and the pl^{tf} to pay other half of the court costs

Willie Barrow lessee vs William McClure and James McMurtry. Motion for a new trial. Defendants motion overRuled

p.--. Grand Jury and Petit Jury discharged

Thomas Watson vs James A Russell. Parties by att^{ys} agree to

MARCH 1817

dismiss suit, defendant paying cost

Willie Barrow lessee vs James McCrory. Agreeable to rule at September Term 1814 agreed by parties that decision of suit Willie Barrow lessee vs James McMurtry shall be the decision in this case; therefore
p.--. Defendant is guilty of tresspass as alledged. Plaintiff recovers his cost of suit.
Court adjourned untill Court in Course. B Searcy

p.-- Dickson, Tennessee, Town of Charlotte. March 3rd 1817. Present the Honorable Thomas Stuart, Esquire Judge

Jurors: William Lucas Sr, Charles Campbell, Hugh Dickson Sr, Hugh Dickson Jr, Samuel Story, John Stafford, George Powell, Peter Gilbert, Thos Pannell, John Nisbitt Senr, John Willey, William Gunn, Jno Dunigan, Jno Nothering, Isaac Hamby, Jesse Epperson, Jas McCauly, Wm Brasher, John Hodge, George Clark,
p.-- Henry Stone, Abraham Robertson.

Grand jurors Hugh Dickson foreman, Isaac Hamby, Wm Brasher, Geo Clark, John Nothern, James McCauly, Thomas Pannell, John Hodge, Jesse Epperson, Jno Dunigan, John Stafford, John Willey, Henry Stone. Benjamin Cruise sworn to attend them

Hugh Dickson Jr and Charles Campbell discharged from further attendance at this Term

Oliver B Hays vs James Watson. Parties by attorneys. Jury
p.-- Wm Lucas, John Nisbitt, Saml Story, Geo Powell, Peter Gilbert, Bartholomew Smith, Wm Miller, Thomas Nisbitt, Alexr Wilkins, Clark Spencer, James L Bell, Edwd Pickett who find for Pltf his debt 100 Dollars, & 9 Dolls 75 cts damages sustained by detention of debt from time due untill 1 January 1817, the damages found by County Court Jury, besides costs. And on motion of Thomas Dunigan, agt his securitys in appeal
p.-- Also 12½ cents present interest from rendition of the judgement in County Court to this Term

Isham Parmer vs George Gallion & Francis Hutton. Si Fa. The Pltf by Atty, recovers agt George Gallion and Francis Hutton 26 dollars 99 1/4 cents, also his costs of suit expended

p.-- Davy Harison vs Bayless E Prince. Parties by attys. Jury William Lucas, John Nisbitt, Saml Story, George Powell, Peter Gilbert, Bartholomew Smith, Wm Miller, Thomas Nisbitt,

MARCH 1817

Alex^r Wilkins, Clark Spencer, Ja^s S Bell, Edward Picket who assess plaintiffs damages to one cent besides costs

Benjamin Joslin vs Jiles Jones. Def^t by att^y, pl^{t}f came not; Order to recover costs from plaintiff

William Sullivan vs Richard C Napier. Parties by attorneys. Jury Wm Lucas, John Nisbitt, Samuel Story, Ge^o Powell, Peter Gilbert, Bartholomew Smith, Wm Miller, Thomas Nisbitt, Alex^r Wilkins, Clark Spencer, James S[L?] Bell, Edward Pickett who find def^t is indebted to pl^t^{f} 287 dollars 30 cents and costs

p.-- Blount lessee vs William Wilkinson. Ejectment. On motion of pltf, order survey of premises in dispute be made by John Humphreys and three fair plats returned to next court. Court adjourned till tomorrow morning nine oclock

Thos Stuart

p.-- Tuesday March 4th 1817. Present Thomas Stewart, Judge

State vs Robert Weakley. Order forfeiture be set aside and the Defendant pay cost of the Scire facias

State vs Joseph Hamilton. Court orders forfeiture be set aside and Defendant pay cost of the Scire facias

p.-- State vs Wilson Blount. Ordered by Court that the forfeiture be set aside and Defendant pay cost of scire facias

State vs Aaron Fletcher. Bond one thousand dollars, to appear before Court September Term

p.-- State vs Aaron Fletcher. Robert Henderson and Moses Fletcher bond, condition Aaron Fletcher appear Sepr term

State vs Aaron Fletcher. Bond of John Scott, Philip Hornbarger, Thomas French, William Lewis, 250 Dollars each, condi-
p.-- tion each appears at Sepr Court to give evidence on behalf the State agt Aaron Fletcher for forgery.

State vs Aculas Straud. Appearance bond of Guidion Francis, John Osbun Roberts & George Michel, 250 dollars to give evidence behalf State Sepr Term agt Aculas Straud

State vs Aculas Straud. Bond of Aculas Straud and John Osbun Roberts, Straud's bond 1000 Dollars, personally to appear at
p.-- September Term. J O Roberts, bond 500 dollars, security

State vs Wilson Blount. Defendant pled Guilty, and is fined

SEPTEMBER 1817

five Dollars and costs

p.-- State vs Joseph Hamilton. Appearance bond, Hamilton 1000 Dollars, Robert Weakly & Wilson Blount 500 dollars each for Hamilton to appear at September Court

p.-- Maxwell Sharp vs Richard C Napier. Parties by att[ys]. Jury Isaac Hamby, W[m] Brasher, Ge[o] Clark, Jn[o] Northern, James McCauly, Tho[s] Pannel, Hugh Dickson S[r], John Hodge, Jesse Epperson, Jn[o] Dunnagan, John Stafford, Jn[o] Willey, Henry Stone who find def[t] indebted to pl[tf] 100 dollars, damage by reason of detention 6 dollars 56 ¼ cents besides cost of his suit

p.-- Joseph Kimble vs William P Hardy. Equity. W[m] P Hardy is inhabitant of Bertie County, North Carolina; order Hardy appear here at Sep[r] term to answer complaint or same will be taken for confession, this order to be published three times in Raleigh Register, at least 30 days previous to Sep[r] Term

p.-- William Newsom vs J Johnson. Pl[tf] maketh oath that Thomas Townsend, Logan County, KY, is a material witness for him. Pl[tf] wishes witness's deposition to be taken to be read at the trial of this case

Benjamin Andrews vs Elias W Napier. At March Term 1816 this cause referred to Sterling Brewer. His award follows: After hearing testimony & examining papers relative thereto, Brewer's decided Elias Napier is in debt to Benjamin Andrews
p.--. eight dollars with Interest from first April 1813 and cost of suit. Pl[tf] to recover ag[t] def[t] his debt and cost.

William Newsom vs James Johnson. Court grants commition to take deposition of Thomas Townsend in Kentucky

p.--. John J Standley vs Alford Cato. Def[t] by att[v]; pl[tf] made default. Def[t] to recover ag[t] Pl[tf] his cost of suit
Court adjourned untill Court in Course. Tho[s] Stuart

p.--. September 1, 1817. Present the Honorable Nathaniel W Williams, Esquire, Judge

Jurors   Isaac Johnson, Robert Lucas, Shedrick Bell, Richard Nall, W[m] White, Thomas Jones, W[m] Goodwin, Willis Walker, Jn[o] Spencer, James McDonal, Joseph Kimble, W[m] Tatum Sen[r], Aaron Vanhook, Jn[o] May, Ja[s] Read, Jn[o] Hall, William Shelton, Elias W Napier, John H Hyde, Raiford Crumpler, W[m] Willey, Lewis

SEPTEMBER 1817

Berry, Jesse Tribble and Absolam Tribble.
Grand Jurors: Raiford Crumpler, William Willey, Robt Lucas, Aaron Vanhook, Wm Tatum, John May, p.--. Willis Walker, Ja^s Read, Jno Hall, William Goodwin, Jno Spencer, Shedrick Bell, Wm Shelton. Sebion Cruise constable to attend the Grand Jury

Ordered that Jurors James McDaniel, John H Hyde, and Elias W Napier be discharged from further attendance at this term

William Peacock vs William Stone. Parties by attys. Cause cont^d until tomorrow by def^t's paying the cost of this day

p.--. Thomas H Perkins vs Reubin Shore. Covenant. Plaintiff came not. Defendant to recover against pl^{tf} has cost of suit

John Gray & Thos Blount vs William Wilkison. Ejectment. John Stafford, Andrew Gammel, John Tally, John Davis being chosen by Nancy Adams, one of the executors of Howel Adams decd, of the one part and William Jones Wilkison of the other part to determine the quantity and value of a tract of land conveyed by s^d Adams to Jesse Straud and by Straud to Wilkison, award as follows: four acres is taken by interference of 2560 acre survey of John G Blount & Thomas Blount; further Nancy Adams ex^{tx} shall pay to Wilkison sixteen dollars and cost of suit now pending s^d Blunts ag^t s^d Wilkison. 20 August 1817. John Stafford, Andrew Gammill, John Tally, Jno Davis. We the contracting parties oblige ourselves to abide by above award. 20 August 1817. Nancy [mark] Adams, William [mark] Wilkison. Test William Herren. Therefore Plaintiffs recover ag^t def^{ts} his term yet to come of the premises also his cost of suit

p.--. Benjamin Thomas vs James Alstin. James Alstin makes oath that Adam Wilson and James Wilson witnesses are old and infirm; he prays their depositions be read. Granted. Also Samuel Spencer is about to remove from state; Court order a deposition be taken of s^d Spencer to be read.
Court adjourned untill to morrow morning 9 OClock
Nath W Williams

September 2nd 1817 Present Hon. Nathaniel W Williams, Judge

State vs Aaron Fletcher. Appearance bond 1000 Dollars
p.--. Indictment for forgery

State vs Aaron Fletcher. Bond of Moses Fletcher and Joseph Stringer, 500 Dollars each, condition Aaron Fletcher personally appear at Court in March

State vs Aaron Fletcher, John Scott, John Fletcher, Philip

SEPTEMBER 1817

Hornbarger, and Thomas French, appearance bond as witnesses

State vs Aaron Fletcher. Solicitor general on behalf of the state. William Lewis called, came not. Scire facias to issue

p.--. State vs Aculas Stroud. Larceny. Def^t by att^y. Jury Jesse Tribble, Thos Jones, Lewis Berry, Richard Nall, Isaac Johnson, Absolam Tribble, Joseph Kimble, William Akin, Abraham Robertson, Thomas Key, William Light, George Light upon oath find defendant not guilty. Pl^{tf} to recover ag^t state

John Nibblett vs William Adams. Parties by attorneys. Deposition of John Nibblett Senr to be taken; also deposition of Valentine D Barry of Kentucky

p.--. State vs Joseph Hamilton. Defendant came not. Recognizance forfeited; scire facias issues returnable next term

State vs Joseph Hamilton. Robert Weakly & Wilson Blount forfeit recognizances; scire facias issue returnable next Term

p.--. Montgomery Bell vs Robert Weakly. Ejectment. Plaintiff made default. Defendant to recover against pl^{tf} his cost

William Peacock vs William Stone. Detinue. Cause continued on Def^t's paying cost of this term. Pl^{tf} to recover agt def^t the cost of this term

Thomas Hill vs Thomas Napier and George F Napier. Parties by attys. Jury James M Ross, Richd Nall, Captain[?] Eason, Danl Williams, Thomas Pannell, Edward Teal, Minor Bibb, David McAdoo, James L Bell, Robert Mason, Robt Nisbitt, William Cox, who find in favour of plaintiff; def^t indebted 400 dollars; assess damages of detention to 17 dollars 66 1/2 cents. Pl^{tf} to recover against def^t, also ag^t Elias W Napier and Henry A Napier his security in appeal bound in sum 400 dollars; also 17 dollars 66 2/3 cents interest at rate of 12½ percent on same from rendition of judgment in County Court to this time and also his costs in County Court and this Court

p.--. State vs Charles Williams. Sci Fa. Def^t made default. State to recover ag^t def^t Charles Williams 500 Dollars, the amount of the recognizance

State vs Nancy Coldman. Alias Sci Fa; def^t came not. State to recover 125 Dollars recognizance and cost of suit

p.--. State vs Rachel Wells. Alias Scire Facias. Defendant Rachel Wells came not; State to recover 125 Dollars, the am^t of the recognizance beside cost of suit

FEBRUARY 1818

State vs Charles Williams, Nancy Coldman, Rachel Wells, Joseph Hamilton. For reasons appearing to satisfaction of Court order the costs of these suits be paid by the County Trustee agreeable to act of assembly in such case made and provided

p.-- Wm Newsom vs Ja^s Johnson. Parties by att^{ys}. Pl^{tf} prosecutes no further, parties recover of each other the costs

James R McMeans vs Henry Lile. Parties by att^{vs}. Pl^{tf} prosecutes no further. Defendant to pay plaintiff's costs of suit

Elias W Napier vs Benjamin Joslin. The parties by attorneys. Plaintiff prosecutes no further; defendant pays costs

p.-- Henry A C Napier vs Benjamin Joslin. Parties by attys and plaintiff prosecutes no further; defendant pays costs

Deed Elias W Napier to Christopher Robertson 103 acres ackd

Thomas Hill vs Thomas and George F Napier. Debt. Appeal. By att^{ys}. Jury Jesse Tribble, Thos Jones, Lewis Berry, Richard Nall, Isaac Johnson, Absolam Tribble, Joseph Kimble, William Aikin, Abraham Robertson, Thomas Key, Wm Light, Thomas Light p.-- who find for plaintiff. Pl^{tf} to recover ag^t defendants and ag^t Elias W Napier & Harry A Napier securities in appeal from the County Court $2462.23 debt, $183.84 damages, also his costs of suit in this behalf expended

Francis Hill vs Thomas and George F Napier. Debt. Def^{ts} pray a writ of error to Supreme Court of Errors & Appeals for 5th Circuit. Elias W Napier security. Appeal allowed.

William Hudson Senr vs Sarah Tatum. A Writ of error issue to Clerk of County Court, Thomas Merrit[Murrel?] security
Court adjourns untill Court in Course.   Nath W Williams

p.-- February 23rd 1818. Present Perry W Humphreys, Judge

Sheriff made return of Venire Facias; jurors summoned to attend the first Monday in March. Said jurors have failed to attend at this term. Ordered by Court that Sheriff summon a sufficient number of by standers to appear tomorrow at 9 OClock to constitute a Grand Jury

p.-- Sarah Tatum vs Wm Hudson. Suit dismissed; d^{ft} pay cost

13

AUGUST 1818

Perry W Humphrey, Esquire, Judge, produced his commission as Judge protempore of the circuit courts vice Hon B Searcy deceased. Signed by Joseph McMinn, Governor, 26 January 1818. Wm Alexander, Secretary of State.
Court adjourned untill tomorrow nine OClock.   P.W. Humphreys

Tuesday, Feby 24th 1818.   Present Perry W Humphreys, Judge

John Malone vs William Penrice. Continued. A Deposition of p.--   Dean Mathew to be read in evidence, giving Bayless E Prince, agent for the defendant, two days notice

Grand Jury John Read foreman, John Northen, Mathew Gilmore, David McAdoo, Sterling May, Ellis Tycer, Jesse Ragan, Andrew Hamilton, James Madlock, Willis Walker, Jn° Bearnard, Marble Stone, Archabald Shelton

Mordecai Johnson vs Joab Copeland. Order pltf give additional security for prosecution of this suit before first day of next term or this cause shall be dismissed

p.-- Mordecai Johnson vs Joab Copeland. Order deposition of Co^l Robert Weakley be taken at two o'clock this evening at Robertsons Hotell in Charlotte to be read in evidence

There being no business, Grand Jury is discharged

Benjamin Thomas vs James Alsten. Deposition of Robert Weakley to be read in evidence on behalf of the plaintiff

James R McMeans vs Aaron James.   Slander. Parties agree to dismiss suit, defendant paying the cost. Confession: p.--   Aaron James declares he never uttered slanders words or words derogatory of sd McMeans character as an Honest man & a gentleman, or if spoken I must have been intoxicated...
February 14th 1818. Aaron James. Test William A Cook, John Montgomery   p.--. Pltf to recover agt deft his costs
Court adjourned untill Court in Course   P W Humphreys

p.--   Court house in Charlotte. August Term 1818. Augt 24th 1818. Present Thomas Stuart, Esquire, Judge

Jurors David McAdoo, Jn° Evens, Allen Howard, Andrew Gamble, Aquilla Tidwell, David Passmore, Ja^s Thedford, Samuel Tubb, Joel Marsh, Wm Tatom, Wm Powers, James Killet, Wm Johnson, Luke Matlock, Edward Lucas, Willis L Dawson, Wm Gilbert, Jn°

AUGUST 1818

Adams, Chas Winsted, Samuel Turner, Tailton Bunch, Mark Reynolds, John Jurden, John W Napier, George Teal.
Grand Jury David Passmore foreman, Aquilla Tidwell, William Powers, James Theadford, Mark Reynolds, p.--. Saml Turner, William Gilbert, Charles Winsted, Willis L Dawson, Luke Medlock, John W Napier, Joel Marsh, David McAdoo. John Nisbitt constable sworn to attend them

Robert Searcy vs Thomas Simmons. Debt. By att^{ys}. Jury Talton Bunch, George Teal, James Kellet, Edwd Lucas, Allen Howard, Jno Jourdan, Samuel Tubbs, John Adams, Andrew Gamble, Wm Tatum, George Lights, John Lucas, who find for plaintiff
p.-- Pl^{tf} to recover against def^t and ag^t George F Napier & Thomas Napier his securities 1000 dollars debt and 30 dollars and interest at rate of 12½ percent, in all $1048.23 as also his cost of suit

Mordecai Johnson vs Joab Copeland. By attorneys. Jury Talton Bunch, George Teal, James Kellet, Edwd Lucas, Allen Howard, John Jourdan, p.--. Samuel Tubb, John Adams, Andrew Gamble, William Tatum, George Light, John Lucas. By consent of Court & with assent of parties, George Teal is withdrawn and a mistrial agreed to. Case stand over for trial at next term of this court
p.-- Margery Boles wife of Thomas Boles, Polly May wife of Jesse May & Peggy Boles wife of Sampson Boles examined apart from their husbands acknowledge they executed power/attorney without compulsion of husbands. Certified 24 August 1818. Power of Attorney from Jane Duning, Thomas Boles & wife Margery, Jesse May and wife Polly, Sampson Boles & wife Peggy, John Duning & Jincey Duning acknowledged. 24 August 1818
Court adjourned untill to Morrow Morning 8 OClock

Thos Stuart

p.-- Tuesday Augt 25th 1818. Present Thomas Stewart, Judge

John Niblett vs William Adams. By attorneys. Deposition of John Niblett Senr to be read in evidence at next term

Mathew Quinn vs William H Burton. Motion to dismiss Certiorari overruled by Court

p.-- Mathew Quinn vs William Easly. Motion to dismiss Certiorari; not dismissed. Fi Fa to Humphreys County levied on fifteen acres and in Hickman County. Fi Fa directed to Hickman was irregular and same should be set aside; plaintiff to pay costs of this proceeding

Mathew Quinn vs William Easley. Court rules that Fi Fa to Hickman was irregular and same be held for nought; plaintiff

AUGUST 1818

to pay costs of this proceeding

p.-- Mathew Quinn vs William H Burton. Considered by Court that defendant recover against Plaintiff cost of his suit

Mathew Quinn vs William H Burton. Considered by Court that defendant recover against plaintiff the cost of his suit

Rogal Furgason vs John George Riner. Parties by attys. Depositions of William Eakins and William Gentry to be taken to be read in evidence giving pltf 10 days notice; also deposition of Charles Riner to be read, giving 30 days notice

Jesse May examined relative to Power/Attorney from heirs of Robert Duning decd to John May; acknowledged

Mordecai Johnson vs Joab Copland. Parties by atty. Jury Talton Bunch, George Teal, James Killet, Edwd Lucas, Allen Howard, Jno Jourdan, Samuel Tubb, John Adams, Andrew Gamble, Wm Tatum, Robert Nisbitt, John Northren who find for plaintiff, assess damage to 149 dollars 75 cents and cost

p.-- William Gordan vs John & Isaac Walker. Parties by att^y. Jury Aquilla Tidwell, Wm Powers, Ja^s Thedford, Mark Reynold, Samuel Turner, Wm Gilbert, Chas Winsted, Willis L Dawson, Luke Medlock, John W Napier, Joel Marsh, David McAdoo, who find in favour of plaintiff, & assess his damages to one hundred dollars. Also to recover cost of his suit.
Court adjourned untill toMorrow Morning 9 OClock.

Thos Stuart

Wednesday Augt 26th 1818. Present Thomas Stewart Esqr Judge

John Baker vs Heslip & Vanlier. Parties by attorneys. Cause is contd until next Term by Defts paying costs of this Term. Plaintiff to recover against def^{ts} his cost of this Term

State vs Aaron Fletcher. Bond 2000 dollars, to make appear-
p.-- ance in Court fourth Monday in February next

State vs Aaron Fletcher. Bond, John A Fletcher 100 Dollars, condition Aaron Fletcher appear in Court

State vs Aaron Fletcher. Cause continued untill next Term

p.-- State vs Robert Weakley and Joseph Hamilton. Sci Fa. Forfeiture set aside by payment of cost of this writ

State vs Wilson Blount. Sci Fa. Def^t by att^y; forfeiture set

AUGUST 1818

aside by payment of cost of this writ

State vs Nathan Nall. A & B. Solicitor Genl will no further prosecute; Nall in proper person assumes payment of all cost

p.-- Thomas Hill vs Thomas Napier & Richard Napier. Parties by attys. Jury Talton Bunch, George Teal, James Kittel, Edwd Lucas, Allen Howard, Jn° Jourdan, Saml Tubb, Jn° Adams, And^w Gamble, Wm Tatum, Wm Johnson, Jn° Stewart who find for def^{ts} indebted to plt^f 375 dollars 65 cents, & 16 dollars 74 cents damages of detention from 9 Octr 1817. On motion of plaintiff, also to recover against James Cummins, Thomas Simpson, Elias W Napier his securities in appeal

p.-- William Peacock vs William Stone. Detinue. Parties by attys. Jury David Pasmore, Aquilla Tidwell, James Thedford, Mark Reynolds, David McAdoo, William Gilbert, Luke Medlock, Joel Marsh, James Kellet, George Teal, Talton Bunch, Edward Lucas who say defendant does not detain the Negro man slave named Monday as the defendant hath alledged
Court adjourned untill to morrow morning 9 OClock

Thos Stuart

p.-- Thursday morning August 27th 1818. Present the Honorable Thomas Stuart Esquire Judge

William Peacock vs William Stone. Parties by attorneys. Pltf withdraws motion for new trial; def^t to pay his own cost and half of attendance of witnesses summoned by both parties

Robert J Nelson lessee vs John Allen and Randolph Harris. Ejectment. Defendants come to Court and plead not guilty

p.-- Mordecai Johnson vs Joab Copeland. Cont^d next Court

Joseph Kimble vs William P Hardy. In Equity. Wm P Hardy is an inhabitant of North Carolina, Burtie County; ordered said deft appear here at next term of this Court in February next

p.-- William P Hardy vs Joseph Kimble. Case. Parties by att^{ys}. Cause continued by plaintiff paying cost of this Term

Buckner Williams vs Elias W Napier. Parties by att^{ys}. Jury Talton Bunch, George Teal, James Kittel, Edward Lucas, Allen Howard, Jn° Jourdan, Saml Tubb, Jn° Adams, Andrew Gamble, Wm Tatum, William Johnson, & John Stuart who find def^t indebted to plaintiff 50 dollars 50 cents. Def^t moves for new trial.

p.-- Wm Carrell vs Thomas Napier & Thomas Simpson. Parties

AUGUST 1818

by att^{ys}. Def^t prays appeal. Granted. Def^t bond with James Cummins & John C Collen securities

William Sanson vs Lewis Joslin. Parties by att^{ys}. Jury David Pasmore, Aquilla Tidwell, Wm Powers, Ja^s Thedford, Mark Reynolds, Saml Turner, Wm Gilbert, Chas Winsted, Willis L Dawson, Luke Medlock, Joel Marsh, Jesse L Kirk. Pl^{tf} came not, Pl^{tf} to be nonsuited; def^t to recover his costs. Pl^{tf} enters motion; nonsuit set aside. Plaintiff to pay costs of Term

United States vs Montgomery Bell. Debt. Defendant came not. On 18 April 1815 deft gave bond payable to U.S. condition he would pay account with collector for debts due for castings by him manufactured on or before due; it further appearing by the collectors book and return made by defendant that dedefendant was indebted to the U.S. on the first July 1816 in sum 96 dollars and that same is due & unpaid Therefore it is considered by court that U.S. recover ag^t s^d Montgomery Bell the sd sum with interest thereon at six per c^t p^r a^n. untill this time, making one hundred eight dollars, also the costs by him about the suit in this behalf expended.

Benjamin Thomas vs James Alston. Pl^{tf} has leave to amend his declaration on the payment of the costs of s^d amendment

William Carrell vs Thomas Napier and Thomas Simpson. Parties by att^{ys}. Jury David Pasmore, Aquilla Tidwell, Wm Powers, Ja^s Thedford, Mark Reynolds, Saml Tubb, Turner, Wm Gilbert, Charles Winsted, Willis L Dawson, Luke Medlock, Joel Marsh, Jesse L Kirk, who find in favour of the plaintiff. Pl^{tf} to recover ag^t def^{ts} & George F Napier their security in appeal $541.75 debt, as also $27.25 damages, beside his cost

p.---. Mathew Quinn vs William Easley & McCracken & Thomason. County Court to issue Venditiori exponas to Humphreys County to sell land levied upon by W^m H Barton sheriff in two cases Quinn vs Easley, McCracken & Thomason

Buckner Williams vs Elias W Napier. Motion for new trial; it is ordered that defendants motion be overruled. Plaintiff to recover 10 dollars 50 cents beside his cost of suit
Court adjourned untill Court in Course   Thos Stuart

FEBRUARY 1819

p.-- Dickson County, Court house in Charlotte. February 22^d 1819. Present the Honorable Afred M Harris, Esquire, Judge

Jury Willis Jackson, William Hightower, William Tatum, John May, Jn° Wadkins, Jesse Epperson, John Nisbitt, Ellis Tycer, Ebenezer Kelly, Willoughby Etheridge, Richd Murrell, William Hudson, Eldridge Bowen, Ge° Tubb, James L Bell, James Hicks, Thomas Simmons, Isaac Tompkins
Grand Jury George Tubb foreman, William Hudson, Richard Murrell, Willoughby Etheridge, Ebenezer Kelly, Jn° Wadkins, Jn° Nisbitt, Jesse Epperson, Thomas Simmons, William Hightower, Eldridge Bowen, Ellis Tysor, James Hicks

p.-- Willie Barrow lessee vs Saml Curtis. Eject. Continued on affidavit of Defendant. Deposition of Abraham Estes taken in suits of Barrow lessee vs James McMurtry & others heretofore decided in this Court be read in evidence of this cause & deposition of Joseph Davidson if Davidson by reason of age or infirmity should not be here or should be dead

William B Haddin Constable to attend Grand Jury

Montgomery Bell vs Richard C Napier. Parties by attorneys. By consent Suit is dismissed, defendant paying cost.

p.-- John Malone vs William Penrice. Parties by attorneys. Continued untill to Morrow, def^t paying cost of this day

George Clark lessee vs Roser Brown. Parties by attorneys. Cont^d untill to morrow by Plaintiff paying cost of this day

John Baker vs Heslip & Vanlier. Parties by att^{ys}, continued to morrow by Defendants paying the cost of this day

p.-- Thomas May vs Elias W Napier. Debt. Parties by att^{ys}. Jury Wm Tatum, Pleasant Crews, Anderson England, Joseph Kimble, Wm Daniel, Wm Rye, Samuel Tubb, Sanford Edwards, Willis Walker, James McKey, Jesse Kirk, W^m B West who find def^t indebted to pl^{tf}. Pl^{tf} to recover ag^t Def^t & ag^t John C Colen & James R McMeans his security, his debt of $120 also $3.60 damages, also his cost of suit

p.-- Thomas May vs Elias W Napier. Parties by att^{ys}. Def^t prays appeal; granted. Def^t enters Bond with George F Napier and L P Cheatham his securities for prosecuting said appeal

John Baker vs Heslip & Vanlier. Parties by attorneys. Demurrer is sustained

James L Bell discharged as a Juror at this Term

FEBRUARY 1819

p.-- Alfred M Harris Judge of 6th Judicial Circuit suggests that Perry W Humphrey Judge, 5th Judicial Circuit, did certify to him in writing that he was incompetent to preside as Judge following cases in Circuit Court of Montgomery County in 5th Judicial Circuit: John W Carroll lessee vs Wm Weeks; William Outlaw lessee vs Williams & Pugh; John Hay vs Jacob Fore; same vs William S White; Same vs Aaron Winters; John McCallister lessee vs Jesse Sullivan guardian; same vs Saml Smith ejectment; Hurt vs Hu F Bell; Walker vs Bell; which fact is ordered to be recorded.
Court adjourns until to morrow morning 9 OClock
Alfred M Harris

p.-- Tuesday morning February 25th 1819. Present Alfred M Harris, Esquire, Judge

Deed Richard Batson Sh^{ff} of Dickson County to Thomas Hickman 640 acres proven by Will A Cook & N H Allen

John McAdo Trustee of Dickson County vs Daniel Perkins Trustee of Williamson County. Certiorari. Parties by att^{ys}. Pl^{tf} motion to dismiss certiorari argued; sustained. Pl^{tf} to recover ag^t Dept/Justice one hundred fifty dollars & all costs

p.-- John Niblett vs William Adams. Def^t by counsel files Bill of Exception, made a part of the record

John Niblett vs William Adams. Trover. Parties by attorneys. Jury John May, Willis Jackson, Benjamin Clark, Benoni Crawford, William Freeman, Mathew Gilmore, John Nisbitt Sr, William B West, Jesse L Kirk, William Thomas, John Evens, John Spencer discharged without rendering verdict

[two blank pages]
p.-- Jeremiah Freeman vs James Young. Plaintiff intends to prosecute no further. Def^t recovers against pl^{tf} his costs

State vs Joseph L Webster. Bond 200 Dollars, condition he makes personal appearance at August Court; Assault & battery

p.-- State vs Joseph L Webster. Henry H Bryan, Thos Napier, William L Brion, N H Allen, J R McMeans, F W Huling, Jehu Neblett, John C Cotten, bond fifty dollars each, condition Joseph L Webster makes personal appearance August Court

p.-- State vs Aaron Brady. It appearing that no charge had been or would be exhibited against Aaron Brady, sd Brady is discharged. County Trustee to pay costs of prosecution

FEBRUARY 1819

Court adjourned until tomorrow morning nine oClock
Alfred M Harris

p.-- Wednesday morning February 24th 1819. Present the Honorable Alfred M Harris, Esquire, Judge

John Niblett[Nibtell?] vs William Adams. Parties by att^{ys}. Plaintiff dismisses suit, defendant assuming cost except the attendance of Benjamin Organ, Sterling Niblett, & John Niblett Senr which is assumed by the plaintiff.

State vs Aaron Fletcher. Forgery. Def^t made default; state recovers against defendant 2000 Dollars, def^t's recognizance

State vs John A Fletcher. Fletcher made default. State to recover against Def^t the 1000 Dollars named in recognizance

p.-- Benjamin Thomas vs James Alston. Ejectment. Parties by att^{ys}. Jury William Tatum, Willis Jackson, William Miller, Joab Leach, Danl Leach, Nathan Tubb, William B West, William Freeman, John B Brown, Benjamin Wallice, Marble Stone, Calvin W Eason who are permitted to disperse until to morrow

Deed Michael Dickson to Francis S Ellis 121 acres proven

p.-- Rogal Furgason vs John George Riner. Parties by att^{ys}. Jury John May, Robt Larkins, Jesse L Kirk, Ja^s L Bell, Randolph Harris, Chas Gunn, William Williams, Francis Balthrop, Aquilla Tidwell, Robt Nesbitt, John Marsh, James Madlock who find for Defendant. Defendant recovers ag^t pl^{tf} his costs
Court adjourned untill tomorrow morning nine OClock
Alfred M Harris

Thursday morning February 25th 1819. Present Alfred M Harris

William P Hardy vs Joseph Kimble. Defendant failed to come agreeably to notice; hearing set next Term of this Court

Benjamin Thomas vs James Alsten. Parties by attys. Jury of yesterday find for Defendant. Def^t recovers costs ag^t pl^{tf}

p.-- John Malone vs William Pinser(?). Parties by attornies; Jury John May, Randolph Harris, Jesse L Kirk, Benoni Crawford, Jno Spencer, Joseph Kimble, Jno Larkins, Wm Cox, Benj^a T Wyatt, Allen C Nimmas, William Thomas, Benjamin Clark who find for pl^{tf}, his damages 55 dollars 37 cents; and costs.

William Sansum vs Lewis Joslin. Parties by attornies. Jury Ge^o

FEBRUARY 1819

Trible, Willough Etheredge, Ebenezer Kelly, Jn° Wadkins, Jn° Nisbett, Jesse Epperson, Thomas Simmons, Wm Hightower, p.-- Eldridge Bowen, Ellis Tycer, Robt Larkins, Ja^s Medlock. Plaintiff, came not. Def^t recovers ag^t pl^{tf} his cost of suit

John Baker vs Joseph Hislip and Anthony W Vanler. Parties by att^{ys}. Jury Ge° Tubb, Willoughby Etheridge, Ebenezer Kelly, John Wadkins, John Nisbitt, Jesse Epperson, Thos Simmons, Wm Hightower, Eldrige Bowen, Ellis Tycer, Robert Larkins, James Medlock, found in favour of plaintiff. Pltf to recover ag^t defendant $338.62½ damages, also costs

p.-- Robert J Nelson lessee vs John Allen & Randolph Harris. Parties by attornies. Jury Ge° Tubb, Willoughby Etheridge, Ebenezer Kelly, John Wadkins, John Nisbitt, Jesse Epperson, Thos Simmons, Wm Hightower, Eldrige Bowen, Ellys Tycer, Robert Larkins, Ja^s Medlock who find def^{ts} guilty of trespass; damage 1 cent; improvements made by def^{ts} previous to commencement of this suit were of value of 1400 dollars.
Court adjourns untill to morrow morning 9 OClock
Alfred M Harris

Friday morning Feby 26th 1819. Present Alfred M Harris Judge

George Ross vs Thomas Simpson & Thomas Napier. Debt appeal. Parties by attornies. Defendants confess they owe plaintiff 221 dollars 58 cents. Plaintiff to recover, also his costs

p.-- Mordecai Johnson vs Joab Copeland. Def^t withdraws his motion, plaintiff assumes costs except the costs of defendant, witnesses, freely admits damages recovered by him

Robert J Nelson lessee vs Allen & Harris. Ejectment. Bill of exception filed

p.-- George Ross vs Simpson & Napier. Def^{ts} pray appeal to Supreme Court of Errors; allowed

Robert J Nelson lessee vs Harris and Allen. Motion for new trial. Prayed for Writ of Error to Supreme Court; allowed

Thomas Collen vs Isaac H Lanier. Debt on demurrer. Considered by Court that plaintiff recover against defendant

p.-- unreadable
Court adjourned till Court in Course.   Alfred M Harris

AUGUST 1819

A Circuit Court held at the court house in Charlotte, Monday August 23rd 1819. Present Alfred M Harris, Esquire, Judge

Jury John Turner, Jeremiah Nesbitt, Mark Reynolds, John Parrot, Jn° Wilson, John Hickerson, John H Humphries, Claiborne Spicer, Ja^s Thompson, John Tatum Senr, Jas Eason, Wm Thomas, Joseph Davidson, David Passmore, Wm Gentry, Ge° Williamson, Daniel Coleman, John Kelly, Thos Matthews, Daniel Hickerson, Edward Hughy, Thomas Simmons, Thomas Hudson, Robert Armour.

Grand Jury: David Passmore foreman, Wm Gentry, Jo^s Davidson, Ja^s Thompson, John Tatum, John Turner, Thos Hudson, Jeremiah Nesbitt, p.-- John H Humphries, John Wilson, Claiborne Spicer, James Eason, Robert Armour. William B Readden constable sworn to attend the grand jury

David Daly, licensed lawyer, admitted to practice in Court

William Banks vs Benjamin Pearsall, Jeremiah Pearsall. Debt. Parties by att^{ies}. Jury John Kelly, Thos Matthews, Mark Reynolds, Jn° Dickson, Edward Hughy, John Parrott, Daniel Coleman, Daniel Hickerson, William Edwards, John W Napier, Green Holland, George Teal who p.-- find for plaintiff. Pl^{tf} to recover debt $732.11, damages $42.50 of detention, and costs

p.-- Willie Barrow vs Samuel Curtis. By att^{ys}. Cause cont^d untill tomorrow by deftendants paying cost of this day

Elias W Napier vs Joseph Hislip. By attornies. Cause continued tomorrow by defendants paying cost of this day

Juror Thomas Simmons discharged from further attendance this term

McRae & Lanier vs Stephen Harris & Dorsett Y Harris by att^{ys} Jury John Kelly, Thos Matthews, Mark Reynolds, John Dickson, Edwd Hughy, John Parrott, Danl Coleman, Daniel Hickerson, Wm Edwards, Jn° W Napier, Green Holland, Ge° Teal p.-- find in favour of Plaintiff. Pl^{tf} to recover ag^t def^t and ag^t John C Collier and Elias W Napier his securities in appeal, $200 debt, also $11, and interest at 12½ percent on same, making debt and damages $214.28½ and also his cost

McRae & Lanier vs James Kirk, parties by attornies. Jury Jn° Kelly, Thomas Matthews, Mark Reynolds, John Dickson, Edward Hughy, John Parrott, Daniel Coleman, Danl Hickerson, William Edwards, John W Napier, Green Holland, George Teal who find p.-- for pl^{tf}. Pl^{tf} to recover ag^t def^t and his security in appeal Jesse G Kirk $105.87½ debt, also interest at 12½ per cent, total $108.15 and his cost about this suit expended

AUGUST 1819

McRae & Lanier vs John Day by att^ies. Jury Jn° Kelly, Thomas Matthews, Mark Reynolds, John Dickson, Edwd Hughy, John Parrott, Daniel Coleman, Daniel Hickerson, William Edwards, Jn° W Napier, Green Holland, George Teal who find for plaintiff. p.-- Pl^tf to recover ag^t def^t debt $201.93 3/4 and damages $7.25, also their cost by them expended in this behalf

McRae & Lanier vs Benjamin Pearsall by att^ies. Jury Jn° Kelly, Thos Matthews, Mark Reynolds, Jn° Dickson, Edward Hughy, John Parrott, Daniel Coleman, Daniel Hickerson, Wm Edwards, Jn° W Napier, Green Holland, George Teal who find defendant owes pltf $177.12½, & $5.50 damages of detention as also his p.-- security in appeal John Refad[Ressad?], & cost of suit

M C Robertson vs Dillard[?] Harris by att^ies. Jury John Kelly, Thos Matthews, Mark Reynolds, Jn° Dickson, Edward Hughy, John Parrott, Danl Coleman, Danl Hickerson, Wm Edwards, John W Napier, Green Holland, George Teal who find for pl^tf. Con- p.-- sidered by Court pltf recover against defendant & his security in appeal David Macadoo $36.83 debt & damages found by Jury and interest at 12½ percent on same, also his cost

Turner Sanders vs John Spencer, by att^ies. Jury John Kelly, Thomas Matthews, Mark Reynolds, Jn° Dickson, Ed^wd Hughy, Jn° Parrott, Danl Coleman, Danl Hickerson, Wm Edwards, Jn° W Napier, Green Holland, Ge° Teal who find for pl^tf. Therefore, p.-- Plaintiff to recover ag^t def^t debt and damages & costs

McRae & Lanier vs Robert Brunnon. By att^ies. Jury Jn° Kelly, Thos Matthews, Mark Reynolds, Jn° Dickson, Edward Hughy, Jn° Parrott, Danl Coleman, Danl Hickerson, Wm Edwards, Jn° W Napier, Green Holland, Ge° Teal who find for pl^tf. Plaintiff to recover against defendant debt, damages, and costs
Court adjourned until tomorrow Morning 9 oclock
                                           Alfred M Harris

Tuesday Morning August 24th 1819.   Present Alfred M Harris

State vs Aaron Fletcher. Forgery. Solicitor General prosecutes no further, assumes payment of all cost in this case

p.--   State vs James Alston. Murder. Solicitor General for State, Def^t brought to Bar, plead Not Guilty, puts himself upon country. Jury John Kelly, John Parrott, David Passmore, Jos Davidson, James Thompson, John Tatum, John Turner, James Eason, John Read, John Shoat, Robert Larkins, Wm Daniel who withdraw until tomorrow morning nine oclock under charge of W^m B Hadden a sworn officer to attend them.

AUGUST 1819

Court adjounred until tomorrow morning nine oclock
                                        Alfred M Harris

Wednesday morning August 25th 1819.   Present Alfred M Harris

State vs James Alston. Murder. Jurors withdraw until tomorrow morning nine Oclock under charge of William B Hadden an officer sworn to attend them.
Court adjourned until tomorrow morning nine oclock

Thursday morning August 26th 1819.   Present Alfred M Harris

State vs James Alston. Murder. Jurors withdraw till tomorrow morning nine oclock under charge of officer William B Hadden

State vs James Alston. Murder. Jurors withrawn until tomorrow morning 9 oclock under charge of officer Wm B Hadden
Court adjourned until tomorrow morning nine oclock
                                        Alfred M Harris

p.-- Friday Augt 27th 1819. Present Alfred M Harris Judge

State vs James Alston. Murder. Jury Jno Kelly, John Parrott, David Passmore, Jos Davidson, Jas Thompson, John Tatum, John Turner, James Eason, Jno Read, Jno Choat, Robert Larkins, Wm Daniel who say James Alston is not guilty of murder in manner and form as charged in Bill of Indictment. James Alston discharged. Hickman County where this prosecution originated pays costs expended by State in this prosecution, including costs of officers of this Court, Hickman Circuit Court, the Jailors fees in Hickman, Dixon & Maury, and the witnesses in behalf of the State

p.-- W Barrow's lessee vs Saml Curtis. Eject. Continued to next Term, Deft pay costs of this Term. Plff to take deposition of Robert McMillon & James Mulherin at house of C Robertson in Charlotte before 12 oClock A.M. On application of Polly Hyre, Squire Little and wife Sally, John Alston, Milly Alston, Jas Alston, Chas Alston by Wm H Benton their guardian, they are admitted codefendants on condition they enter into common rule..., are admitted & plead not guilty

p.--   Mark Reynolds discharged from further attendance as a Juror this Term
Court adjourned until tomorrow morning eight oclock
                                        Alfred M Harris

AUGUST 1819

Saturday August 28th 1819. Present Alfred M Harris Judge

Chris' Robertson lessee vs Wm Turner. Ejectment. Def' agrees to confess lease entry & ouster and rely upon his title only and plead not guilty; thereupon is admitted as defendant.

Christopher Robertson lessee vs William Gilbert. Ejectment. Deft agrees to confess lease entry & ouster, & rely upon his title only & plead not Guilty; admitted as defendant

p.--   State vs Aaron Fletcher. Sci Fa. Demurrer. Solicitor Gen' behalf State, Def' by atty. Demurrer sustained. Sci Fa to issue to Stewart County against said Aaron Fletcher

State vs Joseph P[C?] Webster. A.B. Bond of William L Brown, James R McMeans, Frederick Hueling[Hurling?], John C Collins fifty dollars each, condition that Joseph L Webster appear at February Term

p.--   Sterling Brewer vs Christopher Robertson. Deposition on either side by giving opposite party ten days notice

Elias W Napier vs Joseph Heslip, by att[ies]. Jury John Kelly, Thomas Matthews, John Dickson, Dan' Coleman, Dan' Hickerson, Andw Hamilton, Geo Teal, Wm Henderson, Jos Kimble, Anthony W Vanlier who find defendant does not owe plaintiff anything. Defendant to recover against plaintiff his cost of defence

Ordered by Court that Benjamin T Wyatt be fined two dollars for contempt to the Court for not attending as a Juror when summoned on the suit State vs James Alston

p.--   State vs Wm Edwards. Slander. Solicitor General will no further prosecute said suit.

Sterling Brewer vs Christopher Robertson. Plaintiff by atty is granted to amend his declaration on his paying all costs that have accrued on this suit since the appearance time.

p.-- William R Fluman[?] vs Stephen Howard, Nehemiah Scott, Daniel H Williams, by att[ies]. Debt on Demurrer. Judgment in County Court reversed, and Pl'fs demurrer sustained, and the pl'f recover of def'ts $610 debt and $18.25 damages of detention, and his cost in this behalf expended

W Barrow's lessee vs Heirs of John Alston. The Depositions of Robert McMillen and James Mulherrin taken today on this cause be read at next Term of this Court

MARCH 1820

p.-- Clark Spencer vs Christopher Robertson. Non Suit. The plaintiff came not. On motion, defendant recovers ag^t Marble Stone and William Thomas, plaintiffs securities

James Mulherrin in open Court was sworn to his deposition in the case where Willie Barrow is plaintiff & Samuel Curtis & others are def^{ts}. Robert McMillan in open Court was sworn to his deposition in case where Willie Barrow is pl^{tf} & Samuel Curtis and others are defendants

Court Adjourned until Court in Course

Alfred M Harris

March Term 1820. Circuit Court for County of Dickson, March 6th 1820. Present Honorable Perry W Humphrys, Esquire, Judge

Jury George Adams, Benjn Valentine, John T Hutchison, Jesse Tribble, Olaver Armour, John Nisbitt Sr, James Douglass, Wm McAdoo, John Willy Sr, Sanford Edwards, William Turner, Edwd Lucas, Willis Jackson, Jno B Walker, John Giffin, Archabable Skelton, Drury Adkins, Saml Story, Hugh Dickson Senr, Thomas Murrell, Joseph Larkins, Andrew Gammell, Edmond Tidwell Junr and Curthbird Hudson
Grand Jury Jno Nisbitt fourman, Jno B Walker, Hugh Dickson, Drury Adkins, Ge^o Adams, John Giffen, Edmund Tidwell, Edward Lucas, Archibald Skelton, William Turner, Thos Murrell, Jesse Tribble and Benjamin Valentine
p.-- Wm B Hadden Constable sworn to attend the Grand Jury

James Tidwell vs Richard Tidwell. Parties in proper person; plaintiff to prosecute no further; cost divided equally.

Jane Harris vs Sterling Brewer. Pl^{tf} by att^y prosecutes no further; defendant assumes all costs

Bayless E Prince vs Benjn Williams. Ejectment. Plaintiff to prosecute no further. Defendant to recover ag^t pl^{tf} his cost

Bayless E Prince vs John French. Ejectment. Plaintiff to prosecute no further. Defendant to recover ag^t pl^{tf} his cost
Court Adjourned untill tomorrow morning 9 OClock

P W Humphrey

Tuesday morning March 7th 1820.
Present the Honorable Perry W Humphrey Esquire, Judge

MARCH 1820

p.-- State vs Joseph L Webster. A.B. William L Brown, James R McMeans, Fedrick Huling and John C Collier called to bring Joseph L Webster, made default. State to recover fifty dollars each, the amount in the recognisance

State vs John A Fletcher. Defendant made default. State to recover against defendant 1000 Dollars named in Scire Facias

p.-- Joseph Kimble vs William P Hardy. Parties by attorneys. cause referred to award of Sterling Brewer & Richard Batson

William P Hardy vs Joseph Kimble. By attorneys; referred to award of Sterling Brewer and Richard Batson

Richard C Napier vs Jesse Tribble and Absolam Tribble. Jury James Doughlass, Willis Jackson, Joseph Larkins, John Willy, Oliver Armour, Ge° Sullivand, Benjn Clarke, Isaac Tubb, Edwd Teal, Andrew Hamilton, William Talor, John Evins, find for p.-- plt^f 500 Dollars debt, to be discharged by payment of 50 dollars. On motion, pl^{tf} to recover ag^t defts, also ag^t John Edwards their security in appeal 50 Dollars, interest thereon at 12 ½ per cent, and also his cost of suit

Christopher Robertson vs William Turner. Ejectment. Jury Ja^s Doughlass, Willis Jackson, Joseph Larkins, Jn° Willy, Olaver Armor, George Sullivand, Benjamin Clarke, Isaac Tubb, Edward Teal, Andrew Hamilton, Wm Talor, Jn° Evins who find def^t not guilty of trespass; defendant recovers against pl^{tf} his cost

p.-- George Clarke lessee vs Rosser Brown. Ejectment. Def^t has died. Scire facias issues ag^t W^m F Brown, Robt H Brown, Rosser Brown, Thompson Brown, Arzala Brown
Court adjourned untill tomorrow morning 9 OClock

P.W.Humphreys

Wednesday morning March 8th 1820
Present the Honorable Perry W Humphreys Esquire Judge

Christopher Robertson vs William Turner. Ejectment. Motion for new trial.

p.-- Robert W Green vs John Read. Debt. Def^t confesses debt of 71 dollars 49 cents. Pl^{tf} to recover debt and his cost

Wilkins Tannehill cashier of Nashville Bank vs John Read. Debt. Defendant confesses debt 855 dollars 27 c^{ts}, 31 doll^s 38 cents damage; plaintiff also to recover his cost of suit

MARCH 1820

p.-- Joseph Kimble vs William P Hardy. Bill of Injunction. William P Hardy vs Joseph Kimble. Referees award: Hardy pays Kimble 86 dollars; Hardy pays costs of both suits. S Brewer, Richd Batson

p.-- Jeremiah Baxter vs Montgomery Bell. Jury Ja^s Douglass, Willis Jackson, Joseph Larkins, John Willey, Olaver Armor, Isaac H Lanier, Adonijah Edward, Wm Armor, Jacob Rushing, Thomas Key, William Taylor, And^w Hamilton. Def^t indebted 639 dollars 97 1/4 cents. Defendant by att^y moves for new trial

Charles Teal, Edward Teal vs George Teal Junr and others. Pl^{ts} prosecute no further. In proper person Edward Teal and George Teal assume costs, recover costs of each other

p.-- State vs William Edwards. Jury James Doughlass, Willis Jackson, Joseph Larkins, Jno Willy, Isaac H Lanier, Adonijah Edwards, Wm Armor, Thos Key, Wm Taylor, And^w Hamilton, John Brewer, James Kirk, John Evins who find defendant guilty as charged. Defendant fined 30 dollars and pays cost of suit

State vs Elizabeth Hall, Martha Hall, Susana Hall. Grand Jury retired to consider of presentments

p.-- State vs Mark Holland. No charge; Holland discharged. Court adjourned untill tomorrow morning nine OClock
P W. Humphreys

Thursday morning March 9th 1820
Present the Honorable Perry W Humphreys Esquire Judge

State vs John Grimes. True bill.

p.-- James Kirke vs Francis S Ellis. Jury James Doughlass, Willis Jackson, Joseph Larkins, John Willey, Oliver Armor, David Passmore, Andrew Hamilton, John Spencer, Nathan Tubb, Charles Howard, George Tubb, who find defendant indebted 209 Dollars, also 6 dollars 50 cents damage of detention, & cost

Christopher Strong vs Ja^s Read, Francis S Ellis. Debt. Jury Ja^s Doughlass, Willis Jackson, Jo^s Larkins, John Willy, Olaver Armor, David Passmore, And^w Hamilton, Jno Spencer, Nath^n Tubb, Chas Howard, Ge^o Tubb, Pleasant Crews find def^{ts} debt 248 dollars 4 cents, also 9 dollars 92 c^{ts} damage, also cost

p.-- Christopher Robertson vs Sterling Brewer. Jury James Doughlass, Willis Jackson, Joseph Larkins, Jno Willy, Oliver Armor, David Passmore, Andw Hamilton, Geo Tubb, Jno Spencer, Nathan Tubb, Chas Howard, Pleasant Crews find def^t indebted

MARCH 1820

821 dollars; 61 doll^s 72 c^{ts} damage of detention, and costs

p.-- James Goodrich vs Montgomery Bell. Jury Ja^s Doughlass, Willis Jackson, Jo^s Larkins, John Willy, Oliver Armor, David Passmore, And^w Hamilton, Jno Spencer, Nathan Tubb, Chas Howard, Wm Turner, Jno Giffin find for pl^{tf} debt 645 dollars 10 c^{ts}, 37 doll^s 90 c^{ts} damage by detention, and cost. Also ag^t John Hall & John C Collier, defendants securities in appeal

p.-- James Goodrich vs Montgomery Bell. Jury (as above) find debt 102 dollars, 6 dollars 12 c^{ts} damage, & cost. Also ag^t John Hall and John C Collier def^{ts} securities in his appeal

James Goodrich vs Patrick H Darby, William L Brown. Jury (as above) find debt 155 dollars, damage 10 doll^s 85 c^{ts} & costs

p.-- Louisa Gregham vs Elizabeth Davidel. Jury (as above except John Evins in place of John Giffin) who find def^{ts} debt 200 dollars, damage 12 dollars, & cost, also against John C Collier and Thomas Whitmill, securities in appeal

p.-- Herbert Haynes vs Montgomery Bell. Jury (as above, except Jno Giffin for Jno Evins) find defendants debt 321 dollars 50 cents; 12 dollars 86 cents damages; and costs.

p.-- State vs John Grimes. Defendant submits and is fined five dollars & costs

Charles W Napier vs Rogal Furgason. Jury (as above). James Douglass withdrawn, jurors discharged. Plaintiff nonsuited, defendant to recover against plaintiff his costs

p.-- Daniel Rook vs Isaac H Lanier. Debt on writ of Error. Parties by attornies. Pl^{tf} to recover against def^t, also ag^t Marble Stone his security in appeal, 345 Dollars, damages at 12½ percent, besides cost; def^t appeals, & enters bond with John L McRae and Cave Johnson his securities

p.-- Christopher Robertson vs John H Smith. Injunction. Robertson to pay Smith $934.21; one third to be paid in 3 mo^s, two thirds in 12 months with interest. Richard C Napier voluntarily ack himself security for performance of this decree

p.-- Jeremiah Baxter vs Montgomery Bell. Motion for a new trial. Sustained

Christopher Robertson vs William Turner. Ejectment. Motion for new trial. Sustained

p.-- Deed from Montgomery Bell to Thomas H Perkins & Daniel

SEPTEMBER 1820

Perkins, two lots adjoining Nashville, Davidson County, one on Colledge Hill being same purchased by sd Bell from Alpha Kingsby[Kingsley?] and one in Nashville known as Elk Tavern, same purchased by Bell from Genl Wm Carrel, ack^d by s^d Bell
Court adjourned untill tomorrow morning nine OClock

P.W.Humphreys

Fryday morning March 10th 1820
Present the Honorable Perry W Humphreys Esquire Judge

p.-- State vs James Mallory Sheriff. Sci fa issued agt Aaron Fletcher on behalf State, delivered to s^d Mallory more than 20 days before return day thereof, same not returned. State to recover of James Mallory 125 dollars unless cause shown

John Spencer vs David Hogan. Spencer by att^y. Judg^t by last Court ag^t Jno Spencer for 140.10½ with cost $11.80 in favour of Turner Sanders on a joint note given by Clarke Spencer John Read David Hogan & Jno Spencer. Jno Read, David Hogan & p.-- Jno Spencer were securities for s^d Clark Spencer, judgment & costs amounted to 162 dollars 60 cents had been paid by John Spencer, therefore John Spencer to recover of David Hogan 54 dollars 20 cents. 1/3 part of s^d Judgm^t in^t & costs together with costs of this motion
Court adjourned untill Court in Course. P.W.Humphreys

September Term 1820. Dickson County, first Monday in September, 4th day, 1820. Present Alfred M Harris judge of the 6th Judicial Circuit, Richard Bolton Sheriff of sd County, and John L McRae clerk of Circuit Court for said County

Jurors Robert Whitewill, Charles Thompson, Nehemiah Scott, Daniel Williams, John Stafford, George Powell, Chas Gilbert, Willis Willy, Lebius Richardson, Chris^r Robertson, Mathew Crumpler, William Hudson, Benjamin Clark, John H Stone, John Allen, Alexander Dickson, Hughell Parrish, Thomas Mathews, William Ward, George Clark, William Cox, Jesse Russell.
Grand Jury Daniel Williams foreman, Thomas Mathews, John H Stone, Benjn Clark, Lebius Richardson, George Powell, Jesse Russell, Charles Gilbert, Nehemiah Scott, Wm Hudson, Mathew Crumpler, Robert Whitewill, John Stafford
William B Hadden constable sworn to attend the Grand Jury

p.-- Alfred M Harris orders same entered into Record that he hath interchanged Ridings with the Hon Perry W Humphreys the

SEPTEMBER 1820

Judge of 5th Judicial Circuit. Causes on which Humphreys is incompetent to act are Lem¹ Peters vs Moses Lockharts ex^rs, Debt. Fort vs Woodford & Gold, imployed.
p.-- Sam¹ Williams lessee vs Jnº Duke, imployed. Moses Lockhart vs Lemuel Peters, case. Jnº Allin vs Jnº Haywood; case. Mich¹ Campbell lessee vs George West & Wm Clements, related to persons. Lessee of Ann A Blount vs Wm L Brown, ejectment. Waltons Heirs vs Caleb Williams, ejectment. Ja^s Read vs Thos Napier, Debt, connected by affinity. Ja^s Baxter & Cº vs Geº West, debt, related by affinity. Wm & A McClure vs Thos Napier, Related; Morrison vs Napier same. Robert Peterson vs Napier, affinity. James Rutherford vs Thos Napier; related. James Read vs F Napier; dº. Samuel Smith vs T Napier; dº.
p.-- John McCarrell vs Hamilton & Cook. State vs James West; connected by affinity with def¹. State vs House & Nixon; Geº West is prosecutor; Indictment for feloniously taking slaves property of George West with whom I am connected by affinity

Jesse Sullivan vs Francis S Ellis. Plaintiff prosecutes no further; Defendant to recover against plaintiff his cost

John Walker and wife vs James M Thomas. Securities deliver defendant; sheriff ordered to take him in custody

p.-- Christopher Robertson and Alexander Dickson jurors in original panel discharged from further attendance this term

Isaac Dortch vs Montgomery Bell. By attornies. Jury William Cox, Willis Willy, Charles Thompson, Hughell Parrish, George Clarke, Thomas Hudson, David McAdoo, Jnº Evins, John Giffin, Sanford Edwards, Andrew Hamilton, Jnº Northern who find def¹ indebted 362 dollars, damage by detention 58 dollars 50 c^ts, besides his cost

p.-- Elizabeth Gibson vs Benjn Hudson & wife. Slander. Jury Wm Cox, Willis Willey, Chas Thompson, Hughell Parrish, Geº Clark, David McAdoo, John Evans, John Giffin, Sandford Edwards, Marble Stone, George Tubb, John Wims. Jurors disperse untill to morrow morning nine O'Clock
Court adjourned untill to morrow morning nine O'Clock
Alfred M Harris

Tuesday morning September 5th 1820   Present Alfred M Harris

John Evans fined $2.50 for not attending in time as a Juror

p.-- Francis S Ellis vs Robertson Dickson. Equity. Arbitrators met in Charlotte 8 April 1820 finding the negro property of Dickson, since sold for $700, a loss of $300, which

SEPTEMBER 1820

loss is equally apportioned between Ellis and Dickson. Cost in County & Circuit Courts equally divided. Ellis furnished money that purchased negro from C Strong; he is intitled to the hire of same while in his possession. Therefore Robertson Dickson to pay Ellis $850 & interest; cost to be divided between the parties as above, Ellis has received $700 of the money, leaving a balance due Ellis $150 on which Ellis is to have interest untill paid. James Goodrich, S Brewer, John L McRae, R Batson, Marble Stone

p.-- Elizabeth Gibson vs Benjamin Hudson & wife. Jury [as above] Find for pltf; assess damage by speaking & publishing slanderous words in declaration mentioned $50 besides costs

Deed William Hankins to Thomas Knight 100 acres in Humphreys County on White Oak Creek acknowledged
Deed John Hays to Perry W Humphreys proved by witnesses
Deed George West to Perry W Humphrys, tract of land in Dickson and Montgomery Counties proven by subscribing witnesses

p.-- John Read, Dudly S Jenning, Francis Smith, Jesse Egnue, Esq^{rs}, licensed lawyers admitted to practice in this Court

State vs Morris Blackwell. Jury Thomas Hudson, Nathan Tubb, Solomon Rye, James Williams, Wm Miller, Jno B Walker, Josiah Davidson, W^m McAdoo, Ezra McAdoo, James McKey, George Adams, John Joslin, permitted to withdraw in a Body until tomorrow, Siburn Crews & Wm B Hadden sworn officers to attend them
Court adjourned untill to morrow morning nine OClock
Alfred M Harris

Wednesday morning September 6th 1820. Present the Honorable Alfred M Harris Esquire Judge

p.-- Francis S Ellis vs Robertson Dickson. Equity. Agreeable to award of James Goodrich, S Brewer, John L McRae, R Batson and Marble Stone, considered by Court that pl^{tf} recover ag^t defendant $150 the balance due, and parties recover of each other the cost agreeable to s^d award

State vs John Cleghorn. True bill

p.-- State vs Morris Blackwell. Jurors permitted to withdraw in a Body untill tomorrow morning under same officers

State vs James West & others. Appearance bond of James West and Russell Craft, $500 each, appear at March Court
State vs James West & others. Appearance bond Russell Craft, $250, attend March Court

SEPTEMBER 1820

p.-- State vs James West & others. Appearance bond James West $250 condition Russell Craft appear at March Court Court adjourned untill tomorrow morning nine O'Clock
Alfred M Harris

Thursday morning September 7th 1820. Present Alford M Harris

State vs Morris Blackwell. Jury [selected above] say Morris Blackwell is Guilty of Murder in manner & form as charged in the Bill of Indictment
p.-- Court adjourned untill tomorrow morning nine O'Clock
Alfred M Harris

Fryday morning September 8th 1820 Present Alfred M Harris

John Summerville vs Richard C Napier. Depositions of Duncan Robertson and Wm Robertson to be read in behalf of plaintiff

John Summerville vs Montgomery Bell. Depositions of Duncan Robertson and Wm Robertson to be read in behalf of plaintiff

William M Thomas vs Daniel Owings. Deposition of John Brewer to be taken, giving def^t five days notice of time and place

John Evans exonerated from fine $2.50 for contempt to Court

p.-- John Walker & wife vs James M Thomas. Depositions of Abraham Stanfield & wife Sumner County, William Murry & wife and Thomas Grissom of Wilson County, in behalf of defendant

State vs John Cleghorn. Perjury. Motion by defendant that indictment be quashed is overruled by Court

Petition filed by Eleanor Parrish against Elizabeth Butler; petitioner's security $40

State vs Aaron Fletcher. State to recover against defendant Aaron Fletcher $2000 and costs

p.-- State vs Jno C Collier, W^m L Brown, Ja^s R McMeans, Fedrick W Huling. Forfeitures set aside by payment of Costs

Burwell M Williamson vs Josiah Davidson. Certiorari. By attornies. Order certiorari dismissed; pl^{tf} to recover against deft. On motion against Abner Howell & William P Slaydon his securities $96 with interest from 8th November 1818 untill paid as well all costs in this behalf expended

MARCH 1821

State vs John Cleghorn. Perjury. Def' in proper person sets forth he cannot have an impartial trial in this County. The cause is changed to Hickman County

p.-- State vs Morris Blackwell. Motion for a new trial. The reasons for new trial insufficient; new trial not granted

State vs Morris Blackwell. Prisoner brought to bar and asked by Court if he had anything more to say, why judgment should not be pronounced against him. Blackwell by counsel produced transcript of record from Humphreys Court and alleges record is insufficient. Only name of foreman of grand jury appears in the record.   p.-- Court commands a more complete transcript of the Record in said cause returnable to next Term. Morris Blackwell forthwith taken to jail of Dixon County and there remain until further order of Court

George Clarke lessee vs Rosser Brown. Defendant dead; heirs Roper Brown, Thompson Brown, Arsimina Brown under age 21. William F Brown appointed guardian to defend the suit

p.-- Susan Napier by next friend Richard Williams vs Elias W Napier. Divorce. By attornies. Def' failed to answer petitioner's petition. Elias W Napier guilty of repeated acts of adultery, therefore ordered s^d Susan Napier be divorced from Bonds of Matrimony. Susan Napier to recover of s^d Elias the costs in this behalf expended

State vs M Blackwell. Indictment. Defendant by Counsel filed bill of exceptions to opinion of Court, made part of record

Francis S Ellis exhibited a bill for furnishing the Jury in the case of State vs M Blackwell; admitted
Court adjourned until tomorrow morning nine oclock
                                              Alfred M Harris

Saturday morning Septr 9th 1820   Present Alfred M Harris

Minutes having been read and signed,   Court adjourned until Court in Course.   Alfred M Harris

March Term 1821   Dickson County, Monday 5th March 1821. Present the Honorable Alfred M Harris, Judge of 6th Judicial Circuit who hath changed ridings with Judge of 5th Judicial Circuit. Richard Batson, Sheriff of Dickson, & John L McRae

MARCH 1821

Clerk of Circuit Court for said County

Jury Jesse Ragan, Moses Street, Ashel Vanhook, W^m S Murrell, Thomas Ellis, Jo^s Kimble, Ja^s Hadden, Thomas Nisbitt, Marble Stone, Thomas Hudson, Bartholomew Smith, Austin Richardson, Joshua White, Ebbin Perkins, Edward Perkins, John W Napier, Isaac Tubb, James Mathews, Frederick Collin[Collier?], Jacob Rushing, George Hightower, Maben Gilbert, William McMurry, William Baker, John Baker.

Grand Jury Bartholomew Smith foreman, Jesse Ragan, Wm Baker, Thomas Hudson, Ja^s Hadden, Jno Baker, Thos Ellis, Maben Gilbert, Austin Richardson, Edward Perkins, Eben Perkins, Isaac Tubb, Marble Stone. Benjamin Crews Constable to attend them

p.-- State vs Morris Blackwell. Defendant by attorney moves for new trial

Sterling Brewer vs Christopher Robertson. Ephriam Breeding witness behalf pl^{tf} came not. Pl^{tf} to recover ag^t Breeding $125 unless he appear at next Term of Court

Sterling Brewer vs Chris^r Robertson. On affidavit of pl^{tf}, cause cont^d until next Term, pl^{tf} pays cost of this term

John Walker and wife vs James M Thomas. Depositions may be taken, giving opposite side notice

p.-- McRae & Lanier vs Jesse A Brunson. Debt. Cave Johnson personally appeared, produced Power/Att^y & note of hand executed by sd Brunson to Robert Brunson and endorsed to McRae & Lanier for $1500, 24 March 1819, on which are endorsed two credits, one for $352.68 dated 9 Jany 1820, one for $224.24½ date 1 May 1820. P/A authorized Johnson to confess judgement on sd note & on another note due to John L McRae, which note and P/A are made part of the record. Johnson confesses judgment to McRae & Lanier for $1115.62. John L McRae and Isaac H Lanier to recover of Jesse A Brunson $1115.62.

John L McRae vs Jesse A Brunson. C Johnson produced a P/A in open Court & note of hand signed by Jesse A Brunson payable to John L McRae for $366.35¼ date 1 May 1820 and due one day after date. Judgment confessed by Johnson
p.-- John L McRae to recover $384.66, debt & costs

Sterling Brewer vs Christopher Robertson. Parties by attornies. Deposition of Ephraim Breeding to be taken

John Carothers vs John Epperson. By attornies. Jury John W Napier, Thomas Nisbitt, Ashel Vanhook, James Mathews, George Hightower, W^m McMurry, Joshua White, Moses Street, Jacob

MARCH 1821

Rushing, W^m S Murrell, Sanford Edwards, Ja^s Theadford. Pl^tf came not. Juror John W Napier withdrawn. Remaining jurors from rendering verdict are discharged. Pl^tf nonsuited, def^t to recover against plaintiff his costs

p.-- John Summerville vs Montgomery Bell. Debt. By attornys. Jury [as above] find def^t indebted to pl^tf $324.81¼, damage of detention $21.10. Also his cost

Farmers & Mechanics Bank of Nashville vs Montgomery Bell. By att^ys. Jury [as above] find def^t not indebted to pl^tf. Def^t to recover against pl^tf his costs about his defence expended

Farmers & Mechanics Bank of Nashville vs Montgomery Bell. By attorneys. Depositions of Moses Norville & [blank] Caldwell former clerk of s^d Bank to be taken

Order supersedias issue agreeably to prayer of Jesse Tribble ag^t Martha King to stay collection of $24 by petitioner giving bond security
Court adjourned untill to morrow morning nine O'Clock
Alfred M Harris

p.-- Tuesday March 6th 1821. Present Alfred M Harris, Judge

Anthony W Vanlier vs Joseph Hislip. Def^t's attorney suggests that defendant has departed this life since last Court

George Clarke lessee vs Rosser Brown. Def^t's att^y says that g^dn W^m F Brown app^id for minor infants of Rosser Brown dec^d has departed this life. Robert H Brown appointed guardian to infant heirs of Rosser Brown decd to defend this suit.

Farmers & Mechanics Bank of Nashville vs Montgomery Bell. By att^ys. Order new trial next term by plaintiff paying costs

President, Directors and Company of the Bank of The State of Tennessee vs Montgomery Bell. Debt. Plaintiffs by att^y dismiss suit. Plaintiffs to recover of defendant their costs

p.-- President, directors & Company of the Bank of the State of Tennessee vs Montgomery Bell. Debt. Pl^tfs by att^y order suit dismissed. Defendant agrees to pay all costs

President, Directors & Company of the Bank of the State of Tennessee vs Montgomery Bell. Debt. [decision as above]

President, Directors & Company of the Bank of the State of Tennessee vs Montgomery Bell. Debt. [decision as above]

MARCH 1821

State vs Morriss Blackwell. Motion for mistrial. Blackwell, convicted of murder, appeared at Bar; his att^y read several depositions disclosing probability of testimony in favour of defendant. New trial granted. Blackwell remanded to jail.

p.-- State vs H E Hall. John Hall agrees to pay costs in and about this prosecution expended

State vs James West and Russell Craft. Defendant and security forfeit recognizance

State vs Russell Craft. State to recover ag^t Russell Craft

State vs James West. State to recover against James West

p.-- Christopher Strong vs Montgomery Bell. Deposition of Calvin W Eason of Alabama to be taken and read in evidence, giving defendant twenty days notice

Christopher Strong vs Richard C Napier. Pltf by atty; the deposition of Calvin W Eason of Alabama to be taken

Order Richard Batson Esqr be fined five Dollars for neglect in performance of his duty as Sheriff

David Shropshire allowed $136 for maintaining Morris Blackwell, a prisoner confined in common jail

p.-- Robert Brunson vs John Read. Pl^{tf} by att^y; John Read in proper person ack^d himself indebted to pl^{tf} $2500, damage by nonpayment $121.87. Pl^{tf} to recover, also his costs

Bail for appearance of John Read in following cases: wherein Robt W Green is pltf; 2nd wherein William Tannehill is pl^{tf}; 3rd wherein Robt Brunson is pl^{tf}, in all which Read is deft. Bail surrenders Read. Oliver B Hayes att^y for pl^{tfs} in first two cases, & W^m L Brown, James B Reynolds, & Robert P Dunlap attorneys in last named case, do not require s^d Read in custody. Bail af^{sd} exhonerated from further responsibility

p.-- Robert Brunson vs Richard C Napier. By attorneys. Jury Philip W Austin, Willis Willy, John Giffin, Ezekiel Hickerson, Elisha Gunn, Wm Hightower, Stephen Hostly, And^w Hamilton, Richd Jackson, William Austin, John B Walker, Anthony W Vanlier, assess pl^{tf}'s damage by reason of nonperformance to $2671.87. Pl^{tf} to recover ag^t defendant besides his costs

John Summerville vs Richard C Napier. By att^{ys}. Jury [above] Find for plaintiff his damage by nonperformance

MARCH 1821

p.-- $3155. also his costs about his suit expended

John Summerville vs Montgomery Bell. By att^{ys}. Jury [above] Pl^{tf}'s damage by nonperformance $3155, also costs of suit

p.-- Robert J Clon vs Montgomery Bell. By att^{ys}. Jury [as above] Find def^t indebted to pl^{tf} 237.50, also 6.50 damages by detention, also $11.75 costs

Charles Bailey vs Montgomery Bell. Appeal. By att^{ys}. Def^t withdraws his plea. Pl^{tf} to recover ag^t def^t $79.08 debt, $1 p.-- damage by detention, together with interest, besides his costs by him expended in prosecuting said appeal

President, Directors, & Co of Bank of State of Tennessee vs Montgomery Bell. By att^{ys}. Jury John W Napier, Thos Nisbitt, Ashel Vanhook, James Mathews, George Hightower, William McMurry, Joshua White, Moses Street, Jacob Rushing, William S Murrell, John Winnes[?], Mathew Gilmore, who find for pl^{tf} $1500 debt, damages $106.87½, besides his costs

State vs John Joslin. The fine entered on judgment of County Court ag^t def^t remitted by payment of all costs; & on motion ag^t John Evins and Samuel Joslin his securities

p.-- Gorden F Walker vs Sterling Brewer. By att^{ys}. D^{ft} withdraws plea. Judgement of County Court affirmed. Pl^{tf} to recover ag^t def^t 461.49 balance of debt with $9 damage by detention, also $53.90 damages from date of judg^t to this time

Samuel Turner vs William H & F Balthrop. Debt appeal. By Atty. Jury Philip W Austin, Willis Willey, Jno Giffin, Ezekiel Hickerson, Elisha Gunn, Wm Hightower, Stephen Hosley, Andrew Hamilton, Wm Austin, Richard Jackson, John B Walker, Anthony W Vanlier who say def^t has not paid the debt, the balance of principle and interest to this time 397.76. Pl^{tf} to recover, and also his costs in this behalf expended

p.-- Marble Stone vs James McCauley & Nehemiah Hardy. Debt. By att^{ys}. Def^{ts} withdraw plea. Pl^{tf} to recover of def^t and his security in appeal Drewry Atkins 374.40, interest & cost

Leburn Crews vs Montgomery Bell. Debt. By att^y. Def^t admits judg^t correct. Pl^{tf} to recover of Def^t & ag^t James L Bell & John F Bell his securities in appeal $204, interest, & costs

Darryl Young vs Randolph R Harris. Debt. By att^y. Def^t withdraws plea. Pltf recovers of def^t & Richard N Williams & Wm Blake his securities in appeal $222.14¼, interest, and costs

MARCH 1821

Joseph Saul vs Jesse L Kirk. Defendant withdraws plea. Pltf recovers of defendant and against his securities James Kirk & Sterling Brewer $517, interest, & costs

p.-- Richard C Napier vs Danl Williams. Pl^{tf} by att^y will no further prosecute. Def^t to recover of plaintiff his costs

Joshua G Harkins vs McRae & Lanier. Debt. By attorneys. Def^t admits judg^t. Plaintiff to recover of def^{ts} and ag^t Calvin W Eason security in appeal $1100, interest, and costs

p.-- Elias W Napier vs Danl H Williams. Debt. By att^{ys}. Jury Philip W Austin, Willis Willy, John Giffin, Ezekiel Hickerson, Elisha Gunn, Wm Hightower, Stephen Hostley, And^w Hamilton, Wm Austin, Richd Jackson, John B Walker, Anthony W Vanlier, find for pl^{tf} $205.32 debt, $17.45 damages, and costs

Teagarden & Vingok[?] vs Montgomery Bell. Writ of Enquiry. p.-- By att^{ys}. Jury [above] find pl^{tf} hath sustained damages to amount of $1082.97. Judg^t of Court below affirmed, pl^{tfs} recover of def^t and against James L Bell and John J Bell his securities in appeal aforesaid sum, damages, and costs

Elias W Napier vs Read & Fentress. Appeal. Plaintiff by att^y dismisses suit. Defendants to recover of pl^{tf} their costs

p.-- Gordan & Walker vs Montgomery Bell. Debt. By attorneys. Jury [above] find for Defendant. Def^t to recover his costs

Absalom Baker vs Richard C Napier. Debt. By att^{ys}. Jury Thos Nisbitt, Ashel Vanhook, James Mathews, Ge^o Hightower, W^m McMurry, Joshua White, Moses Street, Jacob Rushing, W^m S Murrell, John West, John Williams, Mathew Gilmore who find for pl^{tf} $651, $19.50 damages. Pl^{tf} recovers of def^t and against Christopher Robertson & John C Collier securities in appeal $670.50, and costs

R Napier vs Jones. Judgment by default set aside & def^t has liberty to plead this time

p.-- Robert Brunson vs Richard C Napier. Deft prays appeal to Superior Court of Errors; granted
Court adjourns until tomorrow morning nine oClock
                                         Alfred M Harris

Wednesday 9th March.   Present Alfred M Harris Judge

John Pursley vs William Herndon, Edward R Bradley, White Cox & David Tally. Attachment. Order writ of attachment or non-

SEPTEMBER 1821

appeal issue commanding sheriff to attach any of the negroes in sd bill mentioned & then in his possession

Rebecca Joslin vs John Joslin. By att^{ys}. Petition dismissed; pl^{tf} pay cost. Def^t recovers ag^t pl^{tf} costs of his defence

Arrington Lowell vs Nancy Lowell. By attys. Petition dismissed, defendant recovers against plaintiff costs expended

Woolfolk & Gerrld[?] vs J H Lanier. By attorney. [illegible] p.-- Appeal to Superior Court of Errors granted

Order fine entered yesterday against Richard Batson, Sheriff for neglect of duty be remitted upon his paying costs

Absolom Baker vs Richard C Napier. Debt. Def^t prayed appeal in nature of Writ of Error; granted

p.-- John Summerville vs Richard C Napier. Debt. Deft prayed appeal in nature of Writ of Error; granted

Grand Jury presentment ag^t Christopher Robertson and others; jury discharged

John Summerville vs Montgomery Bell. Debt. Defendant prayed appeal in nature of Writ of Error; same is allowed
Court adjourned until Court in Course.   Alfred M Harris

September Term 1821.   Charlotte, September 3, 1821.
Present the Honorable Parry W Humphreys Esqr Judge

Jury Shedrick Bell, Wm Gentry, Wm Gunn, Joseph Eason, James Tatum, Jo^s Morris, Archabald Sansell, Jno Lucas, Thos Holloway, Samuel Sparks, John Hand, Edwd Teal, Featherston Cross, Cary Wiggins, Drury Price, Richard Tatum, Solomon Graham, Henry Stone, George Brazell, Thomas Whitmill, Benjn Gilbert, Joseph Kimble, Joseph Rye, Washington Hunter.
Grand Jury Shedrick Bell Foreman, William Gentry, Wm Gunn, Joseph Eason, James Tatum, Joseph Morris, Archabald Sansell, John Lucas, Thomas Holloway, Samuel Sparks, Jno Hand, Edward Teal, Featherston Cross.
Seburn Crews Constable sworn to attend the Grand Jury

William M Thomas vs Daniel Owings. By att^{ys}. Jury Cary Wiggins, Drury Price, Richd Tatum, Solomon Graham, Henry Stone, George Brazell, Thos Whitmill, Benjn Gilbert, Joseph Kimble,

SEPTEMBER 1821

Joseph Rye, Benjamin Clark, & John Toler, who find for pl^{tf}.
p.-- Pl^{tf} to recover ag^t def^t $16.25 besides his costs

John Walker & wife vs James M Thomas. Slander. By attorneys.
Jury [above] find in favour of plaintiff, assess damage to
$47. Plaintiff to recover of defendant said sum and costs

John Walker & wife vs James W Thomas. Eleanor Parrish, appearance bail of James M Thomas, surrendered him. Sheriff to
take James M Thomas into custody untill he gives security

Christopher Robertson vs William Turner. By att^{rs}. Jury Thos
Bullion, Jno Lowel, Alexander Rose, Wm Hollingsworth, George
Light, Jno Grims, William McMurry, Ge^o Tubb, Edward Houston,
Ezor McAdoo, James Gunn, Charles Gunn. p.-- find defendant
guilty of trespass; plaintiff's damage one cent & costs; and
defendant may be taken and pl^{tf} have his writ of possession

Mortgage from Thomas Whitmill to Christopher Strong for 600
acres on Cumberland River proven by Field Farrar and David
Irwin, ordered certifyed for registration

John Wims vs Elisha Gunn. Ejectment. By attorneys. Jury Cary
Wiggins, Drury Price, Richard Tatum, Solomon Graham, Henry
Stone, Ge^o Brazell, Thomas Whitmill, Benjamin Gilbert, Alex^r
Rose, Joseph Rye, Benjamin Clark, John Tolar who are permitted to disperse untill tomorrow morning
Court adjourns untill tomorrow morning Eight O'clock
P. W. Humphreys

p.-- Tuesday September 4th 1821.
Present The Honorable Parry W Humphreys Esquire Judge

Joshua G Harkins vs McRae and Lanier. Plaintiff by attorney
moves to shew cause why execution should not issue ag^t defts

Grand Jury present bill of Indictment against Elias W Napier

John Wims vs Elisha Gunn. Same jury upon their oaths say the
defendant is guilty of trespass; assess pltf's damage to one
cent besides his cost.

Mortgage from Jesse Russell to Christopher Strong for thirty
one acres ackd

p.-- Jeremiah Baxtor vs Montgomery Bell. Upon affidavit of
Defendant, cause is continued to next Term

Stephen Handlin vs Samuel Vance. Depositions of Wm Handlin,

SEPTEMBER 1821

Wm Hankins, Powell Vaughn & Wm Dean to be taken, behalf pl^{tf}

Sterling Brewer vs Christopher Robertson. Deposition of Geo Gallion to be taken; give pl^{tf} 3 h^{rs} notice if in Charlotte; if taken in Alabama, 20 days notice of time and place

Farmers & Merchants Bank of Nashville vs Montgomery Bell. Jury Cary Wiggins, Drury Price, Richd Tatum, Solomon Graham, Henry Stone, George Brazell, Thomas Whitmill, Benjn Gilbert, Joseph Kimble, Joseph Rye, Benj^a Clark, Wm Hudson, who find the def^t not indebted as alleged, def^t to recover his costs

p.-- Order Sheriff summon a pannell of 48 jurymen for trying The State vs Blackwell at this place tomorrow at 8 oclock

David Hogan vs Clark Spencer. Motion of David Hogan by att^y; judgm^t ag^t David Hogan March 1820 in favour John Spencer for 60.95; judgment was on note Clarke Spencer gave Turner Sanders; Jno Spencer, Jno Read, David Hogan were Clark Spencers securities; judgment obtained ag^t Jno Spencer only as one of the securities, judgment satisfied by John Spencer. At March Term 1820 John Spencer recovered agt Hogan $60.95, one third of judgment Turner Sanders vs Jno Spencer, sd 60.95 has been paid by Hogan. Considered by Court that David Hogan recoover against Clarke Spencer $60.95 with cost of this motion

Farmers & Merchants Bank of Nashville vs Montgomery Bell. Jury Wm Gentry, Wm Gunn, Jo^s Eason, James Tatum, Jo^s Morris, Archabald Lansell, John Lucas, Thomas Holloway, Saml Sparks, John Hand, Edwd Teal, Featherston Cross. Wm Gentry withdrawn & jury discharged. Pl^{tf} nonsuited, def^t to recover his costs

p.-- Farmers & Merchants Bank of Nashville vs Montgomery Bell. Ordered nonsuit set aside; hearing set for next Term

Farmers & Merchants Bank of Nashville vs Montgomery Bell. Jury Wm Gentry, Wm Gunn, Jo^s Eason, James Tatum, Jo^s Morris, Archabald Lansel, Jno Lucas, Thos Holloway, Saml Sparks, Jno Hand, Edward Teal, Featherston Cross who find for plaintiff; assess damage to $1114. Pl^{tf} to recover, also his cost. Def^t prays appeal; granted; also files his bill of exceptions

State vs Russell Craft. Ordered that the Forfeiture taken at last Term of this Court be set aside upon payment of cost

p.-- State vs Russell Craft. Riot. Appearance bond $500, on Grand Jury Indictment, Montgomery County. David Irwin and Samuel Craft his securities

State vs James West. Riot. Appearance bond $500, Grand Jury

SEPTEMBER 1821

Indictment, Montgomery County. David Irwin, Saml Craft, sec.

p.-- John Pursley vs White Coxe. Depositions permitted.

William Miller vs Richard C Napier. Deposition of Cyprian Farmer and others in Charlotte to be taken on Saturday next. Court adjourns untill to morrow morning nine OClock
P. W. Humphreys

Wednesday morning September 5th 1821.
Present Parry W Humphreys, Esquire, Judge

Farmers & Merchants Bank of Nashville vs Montgomery Bell. Motion for new trial. New Trial to be had next Term

p.-- John Winn vs Elisha Gunn. Motion for new trial.

Kilpatrick Carter vs Benjamin Joslin. Deposition of [blank] Michel to be taken in Court house this day

State of Tennessee vs Morris Blackwell. Murder. Defendant in proper person pleads Not guilty. Jury Cary Wiggins, Drury Price, Jo^s Kimble, Danl Hickerson, Huel Parish, W^m McMurray, John Sowell, John Willey, Adonijah Edwards, Andrew Hamilton, Robt McMurray, Ge^o Tubbs, withdraw in a Body until tomorrow; Elkanah Parish and Benjamin Crews sworn to attend them Court then adjourned until tomorrow morning seven oclock
P W Humphreys

Thursday morning September 6th 1821
Present the Honorable Perry W Humphreys, Esquire, Judge

State of Tennessee vs Morris Blackwell. Murder. Same Jurors, say Blackwell is guilty. Prisoner remanded to jail

Joseph Hislip vs Anthony W Vanlier. Peter Martin admr of Joseph Hislip decd. Suit revived, Peter Martin to prosecute

Anthony W Vanlier vs Joseph Hislip. Covenant. Suit revived, Peter Martin adm^r of Joseph Hislip dec^d admitted to defence

p.-- State vs Jesse Tribble. A & B. Jury Benj^a Gilbert, Thos Whitmill, Jno H Stone, Richd Tatum, Solomon Graham, Ge^o Brazeal, Jno Davey, Jno Walker, Edward Houston, Wm Bullion, Jo^s Nisbitt, Thomas Hudson. Jurors disperse untill tomorrow

John Walker & wife vs James M Thomas. Judgment obtained ag^t def^t in favour of John Walker and wife at first day of this

SEPTEMBER 1821

Term to be stayed ten months. John Adams and Eleanor Parrish
security for defendant James M Thomas
Court adjourned untill to morrow morning Eight O'Clock

P.W.Humphreys

Fryday morning September 7th 1821
Present the Honorable Parry W Humphreys, Esquire, Judge

Joshua G Harkin vs McRae & Lanier. Harkin had applied for an
exception behalf Joshua G Harkin ag^t John L McRae & Isaac H
Lanier; judgment rendered at March Term 1820, current bank
notes would be taken in discharge of s^d execution. An Appeal
prayed; granted; entered bond

p.-- John Read and Christopher Robertson vs James Douglass.
Ja^s Douglass to recover of Jno Read & Chris^r Robertson, & on
motion Elias W Napier, security, $517.50, & $42.98 interest.

John Winns vs Elisha Gunn. Motion for new trial; overruled

p.-- Christopher Robertson vs John Hinson. Depositions of
Breedlove Bradford and Robertson and others of New Orleans
to be taken in New Orleans giving defendant 30 days notice

Hall vs Elias W Napier. Appearance bond $1000, Richard C
Napier and Montgomery Bell his securities

State of Tennessee vs Isreal Miller. Murder. Jury Jesse Russell, Pleasant Crews, John Adams, Samuel King, Henry A C Napier, Hardeman Stone, Thos Simmons, Jno W Napier, Geo Light,
John C Massie, Samuel D Austin, Alexander Dickson
p.-- find Miller not guilty
Court adjourned untill to morrow morning Eight O'Clock

P. W. Humphreys

Saturday morning September 8th 1824
Present the Honorable Parry W Humphreys, Esquire, Judge

Sterling Brewer vs Christopher Robertson. Deposition of And^w
Hamilton to be taken

John Winns vs Elisha Gunn. Defendant prays appeal to Supreme
Court of Errors; granted; enters bond and security

Kilpatrick Carter vs Benjamin Joslin. The deposition of R J
Miggs to be taken giving plaintiff 40 days notice

p.-- Jurors who served are allowed 75 cents per day

MARCH 1822

Richard C Napier chairman vs Jesse Tribble, Absolom Tribble, John Edwards. Execution to issue against def's in conformity with judgment had at March Term 1820

Richard C Napier chairman vs Jesse Tribble. Defendant to pay costs, and, on motion, his securities Robert Farmer, Absolom Tribble and James Conniway

John Tatum vs Delila Tatum. Petition for divorce. Def't shown guilty of repeated acts of adultery
p.-- Bonds of matrimony dissolved; Delila pays costs

State of Tennessee vs Jesse Tribble. Appearance bond $500, Aberam Coldwell and George West, securities

State of Tennessee vs Morris Blackwell. Murder. Motion for a new trial sustained; verdict set aside

David Shropshire jailor of Dickson County allowed $74.25 for keeping and maintaining Morris Blackwell in the county jail

p.-- Benjamin Crews and Eleanor Parrish fined $25 each for negligence as sworn officers to attend the jurors that were impanneled on trial of Tennessee against Blackwell

Jn° Pursly vs William Herndon, Edward R Bradford, David Tally, and White Cone. Demurrer of White Cone heard; overruled

Jn° Pursly vs William Herndon, Edward R Bradford, David Tally. Def'ts are citizens of Christian County, Kentucky; their appearance is ordered and to be advertised

p.-- George Vinyard vs Patience Vinyard. Petition for divorce. Deft to file answer within sixty days.

Jacob Bredwill vs William Edwards. Depositions of [blank] to be taken in behalf plaintiff, giving notice

Cary Wiggins vs Arthur Bishop. Injunction. Bond to be given. Court then adjourned until Court in Course. P. W. Humphreys

p.-- March Term 1822. March 4th 1822. Present the Honorable Robert Mack, Judge of Sixth Judicial Circuit who suggests he has interchanged ridings with Hon'ble Parry W Humphreys Judge of the 5th Judicial Circuit by agreement dated 2nd February 1822 which is entered in the record

MARCH 1822

p.-- Richard Batson, Sheriff, returns venire facias; following jurors summoned: John Pickett, Thomas May, Jesse P Dees, Amos James, Moses Gammell, Luke Matlock, Michael Light, John Hays, Hugh Dickson, John Grymes, William Hand, Daniel Leach, William Gilbert, John Weems, Elisha Gunn, Jn° Tatom, William Powers, Nelson McClelland, Robert Livingston, Edward Lucas
p.-- Grand Jurors Robt Livingston foreman, Wm Powers, John Hays, Wm Hand, Danl Leach, Moses Gammell, Jn° Weems, Michael Light, Hugh Dickson, Thomas May, John Pickett, John Grymes, Jesse P Dees, attended by Benjamin Crews, Constable

Resignation of John L McRae, Clerk Circuit Court, accepted. John C Collier apptd Clerk; bond $10,000, Securities Thomas Collier, S. Brewer, Field Farrar, Joseph Kimble

p.-- John Tatum a juror discharged from attendance this term

Assignment of plat and survey 50 acres by James Robertson to Mumford Smith proven by Lemuel Russel and Spencer T Hunt

Sterling Brewer vs Christopher Robertson. By att^{vs}. Jury Jn° Hays, Wm Hand, Danl Leach, Moses Gammell, Jn° Weems, Michael Light, Hugh Dickson, Thos May, Jn° Pickett, Jn° Grymes, Jes-
p.-- se P Dees, Nelson McClelland, adjourned till tomorrow Court adjourned untill tomorrow morning 9 o'Clock Robt Mack

Tuesday morning March 5th 1822
Present the Honorable Robert Mack, Esquire, Judge

Sterling Brewer vs C Robertson. Jury above find for the def^t

p.-- George Clarke's lessee vs Heirs of Roper Brown. Ejectment. Jury W^m B Haddin, Thos Hunter, Nathan Tubb, Ge° Tubb, Jn° Rhue, Jesse L Kirk, Jn° West, Ge° Light, James Thompson, William Powers, Robert Livingston, Edward Lucas; W^m B Haddin withdrawn; jury discharged; Malton Dickson appointed to survey the land in controversy

John Pursley vs White Coxe. Thomas Whitmill surrenders the Defendant in discharge of himself as bail
Court adjourned till tomorrow morning 9 OClock.   Robt Mack

Wednesday Morning 6th March 1822. Present Robert Mack, Judge

State of Tennessee vs James West. Riot. Defendant came not

State vs David Irwin & Saml Craft. Recognizance. Indictment

MARCH 1822

for a riot. Defendants came not, forfeit $250 each

Grand Jury present Bill/Indictment against James Glass

p.-- State vs Russel Craft. Riot. Def^t came not; forfeits

State of Tennessee vs David Irwin & Saml Craft. Forfeiture.

State vs James Glass. Defendant in proper person pleads Not Guilty. Jury Amos James, Nelson McClelland, Wm Armour, Wm Floyd, William B Haddin, John Roy Senr, Jno Justice, Rich^d N Williams, Edwd Lucas, Wm Bullion, Willis Norsworthy, Joseph Williams who find defendant not guilty

p.-- State vs Morris Blackwell. Indictment for Murder. Cause continued till next term of this Court

State vs Jesse Tribble. A & B. Bond $250, Absalom Tribble and George West his securities

p.-- David Shropshire jailer allowed $68.12½ for keeping and maintaining Morris Blackwell a prisoner in the Dickson jail

State vs Samuel Rogers. Solicitor General will no further prosecute this suit

State vs Daniel Toler. Writ of Error. Def^t Daniel Taylor in proper person; error in proceedings or in rendition of judgment. Judgment of Court below affirmed. State to recover of Danl Tolar the costs of County Court
Court then adjourned till tomorrow morning 9 oClock
                                              Robt Mack

Thursday morning 7th March 1822. Present Robert Mack, Judge

p.-- George Clark lessee vs Roper Brown heirs.

John L McRae vs Christopher Robertson & Christian Baughman. Trespass. Plaintiff in proper person will no further prosecute his suit. Defendants to recover costs

Christian Baughman vs Marble Stone. In Equity. Pl^{tt} says he will no further prosecute his suit

p.-- Richard R P Powell adm^r of Esther Powell dec^d vs John Hays ex^{tr} of Robert Hays dec^d. Appeal. By attornies. Richard Powell to recover of John Hays $158.26 & costs

Isaac H Lanier vs Ramsey, Green, & Vanlier. Writ of Error.

MARCH 1822

Plaintiff will no further prosecute; defendants recover

Aaron Arnold vs Randolph R Harris. Certiorari. By attorneys. Arnold to recover of Randolph R Harris and against Richard D Sansom & William R Freeman his securities $100 and interest

p.-- Sterling Brewer vs Ephraim Breeding. Forfeiture. Pl^{tf} no further prosecutes; Defendant recovers his costs

Moses Quarles vs Holloway N Merit. Bill/Injunction. By attys Decree Moses Quarles to recover of sd Holloway N Merrit and ag^t Benjamin B Rayburn and Robert Whitledge his securities

State vs James Glass. Dickson Court to pay prosecution costs

State vs Daniel Talor. Appeal to Supreme Court of Errors and appeals granted on his giving bond & security

p.-- State vs Elias W Napier. Perjury. Def^t in proper person pleads not guilty. Jury John Nisbitt, Alex^r Dickson, Robert Larkins, Wm Huston, James Larkins, John Ray Senr, Christian Baughman, Danl Leach, John Weams, Michael Light, Wm Caffrey, James Hunter who are placed in the care of Benjamin Crews & Eleazor Parish two constables until tomorrow
Court then adjourned till tomorrow morning 8 OClock

Robt Mack

p.-- Friday morning March 8th 1822.
Present Robert Mack, Judge

Richard Whitehead vs John Picket. Defendant moves to dismiss supersedeas; supersedeas dismissed; Picket recovers of pl^{tf}

Sterling Brewer vs C Robertson. Motion for new trial Granted

p.-- William Miller vs Richard C Napier. Case. Pl^{tf} recovers $47.21 & costs

State vs Elias W Napier. Perjury. Jury afsd find deft not guilty; county to pay costs of prosecution

William Ward & Daniel Hickison vs Edward Teal. Attachment. Pl^{tfs} recover of def^t their costs expended

Wm Ward & Wm Hickison vs Edwd Teal. In Equity. Pl^{tf} recover

p.-- John Hinson vs Thos Collier. Injunction. Collier moves for dissolution of injunction. Court dissolved injunction & Thomas Collier recovers of John Hinson and of Nehemiah Scott

OCTOBER 1823

and John Adams his securities $858 the debt and $60 interest

George Vineyard vs Patience Vineyard. Petition for Divorce. Defendant came not; evidence of William Fussell that the defendant had been guilty of adultery; divorce granted
p.-- Court adjourned till Court in Course. Robt Mack

End of this Book

Book October 1823 through July 1828

At a court of pleas and quarter sessions begun and held for the County of Dickson at the Courthouse in the town of Charlotte on the first Monday in October in the year of our Lord one thousand eight hundred and twenty three and of the Independence of the United States the forty eighth. Present the worshipful Sterling Brewer, Nathan Nisbitt, Abiram Coldwell, John Johnson, Jesse L Kirk, Esquires, Justices

Christopher Strong app^{td} road overseer in place of [blank]

Following excused from double tax for 1823 on the following property: Joseph Moore 1 white pole; Jesse Ward 114 acres; Mahlam Wood 20 acres; Nathan Ragan 52 acres 1 white pole; Wm Simpson 200 acres 1 white pole

James Douglass app^{td} overseer of road in place of Wm Dunigan

Ebenezer Whitehead produced scalp of wolf over age of 4 mo^s killed within bounds of Dickson, allowed agreeable to law

John Pendergrass, Moses Parker, Minor Bibb Esqrs appointed to lay off one years provision for maintainance of the widow and family of Levi Tidwell decd out of sd estate

Hewel Parrish to adm^r estate of Wyatt Parrish deceased; bond with Enos James & Alexander Dickson, sum Six Hundred Dollars

p.-- Eli Crow app^{td} overseer of road in place of John Right

D H Williams Esqr, John Johnson Esqr, and John May to settle with adm^r of Lewis Berry dec^d, and make return to this Court

W^m McClelland app^{td} overseer of road in place of Wm Fussell

Sterling Brewer, Nathan Nisbitt Esq^{rs}, and Richard Batson to settle with Ja^s Douglass former guardian of Terisa M Bedford

James W Christian app^{td} road overseer in place of Wm Turner

OCTOBER 1823

Robert Nisbitt Senr apptd g^{dn} to Moses Nisbitt minor orphan of John Nisbitt dec^d; no property, so no bond is required

James Rogers adm^r of estate of Lewis Berry dec^d, allowed $22 for his Services in Settling the Estate

Field Farrar allowed $7 for a book for Records of this Court

Archabald Pullen apptd road overseer in place of John Sowell

Richard Waugh, Register, allowed $12 for a book for deeds

Benjamin Sterdevant, Ephraim Ellis, and Alexander Dickson app^{td} to lay off one years provisions for widow & family of Wyatt Parrish dec^d out of said estate & make return thereof

p.-- Polly Burgess to adm^r estate of John Burgess dec^d; gave bond with Absolam Tribble $400; Robert Armour Esqr, William Armour and Samuel Brown app^{td} to lay off one years provision out of s^d estate for widow & family of s^d Burgess

Ordered Joseph Wilson, Benjamin Sturdevant, Esquires, & John Hinson to settle with adm^x of estate of Robert Rogers dec^d. Also divide the estate among the legatees

William Shelton appointed a constable; bond $1250 with James Rogers and Absolam Tribble

Orrin Hogan appointed a constable; having given bond $1250 with Henry Goodrich and James Eason

D H Williams & Benjn Sturdevant to adm^r estate of Alex^r Rose dec^d in place of Aron Vanhook; bond $800 with Alex^r Dickson

Tryphence Smith allowed $50/y^r from 1 July last for keeping Nancy Groce a poor person now in her possession

p.-- Jurors to Circuit Court in November Wm Rye, Jno Witley, Robt Livingston, Danl Coleman, Wm Hutchinson, Newton Sowell, Thomas Simmons, Miles Ashley, Albert Speights, Noah Sugg, Benjn Clark, Ja^s Larkins, Bartholomew Smith, Robt Whitwell, Nathaniel Simpson, Wm Simpson, Jno Adams, Wm Hooper, Charles Thompson, Allen Bowen, James Tatom, Anderson England, Wilkie Myatt, Gabriel Petty, Samuel King

Jurors to March Circuit Court Molton Dickson, John West, Isaac West, Edward D Hicks, Sylvanis Lattimore, Danl Parker, Emsley Seyars, Peter Jackson, Thomas Mathews, Benjamin Cox, Austin Richardson, John H Stone, William Wright, Saml Brown, Willis Collier, Wm Armour, Nehemiah Scott, John May, Sumrel

OCTOBER 1823

Turner, Joel Marsh, Archibald Cox, John Rue, Burwell Myatt, Jesse S Ross, Alsey Semore

Jurors to January County Court Willis Willey, Middleton Higginbottham, Christian Baughman, Hudson Shropshire, Ja^s Ferroll, Jo^s Lampley, Jacob Lampley, Silas Harris, Robt Lucas, James W Christian, Jno Hall, Wm Cox, Thos Bullion, James Epperson, James Armour, Ge^o Baxley, Wm Tauge, Jno Picket, Amos Thompson, Jo^s Eason, Washington England, Elisha Gunn, Brinkley George, Kendrick Myatt, John Reding, George Tubb, Daniel Leach, Jacob Leach

Ge^o F Napier app^{td} road overseer in place of Jonath^n Malugin

Robt Whitledge appt^d road overseer with hands Edward Holly, Horatio Humphries, Hollway N Merit, W^m D Reynolds, Stokely Humphries, Lain Bledsoe, And^w Lewis, C Merit, Robt Whitledge

James R Napier apptd road overseer in place of Wm Gentry

Jesse L Kirk resigned as a Justice of the Peace

Deed Wm Morrisette to John Hall 112½ acres proven by oaths of John B Brown and Harvey Houston
Deed Richard Batson Sheriff to Francis Wisdom 100 acres ackd
Deed Nehemiah Hardy to Wiley Donnell 100 acres ackd
Deed James Hightower, Wm Hightower & Robt T Hightower to Ge^o Hightower 89 acres ackd
Deed James Shelton to Humphries Halliburton 20 acres proven by Nehemiah Hardy and Nicholas Baker
p.-- Deed John Marsh to Wm Stone 30 acres ackd

Assignment of a plat & Certificate by Hiram Dunnagan to Saml King 6 acres on Pine River proven by John Dunnagan & Samuel Dunnagan
Deed Absalom Tribble to John Johnson 121 acres ackd
Bill/Sale Edwd Teal to Chris^r Robertson Negro Girl Arey ackd
Deed/Gift Mary Baker to Absalom Baker for certain property proven by James Eason and Washington England
Deed Edward Faris & Eleanor Faris to Ge^o Clark proven by Jno Piffin & Polly Piffin
Deed/Relinquishment Edward Farris & Eleanor Farris to George Clark for land proven by John Piffin & Polly Piffin

Power/Atty Jesse Seals to John Adams proven by Saml Self who proves the handwriting of Aron Vanhook one of the subscribing witnesses, the execution of sd Power having been before proven by H W Henson the other witness

p.-- Order Cave Johnson solicitor General of 10th Solicitor-

OCTOBER 1823

ial district allowed $35 for exoficio services for 1823
Court adjourned untill to morrow Morning 9 O'Clock
D H Williams, Nathan Nisbitt, A Coldwell

Tuesday October 7th 1823   Present D H Williams, Nathan
Nisbitt, A Coldwell, Esquires, Justices

Grand Jury Drury Atkins foreman, John Grimes, Joel Arrinton, Alsey Seamore, James Donnel, Willis Walker, Washington Hunter, Jas Haddin Sr, Leml Read, Jas McKee, Alexr Southerland, George Powell, Thos Rice; attended by Constable Wm Hightower

Jiles Jones app'td road overseer in place of George Hightower
Deed Adin Bowen to Elisha Stewart 94 acres ackd
James M Ross and Nehemiah Hardy Esqrs to settle with admr of Jeremiah Sullivan decd
p.-- James Jones vs Edwd McCormack. Pltfs atty orders suit dismissed

Kercheville & Bayless assee vs Jesse P Dees. Debt. By Attys. Jury Reese Bowen, Wm Adams, Elijah Dodson, John King, John Picket, Daniel Forsey, Geo Southerland, Wm Rye, Jiles Jones, Elisha Stewart, Richd Tatom, Wm McKee who find $100 debt for pltf, damage $6, & costs

Jno W Napier vs Montgy Bell. Appl. By atties. Jury (above) find for pltf $24.49. Pltf stays execution until 1 April

p.-- John W Napier vs Montgy Bell. Appl. Jury as above find $35 for pltf and costs. Execution stayed as above

Jno W Napier vs Montgomery Bell. Appl. By atties. Jury above find for pltf $22.90. Execution stayed as above

p.-- Jno W Napier vs Montgy Bell. Appl. By attys. Jury above find for pltf $35.26 & costs. Execution stayed as above

Henry A C Napier vs Montgy Bell. Appeal. By atties. Jury as above find for pltf $91.60 & costs. Execution stayed

p.-- Isaac West admr vs Willis Jackson. Appeal. Pltf orders his suit dismissed.
Allen Bowen vs Elisha & Andw Stewart. Pltf in proper person orders his suit dismissed
Elisha Stewart vs Allen Bowen. Pltf in proper person orders his suit dismissed

Reese Bowen vs C Robertson. Debt. By atties. Jury Jno Scott, Wm Adams, Elijah Dodson, Jno King, John Picket, Danl Forsey,

OCTOBER 1823

Geo Southerland, Wm Rye, Jiles Jones, Elisha Stewart, Richd Tatom, Wm McKee find for plff $115, damage $4.87½, & costs

p.-- Robert Stewart vs Nathan Norman. Appeal. Deft by atty; plff came not; deft recovers of plff Robt Stewart his costs

John Adams vs Abram Self. Cause continued

John Marsh vs Montgy Bell. By atties. Jury Reese Bowen, Wm Adams, Elijah Dodson, Jno King, Jno Picket, Danl Forsey, Geo Southerland, William Rye, Jiles Jones, Elisha Stewart, Richd Tatom, William McKee who find for plaintiff $38.45 and costs

William B Ross assee vs Field Farrar. Appeal. By attornies. Jury above find for plaintiff $26.12½ and costs

p.-- Christopher Robertson vs Samuel Craft. Debt. By atties. Jury Jno Scott, Wm Adams, Elish Dodson, John King, Jno Picket, Danl Forsey, Geo Sutherland, Wm Rye, Jiles Jones, Elisha Stewart, Richd Tatom, Wm McKee who find Christopher Robertson was security for Craft in a note of hand on which Judgement in favor of Rees Bowen for $122.87½ was obtained. Said Cr Robertson to recover of defendant $122.87½ besides costs

p.-- A Vanlier, Bernard Vanlier and Robert Baxter vs John C Collins and Christopher Clements exr of Wm Clements decd. By atties. Jury Reese Bowen, Wm Adams, Elijah Dodson, Jno King, Jno Picket, Danl Forsey, Geo Southerland, William Rye, Jiles Jones, Elisha Stewart, Richard Tatom, Wm McKee find that the defts detain $173.42 debt; damage $15.80. And costs. Defendants pray writ of errors; give bond; file bill of exception. Court adjourned untill tomorrow morning 9 OClock

A Coldwell, S Brewer, Nathan Nesbitt

Wednesday Morning October 8th 1823. Present Sterling Brewer, A Coldwell, Nathan Nesbitt, Esquires, Justices

Sheriff to lay off Dower of Nancy Sugg out of real estate of William Sugg decd

p.-- Noah Sugg vs Jno Lucas, Josiah Sugg, Sally Sugg, Howel Sugg, Mary Sugg, Aquilla Sugg. Petition for partition. Order Joseph Morriss, Shaderick Bell, Wm Turner, James W Christian and Robert Duke to make partition of real estate of Wm Sugg decd among heirs of sd Sugg, and make return to next Court

Order Sterling Brewer & Nathan Nisbitt Esqrs superintend repairing of Jail door lately put out of repair by Nathan Norman and White Coxe

OCTOBER 1823

State vs James Scott. Pettit Larceny. James Scott, labourer, appeared. Jury William Adams, Elijah Dodson, John King, John Picket, Dan¹ Forsey, John Choate, Wᵐ Hendrix, Geᵒ Hightower, Thomas Noland, Robert Nisbitt Senʳ, Robert Livingston, Reese Bowen who find defendant guilty; fined $5 and pay cost

p.-- John Johnson vs James Epperson. James Epperson presents petition from a judgment against him in favour of John Johnston for $30 obtained before Robert Armour Esqr. Petition is granted, petitioner having given bond and security

S D Christian vs Polly West. On motion of plᵗᶠ, order Drury Christian a former Sheriff allowed $7.32, the clerk of Court $3 for his fees, in laying off dower of Polly West widow of Isaac West decd

State vs Jesse Hall. Appearance bond, Susannah Hall $250
Court adjᵈ morrow morning 9 OClock
S Brewer, N Nisbitt, A Coldwell

Thursday Morning October 9th 1823   Present the Worshipfull Sterling Brewer, Nathan Nisbitt, Abiram Coldwell, Justices

p.-- State vs Kendley V Parrish. A&B. K V Parrish, labourer, indicted of assault & battery on James Donnel, pleads guilty & is fined $4 & cost; remains in custody of shᶠᶠ until paid

William Hand apptᵈ road overseer in place of Thomas Mathews

State vs Kendley V Parrish. A & B agᵗ Wᵐ Tatum; pleaded not guilty. Jury Drewry Adkins, Jnᵒ Grimes, Joel Arrinton, Alsey Seamore, Willis Walker, Washington Hunter, Jaˢ Haddin, Lemuel Read, James McKee, Alexander Sutherland, Geᵒ Powel, Thoˢ Rice who find defendant guilty; fined 25¢ and cost

p.-- James Ross, Justice/Peace, resigned

Kercheville & Bayless vs Jesse P Dees. Sheriff Richard Batson and H N Allen plᵗᶠ's attʸ in controversial judgᵗ wherein K & B are plᵗᶠˢ as assignees of George West, & Jesse P Dees is Defᵗ. By agreement of Batson and Allen, ordered Batson be exhonerated from liability as special bail in that behalf

State vs Kendley V Parrish. Indicted for Assault on Henry W Hinson. Pleads guilty; fined $8 & costs; remains in custody until said fine and cost be paid

State vs William Edwards. Peace Warrant. William Edwards and

OCTOBER 1823

Elisha Gunn; Edwards to keep peace towards Stephen Tatom for a year and a day and towards all other good citizens

State vs Kendley V Parrish. Riot. John Goodrich prosecutor. Nolle prosequi entered; county to pay costs

State vs Richard Evens. Riot. Nolle prosequi entered. George Evens Senr assumes all costs

State vs William D Evans. Riot. Nolle prosequi entered. Ge^o Evans Senr assumes all costs

State vs Calvin Beter. Riot. Nolle prosequi entered. George Evans Senr assumes all costs

State vs John Tatom. Appearance bond; John Winns & James Tatom his securities

p.-- Oney Harvey vs Montg^y Bell. By att^{ies}. Pl^{tf} to recover of Defendant $108 debt and $4.89 interest besides costs

Sterling Brewer vs Montg^y Bell. By att^{ies}. Jury Allen Bowen, John Dunnegan, Ira A Meck, Wm Dunnegan, James Larkins, John Nolen, Anderson England, Allen Howard, Wm Ward, James Gunn, Pleasant Crews, John Grimes; def^t owes $52.18 3/4 & costs

State vs Elisha Greenwood. Riot. Nolle prosequi entered, and the county to pay cost

p.-- Samuel Smith vs Montg^y Bell. Appeal. By att^{ies}. Jury Drury Adkins, John Grimes, Joel Arrinton, Alsey Seamore, Ja^s Daniel, Willis Walker, Washington Hunter, James Haddin Senr, James McKee, Alex^r Southerland, Ge^o Powell, Thomas Rice find for pl^{tf} $48.86 beside cost expended. Appeal granted

Samuel Smith vs Montg^y Bell. Appeal. Jury named above find for pl^{tf} debt $29.15 & cost. Defendant prays appeal; granted

p.-- John Lee vs Montg^y Bell. Jury named above find for pl^{tf} $98.25 debt, interest $9 and his costs. Appeal granted

John Price vs Nehemiah Scott. Debt. Above jury. Find for pl^t his debt $400 and his costs

p.-- William McCrary vs Montgomery Bell. Pl^{tf} by attorney dismisses suit; defendant recovers of plaintiff his costs

George Evins S^r, Guardian, vs Thomas Hudson, Guardian. Pl^{tf} in proper person dismisses his suit; def^t recovers his costs

OCTOBER 1823

State vs Kendley V Parrish. Appearance bond of K V Parrish, Eleanor Parrish his security. Battery on William Tatom. Court adjourned until tomorrow Morning 9 Clock
S Brewer, Nathan Nisbitt, A Coldwell

Friday Morning October 10th 1823   Present the Worshipful Sterling Brewer, Nathan Nisbitt, Abiram Coldwell, Justices

Spenser T Hunt and L Hunt Adm^r & Adm^x of C Hudson dec^d vs S Croswait & R C Napier. Pl^{tf} recovers of def^t $172.12½ debt and damages together with costs

p.-- Hardin Chambers to oversee road in place of Joel Massie

Order Garret Goodlow excused from paying double tax on 1280 acres for years 1821 and 1822

p.-- Elizabeth Acuff vs Christopher Robertson. Robert Livingston & John Choat, arbitrators, find for Elizabeth Acuff $75 and Christopher Robertson is also to pay costs of suit

p.-- Mack Drummond vs Holloway N Merrit. Continued
John Pursley vs White Coxey. Debt. By att^{ies}. Jury Drury Adkins, John Grimes, Joel Arrington, Alsey Seamore, James Donnell, Willis Walker, James Hadden S^r, Lemuel Read, James McKey, Alexander Southerland, George Powel, & Thomas Rice who find for plaintiff $3124.75 debt and his costs
William H Teagarden vs $Montg^y$ Bell. Pl^{tf} recovers ag^t def^t $372.25 & costs; def^t prays appeal; granted
Peyton R Tunstall vs Benedict Bacon. Ordered execution on a Judgment against def^t in behalf of pl^{tf} on 5 April 1820 for $211.85 debt. Also his costs
p.-- Spencer T Hunt & Lucy Hudson adm vs David Passmore & Wm Austin. By att^{ies}. Pl^{tf} recovers $420 debt & damages besides costs. Def^{ts} pray appeal; granted
James Tidwell vs Jesse P Dees. By att^{ies}. Jury Drury Adkins, Jno Grimes, Joel Arington, Alsey Seamore, Ja^s Daniel, Willis Walker, Ja^s Hadden S^r, Lemuel Read, Ja^s McKey, $Alex^r$ Southerland, Ge^o Powel, Thos Rice find for pl^{tf} $21 debt and his costs. Def^t appeals; John Read & John Montgomery, securities

Deed or quit claim Wm Seals & others to John Adams proven by W^m T Reynolds & Selmon Edwards, 100 acres
p.-- Washington Hunter adm^r of Cary Wiggins dec^d vs $Montg^y$ Bell. By att^{ies}. Pl^{tf} recovers $13.62½ found by jury at last term and costs; def^t appeals; granted
Sterling May vs Wm W Balthrop. Debt. By att^{ies}. Jury Drury Atkins, John Grimes, Joel Arington, Alsey Seamore, Ja^s Donnell, Willis Walker, Ja^s Hadden S^r, Lemuel Read, Ja^s McKey,

OCTOBER 1823

Alex^r Southerland, George Powel, Thos Rice who find for pl^tf $469.45 debt, damage $30.42, and costs
p.-- Jones Williams vs Thomas Wilson & Jno James. By att^ies. Jury Drury Adkins, Jno Grimes, Joel Arington, Alsey Seamore, Ja^s Donnell, Willis Walker, Ja^s Hadden S^r, Lemuel Read, Ja^s McKey, Alex^r Southerland, Ge^o Powel, Thos Rice, who find for pl^tf $141.94 debt, damage $14.88. Also costs
James Lumenenan vs Jiles Jones. By att^ies. Pl^tf recovers ag^t def^t and his security Willis Jackson his costs
Grand Jury presentments: Against George Hightour overseer of Road; ag^t John Toler overseer of road; ag^t Wm Dunnigan overseer of road; ag^t James L Bell overseer of Road
p.-- Deed John Adams to Silmon Edwards 40 acres ackd
John P Chambers vs John Adams. Debt. Pl^tf in proper person orders his suit dismissed; def^t assumes costs
Silmon Edwards admr Palatera Seal decd vs John Adams. Debt. By att^ies. Jury Drury Adkins, John Grimes, Joel Arrington, Alsey Seamore, Willis Walker, Ja^s Haddin S^r, Lem^l Read, Ja^s McKee, Alex^r Southerland, Ge^o Powell, Thos Rice who find for pl^tf $425.25 debt; damage $20. Also costs
p.-- John Bosley vs A W Vanleer. Pl^tf orders suit dismissed; defendant recovers of pl^tf his costs
Thos Hunter ass^ee vs Montg^y Bell. Debt. By att^ies. Jury Drury Adkins, John Grimes, Joel Arrinton, Alsey Seamore, James Daniel, Willis Walker, Ja^s Haddin S^r, Lem^l Read, Ja^s McKee, Alex^r Southerland, Ge^o Powell, Thos Rice find for pl^tf $440 debt; damage $20. Also cost. Def^t prays appeal; granted
p.-- James M Thomas for John Adams vs George Adams. Pl^tfs by att^ies order suit dismissed; def^t pays costs
B and A W Vanleer vs John C Collier & C Clements. Def^ts file bond & security for their Writ of error.
Court adjourned until tomorrow morning 9 oClock
        Nathan Nisbitt, James Eason, S Brewer

Saturday Morning October 11th 1823 Present the worshipful Nathan Nisbitt, James Eason, Stirling Brewer, Justices

Order bastard begotten upon Elizabeth Shelton by Elias W Napier named [blank] about 5 years old bound to John W Napier until age 15; John W Napier gave bond & security
p.-- Elizabeth Steel vs Jno Scott. Motion to dismiss certiorari; so considered; pl^tf recovers ag^t def^t & security John Harley $11.50 & costs; def^ts pray appeal; granted
Sterling May vs W^m W Balthrop. Debt. Def^t granted appeal

Ordered Sheriff sell goods & chattels of Eleakun Raymon dec^d agreeable to Law. Court adjourned until Court in Course
        S Brewer, James Eason, Nathan Nisbitt

JANUARY 1824

Court of Pleas & Quarter Sessions. 5th January 1824. Present the Worshipful Sterling Brewer, Nathan Nesbitt, Abiram Coldwell, D H Williams, James Eason, Minor Bibb

Sheriff D Thompson produced scalp of wolf over age 4 months; Andrew Gammel produced scalp of a wolf over age four months, both killed within county; allowed agreeable to law

Ephraim Roy allowed $4 for keeping Eliakim Raynod
Kindric Myatt app'td road overseer in place of Daniel Nall

Wm Hogan and Andrew Stewart Esq^{rs} to settle with guardian of minor children of Mills Eason dec^d
p.-- Adm^x of estate of Benjamin Cox dec^d permitted to sell twelve negroes
Sh^{ff} to lay off dower of widow of Mills Eason dec^d
Clark Spencer allowed $30.25 for clothing bought for Tereasey M Bedford in 1823; Spencer to draw on the present guardian for same
Sterling Brewer, Joseph Moris Esq^{rs}, & Robt Duke lay off one years provisions for widow & family of Benjn Cox dec^d
County taxes levied same as last year
Will of James Goodrich decd proven by Dorrel Y Harris & Robt P Harris, subscribing witnesses
p.-- Joseph Eason app^{td} g^{dn} for James Eason, Wm Eason, Jane Eason, Savannah Eason, & Joseph Eason minor orphans of Mills Eason dec^d; bond with James Eason & Orrin D Hogan
Henry Richardson app^{td} guardian to Thomas Cox and Sindamilla Cox minor orphans of Benjn Cox dec^d
Wm Tayler app^{td} g^{dn} to Wm Cox and Eldridge Cox minor orphans of Benjn Cox dec^d
Joseph Kimble to adm^r estate of Chesley O Cole
Will of John Turner S^r dec^d proven by John Duning and Willis Norsworthy. Samuel Turner, executor, gave bond
Winneyford Cox to adm^r estate of Benjn Cox dec^d; gave bond
Howard W Turner and Ge^o Sulivan app^{td} constables

Parishioners of this county allowed: Prior Payne at rate of $60. Levi Lovelady at rate of $20. Silas Thompkins at rate of $40. Robert Shelton at rate of $30. Charles Thompson at rate of $40 for keeping two poor children Nancy Tidwell at rate of $30 for keeping Rebeca Strange also $4 for a coffin furnished for William Strange

Hudson Dudley, Andrew Stewart, Wm Hogan, Ge^o Hightower, John Pendergrass, Saml Turner, Jno W Napier, David Smith produced commissions as justices/peace; took oath of office

Wm Lomax app^{td} road overseer from the county line at head of Tumbling creek crossing Garners Creek at Andrew Stewart's to

JANUARY 1824

the road leading from Vernon to Charlotte

George Mitchel app'd road overseer from Minor Bibbs to creek above Mrs Hudsons. Emsley Sears app'd overseer from s'd creek to the Hickman county line

Henry W Hinson apptd road overseer from Esqr Coldwells to 7-mile tree with hands Lebbeus Richardsons, Mark Reynolds, S Reynolds, Herbert Hinson, James Hinson, Abraham Self, Wiley Underwood, Wm Underwood, John B Walker

Richard Batson licensed to keep an ordinary at his dwelling house in Charlotte

p.-- Alex'r Wilkins app'd overseer in place of Eza McAdoo
Henry H Marable app'd overseer in place of Jn° T Hutchison

App't David Smith, Wm Wiley, Elisha Smith, David Wiley & Dan'l George to straiten road from Charlotte to Columbia, the part near Archibald Ponders to the Gum branch

Josiah Davison app'd overseer from Davis ferry to Reynoldsburg, begin at Montgomery line, to foot of ridge at the head of middle fork of Bartons Creek, hands: Joseph Melugin, Sam'l Melugin, Wm Watson, Wm Handlin, Ja's Council, Hiram Washburn, Wm Fleet, Silman Edwards, William Reynolds, Jn° Seals, Peter Seals, Nicholas Baker

John Hutchison app'd overseer of 1/3 of road lately cut from Davis ferry to Reynoldsburg with John Wilkerson, Nathan Dilleyha, Jane Norris, Grainger J Brown, J Brown, hands on waters of Shoulder Strap beginning at Humphreys County line

p.-- Ja's Daniel app'd overseer of 3rd part of new road from Davis ferry to Reynoldsburg with Ja's G Hinson, Powel Sinks, Thomas Mitchel, Jn° Goodrich, Drury Adkins, Ann Brown, Isaac Hill, Thomas Rice, Wm D Jemmison, Woodson Daniel, Allen Daniel, John Daniel & Ephraim Roy to keep road in repair

John McAdoo is allowed $61.62½ for erecting a stove in court house as per account rendered
Settlement with James Douglass former guardian of Tereasey M Bedford is received. James Douglass allowed $50 for services rendered in guardianship

Justices app'd to take lists of taxable property for 1824:
Cap't Nisbitts company, Nathan Nisbitt; Cap't Hunters co., Geo Hightower; Cap't Brown's, Tho's Murrel; Cap't Grimmets, Hutson Dudley; Cap't Tidwell's, Jn° Pendergrass; Cap't Turner's, Sam'l Turner; Cap't Parrish's, Benjamin Sterdevent; Cap't Thedford's

JANUARY 1824

company, Andrew Stewart; Capt George's, Wm Hogan; Capt Reynold's, John Humphreys; Captain Massey's, Robert Armer; Capt Grimes company, John W Napier

p.-- Transfer of plat and certificate from Middleton Higginbotham to Ayer Willey 6 acres ackd
Deed John Walker to Abiram Coldwell 87½ acres proven by Thos Richardson & Thomas M Coldwell
Deed Shadrack Treble to Jesse Epperson 132 acres proven by Henry Collier & Alfred Treble
Deed John T Hutchison to Henry H Marable 100 acres ackd
Deed John J Coppage to Alex^r H Coppage 112 acres ackd
Deed Elijah Ivy to Henry Collier 35 acres ackd
Deed Aaron Vanhook to Moses Streets 110 acres proven by Saml Self and Samuel M Gowen
p.-- Deed Aaron Vanhook to Ashburn Vanhook 50 acres proven by Samuel Self and Peter Self
Deed Stephen Harris & Derely Harris to Alexander Dickson 390 acres ackd
Deed/Gift John Hendricks S^r to heirs of Wm Hendricks certain property proven by Francis S Ellis & Richd Waugh

Agreeable to act of Assembly, Court proceeded to class themselves as follows: 1st class Minor Bibb, John Humphreys, D H Williams, Rich^d C Napier, Robt Armour, Nehemiah Hardy, & Ja^s Eason. 2nd class Thos Murrell, George Hightower, Jno Pendergrass, Jno W Napier, Jno Johnson & S Brewer. 3rd class David Smith, Wm Hogan, Jo^s Morris, Wm White, Ben^J Sturdevant, Saml Tanner. 4th class And^w Stewart, Jno Wilson, Nathan Nesbitt, Hutson Dudley, Montgomery Bell, Abiram Coldwell

Jurors to next term this Court Thos Parmer, Willeyby Etherage, Thos Richardson, Shared D Thompson, Wm Grimmet, William Austin, Luke Medlock, Schelton Choate, Parish Lankford, Wm Morris, John Brown Jr, Wm Tatum S^r, Chas Thompson, John May, Ephraim Ellis, Nathan Ragan, Howel Freeman, Arch^d Shelton, Thos Swift, Jno Giffen, Ja^s Tatum, Allen Bowen, Joel Morris, Redic Myatte, Alexander Myatte, Albert Speight, Esom Breding
p.-- Noah Sugg, Eldrige Bowen, Jesse Russel, Marton H Berton, Thomas Jonakin, Humphreys H Berton
Robert Armour, J W Napier, Samuel Turner

Tuesday Morning January 6th 1824   Present the Worshipful Robert Armour, J W Napier, Samuel Turner, Esquires, Justices

Wm Hogan & Andrew Stewart Esq^{rs} apptd to settle with Joseph Eason guardian of minor orphans of Mills Eason dec^d

p.-- Grand Jurors George Tubb foreman, Jacob Leach, Willis

JANUARY 1824

Willey, Jacob Lampley, Brinkley George, Joseph Lampley, Middleton Higginbotham, Jn⁰ Hall, Hutson Shropshire, John Picket, Daniel Leach, Christian Baughman, Elisha Gunn, attended by William Hightower, constable

John Read vs James H Davie. Appeal. By att^y. Jury Washington England, John Reding, Thos Mcmurry, Hugh Dickson, Holloway N Merit, Thos Edwards, Robt Vanhook, Jn⁰ Dunigan, W^m B Hadden, W^m E Slaten, Morgan Hood, Archibald Cox who find for plaintiff $25.90. Also costs

p.-- John Adams vs Abraham Self. By att^{ys}. Jury George Tubb, Jacob Leach, Willis Willey, Jacob Lampley, Brinkly George, Jo^s Lampley, Middleton Higginbotham, John Hall, John Picket, Daniel Leach, Christian Baughman, Elisha Gunn who say they find for plaintiff $76. Also costs

Bethena Eason widow of Mills Eason decd. Petition for a Distributive share. Joseph Eason guardian, &c. Decree that s^d Joseph Eason divide estate equally amongst legal heirs & pay to Bethena Eason her part of estate, and s^d Joseph Eason pay cost of this suit
Court adjourned until tomorrow 9 oClock
J W Napier, D H Williams, Ge⁰ Hightower

p.-- Wednesday morning Jany 7th 1824   Present Worshipful John W Napier, D H Williams, Samuel Turner, George Hightower

Ordered Nehemiah Hardy Esqr, Joseph Melugins, Burges Wall, & George F Napier & Labon Holt or any three to partition land and negrows belonging to the heirs of Wm Read dec^d

State vs Jesse Hall. On motion of Att^y-General nole prosequi entered; defendant assumes to pay all cost

State vs John Tatum. Def^t pleads not guilty. Jury Washington England, John Reding, James H Davie, Saml Self, Nathan Tubb, W^m B Hadden, Benjamin Gray, Jn⁰ Nothern, Ja^s Vincent, John T Hutchison, Willis Collier, Willeby Etherage, who say def^t is not guilty, county to pay costs

p.-- State vs George Hightower. Def^t at bar with his counsel pleads not guilty. Jury George Tubb, Jacob Leach, Willis Willey, Jacob Lampley, Brinkley George, Joseph Lampley, Middleton Higginbotham, Jn⁰ Hall, Hutson Shropshire, John Picket, Daniel Leach, Christian Baughman who find the defendant is not guilty; county pays costs

State vs John Key. Pettit Larceny. On motion of atty genl,

JANUARY 1824

nole prosequi entered, Willis Collier pays cost

State vs David Mcadoo, Ja^s Nesbitt & Jno Bernard. Defendants confess they owe State $20 as securities for Edwd Teal for maintenance of bastard begotten by Teal on Jane Southerland

p.-- Benjamin Joslin vs Thomas Pennel. By att^{ys}. Jury Washington England, John Redding, Ja^s H Davie, Saml Self, Nathan Tubb, W^m B Hadden, Benjamin Gray, Ja^s Larkins, John Nothern, Willis Collier, Henry Goodrich, Willeby Etherage who say the plaintiff sustained $86.02 damage. Also costs

George F Napier assee vs Elias W Napier admr of Richd Napier decd. By att^{ies}. Jury above. find for pl^{tf} $160 debt, $32.80 interest to be levied on estate of Richard Napier if so much there be, if not then on goods & chattels of Elias W Napier

William & Alex^r McClure vs Rich^d C Napier. Cause transfered to Circuit Court for trial

Samuel C Hawkins vs R C Napier. Transfered to Circuit Court

p.-- Willie Balthrop assee vs Susanah Hall executrix & Jesse Hall executor of John Hall dec^d. Debt. By att^{ies}. Jury above except James Vincent & John Hutchison for Henry Goodrich and Willeby Etherage. Find for pl^{tf} his debt $100 & $6 interest to be levied on estate of John Hall if so much there be, if not then levied on goods of s^d Jesse & Susan

Deed Isaac H Lanier to Marble Stone ½ acre proven by Richard Waugh and Edward D Hicks
Deed Jno L Mcrae to Nathan Nesbitt lots 35 & 36 in Charlotte proven by Field Farrar and Edward D Hicks
Deed Marble Stone to Augustin Roberts ½ acre proven by Field Farrar & Edward D Hicks

Stirling Brewer Esq bond $10,000, Daniel H Williams, Jno Adams, James Kirk, & Jo^s Kimble as Entry Taker of this county

p.-- Timothy Ezell gdn vs Willis Dawson admr. Petitioner by att^y asks for distribution of estate of Isaac Johnson dec^d
Court adjourned until tomorrow morning 9 oClock
       J W Napier, W Hogins, Saml Turner

Thirsday morning 8th January 1824. Present the worshipful John W Napier, William Hogins, Samuel Turner, Esq^{rs} Justices

Deed Christopher Robertson to John E Ellis ½ lot #4 in Charlotte ackd

JANUARY 1824

Mack Drummond vs Holloway N Merit. Covenant. By att^{ies}. Jury Washington England, John Reding, Alexander Chizenhall, Benjn Gray, Jno Choate, Ja^s M Ross, Edwd B Roach, Jno Evins, Alvin Dunigan, Soloman Grayham, Saml Dunigan, Wm Edwards who find for def^t. Def^t recovers his costs. Pl^{tf} is granted an appeal

p.-- William Howard vs Benjamin Joslin. By att^{ys}. Jury Jehu Miller, John Reding, Washington England, Soloman Grayham, Alex^r Chizenhall, Benjn Gray, John Clark, Jo^s Hall, Edward B Roach, Holliway N Merit, Alvin Dunigan, Samuel Dunigan, who find for pl^{tf} his damage $220. Also his costs

Alvin Dunigan vs Wm Edwards. Appeal. By att^{ies}. Jury Washington England, John Reding, Benjn Gray, Jno Clark, Edward B Roach, Holliway N Merit, Jesse Hall, Thos Palmer, Ja^s Douglass, Horatio Humphries, Ja^s H Davie, Wm Mcadoo who find for pl^{tf} $1.50. Also his costs. Appeal to Circuit Court granted

p.-- State vs John Evins. Def^t made default; fined $1 & cost

Willie Baldthrop assee vs Susanna Hall ext^x, Jesse Hall ext^r of Jno Hall decd. Defts' appeal to Circuit Court granted
Court adjourned until tomorrow Morning 9 oClock
                                    S Brewer, D H Williams, J W Napier

Friday morning Jany 9th 1824.   Present the worshipful Stirling Brewer, D H Williams, John W Napier, Esq^{rs} Justices

Deed L P Cheatham to Cave Johnson 800 acres at mouth of Red River in Montgomery County & lots in town of Cumberland ackd

p.-- Power/Atty Wineford Cox to Joseph John Williams proven by Sterling Brewer
Deed Wm Gilbert to Wilson Gilbert 500 acres ackd

State vs John Marsh. Retail spiritous liquors. Def^t pleaded not guilty. Jury Washington England, Jno Reding, Isaac Walker, Drewry Adkins, H A C Napier, Ja^s Medlock, Alex Wilkins, Micajah Mayse, Chr^{ch} Cox, Benjamin Gray, Lem^l Read, Wilkins Tatum say defendant is guilty; fined $1 with costs; appeal to circuit court, writ of error, is granted

p.-- Richard Batson shff & collector, lists insolvents:
John Brice	1821	.56¼
Henry Goodman	1821, 1822	1.12½
Henry Hall	1821, 1822	1.12½
Joseph Hall	1821, 1822	1.12¼
Mark Holland	1819, 1821, 1822	1.75

JANUARY 1824

William Light	1821	.56¼
Acheus Etheridge	1819, 1820, 1821, 1822	2.31¼
John Robertson	1821 1822	1.12½
Jacob Walker	1819 1820 1821	1.75
Randolph R Harris	1821 1 white 2 blacks	3.18 3/4
Randolph R Harris	1822	.56¼
Abraham Robertson	1821 1823	1.12½
Robert Webb	1821	.06
John Wilkerson	1820 1823	1.12½
Nicholas Baker	1820 1821	1.18 3/4
Levi Davidson	1820 1822	1.12½
John McBride	1821	.56¼
Willis Roland	1821 1822	.00
Elisha Shelton	1821 1822	1.12½
Rosamond P Scott	1820	.62½
John Devall	1821	.56¼
Garrett Hall	1821 1822	1.12½
Nathan Davis	1821	.56¼
James Dunlap	1821	.56¼
Edmond Gamble	1819 1821	1.18 3/4
Yelverton Hambric	1818 1819 1820 1821	2.31¼
William Johnson	1821	.56¼
John Chappel	1820	.62½
John Grisham	1819	.56¼
Peterson Vaden	1821	.56¼
p.-- Thomas Barnett	1822	.56¼
Hiram Dunagan	1822	.56¼
James Watson	1822 1823	1.06¼
Jonathan Brown	1823	.56¼
John Gray	1822	.56¼
Elias Abney	1822	.56¼
James Akins	1822	.56¼
John Breeding	1822	.00
Peterson Vaden	1822	.56¼
Nathan Norman	1822 1823	1.06¼
Harrison Fussell	1822	.56¼
Ambrose H Burton	1822	.56¼
Holden Plunket	1822	.56¼
Jesse Sinks	1822	.56¼
James Dawson	1822	.56¼
James McElyea	1822 1823	1.06¼
John Donnell	1823	.50
John Grainger	1823	.50
Richardson L Clark	1823	.50
John Scott Jr	1823	.50
William Dean	1823	.50
George Greger	1823	.50
Elisha Hook	1823	.50
Duncan McDonnell	1823	.50
William McNichol	1823	.50

JANUARY 1824

James Vaughn   1823   .50
Sheriff allowed for above insolvents amount of county taxes

p.-- Richard Batson, Sh^{ff} & Collector, reports town lots &c
given in for taxation which yet remain unpaid and that goods
and chattels cannot be found whereupon to destrain

Owner	date	situation	acres	wh	bl	
James Noland	1820	Salmonds Cr	20	1		.75
Lewis Graham	1819	Leatherwood	20	1		.66¼
Jesse Tribble	'21 '22	Hurricane	230	1		3.46 3/4
Richard Blalock	1820	Beaverdam	23	1		.77
Dempsey Sawyers	1820	Turnbull Cr	32	1		.82
Danl Wheatons heirs	1820	Jones Cr	1040			6.50
Duncan Stuart	'20'21'22	Jones Cr	1640			26.65
Patsy Gower	1822	"	171			.86
Jeremiah Brown	1823	"	350	1		2.32
James G Brehen	1822	Yellow Cr	2374			11.87
Thos B Glosters heirs	'22	Bartons Cr	358			1.79
Marble Stone	1822	Sulpher fork Jones Cr	223	1	1	2.56
Samuel Brook	1822	Bartons Cr	200			1.00
Andw Hamilton	1823	"	230			1.15
Micajah Busby	1823	Shoulder Strap	34	1		.68
Wm Dunnagun	1823	Piney	154			.77

Judgment entered against af^{sd} tracts for sum named to each
being the amount of single taxes due
This order is recinded

p.-- Deed John Lukroy to Jacob Voorhees 35 acres ackd
Pow^r/Att^y Lemuel N Hatch to Daniel Williams proven by Daniel
H Williams and Nehemiah Scott
Court adjourned until tomorrow morning 9 oClock
                    S Brewer, J W Napier, D H Williams

Saturday Morning January 10th 1824   Present the worshipful
Stirling Brewer, John W Napier, D H Williams, R C Napier

p.-- State vs Benedict Bacon. Pettit Larceny. Def^t at bar
with council. Jury Ja^s H Davie, Washington England, Jno Reding, Benjn Gray, W^m S Adamson, Lamuel Read, John Clark, W^m H
Betts, Thomas Palmer, Thos Richardson, W^m S Coleman, Wilkins
Tatom who find def^t not guilty. County to pay costs

James M Brewer, Parry W Humphries, John C Collier appointed
trustees for academy to supply vacancies

Deed Parry W Humphries to L P Cheatham 213 acres, part this
county and part in Montgomery ackd
James Rogers admr the estate of Lewis Berry decd allowed a
credit $32.62 on his settlement of sd estate

APRIL 1824

p.-- Court adjourned until Court in Course
R C Napier, J W Napier, D W Williams

p.-- Monday 5th April 1824   Present worshipful N Nisbitt, A Colewell, John Johnson, D H Williams, Esquires, Justices

Ordered Richard Batson allowed $40 for his exoficio services for 1823 ending last Term
William Houston allowed $40 from January 1st for keeping his son, a poor person of this county
John McAdoo county trustee allowed $5 on his next settlement for an estray taken up by Jesse P Dees & not collected
Stirling Brewer Esqr resigned as justice/peace

Drury Christian, Joseph Morris, George Hightower Esqrs apptd to settle with Washington Hunter admr estate of Cary Wiggins decd and make return thereof
George Davidson appointed overseer of the road in the place of Highram Taylor
Willoby Eatherage allowed $69 for keeping Nathan Jackson and Nancy Eatherage orphans of Phillip Eatherage decd up to this Term
Montgomery Bell admitted to keep a public Ferry on Cumberland River at the mouth of Harpeth

Isaiah Tidwell to oversee road from ford of the creek at Mrs Hudsons to Hickman county line; he and George Mitchel, the other overseer, to make equal division of hands belonging to sd road
A Quoram of justices on the bench; Samuel Tate in open court produced the scalp of a wolf over age 4 months killed within Dickson; he is allowed therefor agreeable to act

p.-- Abiram Coldwell, Jos Morris, Benj Sturdevant, Esqrs, to settle with Willis L Dawson admr estate of Isaac Johnson dec

Alexr Dickson, Benjamin Sturdevant and Hewel Parrish to lay off a years provision for widow & family of Drury Price decd

John Montgomery and Raiford Crumpler allowed $4.50 each for settling with county officers for year 1823
John A Johnson allowed $27.50 pr year from last January for keeping his wife a poor person of this County
Henry G Wells to oversee road in place of Thomas Simmons
Wm Edwards excused from double tax for 1823 on 110 acres and one black pole

APRIL 1824

William Bishop admited to keep an ordinary at his now dweling house in Charlotte

William Bishop allowed $18.50 for keeping John Grainger in jail and discharged by the circuit Court

Archabald Cox to oversee road in place of Joel Marsh

James Tate to oversee road in place of Soloman Marsh

p.-- Joseph Choate appointed to oversee road in the place of Thomas Graves

Rich^d M Jones to oversee road in place of Ben^j Rye

Benjamin Sturdevant, Joseph Willson Esq^{rs} and Hewel Parrish to settle with admr of estate of Robert Rogers decd

Polly West allowed $40 for keeping her son G W West the last year ending this Term, drawing on Stirling Brewer Esqr, his guardian, for same

William Dunigan to oversee road in place of George H Walker

William Taylor to oversee road in place of William Tatom

William Jones to oversee road in place of Jesse May

E Wiley to oversee road from Archibald Ponders to Gum branch with following hands to open said road: James McCord, David Frasier, Willis Dudley, John Peary, William Loftis, George Frasier, Daniel George, James Landers, Josiah Wiley, Burwell Myatt, R Myatt, Aulsey Seamore, Elisha Smith, Brink^y George, Kendrick Myatt

p.-- Robt West, R M Jones, Joseph Wilson, Hugh Dickson, Joseph Kimble to view & turn road from Reynoldsburg to Clarksville, make report to next Court

The Will of Adam Wilson decd proven by Alexander Dickson and Chauncy Davenport. Joseph Wilson & John Wilson qualified as executors, bond $3,000, with Alexander Dickson and Chauncy Davenport

Salley Price & Thomas May to admr the estate of Drury Price decd; bond $1,000 with Sterling May and Jesse May

Catherine Grimes & John Grimes to administer estate of Henry Grimes decd, bond $6,000 with Benjn Crews and Wm Ward

Lucy Vanhook & Henry H Marable to adm^r estate of Aaron Vanhook dec^d; bond $3,000 with John Adams & Samuel Self

p.-- Thomas McMurry, Benjamin Crews, James H Davey and James Williams appointed Constables of this county

Bond of Thomas Williams as County Surveyor, with Saml Self, Joseph Williams & Joseph Wilson

Jurors to next Circuit Court Samuel Self, Ro Vanhook, Rich^d N Williams, Henry A C Napier, James M Ross, Thomas Mathews, James Hicks, Jehu Willis, Francis Tidwell, Henry Lankford, John Wilson, Henry G Wells, Robert Holms, Labon Brown, Robt Harris, Gabriel Petty, Burwell Myatt, Matthew Myatt, Reese Bowen, Christopher Strong, James Nesbitt

Jurors to next County Court James Hartley, Wm Gunn, Thomas

APRIL 1824

Flanery, Thomas Smith, Richd Jackson, Danl Hickison, Elijah Dodson, Thos May, John Turner, John Brown S^r, John Lankford, Jno Linch, William Hutchison, Simon Miers, Thos Ellis, Drury Bonds, Hewel Parrish, Ge^o Baxley, Wm Caffrey, Drury Taylor, Wm Loftes, Kendrick Myatt, James Martin, Robert Nesbitt S^r, Joseph Nesbitt, Jacob Saunderson, Alex^r Dickson, Nehemiah Scott, John H Stone, William Hudson

p.-- Deed John McAdoo to Thos Nesbitt 50 acres ackd
Deed Benjn Pearsall to John Adams 94 acres. The handwriting of Aaron Vanhook decd, one of the subscribing witnesses, was proven by Daniel H Williams
Deed John Adams to Thomas Ellis 94 acres ackd
Deed Brice Prator to Lucreacy Pendergrass 30 acres proven by John Garton and John Parker
Deed Jno Hendricks to Robt Thomas 60 acres proven by Leonard Burnett and James Gilliam
Deed Jno Henricks to Robt Thomas 260 acres proven by Leonard Burnett and James Gilliam
Bill/Sale Joel Marsh to John Choate Negro girl Phereby ackd

p.-- Articles of agreement between Winnefred Dawson and J J Williams and Willis L Dawson proven by Thomas Collier and Joseph Morris
Court adjourned until tomorrow morning 9 oClock
        J Johnson, Pendergrass, Ge^o Hightower, J W Napier

Tuesday Morning April 6^{t}h 1824   Present the worshipful John Johnson, John Pendergrass, George Hightower, John W Napier

Grand Jurors John May foreman, Willouby Eatherage, Humphries H Burton, John Brown Jr, John Giffen, Wm Austin, Noah Sugg, Eldridge Bowen, Albert Speights, Wm Grimmit, Luke Metlock, Parrish Lankford, Charles Thompson
Wm Hightower a Constable sworn to attend them

p.-- John Dunigan vs Wm Edwards. Slander. By att^{ies}. Jury Wm Harper, Alexander Myatt, Martin H Burton, Wm Morris, Redick Myatt, Jesse Russell, Sherod D Thompson, Thos Jernigan, Nathan Ragan, Thos Richeson, Archibald Shelton, Thos Swift who find defendant guilty; assess plaintiffs damage to $50. Plt^f granted appeal to Circuit Court.

John Johnson vs James Epperson. Pl^{tf} in open Court agrees to dismiss Suit; def^t agrees to pay Court cost; pl^{tf} assumes to pay all cost accruing before the Justice of the peace

John Kiser for C Hutchison vs Parry W Humphries. Pl^{tf} by his attorney orders suit dismissed; def^t assumes all cost, $6

APRIL 1824

John Kiser for C Hutchison vs Parry W Humphries. Pl'f by his attorney orders suit dismissed; def' assumes cost

p.-- Samuel Jones vs James M Thomas. Pl'f by attorney orders suit dismissed; def' recovers of pl'f his costs

Hosea C Miller vs Suannah Hall executrix & Jesse Hall executor of Jn° Hall dec'd. By att'ies. Jury Alexander Myatt, James Tatom, Martin H Burton, W'm Tatom S'r, Allen Bowen, W'm Morris, Redick Myatt, Jesse Russell, Sherrod D Thompson, Thomas Jernigan, Nathan Ragan, Thomas Richeson, who find for pl'f his damages $10. Also costs

Deed Samuel Locker to Willis Norsworthey 50 acres proven by William W Baldthrop who also proves the handwriting of John J Lewis the other witness thereto
John Mcadoo duly elected County trustee gave bond & security

p.-- Timothy Ezell g'dn of Dade G Johnson vs Willis L Dawson adm'r of Isaac Johnson dec'd. Petition for distribution. Pl'f by att'y; def' in proper person. Plaintiff recovers of def' $41.11¼ the amount which Isaac G Johnson is entitled to as a distributive share of the estate of Isaac Johnson dec'd. Also further ordered that plaintiff recover of def' his costs

Susannah Hall ex'tx, Jesse Hall ex'tr of Jn° Hall dec'd vs Belfield Carter. Forfeiture. Pl'fs by attorney. Belfield Carter a witness summoned on part of defendants was called to give evidence in suit wherein Hosea C Miller was pl'f & Susannah and Jesse Hall ex'rs of John Hall dec'd def'ts, was called but came not. Order pl'f recover of def' $125 unless def' appear next Term to shew reason why execution shall not be made

Susanna Hall ex'tx & Jesse Hall ex'tr of Jn° Hall dec'd vs Tho's Watson. Forfeiture. Pl'f by att'y & Tho's Watson, witness on part of pl'f (cause as above), came not. Pl'f to recover of def' $125 unless he appear next Term & shew cause why execution shall not be made
p.-- Court adjourned until tomorrow morning 9 oClock
J W Napier, J Pendergrass, John Johnson

Wednesday Morning, April 7'th 1824. Present the worshipful John W Napier, John Pendergrass, John Johnson, Justices

John Nesbitt J'r app'td road overseer in place of James L Bell

Christopher Robertson admited to keep an ordinary at his now dwelling house in Charlotte

APRIL 1824

Nathan Nesbitt to adm^r estate of John Nesbitt decd

Mary Dickson vs James Dickson & others. Cause continued; the defendants pay costs of this Term

p.-- Christopher Robertson, Richard Batson, George Hightower Esq^{rs}, James M Ross app$^{'d}$ to settle with Elias W Napier adm^r of Richard Napier Senr dec^d and make return thereof

Deed Francis V Smitton[Smelton?] to John Reynolds assee for 15 acres ackd

State vs John Toler. Nole Prosequi entered; the county pays costs of prosecution

State vs Wm Dunigan. Nole prosequi entered; the county pays cost

State vs James L Bell. Jury Alex^r Myatt, James Tatom, Martin H Burton, Wm Tatom S^r, Allen Bowen, Wm Morris, Redick Myatt, Jesse Russell, Sherrod D Thompson, Thomas Jernigan, Nathan Ragan, Thos Richeson who find def^t guilty; fined $5 & costs

p.-- State vs Benjamin Cummins. Appearance bond Benjn Cummins, $250; Alex^r Dickson and Wm Morrison each $125

State vs Hugh Dickson. Appearance bond, $250; Alex^r Dickson and W^m McMurry each $125

Peter R Booker vs Francis V Smittoe. Deposition of Jno Brown to be taken for the defendant

p.-- State vs John Evins S^r. Nole prosequi entered; prosecutor George Southerland agrees to pay all costs

State vs Stephen Hostly. Bastardy. Def^t convicted of begeting a bastard upon Jane Craig; bond $500 to keep child from becoming chargable to county. Hostly pays prosecution costs

State vs Benjamin Cummins. Peace Warrant. Cummins bond $500; Alexander Dickson & Wm Morrison each $250; condition Cummins keep peace towards Polly Dickson and her family

State vs Hugh Dickson. Peace Warrant. Dickson's bond $500; Alex^r Dickson and W^m McMurry each $250. Condition Hugh keep the peace towards Polly Dickson and her family

p.-- Sarah Brown vs Resden & Howard Mockbie. By att^{ies}. Jury Jno May, Willoughby Eatherage, Humphries H Burton, Jno Brown Jr, Wm Austin, Noah Sugg, Eldridge Bowen, Albert Speight, Wm Grimmet, Luke Metlock, Parrish Lankford, Charles Thompson, who find for pl^{tf}; damages by trespass $75. Also costs

APRIL 1824

Holleway N Merit vs Mark Drummond. Certiorari. By attornies. Jury Alex^r Myatt, James Tatom, James Tatum, Martin H Burton, Wm Tatum Senr, Allen Bowen, Wm Morris, Redick Myatt, Jesse Russell, Sherod D Thompson, Nathan Ragan, Thomas Richardson, Thomas Swift who find for pl^{tf}. Pl^{tf} to recover of def^t and Thomas Jurnegan his security $7.50. Also his costs

p.-- John Ellis vs Joseph Nesbitt. Certiorari. By Attorneys. Jury Alex^r Myatt, James Tatum, Martin H Burton, Wm Tatum S^r, Allen Bowen, Wm Morris, Redick Myatt, Jesse Russell, Sherod D Thompson, Thomas Jernan, Nathan Ragan, Thos Richardson who find for pl^{tf} $7.20. Pl^{tf} to recover of Nesbitt and of John Marsh his security $7.25(sic) & costs

Henry A C Napier vs Henry G Wells. Pl^{tf} in proper person orders his suit dismissed. Def^t recovers of pl^{tf} his cost

John N Smart vs Eleanor Parrish. Pl^{tf} by attorney orders his suit dismissed. Def^t recovers of pl^{tf} his costs

John N Smart vs John T Hutchison. Pl^{tf} by att^y orders suit dismissed. Def^t recovers of pl^{tf} his costs

p.-- Benjamin Sturdevant moved for appointment of a guardian for W^m H, Patsey, Ja^s, Charlotte, Allis, Jno, Dorothy infant children of James Goodrich dec^d. Court refused so to do, no person present willing to accept s^d appointment

Francis V Schmittoe vs John Reynolds. Award. Pl^{tf} by att^y moves for award in pursuance of award heretofore made by W^m A Cook, R Daily & N H Allen Jany 1823; also Francis had executed a deed agreeably to said award, therefore s^d Francis V Schmittoe recovers of defendant $40.77½ and interest from 23 Jany 1823, also his costs
Court adjourned until tomorrow morning 9 OClock
　　　　　　　　　　　　J W Napier, J Johnson, J Pendergrass

Thursday Morning April 8th 1824. Present the worshipful John W Napier, John Pendergrass, John Johnson, Esquires, Justices

p.-- Deed Jesse L Kirk to Richard Batson town lots 47 and 55 proven by James H Davis & David McAdoo
Dorothy Goodrich app^{td} guardian to Jno, W^m H, Martha, James, Allis H, Charlotte Goodrich, minor orphans of James Goodrich dec^d, she having given bond & security
Samuel Thomas vs Christopher Robertson. By attornies. Jury Alexander Myatt, James Tatom, Martin H Burton, Wm Tatum S^r, Allen Bowen, Redick Myatt, Jesse Russell, Sherod D Thompson,

APRIL 1824

Thomas Jernigan, Nathan Ragan, Thomas Richeson who find in favour of def^t. Def^t recovers of pl^{tf} his cost

Henry A C Napier vs Thomas Wilson. Debt. By attornies. Jury Willoughby Eatherage, Humphries H Burton, Jno Brown Jr^r, John Giffin, Noah Sugg, Eldridge Bowen, Alb^t Speight, Wm Grimmit, Luke Matlock, John May, Parrish Lankford, Charles Thompson who find for pl^{tf} debt and damages $216.50, & cost

p.-- Nathan Nall vs Richard C Napier. Debt. By att^{ies}. Jury Alex^r Myatt, Ja^s Tatom, Martin H Burton, Wm Tatom S^r, Allin Bowen, Wm Morris, Redick Myatt, Jesse Russell, Sherrod D Thompson, Thomas Jurnigan, Nathan Ragan, Thomas Richeson who find for de^{ft}, who recovers of pl^{tf} his cost

Nathan Nall vs Richard C Napier. Debt. By att^{ies}. Jury (as above) find for def^t; who recovers of pl^{tf} costs

Jacob Rape vs Montgomery Bell. By attornies. Jury Willoughby Eatherage, Humphries H Burton, John Brown Junr, John Giffin, Noah Sugg, Eldridge Bowen, Albert Speight, Wm Grimmet, Luke Matlock, John May, Parrish Lankford, Chas Thompson who find for def^t who recovers of pl^{tf} his costs

Gustave Rape vs Jno Noland, Edwd Teal & Thos Noland. Appeal. By att^{ies}. Jury Alex^r Myatt, Ja^s Tatom, Martin H Burton, Wm Tatom Senr, Allin Bowen, Wm Morris, Redick Myatt, Jesse Russell, Sherrod D Thompson, Thos Jurnigan, Nathan Ragan, Thos Richeson who find for pl^{tf} $17.698. Also costs

Robert West vs Montgomery Bell. Debt. By att^{ys}. Jury (above) find for pl^{tf} $425.60 debt, damage $31.84, also costs. Def^t prays appeal in nature of writ of error; granted

p.-- Robt West vs Montg^y Bell. Debt. By att^{ys}. Jury (above) find for pl^{tf} $259.99 debt, damage $11.69, and costs. Def^t prays appeal in nature of writ of error; granted

Robt Dickison, Hugh Dickison, Jo^s Dickison vs Jno Thorn. Firafacias issued in favour Robt Dickson, Hugh Dickson, Joseph Dickson by Benjn Sturdevant J.P. 9 Feby 1824 ag^t John Thorn for $9.25 with interest from 15 Novr 1823, to satisfy which Eleazor Parrish constable for want of other property served same on 95 acres on Salmons Creek of Yellow Cr 10 Feby. Venditionas exponas to issue

p.-- Andrew Vance vs Jno Thorn. Firafacias issued favor And^w Vance by Benjn Sturdevant J.P. 9 Feby 1824 ag^t Jno Thorn for $10 & interest from 3 July 1821 which constable Eleanor Parrish for want of other property levied on 95 acres Salmons

APRIL 1824

C^r of Yellow C^r 10 Feby 1824; venditionas exponas to issue

Henry Hendricks vs John Thorn. Firafacias issued favor Henry Hendricks by Benjn Sturdevant J.P. 9 Feby 1824 ag^t Jno Thorn for $25 & interest from 10 Octr 1823 which constable Eleanor Parrish in default of personal property levied on 95 acres on Salmons Creek 10 Feby 1824; venditionas exponas to issue

Henry A C Napier vs Thos Wilson. Def^t prays appeal [X'd out]

p.-- Thomas Jurnigan vs Mark Drummond. On 1 April 1824 judg^t recovered favor Holliway N Merit ag^t Mark Drummond & Thomas Jurnigan for $7.50 and cost to $12. Jurnigan was security of s^d Drummond. Jurnigan to recover of Drummond $7.50 with cost af^{sd} besides his cost in this behalf expended

Hosea C Miller vs Susannah Hall and Jesse Hall ex^{trs} of John Hall dec^d. Pl^{tf} is granted appeal to Circuit Court
Court adjourned until tomorrow Morning 9 oClock
  Nathan Nesbitt, J Pendergrass, Ge^o Hightower

Friday Morning April 9th 1824. Present the worshipful Nathan Nesbitt, John Pendergrass, George Hightower, Esqrs, Justices

p.-- Ordered that Samuel Turner Esqr, John May, and Charles Thompson lay off 1 years provisions for widow and family of Aron Vanhook dec^d out of s^d estate
Deed John Walker to Abiram Coldwell 18 acres proven by John B Walker and L W Richeson
James M Ross, John Giffin and John W Napier Esqr lay off one years provision for widow of Henry Grimes dec^d, of s^d estate

Henry West vs Susannah Hall & Jesse Hall, ex^{trs} of John Hall dec^d. Debt. By att^{ies}. Jury Alex^r Myatt, Ja^s Tatom, Martin H Burton, Wm Tatom Senr, Allen Bowen, Wm Morris, Redick Myatt, Jesse Russell, Sherrod D Thompson, Thos Jurnigan, Nathan Ragan, Thos Richeson who find for pl^{tf} $485 debt, damage $50. Also his cost, to be levyed on estate of Jno Hall dec^d if so much can be made; if not then to be levied of goods & lands of Susannah Hall and Jesse Hall. Defendants appeal granted

p.-- Isaac Taylor appointed guardian to Lewis, Claibourne, William, James, Daniel Taylor minor orphans; gave bond &c

Edward Picket Jr, Amos Thompson, John Jones ex^{trs} of Edward Picket dec^d for use of W^m W Mallory vs Francis S Ellis & D H Williams. By att^{ies}. Demurer overruled. Def^t to recover his costs. Pl^{tf} granted appeal to Circuit Court

JULY 1824

Francis V Smittoe vs Mark Reynolds & securities. By att[ies].
Motion for judgment ag[t] constable & securities is overruled.
Def[ts] to recover of pl[f] their cost. Pl[tf] granted appeal

p.-- Stirling May vs Andrew M Lewis. By att[ies]. Certiorari
dismissed. Pl[tf] recovers ag[t] def[t] & Holliway N Merit his security in certiorari $55, the judgment before the justice & $1.10 interest, also his costs. Plaintiff granted appeal
Court adjourns until Court in Course
                                    N Nesbitt, Ge[o] Hightower, J Pendergrass

July 5th 1824.   Present the worshipful John Pendergrass, Minor Bibb, David Smith, Hudson Dudley, A Coldwell, Justices

George Clark produced scalps of 7 wolves under age 4 months. Jno Choate produced scalps of 6 wolves under 4 months. James Choate, 1 wolf under 4 months, all killed within bounds of Dickson County. Allowed agreeable to act of Assembly

Wm Tatom Sr allowed $6.50 for coffin and expence of burying Matthew France, a poor person of this county
John Frasier appointed road overseer in place of John Walker

Nehemiah Hardy, Abiram Coldwell Esq[rs] and Molton Dickeson to settle with Robert West ex[tr] of Seth B Jordan dec[d]
p.-- William White produced commission as Justice/Peace
And[w] Stewart & W[m] Hogan Esq[rs] app[td] to settle with Richmond Baker g[dn] for Absolam Baker
David Smith & Andrew Stewart Esq[rs] to settle with Joel Marsh g[dn] for Rebecca C Overton
Hudson Dudley Esq, Moses Parker & Hodge Adams to settle with Minor Bibb adm[r] of Richard Johnson dec[d]
George W Jordan app[td] g[dn] to John A & Robert W Jordan, minor orphans of Seth B Jordan
Jn[o] Adams, Henry H Marable, Jesse May, John May, Robert Vanhook, Ebenezer Whitehead and Sampson Boles to lay off a road from Yellow Creek Road near John Turner's shop to Charlotte

Ebenezer Wiley to oversee road from Archibald Ponders to Gum branch with hands Elisha Smith, William Loftes, David Wiley, David Frasier, Willis Dudley, Nicholas Dudley

p.-- New road from Gum br to old road near Archabald Ponder not to be opened until report is received from Edm[d] Tidwell J[r], Samuel Russell, Isiah Tidwell, Joel Marsh, Ja[s] Thedford, Samuel King, Jesse S Ross, Aquilla Tidwell, Joshua White

JULY 1824

Viewers of road from Clarksville to Reynoldsburgh altered it to leave old road north of Leatherwood Creek, take ridge to mouth of sd creek, follow ridge to intersect old road near a ford of Yellow Creek on Mr Kimbles plantation

Richard N Williams & hands excused from working on road from Elijah Dodsons to head of Hurricane Creek
James Walker to oversee road in place of Solomon Milam
Richard Cocke & hands, John Harris and Jesse Bartee to work under Jiles Jones overseer of road to his house

Sheriff to summon a jury of 12 freeholders to ascertain if Daniel Coleman Junr is a lunatic
p.-- Deed Wm Miller to W^m S Coleman 138 acres proven by Thos Bullian & Danl Coleman
Deed Ambrose H Burton to Francis V Smittoe 150 acres proven by Eleanor Parrish and And^w M Lewis
B/S Drury Taylor to Moses Easley proven by R E Comer & James Rogers
Washington Hunter admr of Cary Wiggins decd allowed $25 for his services
Jurors to next County Court: Thos Matthews Jr, Ja^s Tubb, Wm Gaines, Jno Choate, Danl Coleman, William S Coleman, Sampson Boles, John Jones, And^w Brown, Daniel George, David Frazier, Samuel Sellers, Jno Jones, Jacob Sanderson, Joel Marsh, Joel Arrinton, Lawson Gunn, Samuel Dunigan, John Stafford, Jacob Pucket, Nicholas Dudley, Robert Brown, Robt Easly, Joseph G Davis, Mitchel Jackson, Burwell Jackson, Ja^s Mathews, Howard W Turner, And^w W Lewis, Pinckney T Bledsoe, Isaac Hill, Morgan B Wells, Hasted Parrish
p.-- Will of Moses Easley decd proved by Michael Light and Joel Massey

Seth Richardson extr of Jordan Richardson decd vs Henry H Marable & Ann E Marable. Purported will of Jordan Richardson decd produced by Seth Richardson, extr. H Marable and Ann E Marable his wife, sd Ann one of the children of Jordan Richardson decd, contest will. Seth Richardson by R Daley attorney. Def^{ts} by att^y John Montgomery p.-- Cause continued to next term. Depositions of Edwd Mason & Edw^n Bailey of Greenville County, VA, to be taken for pl^{tf}, they being subscribing witnesses to the will

Reuben Comas qualified as ex^{tr} of will of Moses Easley; bond $1000 with James Rogers and Wm Johnson
Benjn Sturdevant, Jo^s Wilson Esq^{rs} & Alex^r Dickson to settle with Susannah Norris adm^r estate of Robert Norris dec^d. Also to divide estate of Robt Norris decd amongst legatees
Court adjourned until tomorrow morning 9 OClock

JULY 1824

A Coldwell, Geo Hightower, Wm White

Tuesday July 6th 1824   Present the worshipful A Coldwell, William White, George Hightower, Esquires, Justices

Grand jurors: Nehemiah Scott foreman, Drury Taylor, Thomas Smith, Jno Turner, Drury Bonds, William Gunn, Elijah Dodson, Simon Meirs, Jno Lankford, Wm Hutchison, William Loftes, Jno Linch, Richard Jackson. Jas H Davie constable to attend them

Mary Dickson vs Jas, Jos, Adam, Jno, Hugh Dickson. Trespass. By atties. Jury Jno Brown Sr, Hewel Parrish, Jas Martin, Jas Hartley, Danl Hickison, Wm Hudson, Robt Nisbitt Sr, Jos Nisbitt, Joel Massey, Jno May, Molton Dickson, Benjn Gray find plaintiffs damage 1¢; pltf granted appeal to Circuit Court

John McAdoo vs Mark Reynolds. McAdoo by atty proves agt Deft as a Constable agreeable to notice
Peter R Booker vs Francis V Smittoe. Appeal. By atties. Jury Nehemiah Scott, Drury Taylor, Thos Smith, John Turner, Drury Bonds, Wm Gunn, Elijah Dodson, Simon Marr, John Lankford, Wm Hutcheson, William Loftes, Jno Linch, who say deft owes pltf $44.52. Deft granted appeal to Circuit Court

Washington Currie vs Montgy Bell. Pltf by atty orders suit dismissed; defendant recovers of pltf his cost

Susannah Hall extx and Jesse Hall extr of John Hall decd vs Belfield Carter. Pltfs in open court order suit dismissed
p.-- Susannah Hall extx and Jesse Hall extr of Jno Hall decd vs Thomas T Watson. Pltfs order suit dismissed

B/S Thomas Noland to Christopher Robertson ackd
Court adjourned until tomorrow morning 9 oClock
                    B Sturdevant, William White, Saml Turner

Wednesday July 7th 1824.   Present the worshipful Benjamin Sturdevant, William White, Samuel Turner, Esquires, Justices

State vs Benjn Cummins & Hugh Dickson. Riot. Jury Jno Brown, Hewel Parrish, James Martin, James Hartley, Daniel Hickison, Wm Hudson, Robt Nesbitt Sr, Jos Nesbitt, Thos Flannery, John Bradley, Wm Tatom, Wm B Hadden find defts guilty; fined $3 each besides cost

Grand Jury enter bill/Indictment agt Susannah Hall, Berryman Hall & David Hall a True Bill
p.-- State vs Susannah, David, and Berryman Hall. Riot. Jury

JULY 1824

above find def^{ts} guilty. fined $8 each. An Appeal to Circuit Court granted. Appearance bonds Susannah $250 with Francis V Smitton security $125. David Hall & Berryman Hall, $250 each p.-- and Susannah and Jesse Hall $250 each

State vs Christian Baughman. Jury above except Jesse Hall & Hugh Dickson for Jno Bradley & Wm Hadden, find def^t guilty; fined $3 and pay costs of prosecution

p.-- State vs Wm Ward. A&B Pleads guilty; fine $5 & cost
B/S Benjn B Raibourn & Eliz Raibourn to Holliway N Merit for Negroes proven by Penelope Lewis
B/S Eleanor Parrish to Holliway N Merit for Negroes ackd
Court adjourned until tomorrow Morning 9 oClock
R C Napier, Wm White, David Smith

Thursday July 8^{t}h 1824.   Present the worshipful
R C Napier, William White, David Smith, Esquires, Justices

Anthony W Vanleer vs Mark Reynolds, constable, & his securities. By attorneys. Def^t collected for pl^{tf} $53.92 on claims put into his hands by sheriff, pl^{tf} to recover of def^t & his securities Benjn p.-- Sturdevant & James McCauley $53.92 and $5.82 damages besides his cost

Micajah Fly vs Stirling Brewer. Debt. By att^{ies}. Jury John Brown, Hewel Parrish, Ja^s Martin, Ja^s Hartley, Daniel Hickison, Wm Hudson, Robt Nesbitt, Jo^s Nesbitt, Thos Flanery, Wm Tatom, Wm Jones, Wm Adamson, find for pl^{tf} $456.40, & damage $9.12½. Pl^{tf} prays appeal to Circuit Court; granted

Elias W Napier vs John Evins. Plaintiff given leave to take depositions of Wm Hurman, Roger Shakefford, Jesse L Kirk, & also Robert Watson and Turner Evins

Susannah Hall ex^{tx} and Jesse Hall ex^{tr} of John Hall decd by att^{ys} permitted to shew cause why a bill of sale from Ben^j B Raybourn and Eliz^h Reybourn to H N Merit for Negroes should not be admitted to registration

p.-- D H Williams and Abiram Coldwell vs John S Spencer and others. Def^{ts} plea in abatement sustained. Plaintiffs appeal in nature of a Writ of Error is granted

Micajah Fly vs Stirling Brewer. Debt. By att^{ys}. Jury above find for plaintiff $855.63 debt; damage $64.13. Also cost. Pl^{tf} prays appeal to Circuit Court; granted

p.-- Drury Christian vs Wm Ward. Pltf orders suit dismissed

OCTOBER 1824

John McAdoo vs Mark Reynolds. Def^t retains $43.87½ which he should pay over to pl^{tf}; order pl^{tf} to recover; also costs

Elias Tubb vs Joel Massie. Pl^{tf} to take depositions of James Patterson, Andrew Hendricks, Patsey Massie, Silvester Adams

State vs Wm Handlin. Appearance bond of Wm Handlin, securities Hugh Dickson and Hewel Parrish
State vs Wm Handlin. Appearance bond. Securities above
Court adjourned until Court in Course
B Sturdevant, Wm White, David Smith

p.-- October 4th 1824. Present A Coldwell, N Nesbitt, D H Williams, Saml Turner, Jno W Napier, Hudson Dudley, Justices

Wilie B Johnson app^{td} Solicitor Genl Protem
Johnson Edwards produced scalp of wolf over age four killed in this county; allowed
John Nisbitt to oversee road in place of James S Bell
Robert West ex^{tr} will of Seth B Jordan dec^d allowed $105 out of estate for his services
Henry Highland to oversee road in place of Thos Wilson
p.-- Minor Bibb Esq, Hodge Adams, & Thos Gentry to rectify a mistake they made in valuation of property of Cuthbert Hudson dec^d given to his children in his lifetime
George H Walker & Jacob Walker adm^{rs} of Elizabeth Walker dec to sell real estate of decd
Hudson Dudley Esqr, Hodge Adams, and Moses Parker to settle with Minor Bibb adm^r of Richard Johnson dec^d
Trefina Smith allowed $12 keeping Nancy Groce poor person of this County from this Term until January term
Edward Watts to oversee road in place of Oney Harvey
James Medlock to oversee road in place of Daniel Leach
Benjamin Sturdevant, John Humphries Esq^{rs} & Alex^r Dickson to settle with guardian of minor orphans of Robt Rogers dec

James Madison Booker minor orphan bound to John Holliway to age 21, he being now 6 years old; Holliways bond & security $500; to furnish sd boy at age 21 a good horse worth $50, a saddle & bridle worth $25
David Irwin admr estate of W^m B West decd allowed $154 for his services in settling estate
p.-- James Eason & David Smith Esqrs to settle with guardian of Sally Baker
Cave Johnson solicitor general allowed $35 for his exoficio services

OCTOBER 1824

Stirling Brewer Esq[r] to settle with county officers in place of Raiford Crumpler resigned

Jn[o] C Collier & James M Brewer allowed $5 each for repairing the Court House

Rich[d] M Jones allowed $60 for support of Geo W Jordan dec[d], minor orphan of Seth B Jordan dec[d] out of sd G.W.'s estate.

Rich[d] M Jones allowed $36 each for maintaining for one year Jn[o], Rob[t] & Mary Jordan minor orphans of Seth B Jordan dec[d].

Nehemiah Hardy Esq[r] resigned as Justice of the peace

W[m] Hodge & Tho[s] Flannery to settle with Thomas Hudson g[dn] of minor orphans of Lewis Evins dec[d]

Samuel Mitchel to oversee road in place of Burgess Nall

Hodge Adams to oversee road in place of John Tucker

Alfred Norris to oversee road in place of John T Hutchison

Garret Hall to oversee road in place of James Douglass

p.-- Ransom Milam to oversee road in place of Eli Cross

Nathan Tubb to oversee road in place of Jiles Jones

Joseph Kimble to oversee road in place of Hugh Dickson

Reese Bowen to oversee road in place of Christopher Strong

John Dannel to oversee road in place of Ephraim Ellis

George W Highland, James Baxter, Drury Christian, James W Christian, Edward Lucas, W[m] Turner, Silas Harris to mark out a road beginning at Davidson county line on Big Harpeth near Clay lick, down Harpeth intersecting the big road from Charlotte to Nashville by the plantation of Stirling Brewer, and thence to mouth of Harpeth; make return next Court

p.-- Kendrick Myatt to oversee road from Bear creek to Widow Hudsons with hands: Alsey Seamore, Daniel Nall, Brinkley George, Archibald Hogan, Burwell Myatt, Josiah Wiley, John Reding, Redick Myatt, Orran Nall. Cha[s] S Neily

Ja[s] McCord to oversee road Charlotte to Columbia from Coxes cabin to Hickman C[o] line with hands: Nicholas Dudley, David Frasier, Willis Dudley, Azor Wiley, Jacob Picket, David Wiley, Elisha Smith, Peter Picket, W[m] Austin, Nathaniel King.

Thomas Jurnigan to oversee road in place of George F Napier

William Bishop is allowed $68.25 for keeping Jesse P Dees in jail 9 Sept[r] 1822 untill 6 March 1823, previous to change of venue, and 3 Turn keys at 3 p[r] day each

Jo[s] Eason, Jn[o] Dunigan, James Thedford, Jn[o] Wims, Rich[d] Murrell to divide real estate of Gabriel Overton, dec[d].

Benjamin Gummit appointed constable

W[m] B Turley to adm[r] estate of George W Jordan dec[d], a minor orphan of Seth B Jordan dec[d]

p.-- George W Jordan app[td] g[dn] of Mary Jordan, minor orphan of Seth B Jordan dec[d]

Jurors to Circuit Court Thomas Richeson, James Haddin Senr,

OCTOBER 1824

Thos Palmer, Jas Smith, Jno A King, Richd Adamson, Archibald Saneil[Samil?], John Cunningham, Wm Patterson, Wm Simpson, Robert Whitwell, Nathl Simpson, Jno Wims, James Tatom, Allen Bowen, William Loftes, Wm Frasier, Thos Stroud, Wiley Davis, Abesah P Massie, Jesse Stroud, Wm Hudson, John H Stone, Wm Thomas, Alexander Dickson, Hugh Dickson Jr, John Hays

Jurors to next County Court: Joo Wiley, John Bradley, Thomas Nesbitt, Andrew Brown, William W Baldthrop, Jesse Ragan, Jno Haywood, Willis H Cunningham, Jno Edwards, Robt Easly, James Epperson, Jas Armour, George Tatom, Washington England, John Holliway, Orren Nall, Thomas Petty Jr, Jacob Peeler, Benjamin Gilbert, Newby Sowell, James Carter, Jno Parker, William Cox, Eldridge Bowen, Solomon Marsh, Hewell Parrish, Joseph Edwards, Joseph Kimble, John Wilson

William Gravit, orphan boy bound by Court to Jesse L Kierk, being maltreated by Kierk has removed from this County; the object for which he was bound is not likely to be attained; therefore order Kierk appear next Term, and bring Wm Gravit, and shew cause if any why he shall not be taken from him

p.-- Bill/Sale D H Williams to John Johnson 3 Negroes ackd
Deed John Mcadoo to Margret Mcadoo 206 acres ackd
Deed James Salmon to John Wilson 228 acres proven by Alexr Dickson & Stephen Harris
Deed John Thorn to Jno Wilson 90 acres proven by Robert West & Randolph R Harris
Deed Thos Matthews to Saml Mitchel 2 3/4 and 1/8 acres ackd
Deed Christopher Strong to James Matthews 200 acres ackd
Deed Samuel Riley to Lewis D Sowell 43 acres proven by John Sowell and Daniel Harris
Deed Samuel Riley to Daniel Harris 70 acres proven by John Sowell and Lewis D Sowell
Deed James McCallister to John Sowell 100 acres proven by Lewis D Sowell and Daniel Harris
p.-- Deed Francis Wisdom to John Sowell 200 acres ackd

Deed L P Cheatham to Elias W Napier 300 acres land in Shelby County, TN, ackd, & ordered to be certified for registration in Shelby County
Joseph Kimble, William Morrison, and Benjn Rye to distribute estate of George M Jordan decd amongst legatees
Deed Thomas Matthews to Willis Cunningham 157 acres ackd

Jno Turner to oversee opening of road from Yellow Creek road near Jno Turners shop to Charlotte with hands Sampson Boles, Robt Vanhook, Saml Whitehead, John May & hands, John Adams & hands, Geo Adams, Richd Adams, Wm T Hooper, Wm Adams, Samuel Self, Peter Self, Wm Norsworthy & hands, Thomas Norsworthy,

OCTOBER 1824

Jeremiah Nesbitt & hands, Thos May, Joel Boyce, Eliza^b Turners hands, Jno B Jones, And^w Brown, Frank Miscom, Jesse May, Jesse Ragan, H H Ragan, W^m D Turner, H H Marable & hands Court adjourned until tomorrow morning 9 oClock
                         Nathan Nesbitt, A Coldwell, Wm White

Tuesday October 5th 1824.   Present the worshipful Nathan Nesbitt, A Coldwell, Wm White, Esquires, Justices

Grand jury John Stafford foreman, Barnwell Jackson, Robert Brown, Howard W Turner, And^w M Lewis, James Matthews, Nicholas Dudly, Morgan B Wells, James Tubb, W^m S Coleman, Daniel Coleman, Samuel Sellers, John James. James H Davie constable

Benjamin Sturdevant vs Susannah Hall ex^{tx} & Jesse Hall ex^{tr} of John Hall dec^d. Appeal. By att^{ies}. Jury Sampson Boles, Saml Dunigan, Joel Marsh, Mitchel Jackson, Isaac Hill, Jacob Pucket, David Frasier, Jno Clark, Jno Bradley, Wm Hickerson, William C Staley, Matthew Gilmore, who find for def^{ts}. The plaintiff's appeal to Circuit Court is granted

p.-- John Hunter vs William Tatom. Debt. By att^{ies}. Jury as above, except Jesse Hall for Matthew Gilmore, say they find for plaintiff $180, damage of detention $16.35. And costs

Nathan Nall vs William Hudson. By att^{ys}. Jury Sampson Boles, Samuel Dunigan, Joel Marsh, Mitchel Jackson, Isaac Hill, Jacob Pucket, David Frasier, John Clark, Matthew Gilmore, John Bradley, William Hickerson, Wm C Stailey who assess pltf's damage to $118.50 and costs. Appeal is granted to defendant

p.-- Andrew Stewart admr vs John J Bell. Def^t by attorneys, pl^{tt} came not but made default. Def^t recovers of pl^{tt}

Jesse Norris vs James West. Pl^{tt} by attorney orders suit his dismissed. Defendant recovers of plaintiff his costs
Jesse Norris vs Alfred Norris. Plaintiff by attorney orders suit dismissed. Defendant to recover of plaintiff his costs.
Jesse Norris vs Alexander Dickson. Pl^{tt} by att^y orders suit dismissed. Def^t to recover of pl^{tt} his costs

Grand Jury presented bill/indictment against Wm Reynolds Jr, Sampson Camperry, Wm Reynolds Sr, Wm Morrison, Wm Martin, & Thomas Parrish Not a true bill. Also bill/indictment ag^t W^m McNickol & Alexander Hamilton not a true bill & on motion of Sol^r Genl order county pay costs

p.-- Field Farrar vs Elias Fendley. Debt. Pl^{tt} orders suit be dismissed; defendant assumes all costs

OCTOBER 1824

Montgomery Bell vs Elias Fendley. Pl^{tf} by att^y orders suit dismissed. Def^t recovers of pl^{tf} his costs

Montgomery Bell vs William Mcadoo. Pl^{tf} by att^y orders suit dismissed. Def^t recovers of pl^{tf} his costs

Sheriff Richard Batson fined $5 for contempt of Court
Elias W Napier vs John Evins. Parties granted leave to take depositions
Court adjourned until tomorrow morning 9 oClock
Nathan Nesbitt, A Coldwell, J W Napier

Wednesday October 6th 1824.   Present the worshipful
Nathan Nesbitt, A Coldwell, Jno W Napier, Esquires, Justices

Johnson & Hicks vs John C Collier. Writs of supercidias to issue on def^{ts} giving bond and security agreeable to Law

Seth Richardson ext^r will of Jordan Richardson dec^d vs Henry H Marable & wife. By att^{vs}. Jury Sampson Bowls, Saml Dunnegan, Joel Marsh, Mitchel Jackson, Isaac Hill, Jacob Puckett, David Frazier, Jno Clark, Holloway N Merrit, Sylman Edwards, Ellis Tycer, Richd Adams who say the paper writing produced by Seth Richardson is the will of s^d Jordan Richardson dec^d. Will admitted to record. Pl^{tf} recovers of def^t his costs; & enters bond $20 000 with William W Balthrop, Benjamin Sturdevant & Alexander Dickson his securities

p.--Jiles Jones vs James W Christian. Debt. By att^{vs}. Jury above find for pl^{tf} $102, damage $3.16. And cost. Defendant is granted appeal to Circuit Court
William Cox vs Elisha Williams. Pl^{tf} by att^y. Suit dismissed and defendant recovers of plaintiff his cost
State vs Levi Baldwin. Nol Pros entered; county pays cost
State vs Wm Falkner. Nol Pros entered; county pays cost
State vs Isaiah Gray. Nol Pros entered; county pays cost
p.-- George Ross vs Benjamin Joslin & Co. Debt. Pl^{tf} orders suit dismissed; def^t pays half the cost
Christopher Robertson vs George Ross. Pl^{tf} orders suit dismissed; def^t pays half the cost
Benjamin Joslin & Co vs George Ross. Pl^{tfs} dismiss suit; d^{ft} pays one half cost
Jesse Hall vs Holliway N Merit. Each party has leave to take depositions
p.-- State vs William Handlin. Riot. Appearance bond $250; Hugh Dickson and Holliway N Merit his securities
State vs Wm Handlin. Peace Warrant. Bond of Wm Handlin, with Hugh Dickson and Holliway N Merit securities, to keep peace

JANUARY 1825

towards Mary Dickson and her family for 12 months
State vs Thomas Clark. Pettit Larceny. Nol Pros entered. J C
Collier and Jn° Read, defts bail, pay cost
p.-- State vs Alexr Anderson and Henry G Wells. Forfeiture.
Anderson called, came not. Wells, Anderson's bail, made default. State recovers ag^t Anderson & Wells $500 unless next
Term they shew cause why execution should not issue

Mary Dickson vs heirs of John Dickson dec^d. Petiton for her
distributive share. Subpoenas to issue to defendants
Fine of $5 against Sheriff released
p.-- State vs Daniel Peppers. A&B. Nol Pros entered. Henry A
C Napier, def^t's bail assumes to pay costs
State vs Francis V Smitton. Assault. Appearance bond, Francis Smitton and Hugh Dickson
State vs Francis V Smitton. Bond of Anderson M Lewis to give
evidence behalf State
p. Richard C Napier vs Shaderick Harris. Pl^{tf} by att^y orders
suit dismissed; def^t recovers of pl^{tt} his costs
Edward D Hicks presents his commission from the governor as
a justice of the peace
Court adjourned until tomorrow 10 oClock
       A Coldwell, Nathan Nesbitt, E D Hicks

Thursday October 7th 1824   Present the Worshipful
Abiram Coldwell, Nathan Nisbett, E D Hicks, Esq^{rs}, Justices

William Hollingsworth vs Thomas W Schmitton. Smitton petitions to bring up proceedings had before Nehemiah Hardy Esqr
wherein Hollingsworth was pl^{tf} and Schmitton was def^t; Court
granted petition

p.-- B W Raiborn and wife vs H N Merit. Def^t by att^y. Plt^f
failed to shew cause for setting aside the probate of a bill
of sale; said bill of sale admitted to registration
Court adjourned until Court in Course
      A Coldwell, E D Hicks, Nathan Nesbitt

p.-- Monday January 3^d 1825 Present Daniel H Williams, John
Johnson, John W Napier, Thomas Murrell, William White, John
Pendergrass, Minor Bibb, William Hogan, Joseph Wilson, Benjamin Sturdevant, Esquires, Justices

Abiram Coldwell Esqr resigned as justice of the peace

JANUARY 1825

Clark Spencer allowed $59.94¼ for boarding, schooling, and clothing Tereasy M Bedford for 1824; he draws on her guardian John Mcadoo for same

James Tidwell allowed $5.50 for furnishing the guard with provisions that had Jesse Pedeer in custody

Ordered Margaret Evins widow of Lewis Evins decd allowed all previous rents and profits from lands belonging to estate of Lewis Evins dec^d for heretofore educating and schooling the children of sd dec^d.
Ordered Margaret Evins be allowed rents and profits of land belonging to heirs of Lewis Evins dec^d for the educating and schooling of s^d heirs for 1825
Order that taxes for this year be same as Last year

p.-- Mitchel Jackson to oversee road from Charlotte to Jiles Jones as far as the pole bridge with hands on Jones creek in bounds of s^d road, and that Nathan Tubb oversee s^d road from pole bridge to Jiles Jones, and have hands on Johnsons Creek

Jacob Pucket, George Mitchel, Edm^d Tidwell, Lamuel Russell, Aquilla Tidwell, Nich^s Dudley, Hudson Dudley, Wiley Davis to mark a road from where Yellow Cr road intersects old Natchez Trace, to intersect the Franklin road at or near Minor Bibbs

Isaac Hill to oversee road in place of James Dannel
Wm S Coleman to oversee road in place of Wm McClelland
John Parker to oversee road in place of George Mitchel
Howard W Turner Esqr produced a commission from the Governor as Justice/Peace
Joseph Payne to oversee road in place of James McCauly
p.-- Abiram Coldwell apptd to commission to settle with the County officers
Nathan Nesbitt Esqr licenced to keep an ordinary at his now residence in Charlotte. Also Richard Batson licenced to keep an ordinary
Henry Highland to oversee road in place of Thomas Wilson

William Gravel[Gravit?] a minor orphan bound to Wm Bishop to learn the art of sadling until he arrives at age 21 at which time Bishop to furnish him with a good sett of sadlers tools and he is to have him taught reading, writing, & arrithmetic as far as the Rule of three

Minor Bibb, David Gray & Charles Gilbert to settle with Amos James and Enoch James executors of Joshua James decd

Abijah P Massie, Jno Parker, Jno W Fentress, Moses Lankford, & Jno Tidwell to review road from Gum Br to Arch^d Ponder and

JANUARY 1825

say which road shall stand as a public road

Joseph G Davis to oversee road in place of Harden Chambers
David Irwin allowed $30 for services as guardian for George West and that he draw on himself for the amount
James C Hays app^{td} g^{dn} to George M Deadrick minor orphan
p.-- Deed Benjn Matlock to Harden Chamless 12 acres proven by Robert Armour
Deed Thomas Simmons to Wells & Davenport 320 acres proven by Richard D Sansom
Deed Thomas Carns to Thos Simmons 320 acres proven by Joseph Wilson who also proves handwriting of Adam Wilson dec^d
B/S Richard D Sansom to William C Sansom for negroes proven by John W Napier
Deed Henry G Wells & Chancy Devanport to Wm C Sansom for 320 acres proven by Elias Tubb & Rich^d D Sansom
Deed/Gift Shadrack Bell to Thomas Bell for property ackd
Deed William Hudson to Baker Hudson 60 acres ackd
p.-- Deed of Gift William Tatom to George Tatom for property proven by James Eason & Richard Tatom
Deed James Eason to Allen Bowen 225 acres ackd
Deed/Gift Nathan Nall to Danl Nall 198 acres proven by Mumford Smith & Baker Hudson
Deed Robt Weakly to Ausey Burgess 640 acres proven by Evans & Elias Burgess
Deed/Gift Thomas Murrell Senr to Thos Murrell Junr 200 acres proven by Wm Hudson & Ja^s Douglass
Deed/Gift Thomas Murrell S^r to Thomas Murrell J^r Negro Peter proven by Wm Hudson & Ja^s Douglass
Ordered a Precinct Election established at late residence of Thomas Simmons on old Town Creek
p.-- William Hedge app^{td} guardian to John A Evins, Jane Evins, Mahulda Evins, Patsey Evins, Elizabeth Evins, Harriet Evins, minor orphans of Lewis Evins dec^d
Justices to take list of Taxable property for 1825: Captain Tidwells Company, William White; Capt Grimmets, Hudson Dudley; Capt Georges, David Smith; Capt Massies, John Johnson; Capt Turners, D H Williams; Capt Reynolds, Howard W Turner; Capt Grimes, M Bell; Capt Parrish, Benjamin Sturdevant; Capt Nesbitt, E D Hicks; Capt Hunters, Ge^o Hightower; Capt Thedfords, William Hogan; Capt McKees, Thos Murrell

Court proceed to class themselves: First class Hudson Dudley, D H Williams, Wm Hogan, Thomas Murrell, Joseph Wilson, Minor Bibb
Second Class Robert Armour, Nathan Nesbitt, Joseph Morris, Jno Johnson, Ge^o Hightower
Third Class John W Napier, E D Hicks, Samuel Turner, David Smith, Montgomery Bell
Fourth Class John Pendergrass, Howard W Turner, Benjn Stur-

JANUARY 1825

devant, Wm White, R C Napier, Jn° Humphrey, James Eason

p.-- Jurors to April Court Nehemiah Scott, Wiley Baldthrop, W^m D Turner, Woodson Dannel, Nathan Dilleha, Drury Adkins, Reuben P H Burton, Silmon Edwards, Jonathan Malugin, George Gallion, John Crews, Jn° Hand, Jn° A King, Jn° Simpson, Burwell Bosley, Wm Cox, Jn° Hall, Richd Murrell, Jn° Garton, Wm Pendergrass, Alsey Speight, Burton Pope, Shaderick Bell, Jn° Nisbitt Junr, William S Coleman, Hudson J Shropshire, Morgan Hood, Joseph Eason, Henry Goodrich, Orren D Hogan

Parrishoners allowed for this year as follows: Prior Payne $70; Levi Lindsey $10; Charles Thompson $30 for keeping two poor children; Silas Tompkins $35 for keeping his son a poor person; Robert Shelton $20; Wm Houston $40 for keeping his son a poor person; Nancy Tidwell $30; John A Johnson $25 for keeping his wife a poor person; Nancy Groce $40 to be drawn by Mrs Smith

Power/Att^y Lebuous Richeson and Frankey his wife to Ira McPharson proven by Lebius W Richeson & James J Richeson
Court adjourned until tomorrow Morning 9 oClock
    J Pendergrass, Joseph Morris, Wm White, D Smith, Ge°
    Hightower

p.-- Tuesday January 4th 1825   Present John Pendergrass, Joseph Morris, Wm White, Drury Smith, Ge° Hightower Justices

Grand jury: Thos Nisbitt foreman, Robert Duke, John Bradley, Jn° Parker, Benjⁿ Gilbert, Washington England, George Tatom, Soloman Marsh, Joseph Willey, Joseph Edwards, William Turner, Orrin Nall. James H Davie, constable, to attend them

Kendrick Myatt and Daniel Billops elected constables
David Mcadoo constitutionally elected Sheriff for two years; bond $5000, Stirling Brewer, John Mcadoo, John B Brown, Benjamin Clark his securities; & bond for collection of public and county tax $5,000 with the same securities
Andrew Stewart resigns as a Justice of the peace

p.-- Ephraim H Foster, W^m L Brown vs Jehu Miller. Debt. Def^t in proper person says he owes pl^{tfs} $100 with interest from 8 March 1824. Pl^{tfs} to recover of Def^t $105 and their costs

Jehu Miller vs Edmond Miller. Pl^{tf} by att^y moved for judg^t ag^t def^t as security in note to Brown & Foster. Jury Eldrege Bowen, Thos Petty S^r, John Hogwood, Ja^s Eperson, Ja^s Armour, Ja^s Carter, Huel Parish, Thomas McCleland, James McKee, Hugh Dickson, Lemuel Russell, Spencer Brown who say pl^{tf} is cose-

JANUARY 1825

curity with def^t and Mathew Miller. Pl^{tf} to recover $35 and his costs

p.-- Jehu Miller vs Matthew Miller. Pl^{tf} by att^y moved for judg^t ag^t def^t cosecurity in note executed to Brown & Foster for $100. Jury above. Pl^{tf} to recover of def^t $35 and costs

p.-- Samuel Thomas vs Joseph Hunter. By att^{ies}. Pl^{tf} orders suit dismissed. Defendant to recover of plaintiff his costs

Thomas Flanery vs Younger McCaslen. By att^{ies}. Parties order suit dismissed, each pays his costs

Jesse Norris vs Henry G Wells. The plaintiff in open Court orders suit dismissed. Pl^{tf} recovers of defendant the costs
Jesse Norris vs James Wilson. As above.
p.-- Thomas Walker vs Thomas Reynolds and John Wilson. Pl^{tf} by att^y orders suit dismissed; def^t pays costs
Deed B G Stewart to Judith Stewart 6 acres proven by Andrew Stewart and John Arrington
Deed John Arrington to William Lomax 40 acres ackd
Jacob Shipman vs Hugh Dickson. Pl^{tf} by att^y; def^t made default; pl^{tf} to recover of def^t $203
Court adjourned until tomorrow morning 9 oClock
                                J Willson, D H Williams, Wm White

p.-- Wednesday Jany 5th 1825. Present the worshipful Joseph Wilson, D H Williams, William White, Esquires, Justices

Dorothy Goodrich ext^x, Alexander Dickson ext^r, will of James Goodrich dec^d vs David Rushing. By att^{ies}. Jury above except Jno Hall & Raiford Crumpler for Lem^l Russell & Spencer Brown Jury cannot agree. Raiford Crumpler withdrawn and jury discharged. Cause transfered to Circuit Court
Jacob Shipman vs Hugh Dickson [blank]
p.-- State vs William Handlin. Jury Eldridge Bowen, Thomas Petty S^r, Jno Hogwood, Ja^s Epperson, Ja^s Armour, Ja^s Carter, Thomas McClelland, Jno Hall, Raiford Crumpler, Ja^s McKee, Wm Tatom, Lary Burns who cannot agree. Raiford Crumpler withdrawn. Jury discharged. Cause continued to next Term

State vs William McNichol. A&B. Def^t pleads Guilty; fined $1 and pay all costs of prosecution

State vs John Marsh. Nole prosequi entered; county pays cost

John Clark vs Wm Mcadoo. Ordered that each party have leave to take depositions

JANUARY 1825

p.-- State vs Alexander Anderson. Peace Warrant. Appearance bond; Joseph Wilson, Henry G Wells, Richard D Sansom, Daniel Billops, Hugh Dickson, Joseph Edwards, $250 each

State vs James McCauly. Appearance bond with Jesse Hall.
State vs James McCauly. A&B. Appearance bond, John Adams and Holliway N Merit $125 each

p.-- State vs Eleanor Parrish. A&B. Appearance Bond, Eleanor Parrish $250; John Adams $125

State for the use of Jane Southerland vs David McAdoo & John Bernard. Bastardy. Def's as securities for Edward Teal confess judgment $20 and costs

p.-- State vs Robert Rogers. Appearance bond with Jesse Hall

William Hightower took oaths as deputy Sheriff by direction of David Mcadoo high sheriff
Court adjourned until tomorrow morning 9 oClock
Minor Bibb, D H Williams, J Willson

Thursday morning January 6th 1825. Present the worshipful Minor Bibb, D H Williams, Joseph Wilson, Esquires, Justices

Deed Allen Howard & wife to Hudson Shropshire 105 acres Sulpher fork of Jones Creek. Elizabeth W Howard wife of Allen ack[d] she executed deed freely

p.-- Samuel Smith vs Montg[y] Bell. Debt. By Att[ies]. Jury Eldridge Bowen, Tho[s] Petty S[r], John Hogwood, Ja[s] Epperson, Ja[s] Armour, Ja[s] Carter, Huel Parrish, Jn[o] Clark, W[m] Long, Thomas McClelland, Adonijah Edwards, John Choate who find for pl[tf] damage $58.86 & costs

State vs Jeremiah Bruce. Motion of defendant to enquire if illegitimate child charged to him on Ann Rutlege was begotten by him. Jury above find for def[t]. County pays the cost of prosecution $8.50

p.-- Elias W Napier vs Jn[o] Evins. By att[ies]. Jury Rob[t] Duke, John Bradley, Jn[o] Parker, Benj[n] Gilbert, Washington England, Ge[o] Tatom, Silaman Marsh, W[m] Cox, Tho[s] Nesbitt, Jo[s] Willey, W[m] Turner, Orrin Nall who cannot agree. Rob[t] Duke withdrawn; jury discharged. Cause continued to next of Term this court

p.-- Spencer T Hunt vs Montg[y] Bell. Jury above, Jo[s] Edwards for Orrin Nall say def[t] owes pl[tf] $170, damage $5.10, costs.

APRIL 1825

Court adjourned until tomorrow morning 9 oClock
                              Minor Bibb. J Willson. N Nesbitt

Friday morning January 7th 1825.   Present the worshipful
Minor Bibb, Joseph Wilson, N Nesbitt. Esquires, Justices

Elias W Napier vs John Evins. Parties granted leave to take
depositions

p.-- Minor Bibb granted licence to keep an ordinary at his
dwelling house in this county
Order Joseph Kimble, Benjamin Sturdevant, Samuel Turner, and
John Humphries to settle with Joseph Dickson, Robt Dickson,
Hugh Dickson, adm^{rs} of John Dickson dec^d
John Picket to oversee road in place of James Thompson

James M Thomas vs John Hunt. By attornies. Jury above. Def^t
moved Court quash proceedings; motion sustained. Defendant
recovers of pl^{tf} his costs

Theophilus Bullard vs Elias Findley. Pl^{tf} orders suit dismissed. Defendant recovers of plaintiff his costs

p.-- Jacob Shipman vs Hugh Dickson. By att^{ys}. On def^{ts} motion, judg^t by default set aside; pleading set for next Term

Richard Sandsom to oversee road in place of Henry G Wells,
with hands allotted to Wells except Joseph Edwards & hands

Joseph Edwards to oversee road from his house to the road to
Dover down east fork of Wells creek to county line
Court adjourned until Court in Course
                              D H Williams, J Willson, Minor Bibb

p.-- Monday 4th April 1825. Present Daniel H Williams, John
Johnson, Thos Murrell, Minor Bibb, James Eason, Samuel Turner, Benjn Sturdevant, William Hogan, William White, Hudson
Dudley, Howard W Varner, Nathan Nisbitt, Esquires, Justices

John Choate licenced to keep an ordinary at his house
Mary West allowed $40 for keeping her son George W West; she
draws on Stirling Brewer his guardian for same
John W Napier Esqr to take list of taxable property in Capt
Carrolls company for this year
Andrew Flowers to oversee road in place of Thomas Jerrald

APRIL 1825

Lewis Jernigan age 17 bound to Wm Bishop until he arrives at 21 years to learn art of makeing saddles; Bishop is to have him taught reading, writing, arithmetic to rule of three, to keep him well clad and to give him holesome diet & all other necessaries pertaining to an apprentice
p.-- Thomas Murrell and Wm Hogan Esq^rs app^td to settle with Joel Marsh guardian of Moses Overton and Elizabeth Overton
Telman Perry allowed $24/yr from this Term for keeping William Pendergrass S^r a poor person of this County
Benj^a Sturdevant, Samuel Turner Esq^rs & Robert West app^td to settle with adm^rs of estate of John Dickson dec^d
Thos Murrell, David Smith Esq^rs & John Baker app^td to settle with Wm Hudson & Thos C Hudson Ex^trs of Wm Hudson Sr Dec^d

Jesse May to oversee road in place of John Turner, to finish cutting the new road from Yellow Creek to Charlotte, to have same bounds for hands with addition of Wm Baldthrops hands, Wiley Baldthrop and hands, W^m W Baldthrop & hands
Hosea M B Ragan to oversee road in place of Ge^o Davidson
Wm Willey to oversee road in place of Joseph Choate
p.-- Montg^y Bell resigned as Justice of the peace
John A King to oversee road in place of Ja^s Rogers
Samuel Self to oversee road in place of Wm Jones
Deed James McCauly to Aquilla Council and Willis Council, 75 acres proven by Samuel Smith
Deed Isabella Sooter adm^x of James King dec^d to Samuel Brown 90 acres proven by James Rogers
Deed Ryton Robertson to Willoughby Etheredge 300 acres ack^d
Deed Charles Gilbert to John Sowell 100 acres proven by Edmond Tidwell & Jesse Stroud
p.-- Deed John Grimes to Jacob Leach 276 acres proven by Ja^s Matlock and Nathan Tubb
Deed Jesse Benton to George Sullivant certain property proven by John Sowell and Lewis D Sowell
Deed John Lucas and Nancy Lucas to Esam Breeding 72½ acres proven by Joseph Morriss, Jno Gibbs & Robt Lucas
B/S Joseph F Cloud to Richard Batson for Negro girl Seissily proven by John Read
Deed/Gift Thomas Petty S^r to Thomas Petty J^r 100 acres ack^d.
Deed Thomas Epperson to Benjamin Sanders 20 acres proven by John Johnson
Deed Thomas Epperson to Benjamin Sanders 10 acres proven by John Johnson
p.-- Deed/Gift Absolam Baker to Mary Baker, property, proven by John Baker and George Brazel

Will of Ann Marsh dec^d proven by Wm Hudson & Richard Evins; Gilbert Marsh, executor named, qualified
Ceburn Crews, Ge^o Smith, & Thomas Holleway took oath as con-

APRIL 1825

stables, they having given bond & security
Sally Price appointed guardian to Joshua, Thomas, and Willis A Price minor orphans
Alexander Dickson app^{td} g^{dn} to Jonathan Price, minor orphan.
Richard Batson app^{td} g^{dn} to Wm Tuck, minor orphan
Howard W Turner appointed guardian to Polly Linda Dickson, a minor orphan
p.-- James Larkins apptd gdn to John Larkins Sr
Wm Bishop apptd gdn to Lewis Jurnegan a minor orphan
Thomas Holliway apptd gdn to Moses Overton, a minor orphan.
John Adams apptd gdn to Drury Price a minor orphan

James H Davie and Alexander Wilkins app^{td} to adm^r estate of James Kirk dec^d; bond $8,000 with John Adams, George Hightower & Nehemiah Scott
Phillip B Noland & Robert H McCollum admitted to keep an ordinary at their dwelling house in this county

p.-- Jurors to July Term: Ja^s Hightower, John Brewer, Daniel More, Jo^s Williams, Elijah Dodson, Chas Thompson, Wm Lewis, W^m R Gilbert, Chas White, Jesse Hall, W^m McMurry, Jo^s Haney, Willis Collier, Wm Maloney, Burwell Bosley, Wm Lomax, John Flannery, John Watkins, Jno Choate, Thos Drummond, Jno S Roy Jr, John R Tidwell, Orrin Sullivant, Newburn Morris, William Austin, Garret Hall, Benjn Meeker, Soloman Brown, John West, Thomas Bullian

Jurors to Septr Circuit Court: Robert Baxter, Thomas Edwards, Ge^o Gallion, John May, Ge^o Adams, Hartwell Weaver, Alfred H Kenady, Ja^s Baxter, Isaac Hunter, Jo^s Lyle, Samuel W Martin, Robt T Rogers, Absolam Tribble, George Bosley, Samuel King, Brinkley George, John Reding, James D Petty, Edward Parker, Moses Parker, Ja^s Carter, Eldridge Bowen, Ja^s Larkins, Jno B Brown, David Bibb, Edmond Tidwell J^r, Thos Nesbitt, William C Staley, Robert Nesbitt(long bob)

Power/Attorney Daniel Hunt to Spencer T Hunt proven by James H Davie and James Nesbitt
Court adjourned untill to morrow morning 9 oClock
            Nathan Nesbitt, Ge^o Hightower, John Johnson

p.-- Tuesday April 5th 1825. Present the worshipful Nathan Nesbitt, George Hightower, John Johnson, Esquires, Justices

Grand jurors: Nehemiah Scott foreman, Richard Murrell, Alsey Speight, Shederick Bell, Henry Goodrich, R P H Burton, Woodson Dannell, Hudson J Shropshire, W^m S Coleman, John Gaston, J Malugion, Wm Cox, Nathan Dillehay.   James H Davie, a constable, to attend them

APRIL 1825

William W Baldthrop vs Elisha Turner. Debt. By att^{ies}. Jury: Orrin D Hogan, Morgan Hood, Wm Pendergrass, John Hall, John Crews, Drury Adkins, John A King, Silmon Edwards, Matt^w Gilmore, James Malugion, Hugh Dickson, Mark Reynolds, who find def^t doth owe plaintiff $42.49, and damage $4.72. Also costs

p.-- John J Bell vs James Smith. Pl^{ff} by att^y orders suit be dismissed; def^t by att^y assumes all costs
Henry W Hinson vs William Tatom. Appeal. Pl^{ff} in proper person orders suit dismissed. Def^t to recover of pl^{tf} his costs

Bill of Sale Susannah Hall & Jesse Hall to Henry Wert, Negro woman Sarah and child Beckey ackd
William Hightower reappointed g^{dn} to Martha & Mary Hightower minor orphans
Richard M Jones app^{td} guardian to Rosetta M Jones
Court adjourned until tomorrow morning 9 oClock
      Ge^o Hightower, Nathan Nesbitt, John Johnson

Wednesday April 6th 1825. Present the worshipful George Hightower, Nathan Nesbitt, John Johnson, Esquires, Justices

Ordered Richard M Jones gdn of Rosetta M Jones come at next term to give other and further security in his guardianship

State vs William Handlin. Riot. Jury Orrin D Hogan, Morgan Hood, Wm Pendergrass, John Crews, Drury Adkins, John A King, W^m D Turner, Silmon Edwards, Wm Hollinsworth, Thos Drummond, Benjn Gray, Ja^s Malugian who say def^t is guilty; fined $25. Defendant prays appeal; granted
p.-- Appearance bond William Handlin $250, W^m E Slayden and Josiah Davidson $125 each
State vs William Handlin. Riot. Def^t by att^y moves arrest of judgment this day entered against him

William Wallace vs Willis H Cunningham and others. Death of plaintiff suggested; cause continued

Grand Jury presented Bill/Indictment against Eleanor Parrish a true bill; also ag^t Francis V Smitton a true bill; & also two bills against William Ward, true bills

p.-- State vs William Hightower. Bastardy. Def^t found guilty of begetting a child upon Levina Crumpler gave bond & security $500 to keep child from becoming charge to county; order that he pay for first year $35, second year $25, third year $15 for maintenance of sd child, and cost of prosecution

APRIL 1825

Michael Kimes vs Stephen Hostly. Execution levied on goods of Stephen Hostly to make $18.25 & costs, with interest from 6 May 1821 until paid, the amount of judgment Michael Kimes obtained before Aron Vanhook Esqr then a Justice/peace on 31 December 1821. Signed Field Farrar 19 July 1824. Endorsed no personal property found, levyed on 50 acres on Ceder Creek, March 15th 1825. James Williams, Constable. Order sale.
Court adjourned until tomorrow morning 9 oClock
      Ge^o Hightower, Joseph Morris, Nathan Nesbitt

p.-- Thursday April 7th 1825. Present the worshipful George Hightower, Joseph Morris, Nathan Nesbitt, Esqrs, Justices

Henry Johnson vs Eleanor Parish, Danl H Williams, Jno Adams. Pl^{tf} by att^y moved for a judgment against Eleanor Parish and Daniel Williams & Jno Adams his securities for the office of constable. As constable he collected an execution belonging to Henry Johnson & ag^t Reybourn, the principle & interest of which amounts to $29.50. He refused to pay same. Pl^{tf} to recover of the defendants, and also costs

State vs William Hamlin. Fine against deft for $25 released; defendant pays cost

p.-- State vs Alexander Anderson. Riot. Jury Nehemiah Scott, Alsey Speight, Shederick Bell, Henry Goodrich, Richard Murrell, Hudson J Shropshire, Woodson Dannel, William S Coleman, Jona^n Malugian, Wm Cox, Nathan Dillihay, Ge^o Smith who find def^t guilty. Fined $10 and pay the cost of prosecution

State vs Francis V Smitton. A&B. A M Lewis prosecutor. Jury above except George Southerland for Ge^o Smith. Find def^t not guilty. Order def^t taxed with cost and remain in custody of Sheriff until cost is secured. Def^t secures payment of cost

p.-- State vs James McCauly. Ind^t overseer. Jury Orrin D Hogan, Morgan Hood, Wm Pendergrass, Jno Hall, Jno Crews, Drury Adkins, John A King, W^m D Turner, Silmon Edwards, W^m T Reynolds, Robt Maddin, Jno Clark who say def^t is guilty; fined 12½¢ and pay the cost; remain in custody of sheriff until he secures the fine and cost which is accordingly done

State vs James McCauly. A&B. F V Smitton prosecutor. Pleads guilty; fined $5 and cost

State vs Thomas Gafford. Pettit larceny. Nol Pros entered & county pay cost $4.75
State vs William Caffery. Pettit larceny. Nol Pros entered & county pay cost $4.75

APRIL 1825

State vs Elizabeth Hendrix. Nol pros entered; county to pay cost $4.75

p.-- State vs Eleanor Parrish. A&B. Ja^s McCauly prosecutor. fined 12½¢ & pay cost. In custody until paid, which is done

State vs Francis V Smitton. A&B. James McCauly prosecutor. Appearance bond, Smitton $500; Holliway N Merit $250

State vs Francis V Smitton. Peace Warrant. Ja^s McCauly prosecutor. Court of opinion there is no Just Cause; defendant to pay cost of prosecution; defendant prays appeal; granted

p.-- State vs William Handlin. Riot. William Baker and James Malugian agree to pay for Wm Handlin $25 & ½¢, cost of suit agt Handlin; execution stayed three months

State vs Alex^r Anderson. Riot. Alex^r Dickson & Hugh Dickson assume cost of suit $14.25; execution stayed three months

Peter Black vs John Turner & Samuel Turner, executor of John Turner dec^d. Garnishment. Answer of Saml Turner ex^{tr} of Jno Turner dec^d to garnishment: that he had & has $143.56¼ which deft is entitled to as a legatee under will of John Turner; that he has no other effects of John Turner nor had at time he was summoned, that he knows of no debt or effects of John Turner. Court considered that Peter Black recover of Samuel Turner ex^r of Jno Turner $143.56¼ besides his costs expended

p.-- John Clark vs Wm Mcadoo. Motion to dismiss. Parties by att^{ys}. Suit dismissed, plaintiff recover ag^t def^t his costs

William Hollingsworth vs Francis V Schmitton. Certiorari. By att^{ys}. Certiorari dismissed. Pl^{ff} to recover of def^t & also on motion ag^t W^m T Reynolds & Holloway N Merritt securities $12.75, $1 interest, together with costs expended

p.-- W^m S White vs John Montgomery. Debt. By attorneys. Jury Orrin D Hogan, Morgan Hood, Wm Pendergrass, Jno Crews, Drury Adkins, John A King, W^m D Turner, Silman Edwards, William T Reynolds, Robert Maddin, John Clark, who find for pl^{tf} $100 debt, damage $2.50. Also costs. Defendant granted an appeal

p.-- Ephraim Arnold vs Daniel H Williams & Benjamin Sturdevant adm^{rs} of Alex^r Rose dec^d. By att^{ys}. Jury Orrin D Hogan, Morgan Hood, Wm Pendergrass, John Hall, Jno Crews, Drury Adkins, John A King, William D Turner, Silman Edwards, William T Reynolds, Robert Maddin, John Clark who find for pl^{tf} $106 debt, damage $7.95, & costs, to be levied on estate of Alex^r Rose dec^d in hands of adm^{rs}; execution stay of three months

JULY 1825

Court adjourned until tomorrow morning 9 oClock
                    Nathan Nesbitt, Geo Hightower, John Johnson

Friday April 8th 1825.   Present the worshipful Nathan
Nesbitt, George Hightower, John Johnson, Esquires, Justices

p.-- William Rye, C Strong, Reese Bowen, John Mcadoo, Jacob
Leach to lay off one years provision for widow and family of
James Kirk deceased
Simon Myers to oversee road in place of Archd Pullin
Jesse Taylor to oversee road in place of Wm Taylor
John Mcadoo to oversee road in place of Alexr Wilkins

State vs Thomas W Forbush. Bastardy. Order capias issue to
Wilson County for defendant

[4 suits] Willis Norsworthy vs Wm W Baldthrop. Pltf in proper person orders his four suits to be dismissed. Defendant to recover of plaintiff his cost in this behalf expended

Samuel King vs Montgomery Bell. Pltf by attorney orders suit dismissed. Defendant to recover of plaintiff his cost

p.-- William Gibson vs Saml Turner. Garnishment. Saml Turner answered that at time notice was served he had in his hands $133.56¼ as extr of John Turner decd which is due deft as a legatee of sd Jno Turner, which sum Samuel Turner intends to pay toward discharge of an execution of Peter Black agt John Turner, besides which Samuel Turner has nothing belonging to John Turner nor does he know of any property in hands of any other person belonging to John Turner. Considered by Court that pltf Wm Gibson recover of deft $133.56¼ also his cost. Samuel Turner by atty prays appeal to Circuit Court; granted

p.-- John Clark vs William Mcadoo. Deft by atty moves to set aside dismissal of appeal; granted; cause reinstated

John Hall to oversee road in place of James R Napier
James Hicks app'd to oversee road in place of Richard Crunk with hands on east and south sides of Passmores Creek
Court adjourned until court in Course
                    Nathan Nesbitt, Geo Hightower, D H Williams

p.-- Monday 4th July 1825.   Present the worshipful
John W Napier, William White, David Smith, John Pendergrass,

JULY 1825

Hudson Dudly, George Hightower, Jn⁰ Johnson, Thomas Murrell, David Smith, Robert Armour

John Choate produced scalps of eight wolves under 4 months, proving that he killed them within bounds of Dickson County. William Burk produced scalp of 1 wolf over age four months. Mabel Gilbert produced scalps of 8 wolves under 4 months and 1 over 4 months. They proved wolves were killed in Dickson County, & are allowed therefor agreeable to Act of assembly

Benjn Sturdevant, Saml Turner Esqrs to settle with adm^{rs} of Elizabeth Walker dec^d

p.-- Joseph Choate, Burwell Eatherage, Kindrick Eatherage, & Joseph Eatherage are attached to the bounds of Jesse Taylor overseer of road from Charlotte to Reynoldsburgh

Jn⁰ Pendergrass, Hudson Dudley & Wm White Esq^{rs} appointed to settle with James Tidwell adm^r of Levi Tidwell deceased
Huel Parrish vs Chauncy Devanport. Debt. Joseph Edwards, appearance bail for Devanport surrendered him
State agt Jesse P Dees. County trustee to pay State witness.

Stirling Brewer, Augustin Roberts, & Richard Batson app^{td} to see what repairs are necessary to Court House and to let the repairs to lowest bidder
Thomas Palmer is granted licence to keep an ordinary at his house in Charlotte
p.-- Moses Street granted leave to build a mill dam across upper east fork of Yellow Creek and to erect a mill thereon.
Wm White, Hudson Dudley, Richd Batson to settle with Spencer T Hunt surviving adm^r of Cuthbert Hudson dec^d.
Richard M Jones app^{td} guardian to Rosetta M Jones a minor
Jane James app^{td} guardian to Joshua James a minor orphan
Orrin D Hogan app^{td} guardian to Christopher Hudson a minor orphan
Aquilla Council to adm^r estate of Rebecca Council dec^d; bond $400, with Howard W Turner and Wm Hollingworth
Wm Hogins to adm^r with will annexed the estate of Lucy Hudson decd; bond, $2,000 with David Mcadoo and Orrin D Hogins.
Will of Lucy Hudson dec^d proven by David Gray, Minor Bibb, & Edmond Tidwell
p.-- Will of Joseph Davidson proven by Meckins Carr & Edmond Tidwell. John Davidson & Aquilla Tidwell, ex^{trs}, qualified.
Verbal will of Amos James decd proven by Enoch James & Alak James. Jane James to administer estate of Amos James decd
Jesse Smith apptd guardian to Wm Brown a lunatic
Will of Stephen Thomas dec^d proven by David Mcadoo & Robert Livingston
Minor Bibb Esqr resigned as Justice of the peace

JULY 1825

Samuel Turner, Joseph Wilson, Esqrs, and Abiram Coldwell to settle with adm^{rs} of Alexander Rose dec^d
Nathan Nisbitt allowed $6.62½ for work done on the jail
David Mcadoo allowed $3 for iron furnished to repair jail
Field Farrar allowed $95 for exoficio services for two years ending this Term
p.-- Order Mabel Gilbert to oversee road in place of James W Christian and he to have same bounds for hands
Spencer Brown to oversee road in place of James Walker

Benjn Holland, Wm Hodges, James Eason, Wm Pool, Lawson Gunn, Allen Bowen, Jo^s Eason, Ja^s Tatom, Ja^s Thedford, Jno Gunn to mark out a road from Benjamin Holland on Hurricane cr to Co^l Napiers furnace on Jones Creek

Order Lamuel Russell, the officer who arrested Jesse P Dees for Murder, be allowed $2 for services; his guard allowed $1 each to wit Ge^o Sullivant, Isiah Tidwell, John Pendergrass, Robt Lytle, John Parker, Edmond Tidwell Jr, Francis Tidwell, John Tidwell, John Parker, John W Fentress

Deed Samuel Mays to William White Junr 51 acres proven by Wm Morris and Edmond Morris
Deed George Clark to Benjamin Clark 250 acres proven by Thos Williams and John R Cathey
Deed Robert McMurry to William Ragan 6 acres proven by Matthew Gilmore and Hosea M B Ragan
Deed Benjamin Sturdevant to Ransom Ellis 312 acres ackd
Quit Claim from William Giffin to George Black proven by Jno Giffin and Daniel Moore
Deed Minor Bibb to Aquilla Tidwell 90 acres ackd

Jurors to next Term: Meckins Carr, Abijah P Massey, Willis L Dawson, Joseph B Highland, William Turner, Wm Carroll, Ge^o W Logan, Jacob Grymes, Edward Brimm, John Reynolds Jr, Abraham Self, Thos McClelland, Nelson McClelland, John McClelland, A Wilkins, Daniel George, Elisha Smith, Lindley Box, Laury Byrns, William Norsworthy, Absolam Tribble, Danl Forsey, Ge^o Adams, Jacob Leach, George Southerland, John B Brown

Deed George Clark & Mary Clark to William Ward land therein named ack^d by Ge^o Clark; Mary his wife examined apart freely acknowledged she executed s^d deed of her own accord
p.-- George Clark ackd execution of deed for land specified in s^d deed to Wm Ward; Mary wife of sd George Clark examined separately said she executed deed of her own accord
Court adjourned until tomorrow morning 9 oClock
                    J W Napier, Ge^o Hightower, S Turner

JULY 1825

Tuesday July 5th 1825.   Present the worshipful
Samuel Turner, John W Napier, Geo Hightower, Esqrs, Justices

Grand jury: William McMurry foreman, John H Tidwell, John
Choate, John L Roy Jr, John West, Wm R Gilbert, Garret Hall,
Danl Moore, Newburn Morris, William Austin, Wm Lomax, Willis
Collier, Soloman Brown, attended by J H Davie, constable

p.-- John Read vs Thomas Williamson. By atties. Jury William
Lewis, Jno Flannery, Thos Drummond, Joseph Williams, Charles
White, Thomas Bullian, Burwell Boxly, James Hightower, Jesse
Hall, John Watkins, Jno Brewer, William Maloney who find for
plaintiff, assess his damage to $106. Also costs

Deed Samuel Sparks to Daniel Coleman 200 acres proven by
Thomas Bullian and Wm Fussel
Court adjourned until tomorrow Morning 9 oClock
                    J W Napier, Geo Hightower, Saml Turner

Wednesday July 6th 1825.   Present the worshipful
John W Napier, Geo Hightower, Samuel Turner, Esqrs, Justices

Richard C Napier vs Alexander Hamilton. Cov. By attys. Jury
above find for plff. Plt to recover of deft $268 and costs.
Deft appeals to Circuit Court; appeal is granted

Robert West, Jos [blot], & Richd D Sansom to lay off to Mary
Dickson a years provisions from estate of John Dickson decd

A Petition of Mary Dickson having been served by sheriff on
heirs Robert Dickson, Jas W Joseph John James Boatright &
wife, Benjamin Cummins, Adam Dickson, Hugh Dickson, and Jane
Dickson by her guardian Polly Lundy Dickson. Court order the
sheriff to summon twelve men to lay off Mary Dicksons dower
in real estate of her late husband John Dickson. Heirs of
John Dickson decd pray appeal to Circuit Ct; appeal allowed

p.-- Henry M Hinson, M Hinson, Henry W Hinson vs Eleanor
Parrish. Trespass. By attorneys. Jury above find defendant
guilty. Plff to recover $5 damage, and his costs

S & J Kircheville vs James S Bell. Demurrer. By attorneys.
Court overrules demurrer. Because this is an action of debt,
Plaintiff to recover of deft $128 debt and interest, & costs

p.-- Thomas Holliway vs Anderson England. Warrent appeal.
Cause is transferred to Circuit Court

Elenor Parrish vs Thomas Collier. Petition for certiorari.

JULY 1825

Ordered that writs of certiorari & supercedeas issue

State vs William Ward. A&B. John D Edwards prosecutor. Def^t pleads guilty, fined 12½¢ and pay costs of prosecution

State vs William Ward. A & B. Adonijah Edwards prosecutor. Def^t pleads guilty; fined $5 and pay cost of prosecution

Johnson & Hicks vs John C Collier. Petition for supercedias, cause is transferred to Circuit Court

p.-- State vs Francis V Smitton. Appearance bond $500; Hugh Dickson $250. A&B on James McCauly

James Smith vs Montgomery Bell. By att^{ies}. Continued

William McMurry vs Andrew M Lewis & Barney L Bledsoe. Fieri facias favour of McMurry by Howard W Turner Justice/peace on 25 June 1825 ag^t And^w M Lewis & Barney L Bledsoe for $39 & ¼ cts, interest from 1 Jany last, & costs, which came to hands of Thos McMurry, constable, who in default of personal property levyed on 50 acres on Leatherwood fork of Yellow creek, property of Barney L Bledsoe 1 July 1825. Asks order of sale

p.-- Ordered Melisa Vann, Duke Stricklin, Lodwick Stricklin, Henry Vann, minor orphans be bound to Caleb Warren agreeable to act of assembly in such case made

Henry Johnson vs David McAdoo. Pl^{ff} by att^y moved for judg^t ag^t def^t for amount of an execution put into hands of def^t ag^t Eleanor Parrish, D H Williams, & John Adams in favour of plaintiff. Motion overruled, pl^{ff} pays cost of this motion. Plaintiff prays appeal to Circuit Court; allowed

John S Spencer vs Stephen Hostly, Matthew Gilmore, Eleanor Parrish & Wyatt Parrish. Fieri fascias issued favour John S Spencer by Benj^a Sturdevant Justice/peace 17th June 1825 ag^t def^{t}s for $69.44, interest from 12 Decr 1822, & costs, which came to hands of Thomas McMurry, constable, who levyed on 50 acres, property of Stephen Hostly, lying on Ceder Creek fork of Yellow Creek. Asks order of sale

p.-- Elias W Napier vs John Evins. Parties granted leave to take depositions

William Wallace vs Willis H Cunningham, Jesse Cunningham, Archabald Skelton, Edward Ellington & Thomas Matthews. Debt revival. Motion of pl^{ffs} counsel, ordered suit be revived in name of David Read, adm^r of William Wallace dec^d

JULY 1825

Deed/gift Thomas Flannery to John Flannery ackd
J W Napier, James Eason, S Turner

Thursday July 7th 1825.   Present the worshipful
John W Napier, James Eason, Samuel Turner, Esquires

Jesse Hall vs Holliway N Merritt. By attys. Jury Wm Lewis, John Flannery, Thos Drummond, Jos Williams, Chas White, Thos Bullian, Burwell Bosly, William T Rund[?], Jno Whatkins, Jno Brewer, William Maloney, Jos Larkins who find for defendant. Plaintiff prays appeal to Circuit Court; allowed

Willie B Johnson appointed Solicitor ProTem in stead of Cave Johnson who is absent owing to his indisposition

Montgomery Bell vs James W Evins. Appeal. Pltf by atty; deft came not. Pltf to recover of deft & John Evins his security for appeal $20.48 debt and interest, & his costs

William Pendergrass vs James R Napier. Appeal. Deft by atty; pltf came not. Deft to recover of pltf his costs

p.-- John Clark vs William Mcadoo. Appeal. By atties. Jury John K Tidwell, Jno L Roy Jr, Jno West, Wm R Gilbert, Garret Hall, Danl Moore, Newburn Morris, Wm Austin, William Lomax, Willis Collier, Soloman Brown, Wm McMurry who are permitted to disperse untill tomorrow morning
Court adjourned untill tomorrow morning nine oClock
J W Napier, Geo Hightower, D Smith

Friday July 8th 1825.   Present the worshipful
John W Napier, Geo Hightower, David Smith, Esqrs, Justices

Deed James Carter to Archabald Pullin 75 acres proven by Minor Bibb & James [no surname given]
Deed John George Riner to Archabald Pullin and James Carter 150 acres proven by Minor Bibb and John Sowell
Deed John Sowell to Archabald Pullin 12 acres ackd

p.-- Lebues Richardson vs Richard D Sandsom. Debt. By attys. Jury Wm Lewis, Jno Flannery, Thos Drummond, Joseph Williams, Charles White, Thos Bullian, Burwell Boxly, Jesse Hall, John Watkins, John Brewer, William Maloney, Ro Larkins, who find for plaintiff his debt $138.12½, damage $20.70. Also costs

Alexander Dickson, Executor, Dorothy Goodrich extx of James Goodrich decd vs Danl H Williams & Nehemiah Scott. Debt. By atties. Jury William Lewis, Jno Flannery, Thos Drummond, Ro

JULY 1825

Larkins, Charles White, Thomas Bullian, Burwell Boxly, Jesse Hall, John Watkins, John Brewer, Wm Maloney, Ro Larkins[sic] who find for pl^{tf} $184.27 debt, damages $14.60. Also costs

p.-- Francis V Schmitton vs Mark Reynolds. Motion: failing to pay over money as an officer. By att^{ys}. Def^t as constable collected $38.50 from David Irwin, $5 from [blank]Rogers, $4 from William McMurry, $17 from Co^l John Nesbit which sums & interest thereon from time collected untill now make $75.78 which he has failed and refused to pay over to pl^{tf}. Pl^{tf} to recover of def^t. Def^t prays appeal to Circuit Court; allowed

State vs Alex^r Anderson. Peace warrant. Court order Nol Pros entered; county to pay cost $8.52½
State vs Alex^r Anderson. Sci Fa. Court order Nol Pros entered in this case; county pay cost $4.70

p.-- John Clark vs Wm Mcadoo. Appeal. Jury sworn yesterday find for pl^{tf} $29.29. Def^t att^y moves for new trial; granted

James Hogan vs Eleanor Parrish, Const. Motion against constable. Plaintiff attorney orders suit dismissed. Ordered by Court that plaintiff recover of defendant his costs

William B Haddin vs James H Davie. Pl^{tf} by att^y orders suit dismissed. Defendant to recover of plaintiff his costs

John Harmon vs Richard D Sandsom. Debt. Pl^{tf} by counsel orders suit dismissed. Def^t to recover of plaintiff his costs

p.-- State vs Robert Steel. Affray. Def^t with his counsel pleads not guilty. Jury above except Joseph Williams for one Ro Larkins, find def^t not guilty. County to pay cost $6.50

Order the following persons be appointed Judges of elections at the places of holding same in this county
At Minor Bibbs: Arch^d Pullin, John Stafford, Wm Morris
At Rich^d D Sandsoms: Robt West, Jo^s Edwards, Jo^s Wilson Esqr
At Maj^r Adams: Nehemiah Scott, John May, Samuel Turner
At Michael Lights: John Johnson Esqr, Benjamin Holland Esqr, Robert Armour
At Wm Hogins Esqr: Wm Hogins Esqr, Morgan Hood, John Wims
At Charlotte: George Hightower, Co^l John Nesbitt, Robert Livingston
p.-- Court adjourned until tomorrow morning 9 oClock
        N Nesbitt, E D Hicks, Ge^o Hightower

Saturday morning, July 9th 1825. Present the worshipful N Nesbitt, Ge^o Hightower, E D Hicks, Esquires, Justices

OCTOBER 1825

John Clark vs W^m McAdoo. Motion for new trial. By att^{ys}. The verdict of jury is set aside; new trial granted. Defendant granted leave to take deposition of William Hendricks
Court adjourned until court in course
        Nathan Nesbitt, E D Hicks, Ge° Hightower

p.-- Monday 3rd October 1825. Present the worshipful John W Napier, John Johnson, Robert Armour, George Hightower, James Eason, John Pendergrass, William White, Esquires, Justices

Nathan Nesbitt & John Humphries Esqrs resigned as Justices.
Moses White to oversee road in place of James Medlock
Henry Sinks to oversee road in place of John Dannel
Burwell Eatherage to oversee road in place of Jesse Taylor
Enoch James to oversee road in place of Hodge Adams
Daniel Moore to oversee road in place of Samuel Mitchel
Henry Davidson to oversee road in place of Isiah Tidwell

p.-- Barnibas Coldwell to oversee road in place of John Frazier
James H Davie to oversee road from Charlotte to Nashville, working from Charlotte to Sulpher fork of Jones Creek with hands Wm Rye, Wm Kirk, Mrs Kirks Edmond, Jacob Leach, Reese Bowen & hands, Miles Long, Soloman Milam, Jn° B Brown, James Walker
Alexander Southerland to oversee road in place of Reese Bowen beginning at Sulpher fork and work towards Nashville.
Nathaniel Simpson to cut the new road from where it leaves Reynoldsburgh R^d to wolf pen with hands on Little Hurricane.
Josiah Rogers to oversee from wolf pen to head of large hollow one mile & half from Ja^s Tatoms and be allowed all hands on Garners Creek from John Watkins to the county line. James Tatom to oversee there to head of the hollow leading to John Wrights with all hands within two miles of road. John Wright to oversee from there on one miles above George Cathies with hands within one mile & half from sd piece of road

p.-- Old Vernon road from fork at mouth of lane between Thos Williams and Elijah Dodsons discontinued. Hands that formerly worked under William Dunigan to work under John Picket

Thomas May is app^{td} guardian to John H Easly, James V Easly, Eliza C Easly, minor orphans of Moses Easly dec^d
Susannah Swift & James Walker to admr estate of Thomas Swift decd; bond & security $600
Adeline Comer and William Johnson to adm^r estate of Reuben E

OCTOBER 1825

Comer dec^d
Mumford Smith and James Armour app^td constables
C Robertson, Ro Duke, and Washington Hunter app^td Inspectors of Tobacco at the mouth of Harpeth
John Mcadoo County trustee allowed $2.50 for an estray taken up by John Noland which could not be collected
Order Negroes of Estate of Lucy Hudson dec^d sold by adm^r.
p.-- James Priestly, Joseph Edwards, Alex^r Dickson, Samuel Turner and William Blake to settle with Joseph Wilson guardian to John Hays Senr dec^d
James Gilmore to oversee road in place of W^m W Baldthrop
Alsey S Speight appointed to oversee road in place of Washington Hunter
Adm^rs of Levi Tidwell dec^d permitted to sell land

Ordered that William Hedge pay all the money arising on the rents and profits of land belonging to heirs of Lewis Evins decd, and also interest to Margaret Evins for support and education of his children
John W Napier Esqr, Benjn Crews and George Clark to lay off one years provision for widow & family of Thomas Swift dec^d

Joseph Morris, Ge^o Hightower, Edward D Hicks, John W Napier Esquires to settle with Winifred Cox adm^r of Benjn Cox dec^d

Thomas May, William Johnson, Samuel King, Michael Light and William Armour to lay off one years provision for widow and family of Reuben E Comer dec^d out of estate of the deceased

p.-- Deed Williamson Plant to Ebenezer Whitehead 192 acres proven by Richard Whitehead and J H Alexander
Deed Ebenezer Whitehead to Robert Vanhook 92 acres ackd
Deed George H Walker and Jacob Walker adm^rs of Elizabeth Walker decd to W^m B Dodson 56 acres ackd
Deed Humphrey B Dunevant and Nacky Dunevant to Daniel Leach 33 1/3 acres proven by Nathan Tubb and John Crews
Sill of Sale Samuel Self adm^r of John Parrot dec^d to George Tubb negro girl ackd
Mortgage Samuel King to James Rogers 60 acres proven by Jno A King and William Johnson
Bill/Sale John Hays Senr to John Hays Junr Negro boy proven by Alexander Dickson
p.-- William Morrison, Nehemiah Hardy, Ja^s Malugin to settle with Silmon Edwards adm^r of James Seals dec^d
William Morrison, Nehemiah Hardy, James Malugin to settle with Silmon Edwards adm^r of Paletire Seals dec^d

On petition of John Adams, order summons issue to Sally McDearman gd^n of minor orphans of Drury Price dec^d to appear & give security other than s^d John Adams, present security

OCTOBER 1825

Harriatt Evins petition for partition of land of her father Lewis Evins dec^d; subpoena issues to Wm Hedge gd^n of minor orphans of Lewis Evins dec^d

Jurors to next Court Richard Cocke, Adonijah Edwards, Isaac Tompkins, Owen Sullivan, John Cunningham, Wm Hand, Daniel Leach, Gediah Nooner, Wm Caffrey, John Simpson, John Baker S^r, James Hartley, George Brazeal, Wm Grimmet, James Thompson, James Tubb, Reese Bowen, Gabriel Joslin, John Choate, Thomas Ellis, Francis Baldthrop, Silmon Edwards, Nehemiah Hardy, George Clark B C, James Martin, John West

Jurors to March Circuit Court: Ge^o Tubb, Henry A C Napier, James M Ross, Daniel Underhill, Ja^s R Napier, Alex^r Hunter, John D Edwards, Jacob Toland, Jonathan Toland, Dempsey May, Thomas Petty Jr, Gabriel Petty, Joseph Eason, Hodge Adams, Richard Crunk
Court adjourned untill to morrow morning 9 OClock
        J Pendergrass, Ge^o Hightower, James Eason

p.-- Tuesday Octr 4th 1825
Present John Pendergrass, William White, George Hightower

James Smith vs Montg^y Bell. By att^{vs}. Jury Meckins Carr, Jo^s B Highland, Wm Turner, Thomas McCleland, Nich^s Baker, Allen Daniel, Holloway N Merrit, James Tubbs, Benjn Clark, John R Cathey, Gabriel Joslin, John Clark who find pl^{tf}'s damages by reason of nonperformance of promises to $852.21. James Smith to recover of Montgomery Bell af^{sd} sum & costs. The Defendant prays appeal to Circuit Court; granted

p.-- Grand Jury: Jacob Leach foreman, William Carroll, Edwd Brimm, John Reynolds Junr, Abraham Self, Nelson McClelland, Alexander Wilkins, Daniel George, Wm Norsworthy, Ge^o Southerland, Jno McClelland, Elisha Smith, Larry Byrnes, attended by James H Davie, constable

Grand Jury presented Bill/Indictment agt Jesse J Mosley and Esom Breeding a true Bill

John Buckhannon vs John Larkins Jr. By att^{ies}. Jury Meckins Carr, Ge^o W Logan, Jo^s B Highland, Absolam Tribble, William Turner, Danl Forsey, Thos McClelland, Nicholas Baker, Allen Dannel, Holliway N Merritt, James Tubbs, John R Cathey who cannot agree. Nicholas Baker withdrawn; jurors discharged in this case, cause continued until next term

Grand Jury Bill/Ind^t ag^t Henry W Henson Not a true bill

OCTOBER 1825

Grand Jury Bill/Indictment ag^t Henry W Henson, Abraham Self, W^m H Burton, John Toler, Eaton Tatom. A true Bill.
Also Bill/Indictment against Henry W Henson a true Bill

p.-- Wm Grimmet to oversee road in place of And^w Flowers

Henry Hamilton & Thomas Shaw vs Mark Reynolds. Motion. Def^t as constable received of Morgan B Wells $24.50 and interest from 13 July 1820, a claim put in his hands for collection by s^d pl^{tfs}. Mark Reynolds has failed & refused to pay over to pl^f af^{sd} monies. Pl^{tf} to recover of def^t $24.50 with interest from 11 Decr 1823 at 12½ per cent per annum

p.-- Deed Jacob N Miller to John Grimes 162 acres proven by Henry Grimes and Molton Dickson

Elias Tubb vs Joel Massie. Parties in proper persons dismiss their suit; each pays half cost

Alex^r Dickson to adm^r estate of John Hays Senr dec^d
Court adjourned until tomorrow Morning 9 oClock
                    J Pendergrass, Wm White, J W Napier

Wednesday July 5th 1825.   Present the worshipful John Pendergrass, William White, John W Napier, Esq^{rs}, Justices

Nicholas Baker, absent juror, fined $10

p.-- Edward McCormack vs Montg^y Bell. Cause transferred to Circuit Court

Robert West vs Benjamin Sturdevant & Henry H Marable. Debt. By att^{ys}. Jury Meckins Carr, Ge^o W Logan, Jo^s B Highland, Absolam Tribble, Wm Turner, Danl Forsey, Thomas McClelland, Allen Dannel, Holliway N Merritt, James Tubb, Jno R Cathey, Henry W Hinson, who find for pl^{tf} $110.50 debt, damage by detention $8.25. Also costs

Hugh Ross vs Absolam Tribble. Cov. Deft confesses he owes $318 debt and damages. Execution stayed until next Court

p.-- H & J McClure vs Absolam Tribble. Trespass. By att^{ys}. Pl^{tfs} dismiss suit; def^t in proper person assumes costs

Huel Parrish vs Henry G Wells and Chauncey Devanport. Debt. Pl^{tf} by att^y dismisses suit. Def^{ts} pay cost

Huel Parrish vs Henry G Wells and Chauncey Devanport. Debt. Pl^{tf} by att^y dismisses suit; def^{ts} pay cost

OCTOBER 1825

David Read adm^r of Wm Wallace dec^d vs Willis Cunningham, Jesse Cunningham, Archibald Skelton, and others. Pl^{tf} by att^y dismisses suit; def^{ts} pay cost

p.-- State vs John McAdoo. Overseer. Def^t pleads guilty; fined 6¼¢ and cost
State vs Wm Allin. Nolle prosequi entered
State vs Wm Allin. A&B. Def^t at barr pleads guilty; fined $1 & cost
State vs Wm Caffry. A&B. Jury above find def^t guilty; fined $1 and pay all cost
State vs Robt Rogers. A&B. Appearance bond $250; Holliway N Merritt and David Mcadoo $125 each
p.-- John Clark, M[illegible] Mcgee & Samuel Nisbett securities of John Warren in apprentice bond entered into at the last term for orphans bound out to sd Warren as apprentices and which, heretofore, were bound to him in North Carolina: Malisa Van, Duke Stricklan, Lodwick Stricklan, and Henry Vann. Securities being with orphans, Caleb Warren present, surrendered the orphans to Court in discharge of their bond and no one objecting thereto it is ordered that same be entered of record. Upon examination the court is of oppinion that Warren discharge his duty by treating sd orphans properly, and that he retain possession of sd orphans without further restraints

William Nelson, applicant for licence as practicing attorney, proved he has resided in this county 12 months immediately preceeding application, and that he is of good moral character

p.-- George Easly vs Stephen Harris, Dorrel Y Harris, Henry H Marable. By att^{ys}. Demurrer. Jury to enquire pl^{tfs} damage

Crafford Goodwin vs Daniel H Williams, Stirling Brewer, Wm Armour. Debt. Present George Hightower, John Pendergrass, Wm White, Justices. Def^{ts} came not. Pl^{tf} recovers of def^{ts} $124.60 & interest & cost

Deed John Grimes to Daniel Moore 62 acres ackd
Deed John Nisbitt to Elias W Napier 61½ acres proven by Jno W Napier and Peter Mills[Wills?]
Court adjourned until tomorrow morning 9 oClock
          J W Napier, J Pendergrass, Wm White

Thursday October 6th 1825. Present the worshipful John W Napier, John Pendergrass, William White, Esquires, Justices

JANUARY 1826

Thomas Collun Jun[r] vs Eleonor Parrish. Certiorari. Pl[tt] by
att[y]. Petition dismissed. Pl[tt] recover of deft his costs
Court adjourned until Court in Course
                              J W Napier, J Pendergrass, W[m] White

Monday January 2nd 1826.   Present the worshipful
D H Williams, John Johnson, Howard W Turner, Robert Armour,
William White, Joseph Morris, David Smith.

Willie B Johnson Esq[r] app[td] solicitor gen[l] pro tem
Howard W Turner, Joseph Wilson, Esq[rs], and Alex[r] Dickson to
settle with Joseph Kimble adm[r] of Chesly O Cole

Joseph Choate produced scalp of one wolf over age 4 months.
Samuel Sampson 2 scalps over 4 months; they prove the kill
was within Dickson county and are allowed agreeable to law

Abiram Coldwell and James M Brewer allowed $6 each for settling with County officers for 1825, 3 days service.
Samuel Turner, Jn[o] May, & Jo[s] Williams app[td] to settle with
Jacob Walker an adm[r] of estate of Elizabeth Walker dec[d].
Jurors allowed 75¢/day for their services
Joseph Willy to oversee road in place of John Frazier
p.-- Molton Dickson, E D Hicks Esq[rs] & Thomas Shearon app[td]
to settle with Nathan Nisbitt adm[r] of John Nisbitt dec[d].

Alexander Dickson, Henry H Marable, and Willis Norsworthy to
settle with Sarah McDearman former guardian of Joshua Thomas
and Willis A Price minor orphans of Drury Price dec[d]

W[m] Tatom allowed [blank] for keeping Matthew Francis 26 days

E D Hicks, Thomas Shearon, & Stirling Brewer to settle with
John Mcadoo former guardian of Tereasy M Bedford
William Hogan, David Smith Esq[rs] to settle with James Eason
guardian of Lucinda Baker
Cave Johnson Esq[r] allowed $35 for exoficio services for 1825

Joseph Kimble, W[m] Blake, Samuel Turner, Joseph Edwards, and
Rob[t] West settle with Joseph Wilson guardian of John Hays S[r]

Order Parrishoners of this county be allowed for this year:
Charles Thompson at rate of $50 for keeping 2 poor children
Pryor Payne at rate of $70 to be drawn by his wife
Silas Tompkins at rate of $35 for keeping his son

JANUARY 1826

Robt Skelton at rate of $20 to be drawn by Jeremiah Nisbitt
Wm Houston at rate of $40 for keeping his son
John A Johnson at rate of $20 for keeping his wife
Nancy Groce at rate of $40 to be drawn by John Roy
George H Walker to take possession of Elizabeth McDann, poor person of Dickson Co who agrees to keep her for her services

p.-- Samuel Turner, John May and Willis Norsworthy to settle with D H Williams & Benjamin Sturdevant adm^{rs} of Alex^r Rose

D H Williams, Samuel Turner, Henry H Marable to settle with Thomas May adm^r of estate of Drury Price dec^d
Benjamin Sanders to oversee road in place of John A King, to work from Michael Lights to Absolam Tribbles
Thomas Nisbitt to oversee road in place of John Mcadoo.
Joseph Wilson, Joseph Kimble, Robt West to settle with Alex^r Dickson ext^r of James Goodrich dec^d
James M Brewer, John C Collier, & E D Hicks Esqr settle with Alex^r Dickson adm^r of Robertson Dickson dec^d
Winefred Cox adm^x of the estate of Benjamin Cox dec^d allowed $277.13½ for settling s^d estate
Robert Armour Esqr tenders his resignation as Justice/peace.
William Bishop allowed $20.12½ for keeping Wm Allin in jail from 16 July 1825 until 4 Septr 1825 at 37½¢/day, and 2 turn keys at 50 cents each
p.-- Abija P Massey to oversee road in place of John Parker.
James Morris to oversee road in place of Nathan Tubbs
James Gunn to oversee road in place of Soloman Grayham
Wm Austin to oversee road in place of Garret Hall
Zacheas Drummond to oversee road in place of W^m S Coleman

George W Highland, Henry Hiland, Henry J Highland, Joseph B Highland, Ja^s Baxter & T S Williams to mark a road beginning at county line between of Davidson & Dickson, 3½ miles below the narrows of Harpeth and runing down s^d river to intersect the road from Charlotte to Nashville at Henry Highlands

p.-- Court classes themselves for present year:
First class. R C Napier, Molton Dickson, John Pendergrass, Hudson Dudley, Thomas Murrell
2^d class. Wm White, Joseph Wilson, John Grimes, Ezra Mcadoo, Benjamin Grimmit
3^d class. Howard W Turner, William Hogins, D H Williams, Ja^s Eason, Samuel Turner
4th class. Ge^o Hightower, E D Hicks, Jo^s Morris, W^m McMurry, David Smith, John Johnson, John W Napier

Clark Spencer allowed $85 for boarding & clothing Tereasy M Bedford up to this date; to draw on her guardian for same

JANUARY 1826

Hudson Johnson & George Sullivant app'd constables
David Irwin to adm' estate of Robert West J' dec'd
Powel Sinks J' to adm' estate of Powel Sinks S' dec'd
Clark Spencer app'd guardian to Tereasy M Bedford; bond $7 thousand with Benj° Clark and W'" Spencer securities.
John Adams app'd guardian to Joshua, Tho', & Willis A Price, minor orphans of Drury Price dec'd; bond $500. Hewel Parrish security
Plat and certificate of survey of land of Eli Crow proven by Thomas Williams
p.-- Molton Dickson, Jn° Grimes, William Murry produced certificates as Justices/Peace for this county
Joseph Booker, age three, bound to Soloman Grayham
Eliza Austin, age nine, bound to David Austin

Jury next term: Joshua White, Jacob Crouse, Thomas Medlock, Skelton Choate, James Roberts, Jeremiah Nesbitt, Elijah Dodson, Nehemiah Scott, Joseph B Hiland, Ge° W Highland, Plummer Williams, Ge° Mitchel, Samuel Russel, James Tatom, Allin Bowen, Tho' Petty, Pleasant Crews, William Ward, John McCulla, Jn° B Carr, Moses Lankford, Jn° H Stone, Joseph Larkins, Rob' Larkins, Jacob Leach, John Hall, John B Brown

Jurors to next Circuit Court: Silmon Edwards, W'" Reynolds, W'" Baker, Jo' Williams, John Adams, Jn° May, Anguish McLeod, Andrew Gummell, Hodge Adams, Soloman Grayham, Joseph Eason, Richard Tatom

p.--Justices to take list of Taxable property and poles
Cap' Tidwells Company, John Pendergrass Esq'; Cap' Reynolds, Howard W Turner; Cap' Tatoms, Samuel Turner; Cap' Highlands, Joseph Morris; Cap' Browns, Jn° Johnson; Cap' Carrolls, John Grimes; Cap' Bradleys, Thomas Murrell; Cap' Nesbitts, Molton Dickson; Cap' Parishes, Joseph Wilson; Cap' Thedfords, W'" Hogins, Cap' Grimett, Hudson Dudley

Deed Eleanor Parrish to Benjamin Sturdevant & Alex' Dickson 50 acres proven by Enos James
Deed/Gift W'" White to Joshua Burnham for Negro boy proven by Edwin Morris & John Pendergrass
Deed Benjamin Sturdevant and Alex' Dickson to James Piner 50 acres ackd
Deed Soloman Marsh to Tho' N Dunigan 50 acres ackd
Deed Jane McClelland & Jn° McClelland to John West 58½ acres proven by W'" McClelland and Tho' McClelland
p.-- Deed Jane McClelland and Nelson McClelland to John West 58½ acres proven by Tho' McClelland & Sam' W West
Deed Richard Brown to Jonathan Toland 65 acres proven by Laburn Brown & Eli Brown
Deed Edward Stringer to Robert Whitehead 40 acres proven by

JANUARY 1826

Robt Moore & Isaac Flannery
Bill/Sale Mary Kilebro to Sarah Williams wife of Joseph Williams for Negro woman proven by N Scott & J W Scott
Deed Jesse Alexander to Malcom McClellan 160 acres in State of Missoura ackd
B/S Benj^u Sturdevant to Jno Jones for Negro woman ackd
Court adjourned until tomorrow morning 10 oClock
Molton Dickson, Hudson Dudley, J Pendergrass

p.-- Tuesday January 3^d 1826. Present the worshipful Molton Dickson, Hudson Dudly, John Pendergrass, Esquires. Justices

Jones Rivers was quallified an attorney of this bar

Grand Jury: Wm Hand foreman, Adonijah Edwards, Francis Baldthrop, Danl Leach, Ge^o Brazeal, Ja^s Martin, Orrin Sullivant, Gabriel Joslin, John Choate, Isaac Tompkins, Gediah Nooner, Ja^s Tubb, Jno Cunningham. Constable Ge^o Smith to attend them

Grand Jury bill/Indict^t ag^t Augustin Thompson, a true bill; also bill/Indict^t ag^t Epps Jackson, a true Bill

Deed Christopher Robertson to Edward D Hicks 3 town lotts in Charlotte ackd
Deed Montg^y Bell to Chris^r Robertson 657 acres proven by Jno Montgomery & Wm Hightower
Deed & power/atty James Singleton to Jno Montgomery for land proven by James Irwin & Christ^r Robertson

p.-- Deed Peyton Robertson to Wm Willey for land proven by Nathan Nisbett & J W Hicks

Elias W Napier vs John Evins. By att^{ies}. Jury Reese Bowen, Richd Cock, Silmon Edwards, Nehemiah Hardy, Jno Simpson, Jno West, Wm Grimmit, Ira A Meek, John May, Wm Houston, Francis Tidwell, Wm Pendergrass permitted to disperse until tomorrow
Court adjourned until tomorrow morning 9 oClock
     Molton Dickson, Hudson Dudley, J Pendergrass

Wednesday January 4th 1826.   Present the worshipful Molton Dickson, Hudson Dudly, John Pendergrass, Thos Nurrell

Elias W Napier vs John Evins. Jury af^{sd} find for pl^f, assess his damage to $100. Also cost

State vs Robert F Rogers. A&B on Jesse Hall. Jury Wm Hand, Adonijah Edwards, Francis Baldthrop, Danl Leach, George Brazeal, James Martin, Orren Sullivant, Gabriel Joslin, Isaac

JANUARY 1826

Tompkins, Ja^s Tubb, Jno Cunningham, John Tatom who say def^t is Guilty; fined $2.50, and pay cost of prosecution

State vs Ja^s Fussell. Bastardy. Nole prosequi entered
p.-- State vs John Jones. Peace Warrant. Nole prosequi
State vs Edwd B Roach. A&B. Def^t submits; fined 6¼¢ & cost
State vs John Goodwin. A&B. Nole prosequi entered; def^t and David Passmore to pay all cost
State vs Wm Matthews. Bastardy. Bond $50 with Robert Farmbro & Wm Hand, that the bastard child begotton on Agnes Farmbro by Wm Matthews does not become chargable to county
State vs Wm Matthews. Bastardy. Robt Farmbro & Adonijah Edwards pay costs of prosecution
p.-- John Clark vs Wm Mcadoo. Appeal. By att^{ies}. Plt^f orders his suit dismissed; def^t pays all cost except cost of James Tubb and John Hall witnesses for pl^{tf}
Ebenezer Petty vs James W Evins. Pl^f by att^y orders his suit dismissed. Def^t to recover of pl^{tf} his cost
Deed John Wharton to Jno Bradley 100 ac^s proven by E D Hicks and Nathan Nesbitt
Court adjourned until tomorrow 9 oClock
                Molton Dickson, Hudson Dudley, Thos Murrell

Thursday January 5th 1826.   Present the worshipful Molton Dickson, Hudson Dudly, Thomas Murrell, Esquires, Justices

Deed John L McRae to Edward Dickson Hicks and Thos W Shearon lott #34 & 2/3 of #22 proven by Field Farrar & David Mcadoo.
p.-- Deed/Trust Stirling Brewer to John Brewer, Richard Batson, Ja^s M Brown, Abiram Coldwell, P W Humphreys for certain real & personal property ackd by Stirling Brewer.

State vs Harrison Hankins. Bastardy. Appearance Bond $100; Willie B Johnson & Richard D Sandsom $50 each

State vs Jesse Hall. A&B. Jury Reese Bowen, Ge^o Clark, Richd Cock, Silman Edwards, Nehemiah Hardy, Jno Simpson, Jno West, Wm Grimmit, Ge^o Oliver, Luke Medlock, Richd Batson, Midleton Higginbotham who say def^t is not guilty

p.-- State vs Henry W Henson. A&B. Jury Wm Hand, Adonijah Edwards, Francis Baldthrop, Daniel Leach, George Brazeal, James Martin, Orrin Sullivant, Gabriel Joslin, John Choate, Isaac Tompkins, Gediah Nooner, James Tubb who say defendant is guilty; fined $1 and pay cost

State vs Abraham Self. A&B. Jury above find def^t not guilty.
p.-- State vs W^m H Barton. A&B. Jury above find defendant is not guilty

JANUARY 1826

State vs John Toler. A&B. Jury above find def' guilty only of an assault. Fined 6½¢ and cost
State vs Francis V Smitton. Def' moves for continuance; C' orders cause continued; def' to pay cost of this Term.
p.-- State vs Esom Breeding. Appearance bond of Esom Breeding; Francis V Smitton & Wm Hightower, $150 each. A&B.
Court adjourned until tomorrow 9 oClock
     Molton Dickson, Hudson Dudley, Thomas Murrell

Friday January 6th 1826. Present the worshipful Molton Dickson, Hudson Dudley, Thomas Murrell, Esquires, Justices

State vs Henry W Henson. Peace warrant. Prosecutor Francis V Smitton. Defendant not bound to keep the peace

p.-- State vs Thomas J Miller. A&B. Pleads guilty; fined 6½¢ and cost. David Pasmore assumes cost with def'

James McCauly vs Francis V Smitton. The Plaintiff orders his suit dismissed; def' to recover of pl't his cost

Francis V Smitton vs James McCauly. The Pl't orders his suit dismissed. Def' to recover of pl't his cost

Wm Hightower vs Noble Morrison and John Forsythe. By att^{ys}. Jury Geo Clark, Richd Cock, Selmon Edwards, Nehemiah Hardy, Jno Simpson, Jno West, Wm Grimmit, Andw Hamilton, Wm Hickerson, Henry W Henson, Wm Rye, & Holliway N Merritt, who find for plaintiff $125 debt, damage $6. Also his cost

p.-- John Larkins Senr vs Christopher Robertson. Debt. By att^{ys}. Jury above find for pl't $134.10 debt, damage $6 and cost. De't prays appeal to Circuit Court; granted

John Harmon vs Richard D Sandsom. Debt. By att^{ys}. Jury above find for pl't $450 debt, damage $54, besides cost

p.-- James Haynes vs Montgv Bell. By att^{ys}. Jury above find in favour of pl't, assess his damage to $93. Also costs

Henry A C Napier vs Richard D Sandsom & Henry G Wells. Pl't by atty; Rd Sandsom by atty; Henry G Wells came not. Jury above speak upon issues between pl't and Richard D Sandsom; find for pl't the debt due pl't is $154.50; damage is $9.25. Pl't to recover of def'ts Henry G Wells and Richard D Sandsom debt and damage and cost

p.-- Nehemiah Scott vs Daniel H Williams. Motion ag't security. Pl't by atty. Jury above finds pl't was security for

JANUARY 1826

def't in judgment rendered at July Term 1825 ag't Dan'l H Williams and Nehemiah Scott in favour of Alexander Dickson and Dorothy Goodrich ex'r & ex'x of James Goodrich dec'd for debt & interest and cost, in all $640.54. Nehemiah Scott to recover against Daniel H Williams s'd sum & his costs

p.-- David Irwin vs Henry G Wells, Morgan B Wells, Holliway N Merrett & James Priestly. Motion on ca sa. Pl't'f by atty. On 4 Oct'r 1825 writ capias issued by Benj'n Sturdevant J P in favour David Irwin ag't Henry G Wells for $70.87½ & interest from 15 Dec'r 1822 & $1.50 costs which writ came to hands of Tho's McMurry constable. He saw Henry G Wells on 5 Oct'r 1825 execute a bond together with Morgan B Wells, Holliway N Merrett & James Priestly his securities $140 for his appearance at next county court to make payment of monies called for. Henry G Wells hath not made appearance, nor paid money, nor taken oath of insolvency, nor surrendered his property, pl't'f to recover of Henry G Wells, Morgan B Wells, Holliway N Merrett, and James Priestly $85.68 principal, interest, & cost, besides cost in this behalf expended. Def'ts pray appeal to Circuit Court; granted

p.-- George Everly vs Stephen Harris, Donell Y Harris, and Henry H Marable. By att'ys. Jury George Clark, Richard Cocke, Selmon Edwards, Nehemiah Hardy, John Simpson, John West, W'm Grimmet, Andrew Hamilton, W'm Hickerson, Henry W Henson, W'm Rye, H N Merrett who assess damage pl't'fs sustained by reason of def'ts nonperformance of promise $208.17. Pl't'f to recover, also costs. Def'ts pray appeal to Circuit Court; granted

p.-- Robert Jarmon vs Christopher Robertson. Controversy respecting a cotton gin. Cause refered to arbitrament of Richard Batson, Abiram Coldwell, and Reese Bowen. Award of Arbitrators: pltf recovers of deft $89.25, pay for making fifty one gin saws at $1.75/saw from which deduct $12 already paid P W Humphreys by deft leaving balance $77.25. Also cost of suit. The repairs made on sd gin in 1825 we believe pltf not entitled to recover... left to future adjustment between the parties. Jan'y 6'th 1826. A Colwell, R Batson, Reese Bowen

p.-- E W Napier vs Nathan Nisbett adm'r. Pl't'f orders his suit dismissed; def't to recover of pl't'f his cost
Court adjourned until tomorrow morning 8 oClock
                Molton Dickson, Thomas Murrell, E D Hicks

Saturday Jan'y 7'th 1826.   Present the worshipful Molton Dickson, Thomas Murrell, E D Hicks, Esquires, Justices

After the minutes of yesterday was read, the Court adjourned

APRIL 1826

until Court in Course
                                    Thomas Murrell, Molton Dickson, E D Hicks

p.-- Monday April 3d 1826.   Present Daniel H Williams,
Molton Dickson, Thomas Murrell, John Pendergrass, John Johnson, Howard W Turner, Samuel Turner, Esquires. Justices

Alexander Dickson, Joseph Edwards, & Joseph Kimble to settle with Huel Parrish adm^r of Wyatt Parrish dec^d

John Petty produced scalp of one wolf over age four months, proved it was killed within Dickson County; allowed

Samuel Turner, Robert West, and Joseph Kimble to settle with adm^{rs} of John Dickson dec^d
William K Turner Esqr produced his licence and took oaths of an attorney to practice at this bar
Molton Dickson Esqr, Ge^o Hightower and John W Napier Esqr to settle with John Grimes adm^r of Henry Grimes dec^d
Powel Sinks to oversee road in place of Ephraim Ellis
Benjamin Grimmit Esqr produced his commission as Justice of the peace and took oath of office
p.-- Polly West allowed $40 for keeping her son Ge^o W West for 1826, & to draw on his gdn S Brewer for some
Sheriff to lay off the dower of Polly Dickson widow of John Dickson dec^d out of real estate of s^d dec^d
David Mcadoo Sheriff of Dickson gave bond $5000 for collection of public & county tax George Smith, James M Ross, John Mcadoo and Thomas Palmer his securities
John Perry, Benjamin Crews, James Williams, & Thomas McMurry & James H Davie are app^{td} constables
James Tatom app^{td} guardian to Harriett Evins minor orphan of Lewis Evins dec^d
Holliway N Merritt app^{td} gdn to Joshua Hall minor orphan.
James Larkins to adm^r estate of John Larkins Senr dec^d; bond $2000 with Wm Hightower and Richd Batson.
John Jones to oversee road in place of Simon Myers.
Allen Bowen, Henry Goodrich, & Orrin D Hogins to settle with William Hedge former guardian of Harriett Evins & pay amount due to James Tatom the present guardian of sd Harriett.
p.-- Following are attached to bounds of Richard N Williams overseer of road: Joseph Williams & hands and John Picket.

Larry Byrns to oversee road in place of John Picket; to have the following to work under him: Thomas Williams and hands, Richd Tatom, Joel Rogers; and he to work from ford of Yellow

APRIL 1826

Creek near Joseph Williams to Wm Dodsons.
W^m B Dodson to oversee road from his house to what is called the Contrary Pond, with hands: George Brazeal, James Hartly, Jacob Walker, William Dunigan, William Roy.
Following are attached to road bounds of Spencer Brown: Ja^s Walker, Squire Richardson, Henry Gravit, John B Brown, Soloman Milam, Mrs Kirks hands, William Rye.
Benjamin Clark to oversee road from the forks to Vernon road with hands: George Clarks hands, John Barrotts hands, Benjamin Clarks hands, Wm Powers, Henry Bullian, George W Horner.
Thomas Bullian to oversee road begining at old Vernon road, and work to what is called the Contrary Pond with hands: Eli Crow, Isaac Crow, John Meek, Jno Scroggins, Jesse Alexander, Isaac Walker & hands, Wm Willey, Wm Right, Richard Wright.
James Choate to oversee road in place of Wm Willey.
p.-- Wm Adams to oversee road in place of James Self.
James Jones to oversee road in place of Hosea M B Ragan.

George W Highland to oversee the road marked lately by him & others with following hands to open same: Alex^r Brown, John Petty, Robt Garner, Ja^s Garner, Charles White, Plummer Williams, Tippo S Williams, Ja^s Baxter & hands, Benjn Williams, Nicholas Hale, Henry Highland, Joseph B Highland, Wilkinson Garner
George Hightower Esqr resigned as a Justice/Peace
Power/Att^y from Simon Holmes to Thomas Holmes ackd
Deed Sally McDearman to James Price 33 1/3 acres ackd
Deed Absolam Tribble to Wm Lomax 34 acres proven by George H Walker and James King
Deed Jesse Hall to William Shelton 100 acres proven by W^m M Shelton and Susannah Hall
Deed Wm Morris to John Cumming 200 acres ackd
p.-- Deed William Hudson to Jno Holliway 334 acres proven by Thomas Murrell and Washington Smith
Deed James Goodrich to William T Hooper 160 acres proven by George J Goodrich and Nancy Goodrich
Deed John Adams to James Poinier 36 acres ackd
Deed William T Hooper to John Adams 160 acres ackd

Edward Baker vs Christopher Robertson. Def^t in proper person confesses judg^t. Pl^{tf} to recover of def^t $85.32, $3.28 debt & damages, besides cost
William C Sansom and Thomas W Shearon app^{td} commissioners of revenue of Dickson county
p.--Jurors to Circuit Court: Willis Norsworthy, Willie Baldthrop, Jno Adams, Saml King, Drury Taylor S^r, Wm Simpson S^r, Thos Nesbitt, Robt Livingston, Willis Willey, W^m E Slaydon, W^m T Reynold, John Toler, Thomas Holleway, Thos Bullian, Jno Tucker, John Stafford, John Wilson, Isaac Hill, John Cruise, James Matthews, Michael Gafford, John Weems, John Wright, W^m

APRIL 1826

White, Jos Lampley.

Jurors to next County Court: George Adams, Thomas May, Wm Norsworthy, Ezekiel Brown, Minor Marsh, Drury Taylor Jr, Wm McClelland, Robert Nisbitt Jr, Wm Simpson Jr, James Council, James Malugin Sr, Thos Malugin, Andw A Brown, Willis Walker, David Frasier, James McCord, Wm Hutchison, Edwin Morris, Jos Edwards, Jas Wilson, Jos Kimble, Wm Turner, John Garner, Jas White, Morgan Hood, Orrin D Hogins, John Gunn, Arch Skelton, James M Ross, James Medlock, Moses White
p.-- Court adjourned until tomorrow morning 9 oClock
J Pendergrass, Wm McMurry, Jno Grymes

Tuesday April 4th 1826. Present the worshipful John Pendergrass, William McMurry, Jno Grymes, Esquires, Justices

Power/Attorny John Evins to James W Evins & Lorenzo D Evins proven by John B Brown

Grand Jury John B Brown foreman, Jos Larkins, Thos Medlock, Wm Ward, Geo Mitchel, Elijah Dodson, Geo W Highland, Lamuel Russell, Robert Larkins, Allen Bowen, John B Carr, Pleasant Crews, Moses Lankford, attended by James Williams, constable

Field Farrar excused from double tax for 1825.
p.-- Robt West, Saml E Turner Esqrs, D Sansom, Martin H Burton, Jno C Collier to assign Mary Dickson a years provisions

Francis V Smitton vs James McCauley & Wm Handlin. Appeal. By attys. Jury Jas Tatom, Plummer Williams, Jos B Highland, Jas Roberts, Skelton Choate, Graves Ragan, Jas Gilmore, Lorenzo D Evins, Ansemus Merrett, Francis Baldthrop, Jas M Ross, Orrin Nall who find for pltf $73.45. Pltf to recover of deft & on motion agt Jno Giffin & George Gallion his securities for appeal. Also his costs

Robert West vs Henry G Wells & Morgan B Wells. Debt. By atties. Jury above except James McCauley for Orrin Nall. Find for plaintiff $123.81¼ debt, damage $13.61. Also costs

p.-- Jacob Shipman vs Hugh Dickson. By attys. The jury above find for defendant. Deft to recover of pltf his costs

Parrish Lankford vs James Tidwell. Appeal. By attys. Jury above except Orrin Nall for Jas McCauley, say deft owes pltf $10.75. Pltf to recover sd sum besides cost. The defendant prays appeal to Circuit Court; granted

Winstead Davie vs James H Davie. Pltf by attorney orders his

APRIL 1826

suit dismissed; Pl[tf] to recover of def[t] $6.75

p.-- Hicks & Shearon vs Thomas Holliway. Pl[tfs] by att[y] order suit dismissed. Def[t] to pay half cost.

Deed [blot] Leach to John Grimes 276 acres ackd

John Mcadoo elected Trustee of Dickson county; bond $5000 with James Larkins, Rob[t] Larkins, David Mcadoo, Tho[s] Palmer, William Hightower, and George Smith, his securities

Garland Williams admr of Alexander McDowell decd vs R C Foster Jr. Pl[tf] by att[y]. Def[t] called to answer garnishment but came not. Judgment rendered against him for $115.65, unless he appear at next Term and shew good cause to contrary

Garland Williams adm[r] of Alexamder McDowell dec[d] vs Robert C Foster Jr. Pl[tf] by att[y]; def[t] called to answer garnishment came not. Judgment ag[t] him for $149.20, unless he appear at next Term and shew good cause to contrary

p.-- John Forsythe vs Noble Morrison. Motion agt security. Pl[tf] by att[y]. Jury Ja[s] Tatom, Plummer Williams, Jo[s] B Hightower, James Roberts, Skelton Choate, Graves Ragan, Ja[s] Gilmore, Lorenzo D Evins, Ansemus Merrett, Francis Baldthrop, Ja[s] M Ross, Orrin Nall to enquire wheather pl[tf] was security for def[t] in a judgment at last Term against Noble Morrison & John Forsythe in favour of William Hightower for $131 debt & cost $11.22½ say that sd John Forsythe was security of Noble Morrison and say John Forsythe paid $97.92 cents of sd judgment & cost. Considered by Court that pl[tf] recover ag[t] Noble Morrison $97.92 & cost

West H Humphrey having arrived at age 21 and being of good moral character, ordered this certificate issue preparatory to his obtaining licence for practice of the law

[blot] Nesbitt was elected coronor for Dickson County
Court adjourned until tomorrow morning 9 oClock
D H Williams, Molton Dickson, John Grymes

Wednesday April 5th 1826. Present the worshipful D H Williams, Molton Dickson, John Grymes, Esquires, Justices

State vs Francis V Smitton. A&B. James McCauly prosecutor. Jury James Tatom, Plummer Williams, Jo[s] B Highland, Ja[s] Roberts, Skelton Choate, Absolam Tribble, Ephriam S Roy, Josiah Davidson, Hugh McNeely, Woodson Dannel, Cha[s] P Jones, Joseph Handlin who say defendant is guilty. Fined $5 and pay cost.

APRIL 1826

Def^t prays appeal; granted. Appearance bond $500 with Holliway N Merrett, Wm Brasier $250 each.

p.-- State vs Esom Breeding. A&B. Jury John B Brown, Joseph Larkins, Thomas Medlock, Wm Ward, Elijah Dodson, Ge^o W Highland, Saml Russell, Robert Larkins, Allin Bowen, Jno B Carr, Pleasant Crews, Moses Lankford, who find def^t guilty; fined $1 and pay cost

State vs Epps Jackson. A&B. Nole prosequi entered; defendant to pay costs

State vs Jacob Bright. A&B. Jury James Tatom, Plummer Williams, Jo^s B Highland, Ja^s Roberts, Skelton Choate, Absolam Tribble, Ephriam Roy, Josiah Davidson, Hugh McNeely, Wodson Dannel, Charles Jones, Joseph Handlin who find def^t guilty; fined $1 and pay cost of prosecution

State vs Thomas W Forbes. Defendant made default. State to recover ag^t def^t $200, amount of his bond, and on motion ag^t his securities unless he makes appearance next court

State vs Thomas Cox & Moses Ellis. Forfeiture. Def^{ts} called to bring Thomas W Forbes on charge of bastardy, came not. State to recover ag^t them $200 each, amount of their bond

State vs Samuel Petty. Bastardy. Def^t found guilty of begeting a child on Nancy Reding. Samuel Petty and Gabriel Petty bond $100 each condition s^d bastard should not become chargable to county. Def^t Samuel Petty and Gabriel Petty assumes to pay support of s^d child: $40 first year, $30 second year, $20 third year, and also cost of prosecution

p.-- Robert and Francis Squires vs Esom Breeding. Pl^{tfs} by att^{ys} order suit dismissed. Def^t in proper person to pay all cost.

Christopher Robertson vs Phillip B Noland. Appeal. Def^t in proper person confesses he owes pl^{tf} $45. Pl^{tf} is to recover $45 and cost

Hicks & Shearon vs John Mcadoo. Debt. Def^t in proper person confesses judgment for $64.81 3/4 debt and interest. Pl^{tf} to recover sum and cost

Robert West, Jno C Collier, Martin H Burton, Samuel Turner & Rich^d D Sandsom to lay off to Polly Dickson her distributive share of the personal property of late John Dickson dec^d

p.-- Deed Montgomery Bell to Anthony W Vanleer 19 tracts of

APRIL 1826

land and one town lott in Bethall dated 7 July 1825 ackd.
Court adjourned until tomorrow 9 oClock
John Grymes, Molton Dickson, B Grimmitt

Thursday April 6th 1826. Present the worshipful John Grimes, Molton Dickson, B Grimmitt, Esquires, Justices

Molton Dickson Esqr, John Montgomery & Jacob Leach to settle with James H Davie & Alex^r Wilkins adm^{rs} of James Kirk dec^d

State vs John McCrory. Nol Pros entered

State vs Harrison Hankins. Bastardy. Evidence heard, Hankins adjudged father of child of Charlotte O Bair[Barr?]. Hankins to pay $20 for maintenance of child for 1824, $15 for 1825, and $10 for 1826, and cost of suit. Hankins to enter recognizance with security to keep child from becoming chargeable to the county, and recognizance with security to pay sums of money. Defendant bond $500, Jacob Evins and George W Oliver $250 each. Def^t prays appeal to circuit court; granted. Same bond and security.

p.-- Alexander Hamilton vs Montgomery Bell. By att^{ys}. Jury: James Tatom, Plummer Williams, Jo^s B Hightower, Ja^s Roberts, Skelton Choate, Christian Baughman, Jacob Evins, Eldridge Bowen, W^m B Haddin, Richd Batson, Ja^s Irwin, George W Oliver who find for pltf damage $178.50 besides his cost. Plaintiff prays appeal to Circuit Court; granted

A G S Wight for benefit of John Dicks vs Elijah Porter. By att^{ys}. Jury above find for pl^{tf} $114 debt, damage $5, & cost

p.-- Thomas S Slaughter vs Elijah Porter. Debt. By att^{ys}. Jury above find for pl^{tf} $130 debt, damage $20.08, and cost

Hicks & Shearon vs Wm Hudson & Joel Marsh. Debt. By att^{ys}. Jury above find for pl^{fs} $179.07 debt, damage $11.80 & cost

Field Farrar vs Ja^s Priestly. Debt. Field Farrar & Sol Genl pro Tem order suit dismissed

Henry A C Napier vs Holliway N Merrett. On motion of pl^{tf} by att^y, pl^{tf} to recover of def^t and his securities John Hinson and Mark Reynolds $98.25 debt, interest from 1 January 1823 $19.02, & cost. Def^t prays appeal; granted

Aron Arnold vs John J Wells. Forfeiture on Spa. Pl^f by att^y. Def^t called to give evidence on part of pl^{tf} in suit wherein Aron Arnold is pl^{tf} and Richard D Sandsom is def^t, came not.

APRIL 1826

Judgment against defendant John J Wells $125 unless he appear next Term and shew cause to the contrary

p.-- Samuel C Hawkins vs Morgan B Wells. Forfeiture on spa. Def^t called to give evidence for pl^{tf} Saml C Hawkins against Eleanor Parrish made default. Saml C Hawkins to recover ag^t Morgan B Wells $125 unless he appear next Term [as above]

Hicks & Shearon vs Alexander Wilkins. Plaintiffs order suit dismissed; defendant pays cost except attorney's fee
Court adjourned until tomorrow morning eight oClock
Molton Dickson, John Grymes, E D Hicks

Friday April 7th 1826. Present the worshipful Molton Dickson, John Grymes, E D Hicks, Esquires, Justices

Thomas Collier vs M Bell. Plaintiff is granted leave to take deposition of Thomas Jerrall to be read in evidence

p.-- Alexander Dickson & John May vs Daniel H Williams. Summons for adm^{rs} to give counter security. Pl^{tf} by att^y; def^{ts} having failed to give counter security, or to surrender the estate of Alexander Rose dec^d, considered by Court that the def^{ts} deliver to pl^{tfs} the estate of Alex^r Rose dec^d.

A G S Wight vs Beverly A Porter. Pl^{tf} by att^y; the def^t came not. Pl^{tf} to recover against def^t

John Baker vs George Evins and Washington England. Pl^{tf} by att^y; def^{ts} came not. Pl^{tf} to recover against def^{ts}.
Court adjourned until Court in Course.
John Grymes, Molton Dickson, E D Hicks

Monday July 3^d 1826. Present the worshipful D H Williams, John Johnson, Samuel Turner, John W Napier, Howard W Turner

Willie B Johnson app^{td} Solicitor pro tem for this Term.
David Mcadoo, Sheriff, allowed $50 for exoficio services for 1825 ending last January Term
Benjamin Brown, a minor orphan 12 years old, bound to Willis Cunningham until he arrive at age 21 years
Smith Wilkins excused from paying double tax on town lott in Charlotte; he is to pay single tax
Nathan Tubb, Daniel Leach & George Tubb to lay off one years provision for widow & family of Benjamin Crews dec^d

JULY 1826

Absolam Baker produced scalps of 5 wolves over age 4 months killed in Dickson county; allowed
p.-- Selmon Edwards produced scalps of one wolf over age 4 months, 1 wolf under age 4 months, killed in Dickson County; allowed
Pleasant Crews & Robert T Hightower were elected constables.
James W Christian is to adm^r estate of Drury Christian dec^d; bond $20,000, Stirling Brewer and John Brewer securities.
George Hightower to adm^r estate of Benjamin Crews dec^d; bond $400 with John Brewer & Wm Hightower securities

Telmon Perry vs Edwin Morris. Execution recited. Pl^{tf} by att^y. On 20 May 1826 firi facias issued in favour Telmon Perry ag^t Edwin Morris by Benjn Grimmit Esq for $6 & interest from 29 April last & cost; George Sullivan in default of personal property, levyed on 50 acres of def^t lying on Turnbull Creek ad^j land of Adam Weaver, James Ferrall and others. Order of sale issued
p.-- Stephen Eleazer to oversee road in place of John Hall.
James Wilson to oversee road in place of Rich^d D Sansom.
Wm Shearon to oversee road from Hickman Co line with hands: Thomas Petty, Ja^s Petty, John Petty, Ambrose Petty, Wm Gray, Nathan Linn
Daniel W Martin attached to bounds of overseer James Council

Squire Richardson to oversee road in place of Spencer Brown with hands allotted to Brown, except hands allotted to James H Davie, overseer of road from Charlotte to Sulpher fork of Jones Creek on the road Nashville to Franklin

James H Davie to oversee road from Charlotte to Nashville & Franklin, working to the Sulpher fork of Jones Cr with following hands: Mrs Kirk's hands, Wm Rye, James Walker, Henry Gravit, Jacob Leach, Reese Bowen and hands, Peter Jackson & Yelvington Hambrick
Hugh Craig allowed $15 for support as one of the poor from this Term until next Jany Term; Samuel Turner Esqr draw same for his benefit
William Willey S^r to oversee new road from Charlotte Yellow Cr, working from town to Six Mile tree with hands: Burwell Eatherage, Jo^s Eatherage, Thomas Willy, Jno Williams, Hudson Shropshire, John C Collier & hands, Augustin Roberts & hands

p.-- Deed Samuel King to William Johnson 50 acres ackd
Deed Moses Easly to Demsy May 117 acres proven by Eli Brown and Philip May
Deed from Or S Meritt and Nancy Merit his wife to W^m D Reynolds 50 acres proven by B B Corbin & Barney L Bledsoe.
Deed Samuel King to William Johnson 60 acres ackd

JULY 1826

Deed William McMurry to Joseph Malugin 18 acres ackd
Deed Andrew Gammill to Minor Bibb 26 acres proven by Hudson Dudley and Edmund Tidwell
Deed David Hogun to Minor Bibb 75 acres was proven by Edmund Tidwell and Hudson Dudley
p.-- Deed Minor Bibb to Susannah Johnson 213 1/3 acres ackd.
Deed Richard Jackson to Christopher Strong 40 acres proven by Field Farrar and Richard Waugh
Deed Epps Jackson to Christopher Strong 50 acres proven by Field Farrar & Richard Waugh
Bill/Sale Reese Bowen to Christopher Strong, Negro boy Jack ackd
Deed/Gift Christopher Strong to his grandson Robert Dickson, Negro boy Jack ackd
Deed Nathan Nisbitt to Robert S Wilkins part of Lot #45 in Charlotte ¼ acre proven by Augustin Roberts & James H Davie.

Article of an assignment Robert Wilkins Sr to Robert S Wilkins property therein mentioned proven by Richard Batson & William R Hicks
p.-- Commissioners app^{td} to assign to Polly Dickson, widdow of John Dickson dec^d, her years provision made return
Commissioners app^{td} to settle with Sarah McDearman, guardian of minor heirs of Drury Price dec^d, make return
Commissioners appointed to settle with Huel Parrish admr of Wyatt Parrish dec^d made return
Howard W Turner guardian of Polly L Dickson minor orphan of John Dickson dec^d made return
John Adams guardian of Drury Price minor orphan made return

William Jones to oversee new road Charlotte to Yellow Creek, to work from Six Mile tree to Yellow Creek with hands Thomas May and hands, Jesse May and hands, Sterling May and hands, Samuel Turners hands, John Skelton, Amonder Vanhook, Ashburn Vanhook, Moses Street and hands, Hartwell Weaver

Order James Carter, William Hutcheson, James Burnham, James R Napier, Edward Purkins, Moses Parker, John B Carr, Samuel Sellers, Parrish Lankford, Henry Lankford, Isaac Tompkins, & Joshua White to mark a new road from Elijah Jones old place towards Columbia

p.-- Jurors to next Term: Jacob Crous, John Medlock, William Teauge, Wm Mosley, Wm Adams, Danl W Martin, Wm Morrison Jr, Holloway N Meritt, Danl Leach, Nathan Tubb, Ja^s Tubb, Ge^o H Walker, William Flemming, Wm Armour, Willis Dudley, Davidson Crunk, Jno Hays, Bennet B Corbin, George J Goodrich, Stephen Harris, John Wilson, Nehemiah Scott, Jno Holliway, Ge^o Hightower, James Walker, Thomas Bullian, John Bradley

JULY 1826

Daniel H Williams & Samuel Turner Esqrs & Nehemiah Scott to settle with William Tatom guardian of minor heirs of George Right decd and make return to next Court
Court adjourned until tomorrow morning 10 OClock
D H Williams, Saml Turner, Thos Murrell

Tuesday July 4th. Present the worshipful D H Williams, Saml Turner, Thomas Murrell.

Grand Jury: Minor Marsh, George Adams, Ro Nesbitt Junr, William Turner, James McCord, James White, Thomas May, James M Ross foreman, William Simpson, Wm Norsworthy, James Malugin, Ezekiel Brown, Moses White

Labon Holt vs W^m McMurry. Def^t in proper person confesses he owed pl^tf $205.07 and interest. Pl^tf to recover, also costs

p.-- Joseph Kimble, Jo^s Edwards, Robert West, Samuel Turner, Huel Parrish to settle with adm^rs of John Dickson dec^d

Deed Ebenezer Kelly to William Willey Senr 100 acres proven by Abiram Coldwell and Ellis Teas

Will of Ebenezer Kelly dec^d proven by Thomas Richeson & Joseph Willey. Nathan Foster ex^tr, bond $2,000 with A Coldwell and Joseph Willey securities. Nathan Foster returned inventory and account of sales of estate

Huel Parrish app^t^d guardian of Drury Price minor orphan of Drury Price S^r dec^d in place of John Adams former guardian. S^d Parrishs bond $200, John Adams & Samuel Turner securities

Holliway N Merrett appointed guardian to Wesley W Hall minor orphan of John Hall dec^d. Bond $1200, Robert Whitledge and Daniel Billops his securities

Joel Marsh apptd guardian to William Overton minor orphan of Gabriel Overton decd; bond $600, Thomas Holleway and Soloman Marsh securities

p.-- James West to adm^r the estate of George West dec^d; bond $10,000, John Adams and Alexander Dickson securities

Settlement with George H Walker admr of Elizabeth Walker was returned and ordered to be recorded

Francis V Smitton vs Ambrose H Burton. Pltf by attorney. The Deft came not. Pltf to recover damages and cost; a jury to determine damages at next Term

JULY 1826

Cave Johnson vs Edward McCormack. Debt. By att^ies. Jury W^m McClelland, Arch^d Skelton, Orren D Hogins, David Frazier, Wm Hutchison, Willis Walker, Thos Malegin, Morgan Hood, Andrew A Brown, John Gunn, Moses White, James Medlock who say def^t doth owe to pltf $97.50 and damages. Also costs

p.-- James Wilson vs Richard C Napier. Debt. By att^ys. Jury William McClelland, Archibald Skelton, Orrin D Hogins, David Frazier, Wm Hutchison, Willis Walker, Thomas Malugin, Morgan Hood, And^w A Brown, Jno Garner, Moses White, Ja^s Medlock who find def^t owes pl^tf $151.24 debt, damages $12.90. Also cost.

Leonard P Cheatham vs Elias W Napier. By att^ys. Jury above. Def^t hath not kept his covenant, pl^tf damage $314.75. Costs.

p.-- Hicks & Shearon vs David McAdoo. Debt. By att^ys. Jury above find for pl^tf $131.86 debt, damage $1.35. Also cost.

Augustin Gustavis S Wight vs Beverly A Porter. By attorneys. Jury above say pl^tf hath sustained damages of $95. Also cost

Robert Bowers vs James Priestly. Defendant petitions to stop collection of two executions in favour of Def^t & R M Bevins

p.-- Gully Moore vs Simon Holmes. Debt. By att^ys. Jury Minor Marsh, George Adams, Robt Nesbitt J^r, Wm Turner, Ja^s McCord, James White, Thos May, Ja^s M Ross, William Simpson, Wm Norsworthy, Ja^s Malugin, Ezekiel Brown who find for pl^tf $60.50 debt, damage $4.23. Also cost.

Hicks and Shearon vs James H Davie. Debt. By attys. Jury above find for pl^tf $161.90 debt, damage $4.50. Besides cost.

John Baker vs George Evins and Washington England. Pl^tf by att^y orders his suit dismissed. Defendant in proper person assumes to pay cost. Pl^tf to recover of def^t his cost

Shaderick Fluellen vs John J Hutchison, Ambrose Hutchison & William H Earl. Pl^tf by counsel. Def^ts had executed indemnifying bond to pl^tf as constable of Robertson County, also an action by John Bell for trespass committed by pl^tf's selling property mentioned in bond ag^t which def^t covenanted to indemnify pl^tf; judg^t rendered ag^t pl^tf in favour Jno Bell at Circuit Court...therefore pl^tf is to recover of def^t $226.13 and also his costs

p.-- Holloway N Merrett vs Allen Dannel. Cause transferred to arbitrament of Alexand Dickson and Huel Parrish, and a third person to be chosen by them

JULY 1826

Samuel C Hawkins vs Morgan B Wells. Pl^{tf} by att^y dismisses his sci fa, def^t assumes to pay all cost

State vs John Turner. Bastardy. John Turner guilty of begeting a bastard on Jane Lovelady. Turner to enter recogizance with security to keep child from becoming chargable to county: $100, with Henry H Marable, Howard W Turner, Holliway N Merrett and Samuel Turner $50 each
Court adjourned until tomorrow Morning 9 oClock
J W Napier, S Turner, H W Turner

Wednesday July 5th 1826.   Present the worshipful
John W Napier, Samuel Turner, H W Turner, Esquires, Justices

Samuel Turner, Howard W Turner Esq^{rs}, and Thomas May to settle with adm^{rs} of Alex^r Rose dec^d.
State vs Matthew Gilmore. Appearance bond $100, and Howard W Turner & Samuel Turner $50 each.
Silmon Edwards allowed $27.70 as adm^r of James Seals dec^d.
Silmon Edwards allowed $14.55 as adm^r of Palatina Seals dec^d

p.-- State vs Thomas W Forbes. Bastardy. Ordered Nole Prosequi entered. Defendant assumes to pay all cost.
State vs Thomas W Forbes. Case dismissed
State vs Thomas Cox. Case dismissed
State vs Moses Ellis. Case dismissed

Richard Batson vs James Williams. Pl^{tf} by att^y. Motion on ca sa. Sixth April 1826 Molton Dickson J P issued capias Ad in favour of Richd Batson ag^t Ja^s Williams for $72.18 3/4 debt & $1 interest which came to hands of George Smith constable. James Williams 6 April 1826 appearance bond, Edward D Hicks security, sum $146.37½. Williams placed in custody of sheriff until discharged, which is ordered

p.-- Hicks & Shearon vs James Priestly, David Mcadoo, Richd Batson. Pl^{tf} by att^y. Molton Dickson 3 May 1826 issued capias Ad favour of Hicks & Shearon ag^t Ja^s Priestly for $27.07. Ja^s Priestly on 10 May 1826 appearance bond; David Mcadoo & Richard Batson his securities $56.14. Priestly hath not made appearance. Plaintiffs to recover of Priestly and securities

Sheriff to bring child George W Blount to Court next Term

Samuel C Hawkins vs Eleanor Parrish. Motion ag^t constable & securities Daniel H Williams & John Adams for failing to pay over money collected. By att^{ys}. Constable Parrish collected for pl^{tf} of Stephen Hosley $8.52, Benedict Bacon $38.48, M B

OCTOBER 1826

Wells $11.50, Humphries $2, Alexander Rose $2.70, Ja^s Thorne $4.56 making $69.79. Pl^{tf} to recover of def^t and ag^t his securities Daniel H Williams & John Adams s^d sum.

p.-- Thomas Choate vs Absolom Fentress. Covenant. Demurer. By att^{ys}. Demurer overruled. Jury to determine at next Term what damage plaintiff hath sustained by breach of covenant

M Bell vs William Mcadoo. Pl^{tf} allowed to take depositions

Thomas Collier vs M Bell. Pl^{tf} allowed to take depositions

Sally Lile vs Jno Evins. Attachment. The Pl^{tf} by att^y orders suit dismissed; defendant assumes to pay all cost

Deed William Bullian to Elisha Williams 15 acres ackd.
p.-- John B Brown a security of David McAdoo as Sheriff for two years commencing 4th January 1825 and ending 4th January 1827, files petition seting fourth that he is apprehensive he will be injured by negligence of s^d McAdoo. David McAdoo is to give other security for execution of duties of office; John B Brown discharged from further liability. David Mcadoo enters bond with John Mcadoo, Benjamin Clark, Robert Livingston, James Larkins, Thomas Palmer, $5000, and quallified.
Court adjurned until Court in Course
S Turner, E D Hicks, D H Williams

p.-- Monday October 2^d 1826. Present John Pendergrass, Molton Dickson, Samuel Turner, D H Williams, David Smith, Jno W Napier, John Johnson, H W Turner, W^m McMurry, Justices

John McAdoo former guardian of Teresa M Bedford allowed $30 for services in settling sd estate
Robert Nisbitt (long Bob) to oversee road from Charlotte to Irwins Old Mill
George W Blount orphan 7 yrs old bound to Thomas Richardson, who is to furnish orphan with a good hundred dollar horse, a saddle and bridle at age 21, and to have him taught reading, writing & arithmetic to rule of three

George Tatom produced scalp of one wolf aged under 4 months. Lindley Box, scalp of one wolf under 4 months; they proved they killed sd wolves within the bounds of this County

Samuel Turner, D H Williams Esqrs & Nehemiah Scott to settle with Wm Tatom, guardian to Nelly Wright

OCTOBER 1826

Deed Nathan Nesbitt to Anth^y W Vanleer. Isaac H Lanier, Wallace Dixon, and Joseph Harrison, town lott #44 in Charlotte proven by E D Hicks and Molton Dickson
p.-- Samuel Turner Esqr and Willis Norsworthy to settle with John Adams g^{dn} to Drury Price
Jane Baker adm^x of John A Baker dec^d to give other security and release present securities from liability

William Morrison, Joseph Kimble, Alexander Dickson, & Joseph Wilson Esq^{rs} to settle with David Irwin adm^r & g^{dn} to and of Robert West J^r dec^d
Jo^s Kimble, Joseph Edwards, Robt West, Saml Turner, Esq^{rs}, & Howel Parrish to settle with adm^{rs} of John Dickson dec^d.
Reuben McQuarles minor orphan about 11 years old is bound to Spencer T Hunt to learn trade of a potter; Hunt to give him one year schooling between age 15 and 20 years
Matthew Crumpler to oversee road in place of Mitchel Jackson

Wm Morrisons hands, Robert Patterson & hands, John Stewart & hands attached to bounds of Joseph Kimble, road overseer.
Samuel Turner, Joseph Williams, and Nehemiah Scott to settle with Stith Richardson ext^r of Jordan Richardson dec^d.
George Clark to oversee road in place of Daniel Moore.
Deed Nathan Nesbitt to Field Farrar 45 acres proven by Molton Dickson and W R Hicks
p.-- Mumford Smith to oversee road in place of Wm Austin J^r.
Robt Larkins to oversee road in place of Alex^r Southerland.
Wm Simpson to oversee road in place of Moses White
Simon Deloach to oversee road in place of Burwell Eatherage.
William L Mosley to oversee road in place of James Gilmore.
John W Fentress to oversee road in place of Henry Davidson.
John Holliway to oversee road in place of John Bradley
John Saunders and Samuel West attached to bounds of Zacheus Drummond overseer of road

Wm Hogins to open a new road from county line to near Thomas Petty J^r to Wm Hogins, thence to intersect county line near pole bridge; hands to open same, then return to former overseers: Gabriel Petty, Saml Petty, Ja^s Petty, Jonathan Petty, Solomon Petty, Saml King, Abr^m Hogins, A D Hogins, Ja^s Hudson, Chas Hudson, Ja^s D Petty, Ambrose Petty, Thos Petty J^r, Thomas Petty S^r, Allin Wells, Morgan Hood, Alex^r Chezenhall

Deed Claibourn Harris J^r for the heirs of Wm Johnson dec^d to James Hudson 640 acres proven by Stephen Harrison
p.-- Ja^s Hightower, Dempsey Bull, Ransom Bass, & Thos Harvey attached to bounds of Ge^o Clark overseer
William E Slaydon to oversee road in place of Joseph Davidson with hands W^m McMurry, Thomas Malugin, Wm Crain, Selmon Edwards and hands, John Teal, W^m T Reynolds, Nicholas Baker.

OCTOBER 1826

Selmon Edwards, Nehemiah Hardy, Thomas Jurnigan, H W Turner, Esqr to settle with William McMurry Esqr g^{dn} to Washington & Sally McMurry

Daniel Parker to oversee cutting out a new road begining at Elijah Jones old place, leading towards Columbia, with David Bibb, George Mitchel and Thomas Gentry

Deed John Johnson to Jacob Sanderson 60 acres proven by William Gentry and Simon Myers

Deed Samuel King to George H Walker 50 acres ackd

Deed Thomas W Shearon to Edward D Hicks 2/3 of Lott #22 and whole lotts 34 & 27 in Charlotte ackd

Deed Baker Hudson to Thomas Murrell 60 acres proven by Soloman Marsh and Ge^o W Tatom

Deed John Holliway to Thomas Murrell 80 acres proven by Thos Holliway and Soloman Marsh

p.-- Deed Samuel Locker to Joseph Kimble 50 acres proven by Howard W Turner and Francis Baldthrop

Deed Willis Norsworthy and Joseph Trimble to James Dannel 50 acres ackd

Deed John J Lewis to Samuel Locker 50 acres proven by W^m W Baldthrop and Willis Norsworthy

Deed Jacob W Miller to George Ross Senr 200 acres proven by Molton Dickson & James M Ross

Deed Jesse Benton to Simon Myers certain property of estate of Jeremiah Sullivant dec^d proven by Jacob Sanderson & Danl Sullivant.

Power/Att^y Matthew Gilmore, John Gilmore, Wm Gilmore, James Gilmore, James McCrory & wife Jane, George Davidson and wife Elizabeth, Alex^r Scott & wife Mary to Ja^s Gilmore Jr proven & ack^d by Matt^w Gilmore, Jno Gilmore by his Att^y/fact M Gilmore and Wm Gilmore and Ja^s Gilmore by att^y/fact M Gilmore & James McCrory & wife by att^y/fact Wm Gilmore, & Ge^o Davidson & Alex^r Scott & wife by their att^y/fact Wm Gilmore, & Elizabeth Davidson wife of Ge^o Davidson, separately, ackd she executed s^d power freely for purposes therein mentioned.

Field Farrar allowed $20 for 2 blank books furnished by him for use of the Court records

p.-- Jeremiah P Bellemy vs Thos J Paxton. Execution recited. Pltf motion by atty. 15 Sept 1826 firafacias issued favour pl^{tf} ag^t def^t by Howard W Turner Es^q for $40 debt & interest from 13 Augt 1826 & cost. Danl Billops constable levyed same on 228 acres on Salmons Br of Yellow Cr. Order/sale issued

Jurors for next Circuit Court: Francis Baldthrop, Nehemiah Scott, Andrew Brown, Skelton Choat, Absolam Tribble, Malon Wood, Willie Myatt, Stephen Tatom, Ge^o Evins, Jo^s Harrison, Robert Baxter, Jesse Bartee, Reese Bowen, Jacob Leach, John Choate, W^m McMurry, H W Turner, Wm Baker, Jo^s Edwards, James

OCTOBER 1826

Wilson, Randolph R Harris, Jn° Pendergrass, Abijah P Massie, David Passmore, Samuel D Austin
Jurors to next County Court. Moses Street, Wm Tatom S^r, Robt Vanhook, David A Massie, William Wood, Michael Rogers, Redic Myatt, Danl Wall, Jn° Rue, Ja^s Larkins, Wm Cox, Austin Richardson, Waller Bell, Ephriam Garrett, Robt Nesbitt J^r, Benedict Bacon, Moses White, John Kenedy, Thomas Jernigan, Jonah Davidson, Jonathan Malugin, Wm Reynolds, Ja^s Dannel, Robt P Harris, John M Fentress, Ja^s Tidwell, Thos Gentry, Zachariah Allin, Ja^s Walker, Jn° Bradley, Thos Bullian

John C Collier to oversee Street on west boundary of Charlotte; his and hands of Augustine Roberts work on same
p.-- Court adjourned until tomorrow morning 10 oClock
D Smith, John Johnson, J W Napier

Tuesday October 3^d 1826.   Present the worshipful
David Smith, John Johnson, John W Napier, Esquires, Justices

Settlement made with Jn° Grimes adm^r estate of Henry Greymes dec^d. Said John Grymes allowed $110 out of s^d estate for his services in settling estate
Account of sales of estate of Benjamin Crews dec^d returned by Ge° Hightower adm^r
Deed Rich^d M Jones & wife to Robt West life estate in tract of land ack^d & certified in Montgomery County, ordered to be registered
p.-- Grand jurors Nehemiah Scott foreman, Bennet B Corbin, James W McCammon, Ja^s Tubb, Holliway N Merritt, Stephen Harris, Nich^s Dudley, Daniel Leach, Nathan Tubb, Ge° Hightower, William Teague, Jn° Holliway, Ge° J Goodrich. Mumford Smith, constable, sworn to attend them
John Reynolds S^r, Robert Patterson, Wm Morrison J^r, Holliway Merritt, Joshua Hall, H W Turner, Thos McMurry to mark out a new road begining near McMurrys old place and intersect old road near mouth of Leatherwood

William Hodge vs Mary Baker. On petition of def^t Mary Baker, ordered writs of certiorare & supercedeas issue.
Sheriff David Mcadoo resigned.
William Hightower elected Sheriff; gave bond $5,000 with Jn° C Collier, William Ward, Jn° Bernard, Richd Batson, Adonijah Edwards, Jn° Adams his securities
p.-- Stirling Brewer vs David Shropshire & Jesse S Kirk. Execution recited. 5 Sept 1826 execution issued by Field Farrar clerk of Dickson, on judgment rendered by Nathan Nisbitt Esqr 24 Jan 1824 in favour pl^tf for $35.66 & cost. Robt Livingston deputy sheriff, levyed on interest that David Shropshire has in 80 acres on Town branch above Charlotte. Order

OCTOBER 1826

of sale issued
John Barnet vs Daniel H Williams, John Picket, and Nehemiah Scott. Execution issued 26 Sept 1826 by Field Farrar Dickson county clerk on judgment by Robert Armour Esqr 22 May 1826 $70 debt, interest from 22 Sept 1823 and cost. Mumford Smith constable 26 Sept 1826 levied on 160 acres on Yellow Creek on which sd Picket now lives 29 Sept 1826. Order/sale issued

p.-- John Barnet vs Daniel H Williams, John Picket, Nehemiah Scott. Execution issued 26 Sept 1826 by Field Farrar Dickson County clerk on judgment by Robt Armour Esqr 22 May 1824 for $60 debt, interest from 22 Sept 1823 & cost. Mumford Smith, constable, 26 Sept 1826, levied on 160 acres Yellow Creek on which s^d Picket lives Sept 29 1826. Order of sale issued.

William Shigog vs Soloman Petty. Execution 24 July 1826 by Wm Hogins Esqr for $42.75 debt and cost. Kendrick Myatt constable levied on 50 acres west side Turkey Creek adj George Davidsons land. Order/sale issued

p.-- Thomas Choate vs Absolam Fentress. Writ of Enquiry. By att^{ies}. Jury Davidson Crunk, Wm Adams, Wm Armour, Wm Flemming, Stephen Hostly, Ansemus S Merrett, Wm Carroll, David Passmore, Robert H McCollum, John Goodwin, Garrett Hall, Wm Fussell who say pl^{tf} sustained damages by breach of covenant of $119. And cost. Appeal last page.
Jno H Marable vs Montgomery Bell. Case. By att^{ys}. Jury above assess pl^{tfs} damage to $174. And cost
Holliway N Merrett vs Allen Dannel. Alexander Dickson & Huel Parrish to whom this case was refered last court award that H N Merritt pl^{tf} dismiss suit and pay cost thereof, we being of opinion that horse sold as property of Andrew M Lewis was rightfully sold under s^d execution. Court dismiss suit.
p.--   J W Napier, J Johnson, D Smith, Wm McMurry

Wednesday October 4th 1826.   Present the worshipful John W Napier, John Johnson, David Smith, William McMurry, Justices

Francis V Smitton excused from paying tax on 400 acres

p.-- State vs Matthew Gilmore. A&B. Jury Davidson Crunk, Wm Adams, Wm Armour, Wm Flemming, Samuel West, Jno Sanders, Jo^s Howard, Nathan Dillihay, Thos McClelland, Danl W Martin, Jno Kenedy, Robt Nesbitt who find def^t guilty; fined $15 & cost

State vs John Adams. A&B. Def^t pleads Guilty; fine $6 & cost

State vs Wm Adams. A&B. Def^t pleads Guilty; fined $1 & cost

OCTOBER 1826

State vs Edward D Hicks. A&B. Deft pleads guilty; fined 6¼¢ and pay cost
p.-- State vs James Council. Appearance bond $200. Aquilla Council and Willis Council, securities, $100 each
State vs Aquilla Council. Appearance bond $200. James Council and Willis Council $100 each
p.-- State vs Willis Council. Appearance bond $200. James Council and Aquilla Council $100 each
State vs Jacob Bright. Appearance bond, $200. Joseph Handlin and Wm Handlin, $150 each
p.-- State vs Lorenzo Dow Evins. Appearance bond $200; James W Evins & Gabriel P Joslin $150 each

Sarah West and Samuel West to adm^r estate of John West dec^d; bond with John Sanders and Thos McClelland, $1000. S^d adm^{rs} returned inventory of estate; order of sale granted

State vs Henry W Henson and securities. Forfeiture. Def^t on charge of A&B came not. State to recover of Henry W Henson & Mumford Smith, securities, $200

p.-- State vs Henry W Henson & security. Forfeiture. Deft on charge of A&B came not. State to recover of Henry W Henson & Mark Reynolds, security, $200
Samuel McFall vs Elias W Napier, John W Napier, Henry A C Napier. Cause transferred to Circuit Court
Court adjourned until tomorrow morning 9 oClock
                J W Napier, D Smith, John Johnson, W^m McMurry

Thursday October 5th 1826.   Present the worshipful John W Napier, David Smith, John Johnson, William McMurry, Justices

p.-- George Crocket vs Christopher Robertson. Debt. By att^{ys}. Jury Nehemiah Scott, Bennet B Corbin, James W McCammon, James Tubb, Holliway N Merrett, Stephen Harris, Nich^s Dudly, Danl Leach, Nathan Tubb, Ge^o Hightower, Wm Teague, John Holliway who find for plaintiff $251.77 debt, damage $15.75. And cost. Def^t prays appeal; granted.
Soloman Clark vs Christopher Robertson. Debt. Jury above say def^t owes $103.51, damage $6. And cost. Def^t granted appeal

p.-- Stephen Hostly vs James Gilmore. By att^{ys}. Jury Davidson Crunk, Wm Adams, Wm Armour, Wm Flemming, Robt S Wilkins, Edwd McCormack, Jo^s Howard, Richd Whitehead, Jno Baker, Ezra McAdoo, Michajah McGee, Daniel Toler who find for pltf, and assess damage to $10. And cost.
State vs Stephen Harris. A&B. Def^t pleads guilty; fine 6¼¢ & cost.
State vs Alexander Wilkins. A&B. Appearance bond $200; Rich^d

OCTOBER 1826

Batson and Ezra McAdoo $100 each
p.-- Thomas Collier Senr vs Montgomery Bell. Pl^{tf} allowed to take deposition of Thomas Jerrald
William Buckhannon vs Montgomery Bell. Each party permitted to take depositions of Thomas Jerrall

Edward D Hicks and Thomas W Shearon merchants trading under firm of Hicks & Shearon vs John Bradley and Thomas Holliway. Defendants came not; plaintiffs to have execution ag^t def^{ts} for $200.29½ debt & costs

Benjamin Cox vs Robert F Rogers. Judgment by default & writ of enquiry. Pl^{tf} by att^y. The def^t came not. Pl^{tf} to recover damages & costs. A Jury to determine damages at next Court.

p.-- John Picket vs John Barnet. Petition of Jno Picket; the Court order supercedias issue agreeable to petition

Hicks & Shearon vs Joseph Coffee. Pl^{tf} by att^y. 25 Sept 1826 capias by Molton Dickson J P in favour Hicks & Shearon ag^t Joseph Coffee for $19.12½ debt, 48¢ interest, 50¢ cost. Thos Holleway constable took Joseph Coffee who 25 Sept 1826 executed appearance bond together with Richd Waugh, W B Haddin, Andrew Hamilton, Peter Jackson, his securities, $56. Joseph Coffee in custody of sheriff

p.-- Davis Irwin vs Elkana Parrish, Benjamin Sturdevant, and Henry H Marable adm^r of A Vanhook. Motion ag^t constable and his securities for failing to pay over money. Pl^{tf} by att^y. Heretofore an execution in favour pl^{tf} ag^t Daniel H Williams came to hands of def^t Elkana Parrish, then a constable, and of money collected on s^d execution s^d Parrish has failed to pay to pl^{tf} sum of $30. B Sturdevant and A Vanhook were securities of s^d Parrish. No evidence shewing that def^t Henry H Marable administered estate Aaron Vanhook dec^d, H H Marable go hence. Pl^{tf} recover of Elkana Parrish and Benjn Sturdevant af^{sd} sum $30 with cost

p.-- Hicks & Shearon vs Joseph Coffee. Pl^{tfs} by att^y. Molton Dickson J P issued capias 25th Sept 1826 in favour Hicks & Shearon ag^t Joseph Coffee for $26.78, 24¢ interest, 50¢ cost on which Thomas Holleway constable took Joseph Coffee who on 25th Sept 1826 executed appearance bond with Richard Waugh, W B Haddin, A Hamilton & Peter Jackson his securities in sum $38.50. Joseph Coffee in custody of sheriff

John Adams vs Daniel H Williams. Motion ag^t CoSecurity. Pl^{tf} by att^y. Last July Term judgment ag^t John Adams and Daniel H Williams as cosecurities for Eleanor Parrish as constable in favour of Samuel C Hawkins, execution for amount of judg^t, &

JANUARY 1827

cost $103.41 & Sheriffs commission for collecting sum $3.50. Adams paid whole sum. John Adams to recover of Daniel H Williams as cosecurity af^{sd} $53.45½, half am^t paid by Jno Adams

p.-- Robert M Boyers vs James Priestly. By att^{ys}. Motion is dismissed; pl^{tr} to recover of def^t and on motion ag^t his securities George Smith, David Mcadoo, & And^w Hamilton sum $20 debt, interest at 6 percent from 19 March 1822 to 22 October 1825 making $2, interest at 12½ percent from 22 Octr 1825 to this date making $13.25, with 50¢ constable fees

Robert M Boyers vs James Priestly. By att^{ys}. Supercedias is dismissed; pl^{tf} to recover of def^t and on motion ag^t securities Ge^o Smith, David Mcadoo, And^w Hamilton, $14 debt, $5.75 interest at 6 percent up to 22^d Oct 1825, 85¢ interest from April last until this date, $2.75 constables fees, and cost.

p.-- John H Marable vs Montgomery Bell. Def^{ts} appeal granted

Thomas Choate vs Absolam Fentress. Def^{ts} appeal granted.
Court adjourned until tomorrow Morning 9 oclock
        J W Napier, E D Hicks, J Pendergrass

Friday Oc^t 6th 1826.   Present the worshipful Jno W Napier, E D Hicks, Jno Pendergrass, Esquires, Justices
Court adjourned until Court in Course
        J W Napier, E D Hicks, J Pendergrass

Monday January 1st 1827. Present the worshipfull Saml Turner, Molton Dickson, John Johnson, John Pendergrass, William McMurry, Thomas Murrell, John W Napier, William Hogins

Michael Light to oversee road in place of Benjn Saunders.
Thomas Richardson to oversee road in place of Joseph Willey
John McClelland to oversee road in place of Zacheus Drummond
Lemuel Russell to oversee road in place of Abijah P Massie
John Cox to oversee road in place of Squire Richardson
William Tatom to oversee road in place of Henry W Hinson
John Smith to oversee road in place of Thomas Nesbitt
Henry A C Napier to oversee road in place of Robert Nesbitt

p.-- David Irwin adm^r & guardian of Robert West dec^d allowed $86.25 for his services in settling s^d estate
Molton Dickson, Samuel Turner, & John W Napier to take privy exam of Mrs Ann Brewer to a deed of conveyance.

JANUARY 1827

Daniel H Williams, Samuel Turner Esq^{rs} and Nehemiah Scott to settle with William Tatom g^{dn} of Nelly Right.
Stirling Brewer, Thomas W Shearon, & R Batson returned their settlement with John McAdoo guardian of Tereasy M Bedford.
County Tax to be same as last year.
Benjamin Saunders, Ge^o H Walker, & Wm Shelby to settle with Wm Johnson adm^r of Moses Easly dec^d
Huel Parrish guardian of Drury Price made return of settlement of his guardianship
John McAdoo present County Trustee tenders resignation.
Will of Ephriam Breeding decd proven by Robert Duke & Charlotte Duke
Parrishoners of county allowed as follows:
Pryor Payne at rate of $100)
Nancy Groce   ditto   40 | to be drawn by Jesse Smith
Levi Lindsey   "   10)
Charles Thompson   "   50 for two children
Robert Skelton   "   20
John A Johnson   "   20 for keeping his wife dead
William Houston   "   40 for keeping son
David Passmore   "   30 for keeping Sara Miller
Silas Tompkins   "   35 for keeping his son

p.-- The Court classes themselves for present year:
First: William McMurry, James Nesbitt, Saml Turner, Howard W Turner, William Shelby
2^d class: W^m C Sansom, Molton Dickson, Thos Murrell, Joseph Wilson, Hudson Dudley
3^d class: Jo^s Morris, Jo^s Kimble, Jno Johnson, D H Williams, John Pendergrass
4th class: R C Napier, David Smith, Wm Hogins, Jno W Napier, Wm White

Benjamin Grimmit Esqr resigned as Justice/Peace; also James Eason.
Settlement with Joseph Wilson gd^n of John Hays sen^r dec^d was returned into Court
Nehemiah Hardy, Thomas Jurnigan & W^m McMurry Esq^{rs} to settle with Jno Hodges adm^r estate of Maryann Hopper dec^d

Following Justices to take list of Taxable Property & poles:
Capt Thompsons Company   Hudson Dudley Esqr
Capt Browns   William Shelby
Capt Thedfords   David Smith
Capt Carrolls   John W Napier
Capt Tatoms   Samuel Turner
Capt Parrishes   Joseph Kimble
Capt Merritts   William McMurry
Capt McClelland   William C Sansom
Capt Tidwells   John Pendergrass

JANUARY 1827

Capt Bullians   Richard C Napier
Capt Highlands   Joseph Morris

David McAdoo former sheriff allowed $37.50 for his Exoficio services from Jany 1826 to Octr 1826
p.-- Robt P Harris oversees road in place of Alex^r Dickson. Richard Cocks sons, James Matthews, and Alfred Kenedy are to be attached to bounds of James Morris, overseer
Nathan Tubb & hands, George Tubb & hands are allotted to the bounds of Matthew Crumpler overseer of road
Settlement of estate of Chesley O Cole dec^d returned.
Account of sales of the estate of John West dec^d returned.
Settlement with David Irwin gd^n & adm^r of Robt West dec^d was returned into Court.

Howard W Turner to cut out new road from McMurries old place down Leatherwood fork of Yellow Creek to intersect old Road to Dover with hands to open same: Lemuel Read, Aquilla Council, Willis Council, Daniel Martin, John Reynolds hands, Ansemus S Merritt, Gipson Mills, H N Merritt & hands, Wm Morrison J^r, Wm Morrison S^r & hands, Robt Petterson, Robt West & hands, W^m McNickol, John Stewart & hands, Thomas McMurry, Thos Rice, Jno Toler J^r, Jno T Patterson & hands, Edwd Holly and hands, James Council, W^m T Reynolds, Pinckney T Bledsoe, Stokely Humphries & hands

p.-- John B Carr to oversee new road from Elijah Jones's old place to Hickman County line with hands: Wm Pendergrass, Jno Parker, Gideon Cuningham, Martin Garton, John Brown, Henry Lankford, Emsly Sears, Francis Tidwell, Daniel Perkins, Danl Spencer, Newbern Morris, Jno Sellers, Wm Morris, Wm Hudgins, Joshua White, Jno Stinet, Jacob Lampley, Edwd Purkins, Jno K Tidwell.
Settlement with W^m McMurry gd^n of Washington & Sally McMurry returned to Court.
Joseph Kimble, Wm Shelby, W^m C Sansom, & James Nesbitt produced their commissions from the governor as Justices of the Peace & took the oaths.
Settlement of estate of Jordan Richardson dec^d returned.
Nelly Right age 16 bound to Simon Deloach until full age.
Elisha Worley age 10 bound to Joseph Handlin until age 21 to learn the art and mistery of Farming.
Cave Johnson solicitor general allowed $35 for his exoficio services for year ending October Term 1826.
p.-- Jurors to next Court: Arch^d Skelton, George Gallion, Wm Hickerson, Zacheus Drummond, Nelson McClelland, Richard Batson, Thos Stroud, Arch^d Pullin, Jno Holliway, Wm Cox, Edward Purkins, John Perry, Nathan Dillehay, Ja^s Wilson, Hugh Dickson Sr, Wm Gray S^r, Samuel King (Piney), Ambrose Petty, William Caffrey, Elijah Walker, Jo^s Shouse, Ro Nesbitt J^r, Ja^s

JANUARY 1827

Walker, Daniel Nall, Redic Myatt, Moses White, Moses Street, William Tatom, Robt Vanhook, Wm Wood, Ephriam Garrett, Jno W Fentress (the latter part did not attend this Term agreeable to their summons).
Deed Jno Evins to Robert Larkins 100 acres proven by James W Evins and John Larkins
Deed Chris^r Robertson to Thos Armstrong 253½ acres ackd.
Deed Martha King to John King 130 acres proven by Wm [--].
Deed Wm Sooten[Sooters?] to William Flemming 68 acres proven by Washington Douglass
Deed Robert Nesbitt S^r to Hudson Johnson 188¼ acres ackd.
Deed John Hunter to Elijah Walker 40 acres proven by William Shelby & Wm King
Deed John Adams to John Seals 60 acres ackd.
p.-- Deed Wm Turner to Christopher Robertson 3 acres ackd.
Bill/Sale John McAdoo to Robert Livingston Negro woman Charlotte ackd
Deed Christopher Robertson to James Nesbitt 4 3/4 town lotts in Charlotte ackd
Deed Wm Turner to Samuel Vanleer & Co 325 acres ackd
Deed Wm Turner to Saml Vanleer & Co 50 acres ackd
Court adjourned until tomorrow morning 9 oClock
                   Molton Dickson, Wm C Sansom, D H Williams

Tuesday January 2^d 1827.   Present the worshipful Molton Dickson, D H Williams, William Shelby Esq^{rs}, Justices

p.-- Grand Jury: John Bradley foreman, Thomas Bullian, Jonathan Malugin, Austin Richardson, David A Massie, Robt P Harris, Michael Rogers, James Daniel, Ja^s Larkins, William Cox, Thomas Gentry, Zachariah Allen, Josiah Davidson.
Mumford Smith, constable, sworn to attend them.

James Hicks, James Eason, and Daniel Billops appointed constables for 2 years ensuing
James West to admr estate of Levina West decd, bond $1,000, with Joseph Edwards and Robert P Harris his securities.
John May was duly elected coroner.
Will of Jno Humphries dec^d proven by Robt Whitledge & Daniel Billops. John T Patterson, Horatio Humphries, Edward Holly, & H W Turner, executors, quallified; bond $10,000.

Charles Winsted appointed guardian to Terisa M Bedford; bond $7,000 with Henry H Marable, Samuel Turner, Howard W Turner, John May & W^m D Turner securities
p.-- Stirling Brewer, Thomas W Shearon and Richard Batson to settle with Clark Spencer former gd^n of Terisa M Bedford.
James West adm^r of George West dec^d is to sell Negroes of s^d estate for purpose of making a division amongst legatees.

JANUARY 1827

Howard W Turner gd^u of Polly Linda Dickson returns statement of guardianship
Benjamin A Collier elected trustee of this county
Deed John Pendergrass to W^m E Pendergrass 100 acres ackd
[A blot covers most of four lines. Name of Robert Livingston appears, apparently as grantee in a deed.]
Deed James Eason to George Evins 153 acres ackd.
Deed Isaac West Senr to Montgomery Bell 160 acres proven by John Keneda
Deed of bargain & sale Samuel Hogg and John B Hogg to John K Winn 640 acres in Dickson; deed had been certified in Wilson County Circuit Court; ordered registered.

p.-- John Buckhannon vs John Larkins. By att^{les}. Jury John Kenedy, W^m D Reynolds, John Rhen, Ge^o Hightower, Holliway N Merritt, Aquilla Council, James Tatom, Ja^s McCord, Nehemiah Scott, Assemus S Merritt, Edward Holly, Robt Martin who find for defendant. Def^t to recover of plaintiff, also cost.
Court adjourned until tomorrow morning 9 oClock
   James Nesbitt, H W Turner, Wm White, J Pendergrass

Wednesday January 3^d 1827.   Present the worshipful James Nesbitt, H W Turner, William White, Esquires, Justices

p.-- Edward Holly apptd guardian to Clinton, John Sevire[?], & Caroline Reynolds minor orphans; bond $600, with William T Reynolds and Horatio Humphries securities

Bill/Indictment agt John Toler, a true bill

John Bernard vs Alexander Hunter. Pl^{tf} motion by att^y. Pl^{tf} had been security for def^t for prosecution of a suit wherein sd Alex^r Hunter was pl^{tf}, David Roberts was def^t. Hunter had failed in prosecution thereof. Cost of s^d suit had been made out of s^d John Bernard as security afsd amounting to $34.44. Considered by Court that John Bernard recover of Alex^r Hunter s^d sum and cost

State vs Henry W Hinson. Appearance bond $250. Mark Reynolds and Wilkins Tatom $125 each. A&B on Francis V Smitton

p.-- State vs Augustin Thompson. A&B. Pleads guilty; fined 6¼¢ and cost. R D Sansom, Henry A C Napier, & John W Napier agree to pay cost

State vs Jacob Bright. Pettit Larceny. Jury John Kenedy, W^m D Reynolds, Jno Rhue, Benedict Bacon, John Larkins, Thos McClelland, Wm Hickerson, Danl Leach, Rich^d D Sansom, William Grymes, W^m B Hadden, Henry A C Napier find def^t not guilty.

JANUARY 1827

State vs James Council. Appearance bond. $250. Willis Council and Aquilla Council $125 each.

p.-- State vs Willis Council. Appearance bond, $250. James Council and Aquilla Council $125 each.

State vs Aquilla Council. Appearance bond, $250. James Council and Willis Council $125 each.

p.-- State vs Alexander Wilkins. A&B. Jury Thomas Bullian, Jonathan Malugin, Austin Richardson, David A Massie, Robt P Harris, Michael Rogers, James Daniel, James Larkins, Wm Cox, Thos Gentry, Jno Bradley, Zachariah Allen who say defendant is guilty. Fined $12.50 & cost.

State vs Lorenzo Dow Evins. Malicious mischief. Jury William D Reynolds, John Rhue, Benedict Bacon, Thomas McClelland, Wm Hickerson, Danl Leach, Rich^d D Sansom, Wm Grymes, William B Hadden, Henry A C Napier, James Gilmore, John Baker who say def^t is guilty; fined $50. Also cost. Def^t's appeal granted

p.-- State vs Henry W Hinson. A&B. Filed 8 Septr 1826. Def^t pleads guilty; fined $12.50 and cost. John Hinson assumes to pay fine and cost

State vs Joseph Kimble. Ind^t overseer. Pleads guilty; fined 6¼¢ and cost.

State vs Henry W Hinson. Forfeiture on the Scire facias set aside; Def^t and John Hinson to pay cost
State vs Henry W Hinson. Forfeiture on Sci Fa set aside on payment of cost by sd Henry W Hinson and John Hinson
p.-- State vs John Hinson. Sci Fa. Forfeiture set aside on payment of costs by defendant and Henry W Hinson
State vs Mumford Smith. Sci Fa. Forfeiture set aside on payment of cost. Henry W Hinson and John Hinson assume cost.
State vs Mark Reynolds. Sci Fa. Forfeiture set aside on payment of costs. Henry W Hinson & John Hinson assume cost.
p.-- State vs Henry W Hinson. Motion to bind to the peace. Henry W Hinson, bond $500; Abiram Coldwell and Andrew Cole, bond $250 each, condition def^t keep peace towards Francis V Smitton and all good people of this State for twelve months.

State vs Francis V Smitton. Motion to bind to the peace. The bond $500; Daniel Billops & John Bradley $250 each; keep the peace towards Henry W Hinson...for twelve months.

Deed James M Brewer and Nancy H Brewer his wife, one lott in Raleigh, North Carolina, deed for 584 acres in Wake County,

JANUARY 1827

North Carolina to Benjamin S King of North Carolina ackd by James M Brewer; Nancy examined separately acknowledged her voluntary act. Certified.
Court adjourned until tomorrow morning 9 oClock
S Turner, Wm White, James Nesbitt, J Pendergrass

Thursday January 4th 1827. Present the worshipful Saml Turner, William White, James Nesbitt, John Pendergrass, Justices

State vs Lorenzo D Evins. Appearance bond, $500. Gabriel S Joslin and Wm Bishop $250 each. Malicious mischief.

p.-- Adm^{rs} of estate of John Dickson dec^d sell Negroes of s^d estate for purpose of making distribution

Jane Baker admx with will annexed of Jno A Baker dec^d enters bond & security, purpose of releasing her former securities.

Deed/Gift Martin Loftes to Milton Loftes two tracts, one 50 acres, the other 500 acres, proven by oaths of Josiah Thornton and Elizabeth Paskel

Benjamin Ryburn & wife vs Holliway N Merritt. The plaintiffs came not; def^t to recover of pl^{tfs} his costs in this behalf.

Thomas Colliers Senr vs Montgomery Bell. By att^{ys}. Jury Thos Bullian, Jonathan Malugin, Austin Richardson, David A Massie, Robt P Harris, Michael Rogers, Ja^s Daniel, Ja^s Larkins, Wm Cox, Thomas Gentry, Jno Bradley, Zacheriah Allen who find for pl^{tf} damage $44. Cost. Defendant's appeal granted.

p.-- Henry A C Napier vs Joseph Howard. By att^{ys}. Jury John Kenedy, William D Reynolds, Jno Rhue, Benedict Bacon, Edward McCormack, Ja^s McCord, Jno Baker, Wm Grymes, Saml Read, W^m B Hadden, Thos McClelland, Ja^s Gilmore who cannot agree. John Kenedy withdrawn, jury discharged. Cause continued.

Robert F Rogers vs Benjamin Cox. Pl^{tf} orders suit dismissed.
Benjamin Cox vs Robert F Rogers. Pl^{tf} orders suit dismissed.

John C Collier vs James Gould. Pl^{tf} orders his suit be dismissed; defendant to pay all costs.

Stephen Childress vs Joseph Eason. Debt. Def^t confesses he owes plaintiff $427.16 debt and damages. Also costs.

p.-- Joseph Eason vs Carter T Eason. Motion ag^t principal. Jury above inquires if pl^{tf} was security for def^t in note on which judg^t was today rendered ag^t Joseph Eason for $427.16

APRIL 1827

debt & damages, say they find Joseph Eason was security. Motion by pl^{tf} att^y that pl^{tf} recover s^d sum of def^t.

Francis S Ellis vs James Read. Motion Ag^t principal. Pl^{tf} by att^y. Jury above enquires if pl^{tf} was security for def^t on a note by Henry Grymes 7 May 1817 for $625 on which note judg^t was rendered for ballance of debt $107.17½ on 6 Jany 1820, & interest thereon to this time, making $42, cost of suit $10, making in all $149.17½. Pl^{tf} recovers of def^t s^d sum & cost.

p. -- Henry A C Napier vs Joseph Howard. Pl^{tf} orders his suit dismissed
Court adjourned until tomorrow morning 9 oClock
R C Napier, James Nesbitt, W^m C Sansom

Friday January 5th 1827.   Present the worshipful
R C Napier, Ja^s Nesbitt, W^m C Sansom, Esquires, Justices

Hicks & Shearon vs Sally Price. 10th Novr 1826 capias by H W Turner Esqr in favour of Hicks & Shearon ag^t Sally Price for $21.06¼, $3.96 interest, $1.25 cost. Danl Billops constable brought Sally Price who 23 Novr 1826 executed bond with Ja^s Price her security for $55 to appear and make payment. Sarah Price hath failed to comply with her bond. Pl^{tfs} to recover of s^d Sally Price and James Price her security $26.27¼ debt, interest and costs.

p. -- Jno Bradley & Thomas Holliway vs William Hudson. Pl^{tfs} were securitys of s^d def^t in appearance bond to answer Hicks & Shearon for debt; Hudson failed to appear. Judg^t ag^t them for $200.29½ debt, $3.22½ cost. Pl^{tfs} to recover of def^t.

Jacob Voorhies and Robert Steel app^{td} under act of 1825 commissioners of revenue for this year to settle with public officers.
Court adjourned until Court in Course
James Nesbitt, R C Napier, W^m C Sansom

Monday 2^d April 1827. Present the worshipful Molton Dickson, D H Williams, Hudson Dudley, Howard W Turner, Samuel Turner, John Pendergrass, Wm White, W^m McMurry, Jo^s Kimble, Justices

Ordered road Henry Hightower is overseer of discontinued.
Silas Harris to oversee road in place of Mabel Gilbert.
George Cooksey to oversee road in place of James Morris.

APRIL 1827

James Mickle to oversee road in place of Joseph Kimble.
Jacob Leach to oversee road in place of James H Davis.
John Wright to oversee road in place of James Gunn.
Nelson McClelland to oversee road in place of James Choat.
p.-- Gibson Taylor to oversee road in place of James Jones.

Road from Charlotte to Vernon, the part by Ransom Milams to run in the hollow east of his house where it formerly ran.

The Sheriff to cause Joshua Price, Thomas Price and Willis A Price to be brought to Court for purpose of being bound out.

Richard N Williams to oversee road beginning near Eight mile tree the way road was first marked out, down Ragan Branch so as to intersect the road at or near Major Williams

William Morrow to oversee the new road cut out by H W Turner with hands Holliway N Merrett and hands, William Whitington, John Jurdin, John Reynolds and hands, Jesse Sinks, Barney L Bledsoe, Pinckney T Bledsoe, Edward Holly and hands, Clinton Reynolds, Yancy Bledsoe, Thomas McMurry

Wm Wright, Thos Williams, & Danl Williams to settle with Wm Tatom, former guardian of the children of George Wright dec^d

Michael Light, overseer of old road down Hurricane, to over-oversee of new part of s^d road turned by G H Walker

James Walker, Berryman[?] Walker, William Rye and Jno McAdoo and hands attached to bounds of John B Cox, overseer of road

Ordered the Bear Creek road be renewed from where it leaves Dover Road to where it intersects a road from Davis's ferry to Reynolds Burgh, and that Mark Reynolds oversee, and John Hensons hands, Howel Freeman and Abraham Self work under him

p.-- Joseph Kimble, Howard W Turner, Samuel Turner, Esq^{rs} to settle with Susanna Norris adm^x of Robert Norris dec^d

John Cunningham to oversee road from McCallisters to Baxters Iron Works beginning where Montgomery County line crosses sd Road and ending where Brewers Road crosses the road from the mouth of Harpeth to Charlotte. Hands assigned to work road: Baxters hands, Nathaniel Cunningham, Wm Buckhanon, Thos Matthews, John Harris, John McCulla, Archibald Sainsing, Harry Sainsing, William Matthews, Wm Hand, Thos Edwards, Adonijah Edwards, John Edwards, William Simms

James M Brewer, B N Carter, & A Roberts to settle with James Walker adm^r of Thomas Swift dec^d

APRIL 1827

Order Henry Goodrich, James Eason, Orrin D Hogins to settle with William Hedge former guardian of Harriott Evins, & the amount due be paid over to James Tatom, present guardian

Resolved that in the future provision be made for Parrishoners of this County at July Term in place of January Term.

Polly West allowed $40 for keeping her son G W West for the present year ending April Term 1828, & that she draw on his guardian S Brewer Esqr for same

Joseph Kimble Esqr, Thomas C Smith, & Wm Fentress to settle with Jeremiah Brown, former guardian of Stevenson Archer. Jeremiah Brown, former gdn of Stevenson Archer appear before Joseph Kimble, Esqr, Thos C Smith, and Wm Fentress and make settlement of sd guardianship between this and next Term

Order Executors estate of John Humphries decd allowed until next Term of this Court to return inventory of sd estate

Deed Isaac West Senr to Montgomery Bell 160 acres proven by John H Stone
p.-- Orrin D Hogins gd^n of Cuthbert C Hudson returns account of his guardianship
Settlement with adm^r of John Parrel dec^d received.
Settlement with James Walker adm^r of Thomas Swift dec^d rec^d.
Deed Stewart Pipkins to Minor Bibb and Michael Robertson two acres proven by Thomas Gentry and Charles Gilbert
Deed Lewis D Sowell to Henry Harden 30 acres proven by John Garton and Martin Garton
Deed Thomas Wilson to James Baxter 30 acres proven by Henry J Highland and Joseph B Highland
Deed Susannah Johnson to John Garton 50 acres proven by Minor Bibb and Martin Garton
Deed Edmond Tidwell Senr to Silas Tidwell 80 acres proven by John Brown and John Pendergrass
Deed Thomas Wilson to James Baxter 30 acres proven by Henry Highland and Joseph B Highland
Deed William Sooter to William Flemming 68 acres proven by Joseph Shouse
p.-- Deed Daniel Ross to Jno Garner 96 acres proven by Henry J Highland and Nicholas Hale
Deed John Wilson to Elijah Hendrix 90 acres proven by Elijah Hendrix Jr and James Hendrix
Deed James Walker to Labon Hott 215 acres proven by Ja^s Holl and Burgess Wall
Deed Nicholas Hale to Benjamin Williams 2 acres ackd
Deed Daniel Harris to Henry Harden 70 acres proven by John Garton and Martin Garton

APRIL 1827

Deed/Gift John Hinson to his daughter Harriott Hinson, Negro woman Sara ackd
Deed John McAdoo to Isaac Davis town lott in Charlotte No.52 proven by Richard Waugh and Stirling Brewer
Deed Isaac Davis to Richard Waugh one town lott in Charlotte No.52 proven by A Hamilton and James Irwin
p.-- Coburn Crews appointed constable.
Huel Parrish appointed guardian to Stevenson Archer.
James West to adm^r estate of Samuel Richardson dec^d.

Jurors to next Circuit Court: Thomas Jones, Matthew Gilmore, Willie Baldthrop, Augustin Thompson, Henry A C Napier, James M Ross, Wm White, W^m E Pendergrass, Gideon Cunningham, John King, Wm Lomax, Wm Johnson, Thomas Jurnigin, Silmon Edwards, Wm Brazier, Molton Dickson, Ge^o Smith, Thos McClelland, W^m H Goodrich, William Mosley, Thos Ellis, John Grymes, Jno B Cox

Jurors to next County Court: Wm Adams, Asburn Vanhook, Saml Self, Danl Moore, Jno Sullivant, Nehemiah Hardy, Ja^s McCord, Stephen Smith, Danl Forsey, James Epperson, Jesse Epperson, Orsemus S Merrett, Danl W Martin, Lemuel Read, Abiram Coldwell, John McAdoo, David McAdoo, Ge^o Davidson, John Dunigan, Orrin Nall, Thos C Smith, Wm Fentress, Huel Parrish, George Hightower, Jas W Christian, Martin H Barton, Larry Burns, Wm Jones
Court adjourned until tomorrow Morning 9 oClock
Hudson Dudley, Molton Dickson, Thos Murrell.
Wm White, J Pendergrass

Tuesday April 3^d 1827.   Present the worshipful
Hudson Dudley, Molton Dickson, Thomas Murrell, William White, John Pendergrass, Esquires, Justices

Grand Jurors: Wm Tatom foreman, Elijah Walker, Redic Myatt, Moses Street, Moses White, Robert Vanhook, Wm Wood, William Hickerson, Robt Nisbitt Jr, Archibald Skelton, Daniel Nall, Joseph Shouse, Archibald Pullin. Mumford Smith, constable.

Stirling Brewer app^{td} guardian to Ge^o W West minor orphan of Isaac West S^r dec^d; bond $1200, James M Brewer & John Brewer his securities
Bill/Sale Stirling Brewer to Parry W Humphreys & John Brewer for three Negroes Jenny, Lila, and Gilbert proven by James M Brewer and Thomas W Shearon
Deed Daniel Ross to William Turner 325 acres proven by John W Napier and George F Napier
Deed William Turner to Samuel Vanleer, Simon Bradford & John Stacker 375 acres ackd
William Hogins Esqr to take the list of Taxable property for

APRIL 1827

this year in Capt Tidfords Company

p.-- Bill/Sale Wm D Reynolds & wife to Onsemus S Merritt for three Negroes, Charlotte, Artemisa, Silva proven by Bennet B Corbin

Samuel W Handy vs Ephriam Garrett. Fi fa of 20th March 1827 favour Saml W Handy against Eph^m Garrett by Field Farrar on judgm^t by E D Hicks Esqr on 2 May 1826 for $46 & cost, which execution came to Robert Livingston dep^y Sh^{ff}, who levied on 100 acres on Bartons Creek 21 March 1827. Order/sale issued

Samuel W Handy vs Ephriam Garrett. Fi fa of 20 Mar 1827 favour Saml W Handy ag^t Eph^m Garrett by Field Farrar on judgm^t by E D Hicks, Esqr, 7 Octr 1826 for $17 & cost, came to Robt Livingston deputy sh^{ff} who levied on 100 acres on Bartons Cr 21 March 1827. Order/Sale issued.

Elias W Napier vs William McNickol. Def^t allowed to take the deposition of Henry Owens in Davidson County as evidence

Josiah Thornton vs Elisha Smith & others. Pl^{tf} by att^y given leave to take deposition of Mark Thornton as evidence

p.-- Christopher Robertson vs John McAdoo. Cause refered to Robert H Brown and Thomas W Shearon

Robert West vs Richard C Napier. Debt. By att^{ys}. Jury Zacheus Drummond, Wm Caffery, Nathan Dillehay, Saml King, Nelson McClelland, Ambrose Petty, Richd Batson, Ja^s Walker, Wm Cox, Thomas Williams, Richd Murrell, Jno McAdoo who find for pl^{tf} debt $81.60, damage $56.50. Also cost. Def^t granted appeal

James Murry vs Absolam Fentress and others. Pl^{tf} orders suit dismissed. Defendant to recover for pl^{tf} his cost

Gabriel P Joslin vs William Turner and Peter Dozier. Pl^{tf} by att^y orders suit dismissed. Def^{ts} assume to pay costs.

p.-- Thomas L Williams vs George F Napier. Debt. By att^{ies}. Jury above find for pl^{tf} $100, assess damage by detention of debt to $25.50. Also costs. Defendant granted appeal.

John Low[Lau?] and Sarah Sly adm^r and adm^x of Jacob Sly dec^d vs John Forsythe. Debt. By att^{ies}. Jury above, find for pl^{tf} $125 debt, damage $5.90. And costs in this behalf expended.

p.-- Garret Lane vs John N Evins. Defendant orders his suit dismissed.

Mumford Smith app^{td} to collect State and County Tax for the

APRIL 1827

present year; bond $5000 with B H Carter, Geo Evins, William Hedge, Moses T White, E W Napier his securities
Court adjourned until tomorrow Morning 9 oClock
                    Thos Murrell, Molton Dickson, Hudson Dudley

Wednesday April 4th 1827.   Present the worshipful
Thomas Murrell, Molton Dickson, Hudson Dudley, Justices

State vs Henry W Henson. Jury Zacheus Drummond, Wm Caffery, Nathan Dillehay, Saml King, Nelson McClelland, Ambrose Petty, Richd Batson, Jas Walker, Jeremiah Hambrick, Andrew Hamilton Benedict Bacon, Bennet B Corbin find defendant guilty. Fined $12.50. While Court were pronouncing judgt but immediately before Hinson could be taken into custody by Sheriff, Hinson run off to evade execution of judgment. Mark Reynolds & Wm Tatom his securities failed to bring him to Court. The State to recover. Scire facias to issue.

State vs William Anderson. Bastardy. Deft in proper person, guilty of begetting a child on Parthina Young. Ordered deft pay $40 for child's maintenance from 1 March 1826 to 1 March 1827, for 2d year to pay $30, 3 year $20, and to give bond & security. Deft having absconded without having complied with orders of Court. Securities John P Jims[Jerns?] & Reuben McVey failed to bring him to court. State to recover

p.-- State vs James Council. Appearance bond $500. Willis Council and Qualla Council $250 each, his securities.
State vs Aquilla Council. Appearance bond $500, Willis and James Council $250 each, his securities.
p.-- State vs Willis Council. Appearance bond $500, James & Aquilla Council $250 each, his securities.

State vs John Toler. Indt overseer. Defendant with council on arraignment pleads not Guilty. Jury Zacheus Drummond, Wm Caffery, Nathan Dillihay, Saml King, Nelson McClelland, Ambrose Petty, Richd Batson, Jas Walker, William Cox, Benedict Bacon, Wm D Reynolds, Bennet B Corbin who find deft guilty; fined 6¼¢ and pay cost in this behalf expended

State vs William Hambrick. Peace warrant. Nole prosequi entered; defendant to pay cost, and be in custody of sheriff until fine and cost are secured.
p.-- State vs Jeremiah Hambrick. Peace warrant. Nole prosequi entered; Deft assumes cost; in custody until secured.
State vs Uriah Hambrick. Peace warrant. Nol pros entered; & deft assumes cost; in custody of sheriff until cost secured.
State vs Wm Hambrick, Jeremiah Hambrick, Uriah Hambrick, Mathew Gilmore, Mark Reynolds. Defts confessed they owe the

APRIL 1827

State $30, the cost of three suits. State to recover.

William Buckhannon vs Montgomery Bell. By att^{ys}. Jury above except John Roy for Benedict Bacon find for plt^f his damage $719.50. And cost. Defendant prays appeal; granted

p.-- Soloman Marsh vs John Baker. Appeal. By attorneys. Jury Zacheus Drummond, Wm Caffery, Nathan Dillehay, Samuel King, Nelson McClelland, Ambrose Petty, Richd Batson, Ja^s Walker, Benedict Bacon, W^m D Reynolds, Bennet B Corbin, Jeremiah Hambrick find for plt^f $49.84½; & cost. Deft granted appeal.

James W Christian adm^r of Drury Christian dec^d vs John Bernard. Def^t confesses he owes pl^{tf} $37.36 debt & damages, besides cost. Execution stayed until 20 days before next Term.

James W Christian adm^r of Drury Christian dec^d vs John Bernard. Deft confesses he owes pltf $77.12½ debt & interest, & cost. Pl^{tf} stays execution until 20 days before next Term.

E W Napier vs John Keneda. Plaintiff orders suit dismissed & assumes to pay half cost; defendant pays other half

p.-- Henry W Henson vs Simon Bateman. Pl^{tf} orders his suit dismissed; def^t in proper person assumes to pay all cost.

Deed Robert Nisbitt J^r to Augustin Roberts 85 acres ackd. Deed Isaac Davis to Sterling Brewer certain property proven by Robert Livingston and John C Collier.

Nathan Nisbitt vs Henry H Marrable. Debt. By att^{ys}. The pltf hath departed this life. Andrew Nesbitt & William H Maxwell adm^{rs} estate of s^d Nathan dec^d made pl^{tfs} to prosecute suit.

Bill/Sale Sterling Brewer to James M Brewer, two Negroes Joe and Mary plus other property proven by Robert Livingston and John C Collier

James Douglass vs William H Maxwell alias Maxfield. Pltf by atty. Attachment amended [illegible]
p.-- Court adjourns until tomorrow Morning Nine oClock
Thomas Murrell, Molton Dickson, Hudson Dudley

Thursday April 5th 1827.   Present the worshipful
Thomas Murrell, Molton Dickson, Hudson Dudley, Justices

Lewis Thompson vs Elias W Napier. Def^t by att^y; by affidavit of deft: Edward McCormack, pltf^s security, is insufficient. Ordered that unless plaintiff give better security on or be-

APRIL 1827

fore trial, the same shall be dismissed.

James Douglass vs William H Maxwell. Pl^{tf} by att^y. Defendant makes default. Jury at next term to inquire pl^{tfs} damages.

p.-- William D Reynolds vs Orsemus S Merrett. Debt. Att^{ies}. Jury Zacheus Drummond, Wm Caffery, Nathan Dillehay, Samuel King, Nelson McClelland, Ambrose Petty, Richd Batson, James Walker, Wm Cox, Abiram Coldwell, Bennet B Corbin, John Baker who find for pl^{tf} $100 debt, damage $5. And cost.

Arresus W Hicks vs William Bishop & Samuel Heath. Appeal. By att^{ys}. Jury Zacheus King, Nelson McClelland, Ambrose Petty, Soloman Milam, Ja^s Walker, Wm Cox, Abiram Coldwell, Bennet B Corbin, John Baker who find for pl^{tf} $45.48 debt & interest. [details written between lines are too difficult to read on microfilm]. Appeal granted.

Gould & Voorhees vs William H Maxwell. Attachment. Pl^{tf} by attorney, on motion granted to annex oath to attachment.

p.-- Josiah R Rogers vs William Gunn. Pl^{tf} by attorney. Jury Zacheus Drummond, Wm Caffery, Nathan Dillihay, Samuel King, Nelson McClelland, Ambrose Petty, Richd Batson, Ja^s Walker, Wm Cox, Abiram Coldwell, Bennet B Corbin, Jno Baker who find for plaintiff $30 debt, $1.50 interest. And cost

Edward D Hicks vs John Holliway. Execution recited. Fi fa 13 Mar 1827 by W^m C Sansom Esq favour Ed^{wd} D Hicks ag^t Jno Holliway $82.50, interest from 26 Jany 1827, & cost. James Williams constable levied on 250 acres on Jones Cr whereon John Holliway now lives 15 March 1827. Order of sale issued

John Shute vs Christopher Robertson. Debt. Def^t in proper person confesses he owes pltf $115 debt, $1.40 interest.

p.-- Deed Stirling Brewer to Isaac Davis Town Lott No.51 in Charlotte ackd

Sterling Brewer vs Elias W Napier. Caviat. By att^{ys}. Jury Zacheus Drummond, Nathan Dillehay, Saml King, Ambrose Petty, Richd Batson, Ja^s Walker, Abiram Coldwell, Bennet B Corbin, John Baker, John Roy, Ge^o Evins, Benjamin W Thomas who are allowed to disperse until tomorrow morning

A G S Wight vs Thomas Holloway. Garnishment. Pl^{tf} by att^y; Thos Holloway in proper person. 24 March 1827 execution, A G S Wight, pl^{tf}, & Beverly A Porter def^t; Thomas Holloway summoned as garnishee, says he received property of Porter, $60 and agreed to satisfy judg^t of Wight vs Porter. Pl^{tf} to re-

APRIL 1827

cover of Thomas Holloway $60 for satisfaction in part of his execution af^{sd} ag^t s^d Beverly A Porter & costs of garnishee

A W Hicks vs William Bishop & Saml S Heath. Appeal. Def^t by attorney. Amendment of return on warrant refused by Court. Court adjourned until tomorrow morning 9 oClock
                    Hudson Dudley, Molton Dickson, Thomas Murrell

Firday April 6th 1827.   Present the worshipful
Hudson Dudley, Molton Dickson, Thomas Murrell, Justices

Marvel Low vs Montgomery Bell. By Att^{ys}. Demurer overruled, pl^{tf} to recover of def^t $112.50 debt, $5 damage, & cost.
Marvel Low vs M Bell. By att^{ys}. Pl^{tf} to recover of def^t $70 debt, $2.45 damage, & cost.

p.-- Stirling Brewer caveator, vs Elias W Napier. By att^{ies}. Jury above say the black oak marked in Napiers plat south of Reynoldsburgh road is not the true begining corner of Elias W Napiers entry #191. 2d issue: jury say true begining corner of entry #191 is so near Reynoldsburg as to completely include the notorious oarbank. 3rd issue: oarbank north of Reynoldsburg road is the oar bank intended to be included in Elias W Napiers entry #191.... Stirling Brewer to recover of Elias W Napier

p.-- Stirling Brewer vs E W Napier. Def^t, before cause was put to jury for trial, by attorney moved to quash s^d caveat because there had not been a plat and survey shewing the interference. Overruled and submitted to go to Jury

p.-- Sterling Brewer vs E W Napier. Caveat. Def^t by attorney moved an arrest of judgment. Overruled.

Gustavis Rape vs M Bell. Case. By attornies. Jury Wm Tatom, Elijah Walker, Redic Myatt, Moses Street, Robert Vanhook, Wm Wood, Wm Hickerson, Robt Nisbett Jr, Danl Nall, Jo^s Shouse, Archibald Pullin, Wm Bishop who find for pl^{tf}, damages $86. Also costs. Defendant granted appeal.

p.-- Daniel W Maury surviving partner of A Maury & Son vs W^m H Betts. By att^{ies}. Jury above find for pl^{tf} $119.26 debt, damage $52. And cost. Defendant granted an appeal.

Henry V Robertson vs Wm Hickerson & John C Collier. Debt. By attys. Jury William Tatom, Elijah Walker, Redic Myatt, Moses Street, Robt Vanhook, Wm Wood, Moses White, Robt Nisbitt Jr, Danl Nall, Jo^s Shouse, Arch^d Pullin, Wm Bishop, who find for pl^{tf} $160 debt, damage $3.60. Costs. Def^t granted an appeal.

July 1827

p.-- Field Farrar vs Christian Baughman. Defendant in proper person confesses he owed pl^{tf} $90 debt & interest, and cost. Pl^{tf} agrees to stay execution until next term of this Court.

Hicks & Shearon vs James Nesbitt. Debt. By att^{vs}. Jury William Tatom, Elijah Walker, Redic Myatt, Moses Street, Robert Vanhook, William Wood, Wm Hickerson, Nelson McClelland, Danl Wall, Jo^s Shouse, Arch^d Pullin, Wm Bishop. who find for pl^{tf} $206.12 3/4 debt, damage $2. And cost. Def^t granted appeal.

Jacob Grymes vs Jesse Bartee. Debt. By attys. Jury above except Robert Nisbitt J^r for Nelson McClelland find for pl^{tf}. Thereupon, argument on pl^{trs} demurer to defendants pleas being heard, Court says reasons in demurer are insufficient, & demurer overruled. Def^t go hence & recover of pl^{tf} his cost. Plaintiff prays appeal to Circuit Court; allowed

Marvel Low vs Montgomery Bell. Def^t prays appeal to Circuit Court from Judgment against him this Term. Allowed.
Marvel Lowe vs Montgomery Bell. Def^t prays appeal to Circuit Court from judg^t ag^t him at this Term. Allowed.

James Eason, Orrin D Hogins, & Henry Goodrich to settle with Wm Hodge guardian of heirs of Lewis Evins decd

Appoint Abiram Coldwell, John C Collier, & R Batson in addition to present commissioners of revenue, to reexamine last settlement made with the former trustee and sheriff respecting credits allowed sheriff for 1825 & 1826

Gould & Voorhies vs William H Maxwell. Pl^{tfs} by att^y; def^t made default. Pl^f damage to be determined by jury next Term.

p.-- Thomas S Hunter vs Jacob Walker & George H Walker adm^{rs} of Elizabeth Walker dec^d. Pl^{tf} by att^y, Def^{ts} made default. Pl^{tf} to recover of def^t $158.60 debt & damages, also costs, to be levied on estate of Eliz Walker dec^d if so much there be in hands of adm^{rs}, then on goods, chattels, lands of said defendants.
Court adjourned until Court in Course.
     Hudson Dudly, Thomas Murrell, Molton Dickson

Monday, 2^d July 1827.   Present the worshipful Molton Dickson, D H Williams, Joseph Kimble, Thomas Murrell, Howard W Turner, Samuel Turner, Hudson Dudley, Jno W Napier, William McMurray, Esquires, Justices

JULY 1827

Deed Willie Balthrop & wife to Ebenezer Arnold 20 acres & 60 poles land ackd by Willie Balthrop. Polly his wife examined apart acknowledged she executed same without constraint

Deed Ransom Ellis and wife to Ebenezer Arnold 20 acres & 60 poles land ackd by sd Ransom Ellis. His wife Nancy examined apart acknowledged she executed same without constraint

Deed Willie Balthrop & wife Polly & Ransom Ellis & wife Nancy & others to James Green 5 acres ackd by Willie & Ransom. Polly and Nancy examined apart ackd they signed freely

p.-- Deed Samuel Tate to James Tate 40 acres ackd

Deed John Dickson to Hugh Dickson 25 acres. Sd John Dickson has departed life since execution of this deed. There being no witnesses to s^d deed, handwriting of Jn° Dickson dec^d was proven by William Morrison Senr and Joseph Kimble

Power/Attorney Willson Sanderlin to Ira McFarson ackd

Samuel Turner Esqr, Wm Wright & Thos Williams to settle with Wm Tatom Senr guardian of heirs of George Wright Senr dec^d

Joseph Kimble Esqr, Wm Morrison Senr & Robt West settle with Susanna Hall ext^x & Jesse Hall ext^r of John Hall dec^d

Hugh Craig, a poor person of this County, allowed at rate of $37.37 from last January Term until April Term 1828, to be drawn for his support by Samuel Turner Esqr

Joseph Choate produced scalps of 7 wolves under age 4 months that he killed in Dickson County

Willie B Johnson app^{td} Solicitor pro tem

Peter Self to oversee road in place of Wm Adams, having same hands, & also John May & hands and Whitehead & hands
Robert Baxter & hands to keep up the Palmyra road from forks to Creek, Labon Holt to oversee same
p.-- John R Weldron, jailer, allowed $12.25 for boarding Ja^s Watson in jail, 18 April till 17 May at 37½ ¢ pr day, 2 turn keys, also for repairs to jail $14, also for boarding James McCauly in jail 15 days at 37½ pr day 2 turn keys

Jurors for next Court: Robt Vanhook, Willis Norsworthy, Jesse Ragan, William Word, Ge° Gallion, Wm Carroll, Humphries H Burton, Jo^s Melugin, Josiah Davidson, James West, Jn° T Patterson, W^m H Goodrich, John M Selland, W^m T Coleman, Wm Rye,

JULY 1827

Lemuel Russell, Stephen Grigory, John K Tidwell, Jacob Sanderson, Simon Myers, Thomas Bulion, Solomon Marsh, Ja^s Tate, Joseph Williams, Jacob Leach, George Tubbs, Silmon Edwards, Jeremiah Nesbitt, Richard D Sansom, Ellis Ticer

Power/Atty George McMunn to Thomas Palmer ackd
Court adjourned until tomorrow morning 9 oClock
      Joseph Kimbell, J Pendergrass, D H Williams

Tuesday July 3^d 1827.   Present the worshipful Joseph Kimbell, J Pendergrass, D H Williams, Esqrs. Justices

p.-- Grand Jury: Abiram Coldwell foreman, Saml Self, Orsimus S Merritt, Jesse Epperson, Ja^s W Christian, Nehemiah Hardy, Lemuel Read, Oran Nall, Daniel Forsey, Martin H Burton, John McAdoo, Danl W Martin, David McAdoo. Seburn Crews, constable

Deed Claiborn Harris for heirs of William Johnson to James Hudson 640 acres proven by Claiborn Harris Senr
Deed Thomas Nesbitt to Robert Nesbitt Junr 2nd for 102 acres proven by Richard Waugh
Deed John McAdoo to William Bishop lott in Charlotte proven by Richard Waugh & James Nesbitt
Power/Att^y Claiborn Harris Senr to Stephen Harris ackd.
William McMurray appointed guardian to Sally and Washington McMurray; bond $800

L P Cheatham vs F V Schmidt. Execution recited. Fi fa 18 May 1827 favor Leonard P Cheatham ag^t Francis V Schmidt by Field Farrar on judgment by E D Hicks Esqr on 18 July 1826 for $50 debt and cost of suit; to hands of Alex^r Dickson D Shff who levied on 300 acres head of Partins Cr near Schmidts Pond, & also on 50 acres on Williamson Cr of Yellow Cr whereon widow Haily formerly lived. Order of sale issued

p.-- Alsey S Speight vs John F Cotton. Ex^n recited. Fi fa 18 May 1827 favour pl^{tf} ag^t def^t by Joseph Morris J P on judg^t by him 4 Jany for $48.05½ & cost of suit. Seburn Crews, constable levied on 150 acres on the road to Charlotte about 5½ miles from mouth of Harpeth. Order of sale issued

Isabella McClure admx vs Absalom Tribble. Motion. Cause dismissed; defendant to recover of plaintiff his cost.

Aaron Arnold vs Richard D Sansom. By att^{ies}. Jury Thomas C Smith, Ja^s McCord, Ashburn Vanhook, Saml W Handy, Richard N Williams, Ja^s H Davis, Benjn D Pack, Willis Norsworthy, W^m S Mosely, George Davidson, Francis Balthrop, Robt Larkins who find for def^t. Def^t to recover of pl^{tf} his cost. Pl^{tf} prays

JULY 1827

appeal to Circuit Court; allowed.

p.-- George W Lewis vs Wallace Dixon. By attʸs. Jury Abiram Coldwell, Samˡ Self, Orsemus S Merritt, Jesse Epperson, Jaˢ W Christian, Nehemiah Hardy, Lemuel Read, Oran Nall, Daniel Forsey, Martin H Burton, Jnº McAdoo, Danˡ W Martin who find for plᵗᵗ his damage $50. Also cost. Plᵗᵗ prays appeal to Circuit Court; allowed

Lewis Thompson vs Elias W Napier. By attˡᵉˢ, Jury above find for plᵗᵗ his damage $134.18. And cost. Defᵗ prays appeal to the Circuit court; allowed.
Court adjourned until tomorrow morning 9 oClock
        J Pendergrass, H W Turner, Joseph Kimbell

Wednesday July 4ᵗʰ 1827.   Present the Worshipful J Pendergrass, H W Turner, Joseph Kimble, Esquires, Justices

State vs Wilkins Tatom. Indᵗ for rescue. Jury Wᵐ Fentress, Jaˢ McCord, Ashburn Vanhook, Wᵐ Adams, Nicholas Baker, Danˡ Billups, J G Martin, Wᵐ Grimes, Wᵐ Floyd, James Medlock, A Hamilton, Jnº B Walker who find defᵗ guilty; fined $1 & cost

State vs John Hinson. Indᵗ for Rescue. Jury Wᵐ Fentress, Jaˢ McCord, Ashburn Vanhook, Wᵐ Adams, Nichˢ Baker, Daniel Billups, Jeremiah G Martin, Wᵐ Grymes, Wᵐ Floyd, James Medlock, John B Walker, Aquilla Council who find defᵗ is not Guilty.

p.-- State vs Jesse J Mosley. Nol Pros entered
State vs Eaton Tatom. Nol pros entered
State vs Thomas Edwards. Nol pros entered; Adonijah Edwards assumes to pay cost.
State vs James Council. Nol pros entered. State to recover of Joseph Handlin the cost expended
State vs Aquilla Council. Nol pros entered. State to recover of Joseph Handlin the cost expended
State vs Willis Council. Nol pros entered. State to recover of Joseph Handlin the cost expended.
p.-- State vs Allen Wells. James Joslin, defᵗ's bail, brings him to Court; sheriff takes him into custody
State vs Wᵐ Anderson. Sci Fa. Payment of costs is set aside; Wᵐ Anderson, John P Tims, & Reuben McVey assume cost.
State vs John P Tims. Sci Fa. Forfeiture set aside on payment of costs by Jnº P Tims, Wᵐ Anderson, Reuben McVey.
State vs Reuben McVey. Sci Fa. Sci Fa set aside, costs to be paid by Reuben McVey, Wᵐ Anderson, John P Tims.

p.-- State vs Wᵐ P Anderson, John P Tims, Reuben McVey. Bastardy. Defᵗˢ assume cost of suit on which judgᵗ was rendered

JULY 1827

at last Term ag^t Wm Anderson who failed to comply with judg^t of Court. State to recover of defendant the cost in that behalf expended together with cost in this behalf expended.

Augustin Thompson to adm^r the estate of Thomas A Young dec'd; gave bond $700 with E W Napier; returned inventory of estate

Resignation of Joseph Wilson Esqr Justice/Peace received

Green P Rice vs Horatio Bett. On motion of pl^t, order writs of certiorari & supersedeas issue

State vs James Young & John Hinson. Bond $200 condition that the bastard begotton on Parthena Young by Wm Anderson found guilty at last Term shall not become chargable to the county

Thomas Holliway apptd constable

p.-- Willis A Price, Thomas Price, Joshua Price, by Guardian John Adams vs Patrick McDurmond & Letty McDurmond. Petition for distributive shares. Patrick McDurmond is not inhabitant of this state, therefore publication to be made 4 weeks successively in Nashville Gazette requiring s^d def^t to appear

Edward Woodard vs Richard Batson Sheriff. By att^y. Joseph F Cloud, deputy sh^{ff}, collected monies for which he has failed to account. Edwd Woodard to recover of Richd Batson $60 due on a receipt of s^d J F Cloud and cost. Def^t granted appeal.

Field Farrar, Clerk/Court, allowed $50 for exoficio services for last year ending this Term
Court adjourned until tomorrow Morning 8 oClock
    J Pendergrass, Joseph Kimbell, D H Williams

Thursday July 5th 1827.   Present the worshipful
J Pendergrass, Joseph Kimble, D H Williams, Esq^{rs}, Justices

p.-- William H Maxwell & Andrew Nesbitt adm^{rs} of Nathan Nesbitt dec^d vs Henry H Marable. Debt. By att^{ies}. Jury Abiram Coldwell, Saml Self, Orsemus S Merrett, Jesse Epperson, Lem^l Read, Oran Nall, Daniel Forsey, Martin H Burton, Danl W Martin, Nehemiah Hardy, Walker Thomas, Jno Weakley who find for pl^{tt} $202.62½ debt, damage $11. And cost. Def^t prays appeal to Circuit Court; allowed

Elias W Napier vs William McNickel. Plaintiff granted leave to take deposition of Henry Owens of Davidson County

Susannah Hall vs Penelope Lewis. Trial at next Term

JULY 1827

p.-- State vs John Toler Jr., Holliway N Merritt, Thomas McMurry. Defendants confess they owe State $17.21¼, the amount of the ca sa agt s^d Toler. State to recover, & costs.

State vs James W McCammons. Peace Warrant. Nol pros entered.
State vs Allen Wells. A&B. Defendant pleads guilty; fined $1 and costs.

State vs Wilkins Tatom, Holliway N Merritt, & Alex^r Wilkins. Defts confess they owe State $12.75 fine & cost of judgment against s^d Wilkins Tatom. State to recover, also cost.

p.-- State vs Henry W Hinson. Appearance bond $200. Alexander Hickson and Lewis Richardson $50 each.

State vs Henry W Hinson. Sci fa. Nol pros entered.
State vs Mark Reynolds. Sci fa. Nol pros entered.
State vs Wilkins Tatom. Sci fa. Nol pros entered.
State vs James Watson. Peace Warrant. Nol pros entered.

p.-- State vs James Gunn. Appearance bond $100; James Eason and Thomas Hollaway $50 each. To answer bill/indictment for Assault & Battery on Charles E Thompson.

State vs Henry W Hinson. Defendant assumes to pay the fine & cost of prosecution at last Term.

Nehemiah Scott vs David Mcadoo former Sheriff, and Sterling Brewer, Benjamin Clark, John Mcadoo and John B Brown. Cause transfered to Circuit Court.

George H Walker & Jacob Walker, admrs of estate of Elizabeth Walker decd, to appear at next Term and give other & further security for purpose of release of present securities

p.-- Joseph Williams vs D Mcadoo former Sh^{ff}, Sterling Brewer, Benjn Clark, John Mcadoo & John B Brown, his securities. Cause transferred to Circuit Court

Christopher Robertson vs Jno Mcadoo. Award of Robert A Brown & Thos W Shearon, arbitrators: Mcadoo is indebted to Robertson $140.96¼. Mcadoo to pay costs accruing in this cause

James H Davie vs Wm Grimes. By att^{y}s. Jury Thos C Smith, Wm Fentress, Ja^s McCord, Wm Adams, Jo^s Ducard[Durand?], Andrew Hamilton, Wilkins Tatom, Wm Norsworthy, John Adams, Jo^s Haward, Nehemiah Scott, Henry A C Napier who cannot agree. Thos C Smith withdrawn; jury discharged from rendering a verdict.

JULY 1827

Bill/Sale John Holliway to John Sinsing, Negro woman Winney and her child Berry ackd
Court adjourned untill tomorrow morning 8 oclock
                    J Pendergrass, S Turner, W^m C Sansom

Friday July 6th 1827.   Present the worshipful
J Pendergrass, S Turner, W^m C Sansom, Esquires, Justices

Benj^a Collier trustee vs David McAdoo Sh^{ff}, Sterling Brewer, John B Brown, John Mcadoo, Benjamin Clark, his securities. Appeal to Circuit Court granted

p.-- Order Danl H Williams, Jo^s Williams & Willis Norsworthy to settle with Samuel Turner executor of John Turner dec^d

Report of commissioners that accounts of county trustee are correct signed by A Coldwell, John C Collier, R Batson.

p.-- William Hedge vs Mary Baker. By attorneys. Jury Abiram Coldwell, Saml Self, Arsemus S Merrett, Jesse Epperson, Ja^s W Christian, Lemuel Read, Oran Nall, Daniel Forsey, Martin H Burton, Jno Mcadoo, Daniel W Martin, Nehemiah Hardy who find for defendant who recovers of plaintiff the cost expended

Josiah Thornton ext^r & Phereba Loftes ext^x of Martin Loftes dec^d vs Elisha Smith & William Loftes. By att^{ys}. Jury Thos C Smith, Wm Fentress, Asburn Vanhook, Wm Adams, Mumford Smith, Richard Murrell, James W McCammon, Absolam Baker, Nehemiah Scott, Jno Weakley, Wm Gunn, Jesse Alexander who say this is the will of Martin Loftes dec^d. Will is admitted to record. Pl^{ffs} recover of def^{ts} the cost in this behalf expended

State vs James Gunn. Peace warrant. Nol pros entered.
James McClure vs Burwell Bayless. Pl^{ff} by att^y suggests the death of def^t; moves order to revive cause.
Montgomery Bell vs Elijah Porter. The Pl^f by att^y orders his suit dismissed; def^t to recover of pl^{tf} his cost.
Montgomery Bell vs Elijah Porter. Pl^f by att^y orders suit be dismissed; def^t recovers of pl^f his cost.
Court adjourned until tomorrow morning o oClock
                    J W Napier, J Pendergrass, Molton Dickson

Saturday July 7th 1827.   Present the worshipful
J W Napier, J Pendergrass, Molton Dickson, Esq^{rs}, Justices

Thomas Holliway vs Ann Rutledge. Pl^f in proper person orders his suit dismissed; def^t assumes cost except the att^y fee.

OCTOBER 1827

p.-- Phillip Allensworth vs Thos Watson. Deft makes default. Jury at next Term to inquire of plf's damages

Josiah Thornton extr & Pheraba Loftes extx vs Elisha Smith & Wm Loftes. Witnesses summoned for plf be taxed to their cost except the witnesses subscribed to the will.

William Hedge vs Mary Baker. Motion for new trial. Plff by atts introduces affidavit of Mumford Smith. Reasons in support of motion insufficient; motion overruled.
Court adjourned until Court in Course
Wm C Sansom, Molton Dickson, J Pendergrass

p.-- Monday October 1st 1827   Present the worshipful John W Napier, D H Williams, H W Turner, Saml Turner, Molton Dickson, Wm Hogins, Hudson Dudley, Wm McMurry, John Johnson, Joseph Kimble, Esquires, Justices

Absalom Swift to oversee road in place of George Clark
Anderson Gentry to oversee road in place of Enoch James
James R Napier to oversee road in place of John Jones
William Tait to oversee road in place of John Holloway
Henry Southerland to oversee road in place of Robert Larkins
Moran Rose to oversee road in place of John Tolar
p.-- Alexander Dickson allowed $2.75 for furnishing wood for stove and repairing it.
William Shelby Esqr, George H Walker, Benjamin Sanders apptd to settle with Wm Johnson, admr estate of Reuben Comer decd.
Benjamin Pack to oversee road in place of Wm Grimmit.
Joseph Kimble Esqr, Robert West & Wm Morrison to settle with James West admr of George West decd.
Joseph Kimble Esqr, Robert West & Wm Morrison to settle with extrs of John Hall decd.
Benjamin B Dunigan, John Dunigan, John Rhue, and Franklin F Bruce added to hands of William Hogins overseer of new road.
Thos May, Jno May, Saml Turner Esqr, Jos Kimble Esqr, Thomas C Smith and Wm Fentress to settle with Huel Parrish guardian of Stephenson Archer.
Joseph Williams & Alexander Dickson to settle with Lucy Vanhook & Henry H Marable admrs of Aron Vanhook decd.
Alexander Dickson, deputy sheriff, allowed $50 for exoficio services for year ending this Term.
Joseph Kimble, D H Williams, Ro West, Huel Parrish, & Samuel Turner apptd to make division among legatees of the personal property of John Hays Senr decd
p.-- Resignation of David Smith Justice/Peace received.

OCTOBER 1827

John R Weldron, jailer, is allowed $96.75 for boarding David Smith, Rebecca Smith, and Nancy Smith while in jail.

John Hodges, adm^r of Mary Ann Hopper dec^d, allowed $12.40 to be paid out of interest of money of sd estate for schooling of three children.

William Tatom Senr, guardian of heirs of George Wright dec^d, allowed $43.65 for services as guardian

Jesse Smith allowed $7.50 for burial expences of Pryor Payne a poor person who died 22^d Septr 1827.

Joseph Kimbel, Robt West & Thos C Smith app^{td} to settle with Alexander Dickson ex^{tr} of James Goodrich dec^d

Josiah Thornton extr & Pheraby Loftis extx of will of Martin Loftis decd gave bond $1500, Spencer T Hunt, security.

George H Walker, an adm^r of estate of Elizabeth Walker dec^d, entered into new bond in discharge of his former security.

Mumford Smith appointed constable.

p.-- Joel Marsh app^{td} guardian to Wm Overton, minor orphan.

Josiah Thornton extr and Pheraby Loftis extx, will of Martin Loftis decd, returned inventory of estate.

James West, admr estate of George West decd, returned inventory and account of sales of s^d estate

Josiah R Rogers app^{td} gd^n for Elizabeth Evins, minor orphan.

Ruthy Archer files petition for share of estate of John Hays Senr dec^d, against Alex^r Dickson adm^r of s^d estate.

Settlement with Wm Tatom Senr, gd^n of heirs of George Wright dec^d, returned into Court.

Settlement with Wm Hedge, former guardian of Harriatt Evins, returned into Court.

Settlement with Wm Hedge gd^n of Jno, Elizabeth, Patsey, Jane & Hulda Evins, minor orphans, returned into Court.

Deed Nehemiah Scott to William Norsworthy 307 acres ackd.

Deed John Hall to Spencer Brown 30 acres ackd.

p.-- Deed Richard A Roe to Minor Marsh 200 acres proven by Drury Taylor & George W Taylor.

Deed Nicholas Hale to Abraham Hale 100 acres proven by Chas P White and John White

Deed David Passmore to Archibald Pullen 100 acres ackd.

Deed W^m W Balthrop to Francis Balthrop 275 acres proven by Thomas W Shearon and Willie Balthrop.

Deed Solomon Petty to Nathaniel Kimbro 20 acres proven by Wm Hogins & J G Bruce.

Deed Thomas Nisbett to Benjamin Gray 50 acres proven by John McAdoo and Alexander Wilkins.

Deed William B Nesbitt, Moses E Nesbitt and Eliza Nesbitt to Andrew D Clements for lots 17 & 24 in Charlotte proven by W^m H Betts and Wm Nesbitt.

p.-- Jurors to Circuit Court: Willis Norsworthy, Wm Teague, Nehemiah Scott, Franklin F Bruce, Leonard Pinegar, Saml Petty, Risden Mockbee, George F Napier, Edward B Roach, John W Napier, John Sanders, Jno Smith, Saml Simpson, Drury Taylor,

OCTOBER 1827

Saml King, John Perry, Henry Lankford, Jno Toler Senr, Henry Story, John Story.
Jurors to next County Court: Thos May, John May, Saml Brown, John McCormack, Allen Bowen, Ge^o Davidson, Ja^s Medlock, Danl Leach, Nathan Tubb, W^m S Coleman, Ge^o Tilly, Wm Simpson, Eli Southerland, Thomas B McClure, Sandford Edwards, Gideon Cunningham, Abiga P Massie, Thomas Gentry, Wm Gentry, Littleton Story, Neran Rose, Gibson Mills, David Bibb, Willie Davis, Huel Parrish, Dorrel[Dowel?] Y Harris, Ge^o Hightower, Joseph Howard, James W Christian, Washington Hunter.
Dickson County to pay costs of prosecution ag^t Rebecca Smith and Nancy Smith in which case nolle prosequi was entered in Circuit Court, $13.95.
Court adjourned until tomorrow morning 9 oClock
       Molton Dickson, J W Napier, J Pendergrass

p.-- Tuesday October 2nd 1827.   Present the Worshipful Molton Dickson, John W Napier, John Pendergrass, Justices.

Those who have not given lands for taxation allowed from now to first December to pay Clerk/Court.
Grand Jury: Rich^d D Sansom foreman, George Tubb, Jacob Luck, Willis Norsworthy, W^m S Coleman, Stephen Grigry, Ellis Tycer, Jo^s Williams, Jesse Ragan, Simon Myers, Jacob Sanderson, Joseph Melugin, Thos Bullion. Caburn Crews, constable.
Deed Wm Thomas to Augustin Richardson 6 acres ackd.
Deed Drury Adkins to Daniel Hickerson 50 acres ackd.

p.-- Elias W Napier vs Wm McNickle. By att^{ys}. Jury Robt Vanhook, Wm Rye, Wm Tate, Solomon Marsh, Wm Carroll, Wm Ward, Wm Miller, Randolph R Harris, James T Hadden, Green Holland, Ransom Milam, Ge^o Cox who find for def^t. Def^t to recover of pl^{tf} his cost. Pl^{tf} prays appeal to Circuit Court; allowed.

Charles Winstead vs Thomas Palsner & W^m S Adamson. Debt. The Def^{ts} confess they owe pl^{tf} $263.87½ debt & damages. Pl^{tf} to recover of def^{ts} besides cost. Execution stayed to next Term

Batson & Smith vs Henry Tucker. By att^{ys}. 4 Septr 1827 Ca Sa issued by Field Farrar, in favour Batson & Smith ag^t Tucker, for $6.62½ debt with interest from 22 July 1826 & 87½¢ cost. Thomas Holloway constable took (p.--) Henry Tucker who on 5 Sept 1827 made appearance bond. Elias W Napier, C Robertson, and R H Brown security, $15. Henry Tucker took oath in Court he had no debts, land, money, stock, or other estate.

Saml W Handy vs Peter Mills. By att^{ys}. 14 Septr 1827 Ca Sa issued by W^m C Sansom J P, favour S W Handy ag^t Peter Mills for $14.69 & cost. R T Hightower constable took Peter Mills

OCTOBER 1827

who 14 Septr 1827 executed appearance bond with E W Napier & C Robertson security $37.62. P Mills took insolvency oath.

Ja^s Nesbitt vs Peter Mills. By att^y. 14 Septr 1827 Ca Sa issued by W^m C Sansom J P. favour J Nesbitt ag^t P Mills $4.12½ debt & cost. R F Hightower, constable, took P Mills who made appearance bond 14 Septr 1827, with E W Napier & C Robertson security (p.--) $37.62. Peter Mills took insolvency oath. Court adjourned until tomorrow Morning 9 oClock.
            Wm White, J Pendergrass, Wm Sansom

Wednesday October 3rd 1827.   Present the Worshipful John Pendergrass, Wm White, W^m C Sansom, Esq^{rs}, Justices.

p.-- State vs James Gunn. Appearance bond $100; Samuel Bugg & Hiram Dunnagan $50 each.

State vs Archibald Cox. A&B. Def^t with counsel at bar pleads not Guilty. Jury William Austin, Jno Henderson, Jno McNeely, Lewis Thompson, Edwd McCormack, John R Smelly[Smith?], Jesse M Speight, Melenton Reynolds, William Rye, Robt Vanhook, Ge^o Gallion, Solomon Marsh who find defendant not guilty.

State vs Henry W Hinson. Def^t with counsel pleads not Guilty Jury Wm Ward, Wm Carroll, Jno Henderson, John McNeely, Lewis Thompson, Edward McCormack, Jesse M Speight, Wm Gilbert, Wm Rye, Robt Vanhook, George Gallion, Solomon Marsh say def^t is Guilty; fined $5, cost, and be in custody until secured

p.-- State vs Jesse M Speight. Bastardy. Def^t found Guilty of begetting a child on Lavina Crumpler is to pay first year $40, second year $30, third year $20. S^d Jesse Speight gave Bond to keep child from chargeable to County.

State vs Augustin Roberts. A&B. Jury David McAdoo, Gabriel P Joslin, Wm Teague, Ezra McAdoo, Ja^s H Davie, Ge^o Hightower, Ja^s Tate, W^m B Hadden, Ge^o F Napier, Ja^s G Hinson, Spencer T Hunt, Wm Kirk who cannot agree. Ordered nol pros entered.

p.-- State vs Joseph Coffee. Peace Warrant. Bond $200. Alexander Wilkins, John S Walker, B N Carter, Mumford Smith, and R T Hightower, bond $100 each. Joseph Coffee to keep toward Elizabeth Acoff and all other good citizens. Andrew Hamilton assumes cost expended in this behalf.

State vs William D Reynolds. Appearance bond $100; Thos Bullion and Alexander Dickson $50 each.

p.-- State vs Jehu Miller. Peace Warrant. Bond $500; John

OCTOBER 1827

Pendergrass & Archibald Cox $250 each. To keep peace toward Baker Hudson and all good citizens. John Pendergrass assumes to pay cost in this behalf expended.

State vs Baker Hudson. Peace Warrant. Bond $500; Spencer T Hunt and Anderson Gentry $250 each to keep peace toward Jehu Miller and family. Baker Hudson to pay cost.

p.-- State vs Hiram Dunegin. Peace Warrant. Bond $500; Sam¹ Dunigan & John Vineyard $250 each; Hiram Dunigan to keep the peace toward Elizabeth Dunigan. Hiram Dunigan is to pay cost of this prosecution and be in custody of sheriff until paid. Samuel Dunigan & John Vineyard assume sd cost.

State vs Hiram Dunnagan. A&B. Appearance bond $500. Samuel Dunagan and John Vineyard $250 each.

Richard D Sansom vs Claiborne Howse & John W Napier. Pl'f in proper person files his note on which this action is brought in place of his declaration.

p.-- Henry A C Napier vs Joseph Haword. Jury: William Ward, Wm Carroll, John Henderson, Jn° McNeely, Millenton Reynolds, Edwd McCormack, Jesse M Speight, Wm Gilbert, Wm Rye, Robert Vanhook, Ge° Gallion, Salmon Marsh who find for pl'f, assess damage to $64.03¼. Beside cost.

John Larkins & Benjn Clark vs James Nesbitt. Debt. By attys. Jury: Wm Ward, Wm Carroll, Jn° Henderson, Jn° McNeely, Lewis Thompson, Edwd McCormack, Jesse M Speight, William Gilbert, Wm Rye, Robt Vanhook, George Gallion, Solomon Marsh who find for pl^f $200 debt, damage $9. And cost. Def^t prays appeal to Circuit Court; allowed.

p.-- Ja^s Haines for use of Francis Carter vs Holloway N Merritt & Horatio Humphreys. Debt. By att^{ys}. Jury: Wm Ward, Wm Carroll, John Henderson, Jn° McNeely, Lewis Thompson, Edward McCormack, Jesse M Speight, Wm Gilbert, Wm Rye, Robert Vanhook, George Gallion, Solomon Marsh find for pl'f $200 debt, assess damage $20. Also cost. Defendant prayed appeal to the Circuit Court; allowed.

W Vanleer & C° vs Willis Cunningham. Debt. By att^{ys}. Jury above find for pl'f $112.50, damage $3.92. And cost.

p.-- James Gould vs Alias Findley. Debt. By attorneys. Jury above find for pl'f $158.51 debt, damage $6.34. And costs.

William A Cook vs Horatio Bett. Debt. By att^{ys}. Jury above find for plaintiff $100, damage $4.25. And costs.

OCTOBER 1827

p.-- Thomas Wells vs Henry H Marable. Debt. Jury above find for plaintiff $129.89 debt, damage $24.95. And cost. Defendant prays appeal; allowed.

Joseph Kimbell appointed guardian in place of Dorothy Goodrich, former gd^n of Alice Goodrich, Charlotte Goodrich, John Goodrich, James Goodrich, and Martha Goodrich minor orphans.

Molton Dickson, James M Ross, & Abiram Coldwell appointed to settle with ext^r of Ebenezer Kelly make return to Court.
Court adjourned untill Tomorrow morning 9 oClock
J W Napier, Wm White, J Pendergrass

Thursday October 4th 1827.　　　　　Present the Worshipful
John W Napier, William White, John Pendergrass, Justices

John Barnet vs John Picket. Supercedias. By attys. Execution heretofore issued levied on property sufficient to satisfy: property surrendered up to Daniel H Williams principal in sd case, Pickett was only security, & execution had been satisfied. Order execution quashed, and John Barnet pay cost.

John Barnet vs John Picket. Supercedias. By att^{ys}. Levied by constable on property sufficient to discharge execution; s^d Picket was only security; ex^n satisfied. S^d Ex^n quashed, Jno Barnet pay cost.

p.-- Gould & Voorhees vs William H Maxwell. Attachment. The plaintiffs order their suit dismissed. Def^t to pay costs.

Johnson & Hicks vs Field Farrar. Debt. By attorneys. Jury: George Tubb, Jacob Leech, Willis Norsworthy, William S Colemon, Stephen Grigory, Ellis Tycer, Joseph Williams, Jesse Ragon, Simon Myers, Jacob Sanderson, Joseph Melugin, Thomas Bullion who find for pl^{tf} $124.35 3/4 debt, damage $18. And cost. Defendant prayed appeal; allowed

Hicks & Shearon vs Field Farrar. Plaintiffs by attorney order suit dismissed; defendant assumes all cost.

p.-- Hicks & Shearon vs Field Farrar. Debt. By att^{ys}. Jury: Ge^o Tubb, Jacob Leech, Willis Norsworthy, W^m S Colemon, Stephen Grigory, Ellis Tycer, Joseph Williams, Jesse Ragon, Simon Myers, Jacob Sanderson, Jo^s Melugin, Thomas Bullion find for pl^{tfs} their debt $118.17, damage $6.30. And cost. Def^t prays appeal to Circuit Court; allowed.

Henry V Robertson vs William Simpson & Thomas Nesbitt. Debt.

OCTOBER 1827

By att^{ys}. Jury above find for pl^{tf} $160 debt, damage $9. And cost. Defendant prays appeal to Circuit Court; allowed

Deed William Thomas to Spencer Brown 50 acres ackd.

p.-- William T Hooper vs John Adams. Debt. By att^{ys}. Jury above find for plaintiff $175 debt, damage $7.87½. And cost.

James Gould vs John C Collier. Debt. By attorneys. The jury above find for pl^{tf} $80.03 debt, damage $2.20. And his cost. Defendant prays appeal to Circuit Court; allowed.

Deed William Thomas to Spencer Brown 50 acres ackd.

p.-- James Woods & Co for use of John Thompson vs Thomas C Smith. Debt. By att^{ys}. Jury above find for plaintiff $111.06 debt, damage $5.82½. And cost.

Steele & Collier vs Montgomery Bell. Case. By att^{ys}. Jury above find in favour of the def^t. Def^t is to recover of pl^{tf} cost expended. Pl^{tf} prayed appeal to Circuit Court; allowed.

p.-- Phillip Allensworth vs Thomas Watson. Cov. Plaintiff by att^y. Jury above say pl^{tf}'s damages $222.50. Also his cost.

Parry W Humphreys for use of Jacob Voorhies vs Peter Jackson. Debt. Jury above find for pl^{tf} balance of debt and damages $99.16. And cost. Def^t granted appeal to Circuit Court.

James Douglass vs William H Maxwell. Attachment. Pl^{tf} orders his suit dismissed. Defendant to recover of pl^{tf} his cost.

p.-- A G S Wight vs Elijah Porter. Pl^{tf} by att^y orders suit dismissed. Defendant to recover of pl^{tf} his cost expended.

George Clark vs Alex^r Wilkins, E D Hicks, & Thos W Shearon. Debt. Pl^{tf} by att^y, def^t Alexander Wilkins in proper person; def^{ts} Edward D Hicks & Thomas W Shearon came not. Jury above find for pl^{tf} $100 debt, $6.50 damage. Pl^{tf} recovers of def^t Alexander Wilkins, and also E D Hicks & Thomas W Shearon who have made default af^{sd} $106.50 debt & damage, besides costs.

William H Maxwell vs James Douglass and others. Pl^{tf} orders his suit dismissed. Def^t James Douglass assumes all cost.

Thomas Wells vs Henry H Marable. Debt. Def^t prays appeal to Circuit Court from a judgment ag^t him this Term; allowed.

E W Napier vs William McNickle. Case. Pl^{tf} prays appeal to Circuit Court from judgment ag^t him this Term; allowed.

JANUARY 1828

Thomas Clark vs Elias W Napier. Leave granted Defendant to take deposition of Robert H Brown.

George F Napier vs Henry G Wells & Chauncey Davenport. Each party allowed to take depositions.
Court adjourned untill tomorrow morning 10 oclock.
W^m C Sansom, Molton Dickson, J W Napier

Friday October 5th 1827.　　　　Present the Worshipful
W^m C Sansom, Molton Dickson, J W Napier, Esquires, Justices

Austin Thompson adm^r of estate of Thomas A Young dec^d, filed inventory & account of sales of s^d estate.
Mary Rose & others by att^y petition against Benjamin Sturdevant & Daniel H Williams adm^{rs} estate of Alexander Rose dec^d and filed petition for distributive shares of s^d estate
Willis A Price, Thomas Price. Joshua Price by guardian John Adams vs Patrick McDearmon and Sally McDearmon. Petition for distributive shares. Order cause stand trial at next Term.

John H Stone vs Richard Murrell. The pl^{tf} by att^y amends his declaration
Court adjourned till Court in Course.
W^m C Sansom, Molton Dickson, J W Napier

p.-- January Term 1828.
Charles Dunigan to oversee the road from Charlotte to Vernon from the Fussel place to the Hickman line, with hands Henry Goodrich, Armstrong Goodrich, Ja^s Dunigan, Richd Tatom, Ja^s Tatom, Green Tatom, Ellis Newsom, Foster Bruce, Lem^l Bruce, John Bruce, S Bruce, Ja^s Bruce, Charles Turner, James Watson

Jacob Voorhees appointed a trustee of Charlotte Female Academy in place of Doctor James M Brewer resigned.

The Parishoners of this County allowed for present year
Charles Thompson for two poor children　　　　　　　$50
Robert Kelton　　　　　　　　　　　　　　　　　　　　25
William Houston for keeping his son　　　　　　　　　40
Sally Miller to be drawn by Jehu Miller　　　　　　　30
Silas (Nors) Tompkins for keeping his son　　　　　　35
John Waters to be drawn by Alex^r Dickson (removed)　20
James Young for keeping Nancy Groce　　　　　　　　　60
Levi Lindsey --

JANUARY 1828

Orrin D Hogins guardian of Christopher C Hudson returns his account for 1827.
Settlement with James Tidwell adm^r of Levi Tidwell dec^d returned into Court.
James Tidwell adm^r of Levi Tidwell dec^d makes return of sale of a tract of land property of deceased.
Huel Parrish guardian of Stephenson Archer makes return of the account of his guardianship.
John K Tidwell produced scalp of one wolf over age 4 months killed in Dickson County
p.-- John King to oversee road in place of Samuel Brown.
William Caffery to oversee road in place of Joseph G Davis.

William Flemming, Dempsey May, Minor Marsh, Drury Taylor Sr, and Michael Light to mark out a road up Hurricane Creek from the county line to the old line of Dickson.
Richard Batson to oversee road in place of John Smith.
Hudson Dudley, Wm White, and John Pendergrass to make final settlement with James Tidwell adm^r of Levi Tidwell dec^d.
Ordered tax for use of this county be same as last year.
Walker Thomas to oversee road in place of John B Cox.

Joseph Kimble, Daniel Billups, & Wm Fentress to settle with Huel Parrish adm^r of Wyatt Parrish dec^d; to divide personal estate of dec^d; interest that has accrued on money in hands of s^d adm^r to be paid to Elinor Parrish widdow of s^d dec^d as compensation for her expence of raising her children.
p.-- Daniel Nall to oversee road in place of Kendrick Myatt.

Jane Petty formerly wife of Burgess Harris dec^d allowed $40/year from last order, for keeping her two sons minor orphans of sd B Harris decd; she draws on Stirling Brewer for same.
John Adams to adm^r estate of Edward Murfree dec^d.
George Sullivant & William R Light appointed constables.
Minor Bibb to adm^r estate of Daniel Harris dec^d.

Order orphans bound: Adum Harris 12 years old to John R Weldon; Mark Harris 16 yrs old to Minor Bibb to learn Farming; Everitt Harris 13 years old to learn mill right trade; John Harris 7 years old to Archibald Pullin to be a farmer; John Austin 14 years old to Levi H Reeder to be a farmer; William Malugin 15 years old to George Gallion to be a potter.

The Will of William Gilbert decd proven by Henry R Leggett & Richard Cooke. Nicy Gilbert and Mabel Gilbert ext^x and ext^r, and one ext^r declining, gave bond and security.

p.-- Deed Garrett Hall to Squire Richardson 50 acres ackd.
Deed Joseph Spicer to Squire Richardson 50 acres ackd.
Deed Mary Dickson to Joseph Kimble 86 acres proven by Nathan

JANUARY 1828

Ragan and Callum Rogers
Deed Allin Anderson to Joseph Kimble 50 acres proven by Ja^s Dannel and Woodson Dannel.
Deed David McAdoo Sheriff to John McCormac 100 acres ackd
Deed Joel Massey to Ja^s Armour 68 acres proven by Jo^s Neel.
Deed John Wright to Mickins Carr 50 acres ackd.
Deed William Hightower Sheriff to Alfred B Norris 150 acres proven by James Dannel and Alexander Dickson.
p.-- Deed James Dannel to Mary Dickson 50 acres ackd.
Bill/Sale Nehemiah Scott to John Smith, for Negroes, ackd.
Deed Mary Dickson to Woodson Daniel 50 acres proven by Nathan Dillehay and Callum Rogers

Jurors to next County Court: Richard Jackson, Daniel Moore, Thomas Smith, Thomas Brown, Jeremiah Thompson, Larry Burns, Peter Metheny, James Ferrell S^r, Thos McClelland, Wm Turner, Peter Jackson, Thos Graves, Benjn Sanders, Wm King, Nicholas Dudley, David Frazier, Saml Mitchel, Jo^s Payne, Ge^o Oliver, Isaac Hill, Woodson Dannel, Nehemiah Scott, Joseph Williams, Raiford Crumpler, Matthew Crumpler, Jno Brewer, Moses White, John M Williams, James M Ross, Archibald Cox

Ordered by the Court that the following persons to take list of taxable property and poles for present year:
Capt Tatoms Comp^y, Samuel Turner Esqr; Capt Tidwells Comp^y, Wm White Esqr; Capt Carrolls, John Grymes; Capt Browns, Wm Shelby; Capt Merritts, H W Turner; Capt McClellands, James Nesbitt; Capt Tedfords, Kendrick Myatt; Capt Hunnels, Arch^d Pullen; Capt Reynolds, Huel Parrish; Capt Bullian, Thomas Murrell; Capt Hightowers, George Hightower.
Court adjourned until tomorrow Morning 9 oClock
           J W Napier, Molton Dickson, Joseph Kimbell

Tuesday January 8th 1828.   Present the worshipful
John W Napier, Molton Dickson, Joseph Kimble, Esquires

Sheriff made return of Venire Facias: Thomas May, John May, Saml Brown, Jno McCormack, Allen Bowen, George Davidson, Ja^s Medlock, Daniel Leach, Nathan Tubb, W^m S Coleman, Ge^o Tilly, William Simpson, Eli Southerland, Thomas B McClure, Sandford Edwards, Gideon Cunningham, Abija P Massey, Thomas Gentry, Littleton Story, Gibson Mills, David Bibb, Dorrel Y Harris, Willie Davis, Washington Hunter, James W Christian, Jo^s Howard, of which were chosen a grand inquest: John May foreman, Eli Southerland, Allen Bowen, Nathan Tubb, Washington Hunter, Daniel Leach, Jno McCormack, Ge^o Tilly, Thos May, Joseph Howard, Ge^o Davidson, Samuel Brown, William S Coleman. James Williams sworn to attend them.

JANUARY 1828

p.-- Francis V Smitton vs Ambrose H Burton. Writ of Enquiry. By att^{ys}. Jury Willie Davis, Sandford Edwards, Thos Gentry, David Bibb, Ja^s Medlock, Abijah P Massey, Wm Simpson, Joseph Larkins, John T Walker, Ezra McAdoo, Wm Grymes, John McAdoo who say plaintiff sustained damages 1¢, also costs

p.-- James Webb, guardian, vs John Pendergrass. Debt. By attorneys. Jury above find for defendant.
James H Davie vs Wm Grymes. By attys. Jury above except William Harper for John Mcadoo. Find for defendant.
James McClure vs Burwell Bayless. Debt. Pl^{tr} by att^y orders suit dismissed
Hiram Dunigin vs George Cox. The Plaintiff, by his attorney, orders his suit dismissed

p.-- Deed Edward Lucas to Robert Duke 159½ acres lying in Tipton County, TN, proven by Stirling Brewer & John Bernard.
Thomas W Shearon appointed guardian to George W West, minor orphan in place of Stirling Brewer former guardian.
Susannah Reynolds adm^x of John Reynolds dec^d makes return of amount of sales of s^d estate.
Joseph Kimble guardian of heirs of James Goodrich dec^d makes return of his guardianship.
Ordered Samuel Petty to oversee the road from County line to Hurricane fork of Piney at Wm Hogins with hands from County line to Turkey Creek as far as Leonard Pinegers and up Piney as far as Devaneys Branch.
Benj^a B Dunigan to oversee road from Piney to pole bridge on Charlotte Rd, bounds-- up east side of Main Piney to include hands living in Bruce Hollow and up other Piney on east side to include settlement on John Dunigans Spring branch.
Samuel King to oversee road in place of Archibald Cox.
Additional settlement made with Alex^r Dickson ext^r of James Goodrich decd.
Account of doubtful debts due estate of James Goodrich dec^d returned by Alex^r Dickson ex^r.
p.-- Court adjourned until tomorrow morning 9 oClock
Molton Dickson, J W Napier, D H Williams

Wednesday January 9th 1828.   Present the worshipful Molton Dickson, J W Napier, D H Williams, Esq^{rs}, Justices

Anderson England records his stock mark

State vs James Gunn. A&B. Jury Willie Davis, Sandford Edwards, Thomas Gentry, David Bibb, Ja^s Medlock, Abijah P Massey, Wm Simpson, John H Henderson, Danl W Martin, Jeremiah G Martin, Reese Bowen, Jeremiah Nesbitt, who find def^t guilty; fined $1; pay cost of prosecution. James Tedford assumed to-

JANUARY 1828

gether with defendant the payment of fine & cost.

p.-- State vs William D Reynolds. A&B. Def^t pleads guilty; fined $25 and cost; Alexander Dickson and Wm Adams and defendant assume to pay cost and fine.

State vs Benjamin Robertson. A&B. Def^t pleads guilty; fined 6¼¢ besides cost of prosecution.
State vs Hiram Dunigan. A&B. Nol Pros entered. Def^t, Samuel Dunigan and James Tedford assume to pay cost.

p.-- State vs Jeremiah Nesbitt. Peace Warrant. Sally Smith, prosecutor. Jeremiah Nesibtt's bond $500; John Adams & Henry H Marable $250 each.

Robert H McCollom to adm^r estate of Beal Goodwin dec^d.

Isaac Settler vs Holliway N Merritt and Richard Batson. Pl^{tf} by attorney moves to dismiss the petition for Certiorari and Supercedias; petition dismissed, & pl^{tf} to recover of def^{ts}. Court adjourned until tomorrow morning 9 oClock
        D H Williams, J W Napier, Molton Dickson

Thursday Jany 10th 1828.   Present the worshipfull D H Williams, John W Napier, Molton Dickson, Esq^{rs}, Justices

Mary Harrison vs Richard C Napier. Debt. Pl^{tf} by att^y orders suit dismissed. Cave Johnson assumes to pay all cost.

Montgomery Bell vs Christopher Robertson. Debt. By attorneys. Jury Willie Davis, Sandford Edwards, Thomas Gentry, David Bibb, James Medlock, Abija P Massey, Wm Simpson, Wm W Baldthrop, Jno T Walker, Abner Hudgins, Joseph Durard, James Bell, who find for pl^{tf} debt $78, damage $39.78. Also cost.

Solicitor Genl called for the receipts of the Clerk of Court which was produced to the Court

p.-- Montgomery Bell vs Christopher Robertson. Debt. By attorneys. Jury above find for plaintiff $2.000 debt, & damage $123.33 1/3. Also costs in this behalf expended.

p.-- Richard D Sansom vs Claibon Howse & Jno W Napier. Debt. Molton Dickson, Jno Pendergrass, Saml Turner, Justices. Pl^{tf} by att^y. Defendants came not. Plaintiff to recover his debt and interest, $318.75, besides cost.

State vs John Adams. Trespass. D H Williams, prosecutor. Jno Pendergrass, Molton Dickson, John Grymes Justices. Jury Wil-

JANUARY 1828

lie Davis, Sandford Edwards, Thos Gentry, David Bibb, James Medlock, Abijah P Massey, William Simpson, Jnº T Walker, Abner Hudgins, Jos Durard, Jas Bell, Harbert B Hinson who find deft is guilty. Deft fined $35 & cost, and be in custody of sheriff until fine and cost is secured.

p.-- Richard Batson vs John McClelland. Execution recited. Fi Fa issued 23 Octr 1827 by Wm C Sansom J P agt deft favour Richard Batson on judgt by sd Sansom 10 Octr 1827 for $10.35 debt and all cost. Robert Livingston Depy Shff levied on 59¼ acres Sulpher fk of Jones Cr 23 Octr 1827. Order/sale issued

Richard C Napier admited to build a mill on Turnbull on site near east boundary of tract of 2560 acres which he purchased from John J and Thomas Blount

Jacob Voorhies app'd by Legislature of 1827 Entry Taker for this County in place of Stirling Brewer

Sheriff & Collector is allowed for insolvents for 1826: Wm T Reynolds 100, Jesse Sinks 87½, Elisha Neely 37½, Barney Powers 37½, Nichs Baker 87½, Ephriam Garret 37½, Absolam Swift 37½, Jesse Norris 37½, Jas Thorn 37½, Abraham Robertson 37½, Michael Gafford 37½, Thos Anderson 37½, Danl Wheatons heirs $4.15, Samuel Meredith 62½, Richard Watson 37½, Jnº F Catton 37½, Phillip B Noland 79, Wm Baird 1.00, Rhody Abney 56¼, Levi H Reeder 37½, Benjn Meeker 37½, Francis Warden 37½, Jnº Shaddock 37½, James Thompson 37½, Peter Mills 37½, John Forsythe 37½, Jnº Wilson 37½, Saml Forsythe 37½, Francis Myrick 37½, William Carter 37½, Henry Sainsing 37½.
Court adjourned until tomorrow morning 9 oClock
        J Pendergrass, J W Napier, Molton Dickson, D H Williams

Friday January 11th 1828.   Present the worshipful John Pendergrass, John W Napier, Molton Dickson, D H Williams

Deed James Green and Sophronia his wife to Peter Northern 76 acres and 100 poles land in Sumner County ackd. Sophronia M Green examined apart ackd she executed deed voluntarily.

Bill of Sale Alexander Wilkins to James M Kirk, Negro girl Eliza, ackd.
Bill/Sale John Baker to Field Farrar, 2 Negroes, Juda & her child Eve, proven by Jacob Voorhees
Grand Jury presented bill of indictment against Edward Brock and Henry G Wells, a True Bill

p.-- State vs John Adams. Trespass. R N Williams prosecutor. Present Molton Dickson, Wm C Sansom, John Pendergrass. Jury:

JANUARY 1828

Eli Southerland, Allin Bowen, Nathan Tubb, Washington Hunter, Dan¹ Leach, Jnº McCormack, Geº Tilly, Joˢ Howard, George Davidson, Sam¹ Brown, William S Coleman, Jaˢ Price, who find defendant is guilty. Fined $35 and pay the costs.

State vs Jeremiah Nesbitt. A&B. Sally Smith prosecutor. Jury Willie Davis, Sandford Edwards, Thoˢ Gentry, David Bibb, Jaˢ Medlock, Abijah P Massey, Nehemiah Scott, Andrew Hamilton, Harbert B Hinson, John Larkins, Wilkins Tatom, Wᵐ D Reynolds who say defendant is guilty. Fined $35 & pay costs.

p.-- Montgomery Bell vs Christopher Robertson. By attorneys. Jury: Eli Southerland, Allin Bowen, Nathan Tubb, Washington Hunter, Dan¹ Leach, John McCormack, Geº Tilly, Jnº May, Thoˢ May, Joseph Howard, George Davidson, Sam¹ Brown who find for plaintiff, damage $1781.66¾. Also costs.

David Irwin, guardian to Napolian West a minor orphan, makes return of his account as guardian
Thomas Smith to oversee road in place of James Wilson
Court adjourned until tomorrow morning 9 oClock
     Molton Dickson, J W Napier, D H Williams

Saturday January 12ᵗʰ 1828. Present the worshipful John W Napier, Molton Dickson, D H Williams, Esquires, Justices

Matthew Gilmore fined $1 for contempt of Court on yesterday.

Christopher Robertson vs Montgomery Bell. Plaintiff by attʸ orders his suit dismissed.
John Mcadoo & C Robertson vs Montgomery Bell. Plaintiffs by attorney dismissed suit

p.-- John W Lancaster agᵗ Augustine Thomas, admʳ of Thomas A Young decᵈ. Debt. By attᵛˢ. Jury Eli Sutherland, Allen Boen, Mathew Tubb, Washington Hunter, Dan¹ Leach, John McCormack, Geº Tilly, Jnº May, Thoˢ May, Joˢ Howard, Geº Davidson, Sam¹ Brown, who say defᵗ hath not fully admʳᵈ estate of Thomas A Young that has come to his hands, and find for plᵗᶠ his debt $160, damage $4.60; & costs. Plᵗᶠ files bill of exceptions.

p.-- John Adams, guardian of Willis A Price, Joshua Price, & Thoˢ Price vs Patrick McDearman & Sally McDearman his wife. Decree on Petition for distribution. Sally McDearman, former guardian of sᵈ minor children, had received in 1825 $174.11¼ for sᵈ children; $67 allowed defᵗˢ for board & other expences of sᵈ children, adjudged by Court that petitioner recover of defᵗˢ $119.95¼, the balance of sᵈ sum and interest together with cost of this petition.

APRIL 1828

David Pain adm.^r of Robert West dec.^d vs George J Goodrich and Clabon Harris. Demurer. By att.^ys. Demurer sustained; pltf to recover of deft his debt, $626, and $34 interest. And costs. Defendants pray appeal to Circuit Court; allowed.

p.-- Christopher Strong vs Lorenzo D Evins. By att.^ys. Jury Eli Southerland, Allin Bowen, Nathan Tubb, Washington Hunter, Danl Leach, Jno McCormack, Ge.^o Tilly, Jno May, Thos May, Jo.^s Howard, Ge.^o Davidson, Saml Brown who find for plaintiff damages $100. Also costs.

Steel & Collier vs Miles Ashley. Pl.^tf by att.^y; def.^t made default. Pl.^tf to recover. Jury next term to determine damages.

Robert P Currin vs Thomas C Smith. By att.^ys. Jury above find for plaintiff $136.68, damage $10.93 3/4. And costs.

p.-- State vs John Adams. Defendant prays appeal to Circuit Court. Bond $500, Pleasant Crews his security. Allowed.
State vs John Adams. Def.^t prays appeal; allowed. Bond $500. Pleasant Crews, security.

Order John May allowed $5 for holding an inquest over Negro Cary property of David Smith.

p.-- Christopher Robertson vs M Bell. Motion. By attorneys. Motion by plaintiff; the non suit set aside.
John Mcadoo & C Robertson vs M Bell. Motion to set side non suit. By att.^y. Non suit set aside on payment of the cost

John G Blount vs Christopher Robertson. Pl.^tf by att.^y; def.^t made default. Pl.^tf to recover of def.^t $175 balance of debt, $5.25 interest. And costs in this behalf expended.
Court adjourned until Court in Course.
J W Napier, D H Williams, Molton Dickson

April 7.th 1828. Present the worshipful Daniel H Williams, John Johnson, John W Napier, Thos Murrell, John Pendergrass, Saml Turner, William McMurry, William White, Kendrick Myatt, Wm Hogins, Jo.^s Kimble, William Shelby, Esquires, Justices.

Joseph Kimble Esq appointed one of the quoram during present Term in place of Molton Dickson Esqr absent.
Jacob Leach to oversee road in place of Walker Thomas.
David Shropshire former Jailor of this county allowed $5 for keeping William Evins in Jail in a State case.

APRIL 1828

William Turner to oversee road in place of Richard Batson.
Larkin Tate to oversee road in place of John Wright.
Mumford Smith to collect State & County Tax for present year and enters bond & security satisfactory to the Court.
p.-- Wm Hogins, Henry Goodrich & Joseph Eason to settle with Wm Hedge former guardian of Elizabeth and Patsy Evins.
Field Farrar Clerk of Court allowed $12 for Blank books furnished by him for use of the Court.
Woodson Daniel allowed at rate of $20/year for keeping Levi Lindsay, a poor person of this County.
Plummer Burgess, Wm Lomax, & Wm Armour to work under Absolam Tribble, overseer of the road.
Jno Medlock allowed $20 for keeping three orphan children of Daniel Harris dec^d from Jany Term 1828 to Apr Term 1828, to be drawn from Minor Bibb, adm^r of estate of s^d Harris dec^d.
Minor Bibb to keep three of minor children of Daniel Harris, dec^d until next Term of this Court
Huel Parrish & Howard W Turner Esq^{rs} to take privie exam^n of Jane Estes as to execution of a deed for land sold to Joseph Kimble by Tharp R Estis
Account of sales of estate of Martin Loftis dec^d returned.
Berryman Hostley to oversee road from 9 mile tree to 11 mile tree on road down Ceder Creek with hands: Abraham S Hosley, David Hosley, David Robertson, James Daniel, James Gilmore.
William S Mosley oversee from 11 mile tree to Thomas Ellis's and ballance of hands attached to s^d to road work under him.
p.-- James Tatom, guardian of Harriott Evins to pay Josiah R Rogers the rent of land and the interest.
Epps Jackson to oversee road from Nashville to Reynoldsburgh by Richard C Napier's Furnace, from where it leaves the Road from Nashville to Charlotte to where it intersects road from Franklin to Charlotte, with the hands of Richard C Napier to keep up s^d road, and all the hands hired at his furnace.
Josiah R Rogers app^{td} guardian of Martha Evins in room of Wm Hedge.
W^m McMurry Esqr, Nehemiah Hardy, and Burgess Wall to settle with Sally Coleman adm^x of Richard Howard dec^d.
Order Stirling Brewer, former guardian of George W West, to pay Polly West the interest of money belonging to George for his support and tuition.
Robert H McCollom adm^r of Beal Goodwin dec^d says no property of the estate has come to his hands.
Minor Bibb adm^r of Daniel Harris dec^d returns account of the sales of s^d estate.
John Adams adm^r of Edward Murfree dec^d returns an account of sales of s^d estate.
Road from Jiles Jones to Baxters upper forge heretofore discontinued is reinstated; hands living within 1½ miles of s^d road who do not work on other roads are to be attached to s^d road, and James Matthews to oversee s^d road.

APRIL 1828

Graves Ragan to oversee road in place of Nelson McClelland.
p.-- Robert Brown to oversee road lately viewed out, & have hands from forks of Hurricane Creek down to Humphreys county line, and that he work from s^d line to Michael Lights.
Settlement with Wm Johnson, adm^r of R E Bomer dec^d, executor of Moses Easly dec^d, was received.
Ephriam S Roy to oversee road in place of Gibson Taylor.
Albert Speight to oversee road in place of Alsey Speight.
Joseph Highland to oversee road in place of Silas Harris.
William Johnson adm^r of Moses Easly dec^d allowed $45.50 for his services in managing s^d estate.
Deed Richard Fenner to John T Patterson 600 acres proven by Stokely Humphries and John H Patterson.
Deed Daniel Williams to Joseph Rogers 57 acres proven by the oaths of Richard N Williams and Daniel H Williams.
Deed John Larkins and Benjamin Clark to James Nisbitt 1 town lot in Charlotte #14 proven by Richard Waugh and A W Hicks.
p.-- Deed Thomas Nesbitt to Robert Livingston for lot #58 in Charlotte proven by Benjamin A Collier & Theodorick Collier.
Deed/Gift Isaac Stroud to Elizabeth Crow for 2 Negroe slaves proven by George Smith and Meckins Carr.
Thomas McMurry, Jeremiah C Martin, Thomas Holliway and James Williams appointed Constables for two years.
William Smith, age six years, bound to Matthew Gilmore until age 21 to learn art and mistery of a farmer.
William Dungan to administer the estate of Rolly Fann decd.
John Johnson to administer estate of Hudson Johnson decd.
The Will of Robert Harper decd proven by John McAdoo & Hugh McNeely.
p.--Jurors to September Circuit Court: Wm White, Jno Pendergrass, John Perry, Ge^o Davidson, Orrin D Hogins, Wm Carroll, George Clark, Jacob Grymes, Drury Taylor Sn^r, Robt Whitwell, Nathaniel Simpson, Meckins Carr, Eli Crow, Chas Burton, Silmon Edwards, W^m T Reynolds, Jno Adams, Jno May, Willis Norsworthy, James Green, John Tucker, Thomas Stroud.
Jurors to next County Court: Gideon Cunningham, Willis Johnson, Redic Myatt, Spencer T Hunt, Augustin Thompson, Henry Hickerson, Skelton Choate, Ja^s Armour, Mich^l Light, Nehemiah Scott, Ge^o Adams, Wm Norsworthy, Wm Wright, Soloman Marsh, Jno Toler Jr^r, Wm Morrison Jr^r, Thomas McGee, Anderson Gentry, Lemuel Russell, Danl Leach, Ja^s W Christian, Thos W Shearon, Saml West, Allin Bowen, William S Coleman, W^m E Slayden, Jno McCormack, David Bibb.

Mary Thomas has died intestate; she was executrix of will of Stephen Thomas dec^d. Order Wm Rye to adm^r with will annexed on estate of Stephen Thomas dec^d.
Court adjourned until tomorrow morning 9 oClock
                              D H Williams, J W Napier, Joseph Kimbell

APRIL 1828

Tuesday April 8th 1828.   Present the worshipful
D W Williams, J W Napier, Joseph Kimble, Esquires, Justices

Grand jury: Jas M Ross foreman, Moses T White, Saml Mitchel, Matthew Crumpler, Raiford Crumpler, George Oliver, John P Williams, Wm Turner, Woodson Daniel, Wm King, Benjn Sanders, Thomas Brown, Daniel Moore. Robert T Hightower, constable.

Edward McCormack vs Miles Ashley. Execution recited. Fi fa issued 5 April 1828 by James Nisbitt Esq agt Miles Ashley in favour Edwd McCormack for $45 debt and all cost. Robert Livingston, a deputy Sheriff, levied on 50 acres on Jones Creek 5 April 1828. Order of sale issued.

William Kirk infant under age of 21 vs James Nesbett, James H Davie & Jesse L Kirk. Debt. Richard Batson guardian of Wm Kirk admited to prosecute this suit in behalf of his ward.

Susannah Hall vs Penelope Lewis. The cause is refered to the arbitrament of George Lewis and Wm Shelton.

p.-- Satisfactory evidence was adduced in Court proving that Neetly Gunn wife of James Gunn, Sally Gunn wife of Jno Gunn, Susanna Sweany, Alexander W Sweany, Maria Sweany, and Fanny Sweany are the children and heirs at Law to Bernard W Sweany late a soldier in the Seventh Regiment of Infantry.

Copy of a decree in Chancery wherein John Brewer is pltf and George Teal & Edward Teal are defts was produced, it being a decree vesting in sd Brewer the title of 640 acres. Ordered to be certified for registration.

John Rook admr of Rowland Vick decd vs Montgomery Bell. Pltf made default; deft to recover of pltf the cost expended.

Montgomery Bell vs Wm McAdoo. By attys. Jury Peter Jackson, Thos Graves, Richd Jackson, Archd Cox, Jos Payne, Nichs Dudley, David Frazier, James Ferrell, Jno Toler Jr, Benjn Gray, Willis Johnson, Moreau Rose who find for deft. Pltf prays an appeal to Circuit Court; allowed.

p.-- John McAdoo & Christopher Robertson vs Montgomery Bell. By attys. Jury above find for deft. Deft to recover of pltf.

Luke Munsel, acting executor of Achilles Sneed decd, Lucy P Todd extx of Thomas Todd decd, the representatives of Achilles Sneed & Co vs Montgomery Bell. By attys. Jury above find for deft. Deft to recover of pltf his costs expended. Pltfs pray appeal to Circuit Court; allowed.

APRIL 1828

p.-- George F Napier vs Henry G Wells and Chauncy Devanport. By att^{ys}. Jury above find for defendants. Def^{ts} to recover of pl^{tf}. Plaintiff prays appeal to Circuit Court; allowed.

Charles C Thompson vs James Gunn. Plaintiff by att^y orders his suit dismissed. Def^t assumes all costs except att^y fee. Court adjourned until Tomorrow Morning 9 oClock
J W Napier, Joseph Kimbell, J Pendergrass

p.--Wednesday April 9th 1828. Present the worshipful John W Napier, Joseph Kimble, John Pendergrass, Esquires, Justices

State vs Joseph Handlin. Garnishment. Isaac H Lanier, of the firm of Anthony W Vanleer & Co acknowledged that s^d firm was indebted to Joseph Handlin $24.79 3/4. State to recover of Anthony W Vanleer, Isaac H Lanier, and Wallace Dixon s^d sum.

State vs Henry G Wells. A&B. Nol prosequi entered. Henry G Wells and Daniel Billups assume to pay cost.

Jesse A Brunson vs Parry W Humphreys. Debt. By att^{ys}. Jury Peter Jackson, Thos Graves, Richd Jackson, Arch^d Cox, Joseph Payne, Nich^s Dudley, David Frazier, Ja^s Ferrell, Peter Methena. William B Haddin, Ge^o W Caffery, David McAdoo who find for plaintiff $424.97½ debt, damage $28.61. And cost.

p.-- William Nall vs Empson Bishop. Appeal. By att^{ys}. Jury above find for defendant; new trial is granted in this case.

Green P Rice vs Horatio Bell. Pl^{tf} by att^y orders his suit dismissed. William K Turner assumes to pay cost.

John H Stone vs Richard Murrell. Debt. Jury above find for pl^{tf} $100 debt, damage $30. And cost. Def^t prays appeal to Circuit Court in nature of writ of Error; allowed.

p.-- John Nichol vs Christopher Robertson. Debt. By att^{ys}. Jury above find for pl^{tf} $394.93 debt, damage $21.89. & cost

Edward Taylor vs John Adams. Cov. Pl^{tf} by att^y; def^t came not. Pl^{tf} to recover of def^t, damages to be determined by a jury at next Term of this Court.

Joshua Brockman & L Lindsey, adm^{rs} of Joseph [smeared] dec^d, vs Elias W Napier. Cov. By att^{ys}. Jury above find for pl^{tf} damage $96.87½. And cost.

p.-- Elijah Lowery vs Alexander Dickson Ext^r & Dorothy Good-

APRIL 1828

rich ext^x of James Goodrich dec^d. Debt. By att^{ys}. Jury above find for plaintiff debt $37.08; damage $19.82. And costs.

William W Baldthrop vs Jeremiah Nesbitt. Pl^{tf} in proper person orders suit dismissed. Def^t recovers of pl^{tf} his costs.

p.-- Deed Jacob Voorhees to Daniel Toler 35 acres ackd.

Elias W Napier vs Montgomery Bell. The Pl^{tf} orders his suit be dismissed. Def^t to recover of pl^{tf} his costs expended.

Henry G Wells for Joseph Anderson vs Richard D Sansom. Cov. Pl^{tf} by att^y orders suit dismissed. William C Sansom assumes to pay all cost.

Elias W Napier vs Hansil Tucker. Pl^{tf} orders his suit to be dismissed. Defendant to recover of pl^{tf} the costs expended.

James West admr of George West decd vs Claiborne Harris. The Plaintiff moves to amend his declaration; permitted. Name of Stephen Harris stuck out. Trial tomorrow.

John McSwain vs James C Price. Pl^{tf} by att^y orders suit dismissed and assumes all cost.

p.-- John W Napier vs Nicholas Hail. Pl^{tf} by att^y; def^t came not. Damages to be determined by jury.
Court adjourned until tomorrow morning nine oClock.
      Joseph Kimbell, H W Turner, Joseph Morris

Thursday April 10th 1828. Present the worshipful Joseph Kimble, Howard W Turner, Joseph Morris, Esquires, Justices.

John T Chiles to oversee road in place of Labon Holt.
John Brewer to oversee road in place of Robert Collier.

Obligation from Nathan Nesbitt to Samuel Bowker for conveyance of town lott in Charlotte was produced. Handwriting and death of Nathan Nesbitt proven by Richard Waugh and Benjamin A Collier who also proved handwriting of Samuel M Handy, the only subscribing witness thereto, & also proved s^d Handy is without the limits of the United States.

p.-- Susannah Reynolds ext^x of John Reynolds dec^d vs Francis V Smitto, William T Reynolds, & Mark Reynolds. Will contested. By att^{ys}. Jury Ja^s M Ross, Moses T White, Saml Mitchel, Matthew Crumpler, Raiford Crumpler, Jno P Williams, Wm Turner, Woodson Daniel, Wm King, Benjn Sanders, Thos Brown, Danl Moore who find the will to be the last will and testament of

JULY 1828

s^d Jno Reynolds S^r dec^d; will to be recorded & Susannah ext^x as af^{sd} to recover of Mark Reynolds & Francis V Smitto & W^m T Reynolds the cost by her about her suit expended.
Susannah Reynolds ext^x of will of John Reynolds dec^d entered bond and security and qualified.

p.-- Steel & Collier vs Miles Ashley. Writ/Error on attch^t. Pl^{tf} by att^y. Jury Ja^s M Ross, Moses T White, Saml Mitchel, Matthew Crumpler, Raiford Crumpler, Jno P Williams, Wm Turner, Woodson Daniel, Wm King, Benjn Sanders, Thos Brown, Danl Moore who find plaintiffs damage $50.50. And cost.

Mary A Napier, wife of George F Napier, being examined apart from her husband ack^d deed executed by Ge^o F Napier and his wife Mary A, Martha W Wills & Ann G Wills to Guildford Mills for an undivided interest in 330 acres in Montgomery County was by her executed freely and without any constraint.

James West admr George West decd vs Clabon Harris. Pl^{tf} by att^y; defendant came not. Pl^{tf} to recover of def^t $142.12½ debt and damages besides his cost expended.

p.-- James Williams and Pleasant Crews appointed constables to wait on the Court at their next Term.
Court adjourned until Court in Course.
                    D H Williams, J W Napier, Joseph Kimbell

p.-- Monday July 7th 1828.   Present the worshipfull Molton Dickson, Jno Pendergrass, Wm Hogins, Jno W Napier, Ge^o Hightower, Wm White, John Johnson, Joseph Kimbell, Thos Murrell, D H Williams, William C Sansom, R C Napier, Archibald Pullin, Huel Parrish, Esquires, Justices.

Lindley Box produced scalps of 7 wolves under age 4 months & one over age 4 months, killed within Dickson County. Silas Harris produced scalp of one wolf over 4 months, killed &c.
Mary West allowed $40 for keeping her son, George W West, up to last April Term, draw on Thos W Shearon his gd^n for same.
Henry Goodrich, Jo^s Eason, Wm Hogins to settle with William Hedge former guardian of John Evins and make return thereof.
Thomas Murrell allowed $5 for keeping Richd Harris minor orphan of Danl Harris dec^d until next Court, to be paid out of of the estate of s^d Daniel Harris dec^d.
p.-- Lindley Box, Joel Arrington, Wm Shearon, Gabriel Petty, & Wm Gray S^r to view and turn road from Pine River down dry fork of Garners Cr, to intersect s^d road at Lindley Boxes, &

JULY 1828

s^d Box to open s^d road with hands: Joel Arrinton, Thos Hart, Samuel J Austin, Calvin H Tharp, Eleanor Flannery, Jno Flannery, Josiah R Rogers, Wm Hedge, Joshua Pool, James Wadkins, Richard Wadkins.

Willie B Johnson app^{td} Solicitor pro tem for this Term.

Molton Dickson, Ge^o Hightower, Esq^{rs} & Jacob Leach to settle with Wm Rye adm^r with will annexed of Stephen Thomas dec^d.

Robt T Hightower & Pleasant Crews apptd Constables.

Orrin Nall appointed guardian to William Overton, minor orphan; bond $600, with Joel Marsh and John Pendergrass.

Josiah R Rogers appointed guardian to John Evins, minor orphan; bond $100, with George Evins and Stephen Tatom.

Minor Bibb allowed $5.37½ for furnishing Sarah and Richard, orphans of Daniel Harris decd, with clothes.

Settlement with Huel Parrish, adm^r of Wyatt Parrish dec^d returned into Court and ordered to be recorded.

Account of sales estate of Stephen Thomas dec^d, was returned into Court and ordered to be recorded.

Wm Hogins, Thos Murrell, Esq^{rs}, and Thos Holliway to settle with Joel Marsh former guardian of Wm Overton, minor orphan.

p.-- Huel Parrish & Howard W Turner Esq^{rs} to take the privy examination of Jane Estes as to deed for land sold to Joseph Kimble by Tharp R Estes.

Account of sales of estate of Raleigh Fann dec^d returned.

Woodson Dannel, Nathan Dellihay, & Isaac Hill to settle with Powel Sinks adm^r of Powel Sinks dec^d.

Settlement with James West adm^r George West dec^d received.

George Smith, Richd Batson, & Molton Dickson Esq^{rs} to settle with George Hightower adm^r of Benjamin Crews dec^d.

Ja^s T Hadden attached to road from Charlotte to Giles Jones, and he to oversee s^d road in place of Robert Collier.

Settlement with William Hodge late guardian of Betsy & Polly Evins minor orphans of Lewis Evins dec^d ordered recorded.

Orrin D Hogins, Ja^s Tatom, Ge^o Brazeal to turn road from Ja^s Tatoms field to the Nine mile tree towards Charlotte; Orrin D Hogins to oversee thereof with hands: Stephen Tatom, Ja^s M Sizemore, Absolam Baker J^r, Jno Baker, Richard Evins, George Evins, Armstrong Baker, Jno A Baker, Washington England, Absolam Baker S^r, Henderson Dunigan, Stanford Dunigan, George Brazeal, James Hartly, James Eason.

James Carter app^{td} to oversee Franklin road from Minor Bibbs to Williamson County line.

Sidney Whitehead to oversee road in place of Peter Self.

p.-- Armstrong Hickerson to oversee road in place of William Simpson.

Jurors to Octr Term: Arch^d West, W^m T Perry, Samuel Dunigan, Wm Shearon, John Flannery, Josiah R Rogers, John W Fentress, Isiah Tidwell, Saml Brown, H B H Williams, Wm Hand, Benjamin Williams, Thos Armstrong, Felix Gilbert, Young Jolly, Labon

JULY 1828

Brown, Dempsey May, Ja^s Morgan, Zacheus Drummond, Wm Turner, Jno McAdoo, Hudson Shropshire, Raif^d Crumpler, Jesse F Thomas, Alexander H Coppage, Thomas W Shearon, Abiram Coldwell, James M Ross, John B Brown, William S Coleman.

Deed Riley Cassel to William Shearon 50 acres proven by Chas Dunigan and George Evins.
Deed Thomas Holliway to Orrin Hogins 283 3/4 acres ackd.
Deed James Barr to Enos James 300 acres ackd.
Deed Jacob Harder, att^y/fact for heirs of William Slader, to Jeremiah Nesbitt 357 acres proven by Willis Norsworthy.
Deed/trust Christopher Robertson to Robert H Brown proven by Elias W Napier and B C Robertson.
Order^d all who failed to give in their list of Taxable property for this year to give in and pay Clerk/Court.
p.-- Deed Jesse Bartee to William B Bartee 100 acres ackd.
Deed Robert Dickson, J W Dickson, Hugh Dickson, Joseph Dickson, Adam Dickson, John Dickson, T R Estes to Joseph Kimbell 264 acres proven by William Morrison.
Deed Willis Cunningham to Isaac Grove 157 acres proven by Benedict Bacon.
Deed Orrin Nall to Leonard Pineger 83 acres ackd.

Justices present: Molton Dickson, John Pendergrass, Wm Hogins, Jno W Napier, Ge^o Hightower, Wm White, Jno Johnson, Jo^s Kimble, Thos Murrell, Danl H Williams, Rich^d C Napier, Arch^d Pullen, Huel Parrish; Dickson County is by law bound to pay costs/prosecution of case State vs John Law[Lain?] for Perjury, def^t having been discharged from s^d Indictment by Circuit Court; bill/costs certified by Sol.Genl [p.--] [list of costs to be paid by county Trustee, John C Collier, follows] ...Witnesses for State in s^d cause: Wm Adams $5, John Adams $6.50, John Gilbreath $21.77+, Elisha Turner $20.50.

John McAdoo, former Trustee, had in 1825 & 1826 accounted to County for State Tax on Stud horses which was not allowed by State Treasurer in settlement with Collector amounting to $37.50; order Clerk pay John McAdoo s^d sum.

Robt Williams to oversee Nashville road from Strongs hill to Co^l Napiers furnace road; hands north of furnace rd & Benjn D Packs corn road to county line.
p.-- Power/atty from Burwell Myatt & Polly his wife to John Bowden ack^d; Polly Myatt, his wife, examined apart ack^d she she executed s^d Power freely and without constraint.
Court adjourned until tomorrow Morning 9 oClock
                    J W Napier, D H Williams, Molton Dickson

Tuesday July 8th 1828.   Present the worshipful

JULY 1828

John W Napier, D H Williams, Molton Dickson, Esq^{rs}, Justices

John Hodges adm^r of Mary Ann Hopper dec^d allowed $30.22 for his services in settling s^d estate.
Order Huel Parrish adm^r of Wyatt Parrish dec^d to pay to Elinor Parrish, guardian of minor orphans of Wyatt Parrish dec^d all money in his hands belonging to said estate.
p.-- Elinor Parrish app^{td} guardian to Huel, Eliza, Jane, Jno G and Ezekel Parrish, minor orphans of Wyatt Parrish dec^d.
Spencer T Hunt app^{td} guardian to Christopher C Hudson, minor orphan.
Deed/assignment of claims from Samuel W Handy to Joseph Anderson proven by Robert Steele.
Articles of agreement between Josiah Davidson and William E Slayden ackd.
Deed William Hightower Sheriff to Montgomery Bell 1550 acres and lotts 30 and 50 in Charlotte proven by Washington Hunter and Robert T Hightower, subscribing witnesses.
Bill of Sale Stirling Brewer to James M Brewer, Negro slave Joe, ackd.
Deed/Trust Stirling Brewer to Ja^s M Brewer & Jno Brewer ack.

Grand Jury: Raiford Crumpler, Henry Hickerson, W^m S Coleman, Orrin D Hogins, David Bibb, Michael Light, Ja^s W Christian, James M Ross, Ja^s Armour, Saml West, Gid Cunningham, Jno McCormack, Danl Leach. Ja^s Williams, Constable, attends them.

p.-- Deed/trust Thomas C Smith to Matthew Watson and Simpson Shepherd ackd.
Settlement with John Hodges adm^r of Mary Ann Hopper dec^d returned into Court and ordered to be recorded.
Will of John R Cathey dec^d proven by John Forsythe.

Gould & Voorhees vs James Gunn. Execution recited. April 2^d 1828 issued execution by Ja^s Nesbitt Esqr J P favour Gould & Voorhees ag^t Ja^s Gunn for $45.12+ due 8 Jany 1828. Jeremiah Martin constable levied on 54 acres on Piney, adj Saml Bugg. Order of sale issued.

Matthew Gilmore vs Wm Hambrick, Jere^h Hambrick, Uriah Hambrick, Mark Reynolds. Motion of pl^{tf} by att^y. Pl^{tf} and Mark Reynolds became security of W^m, Jeremiah & Uriah Hambrick in State prosecution ag^t them wherein judg^t was rendered April 1827 Term for $30 & cost; 23 April 1828 ex^a issued ag^t def^{ts} & pl^{tf} in favour State for Judg^t and cost $32.80 with credit of $10; further, Matthew Gilmore had paid $21.71 of s^d execution. Therefore, considered by Court that Matthew recover of defendants $21.71 besides cost of this motion.

Shaderick Bell vs Christopher Robertson. By att^{ys}. Jury John

JULY 1828

Toler Junr, Shelton Choate, Redic Myatt, Soloman Marsh, Wm Norsworthy, Wm Wright, Augustin Thompson, Abraham Self, Ja^s Gunn, William Tatom, Burwell Jackson, John Bernard who find for plaintiff damage $453.12¢. And cost.

William Simpson vs Alias Findley. By att^ys. Jury Henry Hickerson, W^m S Coleman, Orrin D Hogins, Dav^d Bibb, Mich^l Light, James W Christian, Ja^s Armour, Saml West, Gideon Cunningham, John McCormack, Daniel Leach, Raiford Crumpler cannot agree. Raiford Crumpler withdrawn; jury discharged from rendering a verdict; cause to stand trial at next Term.

p.-- Justices present Molton Dickson, John Pendergrass, William Hogins, Jno W Napier, Ge^o Hightower, William White, Jno Johnson, Jo^s Kimbell, Thomas Murrell, Daniel H Williams, R C Napier, Arch^d Pullin, Huel Parrish: following persons, def^ts in State cases are insolvent and unable to pay cost they are taxed with; items to be paid by trustee of Dickson County:

State vs Jesse Tribble atty genl $5, clerks fee $3	8.00
State vs Elizabeth Shelton	8.00
State vs Jesse Alexander	11.00
State vs Jesse Alexander	9.00
State vs Ambrose H Burton	8.00
State vs Soloman Grayham	9.00
State vs John Edwards and James W McCammon a witness for the county	12.00
State vs John Edwards and James W McCammon a witness for the State	16.50
State vs John Goodrich	8.00
State vs John Goodrich	8.00
State vs John Goodrich	8.00
State vs William Allin	8.00
State vs William Caffery	8.00
State vs Robert F Rogers	11.00
State vs John Jones	8.00

Ordered by the s^d Court that Field Farrar be allowed $50 for his exofficio services for 1827 ending this Term.
p.-- Court adjourned until tomorrow 9 oClock
                    D H Williams, J W Napier, Molton Dickson

Wednesday July 9th 1828.   Present the worshipful
D H Williams, John W Napier, Molton Dickson, Esq^rs, Justices

A second inventory of estate of John Hall dec^d returned.
Deed Willis Cunningham to Isaac Grove 157 acres ackd.
Thomas Bullian to oversee road in place of John Tatom.

Saml C Hawkins & Co vs James Council & Aquilla Council. Execution recited. Fi fa issued 23 Jany 1828 by W^m C Sansom J P

JULY 1828

favour pl^{tf} for $13.25 debt with interest from 1 Jan^s 1827 & cost to satisfy judg^t before W^m C Sansom 27 Octr 1827. Robt Livingston dep^y sh^{ff} levied on 50 acres on Leatherwood property of James Council on 8 Feby 1828, with credit of 71¢ on book. Order of sale issued.

p.-- Samuel C Hawkins & Co vs Aquilla Council. Execution recited. 17 June 1828 ex^n by Ja^s Nesbitt J P for $24.34 debt & cost with interest from 1 Jany 1828 to satisfy judgment that Saml C Hawkins & Co recovered ag^t Aquilla Council before Ja^s Nesbitt 26 Ap^l 1828. Robt Livingston dep^y sh^{ff} levied on 36½ acres on Leatherwood, the property of Aquilla Council. Order of sale issued.

Samuel C Hawkins & Co vs Willis & Ja^s Council. Execution recited. Jany 23^d 1828 W^m C Sansom J P issued ex^n for $7.50 & interest from 1 Jany 1827 & cost, to satisfy judg^t that Saml C Hawkins & Co recovered ag^t Willis & Ja^s Council on 27 Octr 1827. Robert Livingston dep^y sheriff levied on 36½ acres on Leatherwood 8 February 1828. Order of sale issued.

p.-- Samuel C Hawkins & Co vs Willis & Aquilla Council. Ex^u recited. Jany 23^d 1828 ex^n issued by W^m C Sansom J P for $5 & interest from 4 Octr 1827 & cost to satisfy judg^t pl^{tf} recovered ag^t def^{ts}. Robert Livingston dep^y sh^{ff} levied on 36½ acres Leatherwood. Order of sale issued.

Thomas May vs Aquilla Council, John C Collier & Lemuel Read. Ex^u recited. Ex^n 28th Jany by W^m C Sansom J P for $5 & cost to satisfy judg^t Thos May recovered ag^t s^d Council & Read, 8 Septr 1827. Robt Livingston dep^y sh^{ff} levied on 36½ acres on Leatherwood. Order of sale issued.

Shearon Batson & Co vs Richard Waugh. Execution recited. Ex^u issued 9 July 1828 by Ja^s Nesbitt J P for $7.62½ & interest from 12 Jany last & cost to satisfy judg^t ag^t Richard Waugh. Jeremiah G Martin, constable, levied on a lott in Charlotte property of Richard Waugh including s^d Waugh's house. Order sale issued.

p.-- Hicks & Shearon vs Richard Waugh. Ex^u recited. July 9th 1825 exn issued by James Nesbitt J P for $32.44¼ & interest from 11 Jany last & cost to satisfy judgment Hicks & Shearon recovered ag^t Richard Waugh 5 July 1828. Jere^h G Martin constable, levied on lot in Charlotte property of Richard Waugh incl Waugh's house. Order of sale issued.

State vs John Crews. A&B. Nol Pros entered.
State vs Samuel W Handy. A&B. Nol Pros entered.
Tax collector to receive in payment of county taxes the jury

JULY 1828

tickets of 1827 & 1828 for taxes of 1828.

p.-- State vs James Hightower. A&B. Jury: John Toler, Skelton Choate, Redic Myatt, Soloman Marsh, Wm Norsworthy, Wm Wright, Wm Long, Matthew Crumpler, Abiram Coldwell, Ja^s Larkins, John R Smelly, W^m B Haddin who say def^t is not guilty.

State vs Edward Brock. A&B. Nol pros entered.

State vs Holliway N Merritt. Appearance bond $500; Jno Adams & William Adams $250 each.

p.-- State vs Robt Collier. Presentment Overseer. Jury above except Willoby Eatherage & Ransom Ellis for Matt^w Crumpler & Ja^s Larkins. Jury find defendant Not Guilty.

State vs Wm Simpson. Present. overseer. Def^t pleads guilty; fined 6¼¢ and cost.

Thomas Clark vs Elias W Napier. By attys. Jury Jno Toler Jr, Skelton Choate, Redic Myatt, Sol Marsh, Wm Wright, Wm Long, Matthew Crumpler, Abiram Coldwell, Ransom Ellis, Wm Turner, Jesse M Speight, Willoby Eatherage who are permitted to disperse until tomorrow morning.

p.-- Jno Johnson, Daniel H Williams, Thos Murrell, Justices, for benefit Terisa M Bedford vs Benjamin Clark. Deft confesses he owes pl^{tf} $568.40. Pl^{tfs} to recover, besides cost.

Henry A C Napier vs Joseph Edwards and James Trousdale. Pl^{tf} by attorney orders suit dismissed.

Jacob Voorhies vs Thos W Shearon. By att^{ys}. Jury Henry Hickerson, W^m S Coleman, Wm Simpson, David Bibb, Michael Light, James M Ross, Ja^s Armour, Saml West, Gideon Cunningham, John McCormack, Danl Leach, Raiford Crumpler who are permitted to disperse until tomorrow.
Court adjourned until tomorrow morning 9 oClock
       D H Williams, Molton Dickson, Wm White

Thursday July 10th 1828.   Present the worshipful D H Williams, Molton Dickson, William White, Esq^{rs}, Justices

Power/Atty from Henry S Palmer & Eliza Palmer, his wife, to Thomas Palmer ackd by Henry S Palmer. Eliza Palmer examined apart ackd she executed s^d Power voluntarily.

J[or I] Gray vs William Thomas and Benjamin W Thomas. Execution recited. Ex^n issued 1 Ap^l 1828 by John Pendergrass J P

JULY 1828

for $22.75 & interest from 24 Novr 1826, and cost to satisfy judg^t ag^t def^ts. George Sullivant constable levied 17 April 1828 on 87 acres on Jones Creek adjoining land of A Richardson, George Clark, and others. Order of sale issued.

p.-- Jacob Voorhees vs Thomas W Sharon. Again came jury af^sd find for defendant.

Thomas Clark vs Elias W Napier. Again came the jury af^sd who find for pl^tf his damage $22.39½. Also cost. Defendant prays appeal to Circuit Court; allowed.

Alexander Dickson ext^r & Dorothy Goodrich ext^x of Ja^s Goodrich dec^d vs W^m W Balthrop. Debt. By att^ys. Jury Jno Toler, Skelton Choate, Redic Myatt, Solomon Marsh, Wm Wright, William Long, Matt^w Crumpler, Wm Turner, Jesse M Speight, Wiloby Etherage, Ge^o Tilly, W^m B Hadden who cannot agree. John Toler withdrawn, jury discharged from rendering verdict; the cause to stand for trial next Term.

p.-- Susannah Hall vs Penelope Lewis. Award of arbitrators: suit to be dropped by defendant paying all cost.

Hynes Knowles & Woods vs Josiah Davison & William E Slayden. Debt. By att^ys. Jury above find for pl^tf $100 debt, damage $7. And cost. Def^ts pray appeal to Circuit Court; allowed.

Francis Merick vs Elias W Napier. Plaintiff orders his suit dismissed. Def^t to recover of pl^tf his costs.
Francis Merick vs Elias W Napier. Pl^tf orders his suit dismissed. Def^t to recover of pl^tf his costs.

Montgomery Bell vs Christopher Robertson. Garnishment served on W^m C Sansom. By att^ys. Answer of W^m C Sansom, that he is not indebted to C Robertson. W^m C Sansom is discharged from garnishment and recovers of Montg^y Bell his cost expended.

p.-- Benjamin Clark vs Clark Spencer. Motion by security ag^t principal. Pl^tf was security of def^t in bond as guardian of Tereasy M Bedford; judg^t this Term ag^t pl^tf on suit ag^t him on s^d gd^n bond, favor of Jno Johnson, Danl H Williams & Thos Murrel, Justices, benefit of Tereasy M Bedford for $568.40. On motion of pl^tf by att^y, considered by Court that pl^tf recover of def^t s^d sum & his cost about this motion expended.

Benjamin Clark vs William Spencer. Motion by security ag^t Co-Security. Def^t Co-security with pl^tf in gd^n bond by Clark Spencer as gd^n for Tereasy M Bedford; further a judgm^t this Term ag^t pl^tf on suit brought ag^t him in favor John Johnson, Danl H Williams & Thos Murrell for benefit of Tereasy M Bedford for $468.40; considered by Court that pl'f recover of def' as Co-security the sum $284.20, besides cost of motion.

Francis V Smittoe vs Horatio Humphrey and Holloway M Merit. Motion by security ag' principal. Pl'f & O S Merit security of def's in appeal bond to Circuit Court on judgm' ag' def's in favor of John Haynes for benefit Frances Carter; further, s'd judg' affirmed in Circuit C' ag' s'd def's, s'd plaintiff & Orsemus Merit as securities af'sd; execution had issued on s'd judg' ag' s'd def's, & s'd pl'f & O S Merit as securities afsd for $284.70 debt & cost; whereupon on motion of pl'f by atty considered by Court that pl'f recover of def's $124.35 besides the cost of this motion.

Will of Richard D Sansom dec'd proved by Thomas H Handy and Benjamin C Robertson; William C Sansom and Henry A C Napier, executors entered bond $5000, with John W Napier, security.

Montgomery Bell vs Christopher Robertson. Garnishment served on W'm C Sansom. W'm C Sansom is not indebted to s'd C Robertson; is discharged, & recovers of M Bell his cost expended.

William McMurry vs Mark Reynolds. Motion by Security against principal. Pl'f was security of def' in appeal to Circuit C'; judg' ag' def' together with pl'f & Henry W Hinson coSecurity with pl'f in Circuit C'. Execution issued on s'd judg' for $340.39 debt & cost. W'm McMurry discharged $252.99 of s'd execution. Therefore pl'f William McMurry is to recover of the defendant Mark Reynolds $252.99 and the cost of this motion.

p.-- W'm McMurry vs Henry W Hinson. Def' coSecurity with pl'f in appeal bond to Circuit Court from Judg' ag' Mark Reynolds favour of Francis V Smitto. Judg' in Circuit Court ag' Mark Reynolds with McMurry & Hinson. Execution issued for $340.39 of which Pl'f discharged $252.99. Court considers that pl'f recover of defendant $126.49½ besides cost of this motion.
Court adjourned until tomorrow Morning 8 oClock
                      Sam'l Turner, Molton Dickson, J Pendergrass

Fryday July 11'th 1828.   Present the worshipful Sam'l Turner, Molton Dickson, J Pendergrass, Esq'rs, Justices

p.-- Madison King vs James H Davie, W'm Hightower. Motion ag' Constable and his securities for failing to pay over Money. Defendant collected, as constable, from Montgomery Bell for plaintiff $43.84. Plaintiff to recover of defendants s'd sum.

John W Napier vs Nicholas Hail and Daniel Ross. Writ of Enquiry. Present M Dickson, S Turner, J Pendergrass. Jury Sam'l

JULY 1828

West, Skelton Choate, Henry Hickerson, Raiford Crumpler, Jno McCormack, David Bibb, Michael Light, Ja^s W Christian, Ja^s M Ross, James Armour, Gideon Cunningham, Daniel Leach who find for plaintiff damage $330. Also costs.

p.-- Edward Taylor vs John Adams. Writ of Enquiry. Jury: Jno Toler, Redic Myatt, Soloman Marsh, Wm Norsworthy, Wm Wright, Augustin Thompson, Henry W Hinson, William B Hadden, John Clark, Abiram Coldwell, William Turner, Nelson McClelland who find for plaintiff damages $109. And cost.

Henry H Johnson vs Noble Morrison & Washington Curry. Debt. Jury: Skelton Choate, Henry Hickerson, David Bibb, Michael Light, Ja^s W Christian, Ja^s M Ross, Ja^s Armour, Samuel West, Gideon Cunningham, Jno McCormack, Danl Leach, Raiford Crumpler find for pl^{tf} $140 debt, damage $22.73 1/3. And costs.

Robert Barter vs Jesse Barter. By att^{ys}. Pl^{tf} dismissed his suit; defendant assumes to pay all cost.

p.-- William Nall vs Empson Bishop. Appeal. Jury above find defendant owes plaintiff $25.32 debt and damages. And costs.

Sally Smith vs Jeremiah Nesbitt. Trespass. Jury John Toler, Redic Myatt, Sol Marsh, Wm Wright, Augustin Thompson, Henry W Hinson, John Clark, Abiram Coldwell, Wm Turner, Nelson McClelland, Ja^s Cunningham, Willis Cunningham who find for the defendant. Defendant to recover of plaintiff his costs.

Augustin Thompson vs Elias W Napier. Pl^{tf} orders his suit be dismissed. Def^t pays half the cost; pl^{tf} pays other half.

p.-- Order John W Napier, Thomas Terrell, B A Collier settle with Augustin Thompson adm^r of Thomas A Young dec^d.

J Ogburn vs William W Balthrop. Debt. Jury Henry Hickerson, W^m S Coleman, David Bibb, Michael Light, James W Christian, James M Ross, Ja^s Armour, Saml West, Gideon Cunningham, John McCormack, Daniel Leach, Raiford Crumpler who find for pl^{tf} $100 debt, damage $3. And cost.

State vs Daniel H Williams. A&B. Def^t pleads guilty; fined 1¢ and cost in this behalf expended.
State vs Willis Norsworthy. A&B. Def^t pleads guilty; fined 1¢ and pay cost in this behalf expended.

Willis Norsworthy vs William C Sansom. Pl^{tf} orders his suit dismissed. Def^t assumes to pay all cost except att^y fee.
Court adjourned until tomorrow Morning 9 oClock.
                      J W Napier, D H Williams, Molton Dickson

WITNESS DOCKET

Saturday July 12¹ʰ 1828.   Present the worshipful
John W Napier, D H Williams, Molton Dickson, Esq^rs, Justices

James W Christian vs William C Sansom & Elias W Napier. Pl^tt orders his suit dismissed; def^ts pay all cost.

On petition of Washington Hunter & Sally Hunter adm^rs of Wm Speight dec^d, order they sell Negroes of estate for purpose of making equal distribution amongst heirs.
Washington Hunter app^td guardian to William Speight and John Speight minor orphans.

p.-- Will of Richard D Sansom dec^d produced; codical to will proven by A W Hicks and B N Carter witnesses. Barbary Sansom executrix apptd by codicil qualified; bond $5000.

Deed Edward B Roach & Thomas Jerrall to William C Sansom 935 acres in Haywood County, Tennessee, proven by oaths of Belfield N Carter and George F Napier.
Court adjurned until Court in Course.
                    J W Napier, Molton Dickson, D H Williams

End of the Minutes in this book.

Witness Docket for January 1824
Hosea C Miller vs John Halls Executors. Wm Morrison 1 day.
John Adams vs Abram Self. John P Chambers 2 days 90 miles.
State vs John Tatom. James Larkins 2 days. George Lewis 1 day. Henry Goodrich 2 days.
Mary Dickson vs Hugh Dickson & others. John Stewart 2 days.
State vs John Kee. David Owen 1 day; Joseph Parker 1 day.
Mark Drummond vs H N Merit. Matthias Kean 5 days in all. Horatio Humphries 3 days; W^m D Reynolds 5 days.
John Dunegan vs Wm Edwards. Henry Goodrich 3 days; John Miller 6 days; John Wim 1 day; William Hogan 2 days
Alvin Dunegan vs Wm Edwards. Elisha Gunn 3 days; Richd Tatom 2 days; Soloman Grayham 2 days; Saml Dunigan 4 days; Morgan Hood 2 days; Archibald Cox 3 days; Sandford Edwards 3 days; Reubin Edwards 3 days; Alfred Edwards 3 days; Thomas Holliway 3 days.
State vs John Marsh. William Hendric 1 day.
State vs Benedict Bacon. W^m M Thomas 1 day; John Mockbee 4 days; Anthony W Vanleer 4 days 38 miles; Wm Hand 4 days; Elias W Napier 3 days.

April 1824
Hosea C Miller vs John Halls ext^r. Wm Morrison 1 day; John H Marable 2 days, 40 miles.

WITNESS DOCKET

p.-- Mary Dickson vs James Dickson & others. John Stewart 1 day; John H Marable 2 days; Jn° Kernan 11 days 150 miles.

John Dunigan vs Wm Edwards. Jn° Tatom 10 days; Elisha Gunn 1 day this & 4 days last Term; Soloman Grayham 1 day, Wm Hogan 1 day; Jn° Weems 1 day; Morgan Hood 1 day this Term, 2 days at last; Henry Goodrich 1 day; Ja^s Tatom 1 day; Allen Barber 1 day; Jehu Miller 1 day.

F V Smitton vs Mark Reynolds. William McMurry 2 days; Nehemiah Hardy 2 days; Robert Haddin 2 days; Drury Adkins 5 days; Horatio Humphries 4 days; Andrew M Lewis 2 days; Stirling May 2 days

Sarah Brown vs Resden and Howard Mockbee. Molton Dickson 2 days; Mathew Gilmore 2 days; Thos McCrory 2 days; Thomas Smith 3 days

Samuel Thomas vs C Robertson. Willis L Dawson 3 days 35 mi; Wash^a Hunter 11 days; Wm Hunter 7 days; Jn° McAdoo 1 day

Henry A C Napier. Thos M Ross 4 days 200 miles 2 ferriages.

Jacob Raper vs M Bell. Benjamin D Pack 3 days 20 miles; John Johnson 3 days 90 miles; Edward McCormack 4 days 30 miles.

H N Merit vs Mark Drummond. Horatio Humphries 2 days; F V Smittoe 2 days

p.-- Henry Wert vs Susannah Hall & Jesse Hall Ex^rs. William Morrison 3 days; Horatio Humphries 4 days; John Reynolds Senr 3 days; Mathias Gilmore 2 days; F V Smittoe 4 days.

July Term 1824

Mary Dickson vs Hugh Dickson & others. Chauncey Devanport 6 days; Lucy Anderson 2 days; John Stewart 2 days; John McKernan 1 day 50 miles for Def^t; Lucy Anderson 14 days up to this Term.

Elias W Napier vs John Evins. Elizabeth Joslin 1 day; Benjn Clark 4 days; James W Evins 1 day.

State vs Hugh Dickson & others. Lucy Anderson 1 day; Polly Dickson 1 day.

M Bell vs Wm Mcadoo. W^m B Haddin 3 days.

D Christian vs Wm Ward. Howel Harris 2 days, 28 miles.

D Williams & A Coldwell vs John S Spencer. B Sturdevant 3 days.

October 1824

p.-- Elias W Napier vs John Evins. Ben^J Clark 5 days; John Hall 5 days; Eliz^h Joslin 1 day; Margrit Nesbitt 1 day.

R C Napier vs Alex^r Hamilton. E W Napier 4 days; Richard D Sansom 4 days this & Last, 64 miles; Francis Myrick 4 days

Henry W Hinson vs Eleanor Parrish. Thomas Williams 2 days; William Adams 1 day

Jesse Hall vs H N Merit. B Sturdevant 1 day; Andrew Lewis 2 days.

Goodrich's Extrs vs David Rushing. John Worden 2 days 40 mi; Robert Aronsby 2 days 52 miles; Elisha Turner 3 days 50

WITNESS DOCKET

miles; John Adams 2 days; William Adams 2 days.
James M Thomas vs John Plant. David Mills 3 days 50 miles.
Bell vs Wm Mcadoo. Wm B Haddin 1 day.

p.--   January Term 1825
Goodrich's Extrs vs D Rushing. Elisha Turner 1 day 50 miles;
  John Warden 2 days 42 miles; Robt Ormsby 2 days 52 miles;
  Wm Adams 2 days; Jno [illegible] 2 days; Daniel Billops 2
  days last & 2 this Term; R D Sansom 2 days 40 miles.
State vs Wm McNichol. Wm Adams 2 days; Jno Adams 2 days; W^m
  B Hadden 3 days.
R C Napier vs Alex^r Hamilton. R D Sansom 2 days.
James M Thomas vs John Plant. Eleanor Parrish 2 days; John
  May 2 days; Eliz^h May 2 days; David Mills 3 days 50 mi; W^m
  Adams 4 days; Chas Thompson 3 days; Ja^s Thompson 2 days.
State vs Jeremiah Bruce. Anderson England 2 days; Franklin F
  Bruce 2 days, Charles Terren 2 days.
p.-- Elias W Napier vs John Evins. Eliz^h Joslin 4 days; Jno
  Hall 3 days; John B Brown 5 days; W^m McNickol 5 days; Robt
  Watson 2 da 44 mi; Benjn Clark 3 da; Margaret Nesbitt 2 da
John Clark vs Wm Mcadoo. James Tubb 3 days; Ja^s Bell 3 days.

                        April Term 1825
E W Napier vs Jno Evins. Ja^s Larkins 1 day; Wm Hickerson 2
  days; Samuel Rogers 2 days 60 miles; John Hall 1 day
Elias Tubb vs Joel Massie. Silvester Adams 1 day 36 mi; Thos
  B McMurtrey 2 days 50 mi; Jno H Tubb 2 days 40 mi; William
  H Varnal 1 day 46 miles
R C Napier vs Alex^r Hamilton. Wm Wickham 2 days 38 mi; Rich^d
  D Sandsom 1 day.
Jesse Hall vs Holliway N Merritt. Jo^s Handlen 1 day, Horatio
  Humphries 2 days; Francis V Smitton 2 days Oct and 2 days
  this Term; James Malugian 1 day
Francis V Smitton vs Mark Reynolds. Wm Brasier 2 days; Alex^r
  Dickson 3 days for pl^t^{f}; W^m T Reynolds 2 days; Jno Nisbitt
  4 days; Stirling May 4 days.
State vs William Handlin. Francis Carter 2 days 32 miles;
  Horatio Humphries 1 day; Eleanor Parrish 2 days
M Bell vs Wm Mcadoo. W^m B Haddin 2 days; Ben^j Gray 4 days.
Susannah Hall vs Penelope Lewis. Horatio Humphries 2 days.
State vs James McCauly overseer. John Toler 3 days; James
  Malugian 3 days; Joseph Handlin 2 days.
State vs F V Smitton. Wm Hollinsworth 3 days; And^w M Lewis 3
  days; James Council 3 days.
State vs Ja^s McCauly. A&B. Wm Baker 2 da; Jo^s Handlin 2 da.
Wm Hollinsworth vs Francis V Smitton. James McCauly 3 days,
  24 miles; Lamuel Read 3 days.
John Clark vs Wm Mcadoo. James Bell 3 days; Ja^s Tubb 3 days.
F V Smitton vs Mark Reynolds. Drury Adkins 4 da; W^m McMurry
  4 days; Lamuel Read 4 days; Nathan Dillehay 4 day; Eleanor

WITNESS DOCKET

Parrish 4 days; Robert Maddin 4 days; Wm Blount 4 days; Wineford Richardson 4 days.

July Term 1825

R L Napier vs Alex^r Hamilton. E W Napier 6 days Jan^y & Ap^l; Wm Wickham 2 days 38 miles; Francis Myrick 6 days; Richard Sandsom 2 days; Spencer T Hunt 2 days 36 mi; Ja^s R Napier 7 days.

Thomas Holliway vs Anderson England. Josiah Rogers 2 days; Thomas Flannery 2 days; Jno Baker 3? days; Absolam Baker 2 days; John Wims 2 days; Isaac West 3 days.

Eli Napier vs Jno Evins. Ja^s Larkins 1 day; Jno Hall 2 days.

Henry W Hinson vs Eleanor Parrish. W^m W Baldthrop 1 day; Matt^w Gilmore 2 da; Thos Williams 4 da; Mark Reynolds 5 da

Jesse Hall vs H N Merritt. Ja^s Malugian 3 da; Jo^s Handlin 3 days; Horatio Humphries 3 days; Eleanor Parrish 3 da; Ge^o Lewis 3 days; Wm D Reynolds 3 days; Andrew M Lewis 9 days; Francis V Smitton 3 days; Mark Reynolds 2 days.

Francis V Smitton vs James McCauly. Eleanor Parrish 1 day.

John Clark vs Wm Mcadoo. Jno Mockbee 1 day; Ja^s Bell 3 days; James Tubb 3 days.

State vs Francis V Smitton. Wm T Reynolds 1 day.

Francis V Smitton vs Mark Reynolds. Eleanor Parrish 4? days.

Susannah Hall vs Penelope Lewis. Horatio Humphries 3 days.

M Bell vs William Mcadoo. Benjamin Gray 3 days 120 miles; W^m B Hadden 3 days.

John Read vs Thos Williamson. And^w Hamilton 1 day 120 miles.

Francis V Smitton vs Mark Reynolds. Wineford Richeson 4 day; John Nesbitt 3 days; Wm T Reynolds 3 days; Lamuel Read 2 days; Nathan Dillehay 4 days; Drury Adkins 4 days; William Blount 4 days; William McMurry 4 days

John Buckhannan vs John Larkins. Ja^s Larkins 4 days; Joseph Larkins 4 days; John Larkins Jr 4 days; James Larkins Jr 4 days; Robert Larkins 4 days.

Edward McCormack vs M Bell. Willis Jackson 4 days.

October Term 1825

John Clark vs Wm Mcadoo. Wm Hendricks 1 day 130 mi; Augustin Roberts 1 day; James Tubb 1 day.

Elias W Napier vs John Evins. Saml Rogers 1 day 40 m; 2 days 40 mi last Term; W^m McNickol 1 day this 3 days last Term; Jno Hall 1 day; James R Napier 1 day; Gabriel P Joslin 1 day; Elizabeth Joslin 1 day this, 2 July, 1 Ap^l Term; Jno B Brown 1 day this 1 day last; James Larkins 1 day; Benj Clark 1 day last 1 day this; John Sullivant 1 day this 1 day last; Stephen Eleazer 1 day; Robert Watson 2 days last 1 day this 20 miles.

M Bell vs Wm Mcadoo. Ben^j Gray 1 day 120 miles; W^m B Hadden 1 day this Term.

Susannah Hall vs Penelope Lewis. Horatio Humphries 1 day.

WITNESS DOCKET

Elias Tubb vs Joel Massie. Ja⁵ Patterson 1 day 50 mi at July
  1 day at April & 50 miles for pl'f; Thos B McMurtry 2 days
  50 miles at July for pl'f.
John Buckhannon vs John Larkins Jr. Jos Larkins 1 da; Robert
  Larkins 1 day; Jas Larkins Sr 1 day; Jas Larkins Jr 1 day;
  John Larkins Jr 1 day; Robert H McCollum 2 day last 1 day
  this; Richard C Napier 1 day
State vs Elizabeth Gunn. Solaman Grayham 1 day.
Ro Jarmon vs C Robertson. Benj Clark 2 days; Richd B Jarmon
  2 days 68 mi; John Bernard 2 da; John Adams 2 da; Augustin
  Roberts 1 day.
State vs Ro Rogers. Jesse Hall 1 day.
Edward McCormack vs Montgy Bell. Geo W Curry 3 days 72 miles
  4 ferriages; James M Ross 4 days; William McNickol 4 days;
  Benjamin Pack 3 days; Joseph Victor 2 days 70 miles.
Hamilton & Shaw vs Mark Reynolds. Morgan B Wells 1 da 20 mi.
Samuel C Hawkins vs Eleanor Parrish. Morgan B Wells 2 days
  20 miles.
State vs Francis V Smitton. Wm Baker 1 day.
State vs Henry W Henson. Wm Baker 1 day; Jos Handlin 1 day.
Francis V Smitton vs James McCauly. William Baker 2 days.

January 1826

E W Napier vs John Evins. Jno Hall 1 day; Elizabeth Joslin 1
  day; Gabriel Joslin 1 day; Clinton Richardson 1 day; Benjn
  Clark 1 da; Wm McNickol 1 da; John B Brown 1 da; Jas Larkins 1 day; Saml Rogers 2 da 40 mi; Robt Watson 1 da 40 mi.
Jno Buckhannon vs Jno Larkins. Jno Bradley 2 da; Jno Goodwin
  2 days; Augustin Roberts 2 days; Robt McCollum 2 days; Jas
  McCollum 2 days; James Larkins Jr 2 days; Jno Larkins Jr 2
  days; Jos Larkins 2 days; Robt Larkins 2 days; David Pass-
  more 2 days; Wm Houston 2 days.
State vs John Goodwin. Richd Nall 1 day; Thos Gentry 1 day.
State vs Robert Rogers. Francis Carter 1 day for plaintiff
  32 miles; Jesse Hall 1 day.
State vs Edward B Roach. James W Evins 1 day.
p.-- State vs Jesse Hall. Francis Carter 2 days 14 miles.
State vs F V Smitton. Wm T Reynolds 2 days.
State vs H W Hinson. Saml Smith 2 days 14 mi; H N Merritt 2
  days; Jos Handlin 2 da; Wm Baker 2 da; Dan Billops 2 days.
State vs Wm H Burton. Saml Smith 2 da 14 mi; Howard W Turner
  2 days; H N Merritt 2 days; Joseph Handlin 2 days; Wm Hol-
  lingsworth 2 days; Wm Baker 2 days; Daniel Billops 2 days.
Allin Dannil vs H N Merritt. John Rogers 1 day 76 miles.
State vs H W Henson. John Rogers 3 days 76 miles.
State vs John Toler Jr. H W Turner 1 da; H N Merritt 2 days;
  Joseph Handlin 2 day; Wm Baker 2 day; Danl Billops 2 days.
State vs Abraham Self. H W Turner 1 day; H N Merritt 2 day;
  Joseph Handlin 2 days; Wm Baker 2 da; Danl Billops 2 days.
Robert Jarmon vs C Robertson. John Adams 3 days; John May 3

WITNESS DOCKET

days; Augustin Roberts 3 days; Jn° Bernard 3 day; Benjamin
Clark 4 days; Richard B Jarmon 4 days 68 miles; John H
Burton 4 days 50 miles; Adonijah Edwards 6 days.
Sam¹ C Hawkins vs Eleanor Parrish. Morgan B Wells 4 da 36 mi
State vs H W Hinson. John Toler 3 days; Nicholas Baker 3
days; Joseph Handlin 3 days; William Baker 3 days.
John Larkins Sen' vs C Robertson. John Larkins Jun' 3 days;
Gabriel Joslin 3 last 4 this; Ro Larkins 4 days.
F V Smitton vs James McCauly. Damage. Wm Baker 4 days; James
Council 3 days.
James McCauly vs F V Smitton. William Baker 2 days.

April 1826

H N Merritt vs Allin Dannel. John Rogers 1 day 76 mi; David
Robertson 1 day; Thomas McMurry 1 day.
John Buckhannon vs John Larkin. David Passmore 1 day; John
Goodwin 1 day; Robt H McCollom 1 da; Ja^s Larkins S^r 1 day;
Wm Houston 1 day; Ja^s Larkins J^r 1 day; Jo^s Larkins 1 day.
Francis V Smitto vs James McCauley and William Handlin. John
McCauley 1 day 25 mi; Jn° McCauley 5 days 25 mi last Term;
Stephen Handlin 1 day 36 miles.
Parrish Lankford vs James Tidwell. John Pendergrass 1 day
this 1 day last Term
State vs Esom Breeding. Hardy D Miles 1 day 36 miles; Sally
Hunter 1 day this and 2 days last Term; Lucy Morris 1 day;
Willis L Dawson 7 days 40 miles.
State vs F V Smitton. Joseph Handlin 1 day.
M Bell vs Wm Mcadoo. Wm B Haddin 3 day last; 1 day this Term
p.-- Alexander Hamilton vs M Bell. John Parr 3 days 50 mi;
Robert Collier 3 days; William Fussel 3 days.

July 1826

Aron Arnold vs R D Sansom. John J Wells 1 day 300 miles 4
ferriages.
John Buckhannon vs John Larkins. Joseph Larkins S^r 1 day; Ro
Larkins 1 day; R C Napier 1 day; James Larkins 1 day; W^m
Houston 1 day; David Passmore 1 day; Ro H McCollum 1 day.
Stephen Hosley vs Ja^s Gilmore. David Robertson 1 day; Richard Whitehead 1 day.
Henry A C Napier vs Joseph Howard. Daniel Toler 1 day; Jn° W
Napier 1 day.
Thomas Collier Sen' vs M Bell. Benedict Bacon 1 day.
p.-- Sally Lile vs John Evins. Gustavis Rape 2 day 30 miles;
Lorton Cox 2 days 60 miles.
Holliway N Merritt vs Allin Dannel. David Robertson 1 day;
John Rogers 1 day 72 miles.
E W Napier vs W^m McNickol. Henry A C Napier 1 day; William
Hickerson 1 day.
Sam¹ C Hawkins vs Eleanor Parrish. Morgan B Wells 2 days 300
miles 4 ferriages.

WITNESS DOCKET

State vs Henry W Hinson. Nicholas Baker 1 day and 1 day last
Term; John Toler 1 day; Joseph Handlin 1 day.

October Term 1826

John Buckhannon vs John Larkins. Wm Houston 1 day; Jo^s Lark-
ins 1 day; Jno Larkins J^r 1 day; R C Napier 1 day; David
Passmore 1 day; Ro H McCollum 1 day; John Goodwin 1 day.
State vs Jacob Bright. Pettit Larceny. H W Turner 1 day.
State vs James Council. H W Turner 1 day; Stephen Hostly 1
day; Williamson Sullivant 1 day 20 miles; W^m T Reynolds 1
day; Thomas McMurry 1 day; Thomas McGuire 1 day; Daniel W
Martin 1 day; William Handlin 1 day; H N Merritt 1 day.
State vs Willis Council. Williamson Sullivant 1 day 20 mile;
Stephen Hostly 1 day; F V Smitton 1 day; H W Turner 1 day;
Wm Handlin 1 day; W^m T Reynolds 1 day; H N Merritt 1 day;
James Malugin 1 day; Daniel W Martin 1 day.
State vs Aquilla Council. H W Turner 1 day; W^m T Reynolds 1
day; Ja^s Malugin 1 day; Stephen Hostly 1 day; Thos McGuire
1 day; Danl W Martin 1 day; Wm Handlin 1 day; F V Smitton
1 day; H N Merritt 1 day; Tho McMurry 1 day.
Elias W Napier vs W^m McNickol. Thos H Green 3 days 30 miles;
Jno Kennedy 3 days; Henry A C Napier 3 days.
State vs James W McCammon. Jesse Ward 1 day; William Simpson
1 day; Samuel Simpson 1 day.
State vs Wm Adams. James W McCammon 1 day.
State vs Jno Adams. James W McCammon 1 day.
Stephen Hostly vs James Gilmore. David Robertson 4 days,
Thomas McMurry 3 days; Richard Whitehead 3 days.
David Nevin[?] vs Eleanor Parrish & securities. Thos McMurry
3 days; D H Williams 7 days in all.
p.-- Henry A C Napier vs Joseph Howard. Daniel Toler 3 days.

January 1827

M Bell vs Wm Mcadoo. W^m B Haddin 1 day this 1 day Apr 1 day
Oct; Benja Gray 1 day 40 miles.
John Buckhannon vs Jno Larkins. Wm Houston 1 day; Ro Larkins
1 day; R H McCollum 1 d; Jno Larkins Jr 1 d; Ja^s Larkins
Jr 1 d; Jo^s Larkins 1 d; Jno Bradley 1 d; Ja^s Larkins 1´d.
State vs Jacob Bright. Jane Craig 1 day; James Williams 1 d;
D H Williams 1 d; Howard W Turner 1 d; Saml Turner 2 days.
State vs Ja^s Council. W^m T Reynolds 1 d; Nicholas Baker 1 d;
Thomas McGuire 1 day; D W Martin 1 day; H W Turner 1 day;
Joseph Payne 1 day; Jno Story 1 day; Stephen Hostly 1 day.
State vs Willis Council. William T Reynolds 1 day; Nicholas
Baker 1 day; D W Martin 1 day; H W Turner 1 day; Jo^s Payne
1 day; John Story 1 day; Stephen Hostly 1 day.
State vs Aquilla Council. W^m T Reynolds 1 day; Thos McGuire
1 day; Nich^s Baker 1 day; D W Martin 1 day; H W Turner 1
day; Jo Payne 1 day; Jno Story 1 day; Stephen Hostly 1 day
p.-- State vs James W McCammon. Wm Simpson 1 day; Saml Simp-

WITNESS DOCKET

son 1 day; Jesse Ward 1 day.
State vs L D Evins. Robert Williams 1 day; Ailsey Williams 1 d; Alex^r Y Brown 1 d; Reese Bowen 1 d; Matilda Gafford 1 day; Gabriel P Joslin 1 d; Ro Nisbett J^r 1 day 100 miles.
Josiah Thornton vs Elisha Smith and others. Mark Thornton 3 days 80 mi; Reuben Thornton 2 d 36 mi; Isbel Griffin 3 d; Jo^s McReary 2 d 36 mi; Easter Thornton 1 d 38 mi; Elizabeth McCord 3 days; Archibald Ponder 3 days 30 mi; Elisha Pascal 2 days 30 miles; Nicholas Dudley 5 days 30 miles.
S Brewer vs E W Napier. John Choate 4 days; Wiloby Eatherage 3 days.
Wm Buckhannon vs M Bell. Ge^o Hightower 3 d; Thos Clark 1 d.
H A C Napier vs Jo^s Howard. Danl Toler 3 days; Joseph Howard 7 days in all; William Howard 8 days in all.
Ja^s H Davie vs Wm Grymes. Sion Jones 3 days.
p.-- E W Napier vs W^m McNickol. John Kennady 3 days.
George W Lewis vs Wallace Dixon. John Kenedy (no days)
Ja^s H Davie vs Wm Grymes. Jno McAdoo 4 day; Jno McNeely 4 d; Trinstan Rye 4 days; G P Joslin 4 days; Betsey Crumpler 3 day; L D Evins 3 d; Walker Thomas 3 d; Thos Holliway 3 d.
Thomas Collier vs M Bell. Alex^r Hamilton 9 days 200 miles 3 ferriages up to this Term for the pl^{ff}.
W^m D Reynolds vs Arsemus S Merritt. Daniel Billops 3 days.
Hicks & Shearon vs Sally Price. Daniel Billups 3 days.

April Term 1827

Bell vs Wm Mcadoo. W^m B Haddin 1 day last & 1 day this Term.
James H Davie vs Wm Grymes. W^m B Haddin 3 day last & 2 days this term.
Josiah Thornton vs Elisha Smith & others. Ja^s McCord 1 day; Archibald Ponder 1 day 30 miles.
State vs John Toler. Ausy Burgess 1 day.
State vs Ja^s Council. Howard W Turner 1 day; Stephen Hostly 1 day; Thomas McGuire 1 day; Joseph Payne 1 day; Daniel W Martin 1 d; Wmson Sullivant 1 d this 2 d last 30[?] miles.
State vs Willis Council. H W Turner 1 d; Stephen Hostly 1 d; Jo^s Payne 1 d; Danl W Martin 1 day; Williamson Sullivant 1 day this 2 days last Term; Jno Story 1 day; Nicholas Baker 1 d; Wm Baker 1 d; F V Smitton 1 d this & 1 at last Term.
State vs Aquilla Council. H W Turner 1 day; Stephen Hostly 1 day; Thos McGuire 1 d; Jo^s Payne 1 day; Daniel W Martin 1 day; Williamson Sullivant 1 day this 2 days last 40 miles; John Story 1 day; Nicholas Baker 1 day; Wm Baker 1 d; Thos McMurry 1 day; F V Smitton 1 day this and 1 day last Term.
p.-- Ja^s W Christian adm^r vs John Bernard. Ceburn Crews 2 d; Benja Andrews 2 days.
State vs Henry W Hinson. Jo^s Handlin 1 d; Nich^s Baker 1 day.
Wm Buckhannon vs M Bell. John Mockbee 1 d; Thomas Clark 1 d; Robert Collier 1 d; John McCormick 2 d this term 2 d last; Ja^s H Davie vs Wm Grymes; Gabriel P Joslin 3 d; L D Evins

WITNESS DOCKET

2 days 24 mi; Thos Holliway 3 d this Term; Jn° Mcadoo 3 d; Jn° McNeely 3 d; Tristrian Rye 3 d; Benja W Thomas 3 days.

N Scott vs David McAdoo. Willis Norsworthy 2 days last and 2 days this Term.

Jo Williams vs David McAdoo. Willis Norsworthy 2 days last & 2 days this Term.

William D Reynolds vs Orsemus S Merritt. Ciras Bledsoe three days in all 2 days for pl^{ff} & 1 for def^t with one pays his own witness; Bennet B Corbin 3 days for pl^{tf}

p.-- Stirling Brewer vs E W Napier. Thomas Williams 3 days for pl^{tf}; Jn° Choate 3 days for pl^{tf}; Joseph Choate 3 days pl^{ff}; Willoby Eatherage 3 days pl^{ff}; Thomas McClelland 3 d Def^t & 3 days this Term.

William Hedge vs Mary Baker. Orrin D Hogins 3 d pl^{tf}; George Evins 3 d for pl^{tf}, 2 days last; Ann Rutledge 6 d in all.

Gustavis Rape vs M Bell. Wm Rye 4 days pl^{tf}; Soloman Milam 4 days for plaintiff.

Jacob Grymes vs Jesse Bartee. W^m McNickol 4 d def^t 315 mile.

Lewis Thompson vs Elias W Napier. W^m McNickol 4 d 30 mi pl^t.

E W Napier vs W^m McNickol. Wm Hickerson 2 d last & 4 d this.

July Term 1827

Aron Arnold vs R D Sansom. John J Wells 1 day, 300 miles for plaintiff, 6 ferriages.

Elias W Napier vs W^m McNickol. Thos H Green 1 d, 30 mi def^t, 3 d Jany 1827, 30 mi; Jn° Kenedy 2 d last 1 d this; And^w A Brown 3 days up to this Term; Wm Hickerson 1 day this Term

p.-- Ge° W Lewis vs Wallace Dickson. John Kenedy 2 days last 1 day this Term; Ja^s Cricket 6 d in all, 72 miles in all.

Lewis Thompson vs Elias W Napier. W^m McNickol 1 day; Robert H Brown 1 day this Term for defendant.

Edward Woodard vs Richard Batson. Jeremiah Baxter 2 days and 30 miles for the plaintiff.

State vs James Council. Stephen Hostly 1 day for State; Thos McGuire 1 day for Def^t; Wmson Sullivant 1 d Def^t; Daniel W Martin 1 day Def^t; Jo^s Payne 1 day pl^{tf}; H N Merritt 1 day pl^{tf}; H W Turner 1 day pl^{tf}; John Story 1 day pl^{tf}; Thomas McMurray 1 day for defendant; Nicholas Baker 1 d for pl^{tf}.

State vs Willis Council. Stephen Hostly 1 d pl^{tf}; Thomas McGuire 1 d def^t; Wmson Sullivant 1 d def^t; Danl W Martin 1 d Def^t; Jo Payne 1 d pl^f; H N Merritt 1 d pl^f; H W Turner 1 day plaintiff; John Story 1 day pl^{tf}; Nicholas Baker 1 d plaintiff; Thomas McMurray 1 day defendant.

State vs Aquilla Council. Stephen Hostly 1 day pl^t; Williamson Sullivant 1 day def^t; Danl W Martin 1 d Def^t; Jo Payne 1 day pl^t; H N Merritt 1 day pl^{tf}; H W Turner 1 day pl^f; John Story 1 day pl^{tf}; Nicholas Baker 1 day for plaintiff.

p.-- Nehemiah Scott vs David Mcadoo. Willis Norsworthy 2 day for pl^f; Rich^d N Williams 2 days pl^{tf}; Ja^s Williams 3 days for plaintiff; John S Williams 10 days in all for def^t.

WITNESS DOCKET

Joseph Williams vs David Mcadoo. Willis Norsworthy 2 day for plaintiff; Richard N Williams 2 days for plaintiff; John S Williams 10 days in all for defendant.

James H Davie vs Wm Grymes. B W Thomas 3 d pl^{tf}; G P Joslin 2 d pl^f; Robt Peacock 2 d this 1 last for def^t; Lorenzo D Evins 3 d pl^f, 24 miles; Jno McAdoo 3 d pl^f; Jno McNeely 3 d pl^f; Tristam Rye 2 d Def^t; Benja Pack 3 d Def^t; Reese Bowen 5 day in all for def^t; Thos Holliway 3 days for pl^f.

Wm Hedge vs Mary Baker. George Evans 3 days for pl^{tf}; Joseph Eason 5 days in all for plaintiff.

C Strong vs Lorenzo D Evans. Robt Larkins 2 days for plaintiff; Robt Williams 3 day pl^f; Elsy Williams 3 day pl^f; Jacob Leech 1 day pl^f; Gabriel P Joslin 3 d def^t; Henderson Joslin 2 days def^t; Lewis Richardson 5 days pl^{tf}; Matilda Gafford 3 days for pl^{tf}; Reese Bowen 4 days for plaintiff.

Josiah Thornton ext^r & Pheriba Thornton ext^x of Martin Loftes dec^d vs Elisha Smith & others. Joseph McCreary 3 days & 1 day last Term & 72 miles; Robt Lyle 5 d & 72 mi for pl^f; James McCord 4 days for pl^f; Archibald Ponders 4 d & 30 mi pl^f; Elisha Paschal 3 days this & 2 last for def^t; Reuben Thornton 4 days this Term, 1 last, for pl^{tf} 72 mi; Hudson Dudley 8 days in all pl^f; Easter Thornton 4 day 36 mi pl^f; Ibby Griffin 2 days last Term, 4 this term, for defendant.

John Barnet vs Jno Picket. Jno Adams 4 days in all for deft.

April 1827

State vs James Gunn. James Eason 1 day for defendant; William Gunn 1 day for defendant.

October 1827

M Bell vs W^m McAdoo. W^m B Hadden 1 day for pl^f; Benjⁿ Gray 1 day for defendant.

E W Napier vs Wm McNickles. Andrew A Brown 1 day for def^t; Sally Thompson 10 d pltf; Lewis Thompson 10 days for pl^{tf}.

James H Davie vs Wm Grimes. Tristram Rye 1 day for pl^{tf}; L D Evins 2 days 24 miles; Wm Rye 2 days; John McNeely 2 days; F Joslin 2 days; Ben W Thomas 3 days for plaintiff.

State vs Jehu Miller. Peace warrant. William Austin 2 days for plaintiff; James Hicks 1 day.

State vs James Gunn. Saml Bugg 1 day for pl^f; Elizabeth Bugg 1 day for plaintiff; Solomon Marsh 1 day; Ja^s Tate 1 day.

Henry A C Napier vs Jo Howard. Danl Toler 2 days.

p.-- C Strong vs L D Evans. Robert Williams 2 days for pltf; Alsey Williams 2 days defendant; Gabriel P Joslin 2 days pl^{tf}; Elizabeth Joslin 1 day pl^{tf}; Matilda Gafford 2 days for plaintiff; Reese Bowen 2 days for plaintiff.

John Barnet vs John Picket. Jesse H Alexander 3 days in all for def^t; John Johnson 3 days last Term, 3 this for def^t; John Adams 1 day for defendant.

WITNESS DOCKET

January Term 1828

Hiram Dunigan vs Geo Cox. Saml Bugg 1 day Deft.
James H Davie vs Wm Grymes. Gabriel P Joslin 1 day for pl'f;
  L D Evins 1 day plf 24 miles; Reese Bowen 1 day deft; John
  McNeely 1 d deft; Jos Nesbitt 1 d 90 miles; Wm Rye 1 day.
Shadk Bell vs C Robertson. Jos Morris 2 d; Jno J Williams 2
  d 15 mi 1 fer; J Brewer 2 d plf, 2 fer; Washn Hunter 2 d.
Francis V Smitto vs Ambrose H Burton. Wm Reynolds Sr 3 days
  in all; Catherine Reynolds 2 days in all.
Susannah Reynolds Exr vs F V Smitto & others. Robert West 3
  days. Wm Morrison 3 days; Jos Kimble 3 days; John H Burton
  2 days 50 miles; H W Turner 2 d; Jacob Evins 2 day; Silmon
  Edwards 2 days; Daniel W Martin 2 days; Wm D Reynolds 2 d.
State vs James Gunn. Solomon Marsh 1 day; Samuel Bugg 1 day;
  Elizabeth Bugg 1 day; James Tate 1 day.
C Robertson vs M Bell. Thomas Armstrong 3 days.
State vs Wm D Reynolds. H W Turner 1 day; Hanna Reynolds 1 d
  this. 1 d last; Benja Darrow 2 days in all; H N Merritt 1
  day; Daniel W Martin 1 day; John Henderson 2 days in all.
p.-- Sally Smith vs Jeremiah Nesbitt. James Gilmore 2 days.
Thomas Clark vs Elias W Napier. Jesse Bartee 3 days; Robert
  Nesbitt Senr 4 days.
State vs John Adams. R N Williams pros. Chas Thompson 1 day.
State vs John Adams. D H Williams pros. Chas Thompson 2 day
State vs Jeremiah Nisbitt. A&B. Jane Craig, 1 day; Willie
  Baldthrop, 1 day; Mary Baldthrop, 1 day; William Adams, 2
  days; Ephriam Roy, 1 day.
Charles C Thompson vs James Gunn. Samuel Bugg 2 days; Isaac
  Hedge 2 days; James Tate 3 days.
Goodrich's Exrs vs Wm W Baldthrop. Wm Adams 2 days.
John Adams vs McDearman & wife. Thomas May 2 days.
p.-- C Strong vs L D Evins. Lewis Richardson 5 days; Robert
  Williams 4 days; Ailsy Williams 1 day.
M Bell vs Wm McAdoo. Benja Gray 1 day.

April 1828

C C Thompson vs James Gunn. Isaac Hedge 1 day for plaintiff.
George F Napier vs Henry G Wells & Chauncey Devanport. John
  Thompson 1 day 25 miles 2 ferriages.
M Bell vs Wm McAdoo. Wm B Haddin 1 day last 1 day this Term.
Goodriches Exrs vs Wm Baldthrop. Jno Adams 1 day this 2 days
  last Term; Wm Adams 2 days.
William Nall vs Empson Bishop. Willis Johnson 7 days in all;
  Jno Pendergrass 8 days in all up to this Term; George Sul-
  livant 2 days this term.
E Lowery admr vs Goodriches Executors. Gladdin Gorin 2 days
  44 miles for defts; Hugh McMillan 2 days 52 miles for defts.
Wm Simpson vs Alias Finley. Wm B Haddin 2 days.
p.-- Sally Smith vs Jeremiah Nesbitt. Stephen Hostly 1 day.
S Bell vs C Robertson. S Brewer 3 days 80 mi for plaintiff;

WITNESS DOCKET

Joseph Morris 3 days; J J Williams 3 days 30 miles, 2 ferriages; Charles H Pickering 3 days this & 2 last Term; Andrew Stewart 3 days, 17 miles, 2 ferriages.
Susannah Reynolds vs Francis V Smitto. Will case. W^m D Reynolds 2 days; Silmon Edwards 2 days; Benj^u Darrow 2 d; Wm Morrison 3 days; H W Turner 2 days; D W Martin 2 days; Jo^s Kimble 3 days; Jacob Evins 2 days; Levina Brashier 2 days; Cealy Irwin 2 d; Sophia Holly 2 d; Martha Baker 2 d; Ge^o Oliver 2 day; Jno H Burton 3 day 50 miles; Ro West 2 days.

July Term 1828

Shaderick Bell vs Christopher Robertson. Joseph Morris 1 day for plaintiff; Andrew Stewart 1 day for pl^f 34 miles; Joseph Williams 1 day, 34 miles for pl^{tf}; Washington Hunter 8 days up to this Term for pl^f; John Jones 4 days up to this Term for def^t; Stirling Brewer 1 day, 80 miles, for pl^{tf}; Charles H Pickering 1 day for plaintiff.
p.-- State vs H N Merritt. Daniel W Martin 1 day for def^t; William Morrison 1 day for the State.
State vs Ja^s Hightower. Balam Bull 1 day 24 miles for deft; Jacob Sanderson 5 days in all for the State; Simon Myers 5 days in all for the State.
C Robertson vs M Bell. Thomas Armstrong 2 days for pl^{tf}
J Voorhies vs T W Shearon. Benjamin D Pack 2 days for pl^{tf}; Andrew Nesbitt 3 days, 300 miles 2 ferriages for pl^f; John Bernard 6 days in all for defendant.
State vs Robert Collier. Matthew Crumpler 2 days for State.
Thomas Clark vs E W Napier. Robert Nesbitt Senr 3 days 140 miles for pl^{tf} 2 ferriages; John Griffith, 7 days to this Term, 64 miles for pl^f; John Adams 2 days for def^t; Robert H Brown, 5 days, 200 miles for defendant.
Sally Smith vs Jeremiah Nesbitt. Samuel Turner (blank)
Goodriches Exrs vs W W Balthrop. John Adams 3 days for pl^f; William Adams 3 days for plaintiff.
p.-- Francis Myrick vs E W Napier. John W Napier 3 days for def^t; George F Napier 3 days for def^t; Robert N Brown 3 days in all; Henry A C Napier 3 days for def^t.
William Nall vs Empson Bishop. John Arthur 4 days 50 miles for plf; Willis Johnson 4 days plf; Jno Pendergrass 4 days pl^f; Ge^o Sullivant 4 days pl^f.
Sally Smith vs Jeremiah Nesbitt. Willie Balthrop 4 days for plf, 1 day last Term; Stephen Hostly 4 days for pl^f; Jane Craig 3 days for pl^f; Matthew Gilmore 3 days last Term, 4 days this Term for def^t; Samuel Turner 4 days for def^t; John Adams 4 days for def^t; Sally Underwood 4 days for the defendant; Ephriam L Roy 5 days in all for the plaintiff.
James G Hinson vs William Hightower. Henry W Hinson, 1 day for pl^f; John B Cox 1 day for pl^f; Thomas McMurry 3 days for pl^f; Abraham Self 3 days for pl^f.

INDEX

--, Joseph 175
ABNEY Elias 5 65 Rhody 169
ACOFF/ACUFF Elizabeth 57 160
ADAMS George 27 33 58 81 92 98 117 124 125 173 Hodge 2 75 79 80 103 105 110 Howel 3 11 John 15-17 45 50-52 54 57 58 62 63 68 69 75 81 89 92 94 100 104 110 116 123 124 126-128 130 131 133 134 137 154 155 163-165 168-173 175 179 183 186 187 189 191-193 196-198 Major 102 Nancy 11 Richard 81 83 Silvester 79 189 William 1 3 4 6 12 15 20 21 53-55 81 116 123 131 132 144 151 153 155 156 168 179 183 188 189 193 197 198
ADAMSON Richard 81 William 66 78 159
ADKINS Drewry/Drury 27 55-58 60 64 87 93-95 159 188-190
AIKIN/AKIN/AKINS James 65 William 12 13
ALABAMA 43
ALEXANDER J 104 Jesse 111 116 156 181 196 William 14
ALLEN/ALLIN H 55 John 17 22 31 32 N 20 72 William 3 107 109 181 Zachariah 130 137 139 140
ALLENSWORTH Phillip 157 163
ALSTEN/ALSTIN/ALSTON Charles 25 James 11 14 18 21 24-26 John 25 26 Milly 25
ANDERSON Alexander 84 89 94 95 102 Allin 166 Joseph 176 180 Lucy 188 Thomas 169 William 146 153 154
ANDREWS Benjamin 3 10 194
ARCHER Ruthy 158 Stephenson/ Stevenson 143 144 157 165 AREY (slave) 52
ARMER/ARMOR/ARMOUR James 52 81 87-89 104 166 173 180 181 183 186 Olaver/Oliver 27 28 30 Robt

ARMER/ARMOR/ARMOUR (continued) 23 51 55 61 86 97 102 103 108 109 131 William 29 48 51 104 107 123 131 132 172
ARNOLD Aaron/Aron 49 120 152 192 195 Ebenezer 151 Ephraim 95
ARRINGTON/ARRINTON &c Joel 53 55-58 76 177 178 John 88
ARTEMISA (slave) 145
ARTHUR John 198
ASHLEY Miles 51 171 174 177
ATKINS Drewry &c 39 53 57
AUSTIN David 110 Eliza 110 John 165 Philip 38-40 Samuel 45 130 178 William 38-40 57 61 69 71 80 92 99 101 109 128 160 196
BACON Benedict 57 66 126 130 138-140 146 147 179 187 192
BAILEY Charles 39 Edwin 76
BAIR Charlotte 120
BAIRD William 169
BAKER Absalom/Absolom &c 40 41 52 75 91 122 156 178 190 Armstrong 178 Edward 116 Jane 128 140 John 16 19 22 36 91 105 121 125 128 132 139 140 147 148 Lucinda 108 Martha 198 Mary 52 91 130 156 157 195 196 Nicholas 52 60 65 105 106 128 153 169 192-195 Richmond 75 Sally 79 William 36 95 110 129 189 191 192 194
BALDTHROP/BALTHROP F 39 Francis 105 111 112 117 118 129 152 158 Mary 197 Polly 151 W 198 Wiley 87 91 William 6 21 39 57 58 63 64 70 81 83 91 93 96 104 129 158 168 176 184 186 190 197 Willie 116 144 151 158 197 198
BALDWIN Levi 83
BANK OF STATE OF TENN 37 39

BANKS William 23
BARBER Allen 188
BARNARD John 5
BARNET John 131 133 162 196
BARNETT Thomas 65
BARR Charlotte 120 James 179
BARROTT John 116
BARROW W 25 26 Willie 6 7 8 19 23 27
BARRY Valentine 12
BARTEE Jesse 76 129 150 179 195 197
    William 179
BARTER Jesse 186 Robert 186
BARTON Martin 144 Wm 18 112
BARTONS CREEK 60 66 145
BASS Ransom 128
BATEMAN Simon 147
BATSON R 33 135 150 156 Richard 20
    28 29 35 38 41 47 50 52 55 60 64 66
    67 71 72 83 85 91 92 97 112 115 120
    123 126 130 133 136 137 145-148 154
    165 168 169 172 174 178 182 195 --
    159
BAUGHMAN Christian 48 49 52 62 78
    120 150
BAXLEY George 52 69
BAXTER/BAXTOR James 32 80 92 109
    116 143 Jeremiah 29 30 42 195 Robert
    54 92 129 151 -- 142 172
BAYLESS Burwell 156 167 -- 53 55
BEAR CREEK 80 142
BEAVERDAM CREEK 66
BECKEY (slave) 93
BEDDLE -- 5
BEDFORD Teresa/Tereasey &c 50 59 60
    85 108 109 110 127 135 137 183 184
BELL Horatio 175 Hu 20 James 8 9 19 21
    39 40 58 70 71 79 99 168 169 189 190
    John 39 40 82 93 125 M 86 121 127
    171 188-190 192-198 Montgomery 2 7
    12 18 19 29-32 34 37-45 53 54 56-58
    61 67 73 77 83 86 89 91 96 100 101
    105 106 111 113 119 120 131 133 134
    138 140 143 147 149 150 156 163 168
    170 174 176 180 184 185 191 S 197
    Shadrack &c 10 11 41 54 86 87 92 94
    180 197 198 Thomas 86 Waller 130 --
    20 189
BELLEMY Jeremiah 129
BENTON Jesse 91 129 Wm 25
BERNARD &c John 14 63 89 130 138
    147 167 181 191 192 194 198
BERRY (slave) 156

BERRY Lewis 11 12 13 50 51 66
BERTIE COUNTY NC 10
BERTON Humphreys 61 Marion 61
BETER Calvin 56
BETHALL TN 120
BETT Horatio 154 161
BETTS William 66 149 158
BEVINS R 125
BIBB/BIBBS David 92 129 159 166-169
    173 180 181 183 186 Minor 50 59-61
    75 79 84-86 89 90 97 98 101 102 123
    143 165 172 178
BILLOPS/BILLUPS Daniel 87 89 124
    129 137 139 141 153 165 175 189 191
    194
BISHOP Arthur 46 Empson 175 186 197
    198 William 68 80 85 91 92 109 140
    148 149 150 152
BLACK George 98 Peter 95 96
BLACKWELL Morris 33-36 38 44 46 48
    -- 43
BLAKE William 39 104 108
BLALOCK Richard 66
BLEDSOE Barney 100 122 142 Ciras 195
    Lain 52 Pinckney 76 136 142 Yancy
    142
BLOUNT Ann 32 George 126 127 Jesse 6
    John 11 169 171 Thomas 11 169
    William 190 Wilson 3-6 9 10 12 -- 9
BOATRIGHT James 99
BOLES Margery 15 Peggy 15 Sampson
    15 75 76 81-83 Thomas 15
BOLTON Richard 31
BOMER R 173
BONDS Drury 69 77
BOOKER James 79 Joseph 110 Peter 71
    77
BOSLEY Burwell 87 92 101 George 92
    John 58
BOWDEN John 179
BOWEN/BOEN Allen/Allin 51 53 56 61
    70-74 81 86 98 110 115 117 119 159
    166 170 171 173 Eldridge 19 22 61 69
    71 73 81 87-89 92 120 Rees/Reese 53-
    55 68 80 96 103 105 111 112 122 123
    129 167 194 196 197
BOWERS Robert 125
BOWKER Samuel 176
BOX Lindley 98 127 177
BOXLY Burwell 99 101 102
BOYCE Joel 82
BOYERS Robert 134

BRADFORD Edward 46 Samuel 144 -- 45
BRADLEY Captain 110 Edward 40 John
  77 78 81 82 87 89 112 123 128 130
  133 137 139-141 191 193
BRADY Aaron 20
BRASHER/BRASHIER Levina 198
  William 8 10 119 189
BRAZEAL/BRAZELL George 41 43 44
  91 105 111 112 116 178
BRAZIER William 144
BREDWILL Jacob 46
BREEDING/BREDING Ephraim/Ephriam
  36 49 135 Esam/Esom 61 91 105 113
  119 192 John 65
BREEDLOVE -- 45
BREHEN James 66
BREWER Ann 134 J 197 James 66 80 108
  109 139 140 142 144 147 164 180
  John 29 34 92 99 101 102 112 122 144
  166 174 176 180 Nancy 139 140 S 33
  47 61 115 143 144 148 194 197 Ster-
  ling/Stirling 2 3 10 26-29 36 39 40 43
  45 47 49 50 54-59 63 64 66-68 78 80
  87 90 97 107 108 112 122 130 135 137
  144 147 149 155 156 165 167 169 172
  180 195 198 -- 142
BRICE John 64
BRIGHT Jacob 119 132 138 193
BRIM/BRIMM Edward 98 105
BRION William 20
BROCK Edward 169 183
BROCKMAN Joshua 175
BROOK Samuel 66
BROWN Alexander 116 194 Andrew 76
  81 82 117 125 129 195 196 Ann 60
  Arzala 28 Arsimina 35 Benjamin 121
  Captain 60 110 135 166 Eli 110 122
  Ezekiel 117 124 125 Grainger 60 J 60
  James 112 Jeremiah 66 143 John 21 52
  61 69 71 73 77 78 87 92 98 103 110
  116 117 119 127 136 143 155 156 179
  189 190 191 Jonathan 65 Labon 68
  179 Laburn 110 R 159 Richard 110
  Robert 28 37 76 82 145 155 164 172
  179 195 198 Roper 35 47 48
  Roser/Rosser 6 19 29 35 37 Samuel 51
  91 159 165 166 170 171 178 Sarah 71
  188 Soloman 92 99 101 Spencer 87 88
  98 116 122 158 163 Thomas 166 174
  176 177 Thompson 28 35 William 26
  28 30 32 34 35 37 38 87 97 -- 87 88
BRUCE Foster 164 Franklin 157 158 189

BRUCE (continued)
  J 158 James 164 Jeremiah 89 189 John
  164 Lemuel 164 S 164 Bruce Hollow
  167
BRUNSON Jesse 36 175 Robert 36 38 40
BRUNNON Robert 24
BRYAN Henry 20
BUCKHANNON John 105 138 190 191
  192 193 William 133 142 147 194
BUGG Elizabeth 196 197 Samuel 160 180
  196 197
BULL Balam 198 Dempsey 128
BULLARD Theophilus 90
BULLIAN/BULLION &c Capt 136 166
  Henry 116 Thomas 1 2 3 42 52 76 92
  99 101 102 116 123 130 137 139 140
  152 159 160 162 181 William 44 48
  127
BUNCH Tailton/Talton 15 16 17
BURGESS Ausey/Ausy 86 194 Elias 86
  Evans 86 John 51 Plummer 172 Polly
  51
BURK William 97
BURNETT Leonard 69
BURNHAM James 123 Joshua 110
BURNS Larry/Lary 88 144 166
BURTON Ambrose 65 76 124 167 181
  197 Charles 173 Humphries 69 71 73
  151 John 192 197 198 Martin 69-74
  117 119 152-154 156 R 92 Reuben 87
  William 16 106 191
BUSBY Micajah 66
BUTLER Elizabeth 34
BYRNS Larry/Laury 98 105 115
CAFFERY/CAFFREY &c George 175
  William 49 69 94 105 107 136 145-
  148 165 181
CALDWELL/CALWELL Andrew 4 6 7 --
  36
CAMPBELL Charles 8 Michael 32
CAMPERRY Sampson 82
CAPLING John 5
CARNS Thomas 86
CAROTHERS John 36
CARR John 110 117 119 123 136 Meck-
  ins/Meekins/Mickins 97 98 105 106
  166 173
CARROLL/CARELL Captain 90 110
  135 166 John 20 William 18 31 98 105
  131 151 159 161 173
CARTER B 142 146 160 187 Belfield 77
  187 Francis 185 189 191 James 81 87

CARTER (continued)
　88 89 92 101 123 178 Kilpatrick 44 45
　Wm 169
CARY (slave) 171
CASSEL Riley 179
CATHEY John 98 105 106 180
CATHIE George 103
CATO Alford 10
CATTON John 169
CEDER CREEK 94 100
CHAMBERS/CHAMLESS Hardy/Harden
　4 57 86 John 58 187 Reuben 4
CHAPPEL John 65
CHARLOTTE (slave) 145
CHARLOTTE FEMALE ACADEMY 164
CHEATHAM L 19 64 66 81 152 Leonard
　125 152
CHEZANHALL / CHISENCHALL /
　CHIZANHALL Alexander 4 6 7 64
　128
CHILDRESS Stephen 140
CHILES John 176
CHOAT/CHOATE James 75 116 142
　John 2 25 55 57 64 69 75 76 89 90 92
　97 99 105 111 112 129 194 195 Joseph
　68 91 97 108 151 195 Schelton/Skel-
　ton 61 110 117-120 129 173 181 183
　184 186 Thomas 127 131 134
CHRISTIAN D 188 Drury 55 67 78 80
　122 147 James 50 52 54 80 83 98 122
　144 147 152 153 156 159 166 173 180
　181 186 187 194 S 55
CHRISTIAN COUNTY 46
CLARK/CLARKE Benjamin 2 20 21 28
　31 42 43 51 87 98 105 110 116 127
　155 156 161 173 183 184 188-192
　George 8 10 19 28 31 32 35 37 47 48
　52 75 98 105 112 113 116 128 157 163
　173 184 John 64 66 82 83 88 89 94-96
　101-105 107 112 186 189 190 Mary 98
　Richardson 65 Soloman 132 Thomas
　84 164 183 184 194 197 198
CLARKSVILLE TN 76
CLAY LICK 80
CLEGHORN John 33 34 35
CLEMENTS Andrew 158 C 58 Christo-
　pher 54 William 32 54
CLON Robert 39
CLOUD Joseph 91 154
COCK/COCKE Richard 76 105 111-113
　136
COFFEE Joseph 133 160

COLDMAN Daniel 2 Nancy 5 12 13
COLDWELL A 53 75 77 79 82-84 124
　156 188 Abiram 46 50 54 55 57 59 61
　67 74 75 78 84 85 98 108 112 124 139
　144 148 150 152 153 154 156 162 179
　183 186 Barnibas 103 Esqr 60 Thomas
　61
COLE Andrew 139 Chesley 59 108 136
COLEMAN Daniel 23 24 26 51 76 82 99
　Sally 172 William 66 76 82 85 87 92
　94 109 151 159 162 166 170 173 179-
　181 183
COLEWELL A 67
COLLEN/COLEN John 18 19 Thos 22
COLLIER/COLLIERS B 186 Benjamin
　138 156 173 176 Frederick 36 Henry
　61 J 84 John 23 28 30 34 40 47 58 66
　80 83 100 109 117 119 122 130 140
　147 149 150 156 163 179 182 Robert
　176 178 183 192 194 198 Theodorick
　173 Thomas 47 49 69 99 121 127 133
　140 192 194 Willis 51 63 92 99 101 --
　163 171 177
COLLIN/COLLINS/COLLUN Frederick
　36 John 26 54 Thomas 108
COLUMBIA TN 60 80 123 129
COMAS Reuben 76
COMER Adeline 104 R 76 Reuben 104
　157
CONE White 46
CONNIWAY James 46
CONTRARY POND 116
COOK William 14 20 72 161 -- 32
COOKSEY George 141
COPELAND/COPLAND Joab 14-16 22
COPPAGE Alexr 61 179 John 61
CORBIN B 122 Bennet 123 130 132 145-
　148 195
COTTEN/COTTON John 20 152
COUNCIL Aquilla/Qualla 91 97 132 136
　138 139 146 153 181 182 193-195
　James 60 117 122 132 136 139 146
　153 181 182 189 192-195 Rebecca 97
　Willis 91 132 136 139 146 153 182
　193-195
COX/COXE/COXEY Archibald 52 62 68
　160 161 166 167 174 175 187 Benja-
　min 51 59 104 109 133 140 Church 64
　Eldridge 59 George 159 167 197 John
　134 142 144 165 198 Lorton 192
　Thomas 59 119 126 Sindamilla 59
　White 40 44 47 54 57 William 21 31

COX/COXE/COXEY (continued)
 32 52 59 81 83 87 89 92 94 130 136
 137 139 140 145 146 148 Winneyford
 / Wineford / Winifred 59 64 104 109 --
 80
CUMBERLAND TN 64
CRAFT Russell 33 34 38 43 48 Samuel 43
 44 47 48 54
CRAIG/CRAGUE Hugh 122 151 Jane 71
 193 197 198 John 1 2 3
CRAIN William 128
CRAWFORD Benoni 20 21
CREWS Benjamin 36 44 46 47 49 68 104
 115 121 122 130 178 John 87 93-95
 104 182 Seburn/Ceburn/Leburn &c 33
 39 41 91 144 152 159 194
CRICKET James 195
CROCKET George 132
CROSS Eli 80 Featherston 41 43
CROSWAIT S 57
CROUS/CROUSE Jacob 110 123
CROW Eli 50 110 116 173 Elizabeth 173
 Isaac 116
CRUISE Benjamin 8 John 116 Pleasant 3
 Sebion 11
CRUMPLER Betsey 194 Levina 93 160
 Matthew 1 31 128 136 166 174 176
 177 183 184 198 Raiford 10 11 67 80
 88 166 174 176 177 179 180 181 183
 186
CRUNK Davidson 123 131 132 Richard
 96 105
CUMBERLAND RIVER 42 67
CUMMING John 116
CUMMINS Benjamin 71 77 99 James 17
 18
CUNNINGHAM Gideon 136 144 159 166
 173 180 181 183 186 James 186 Jesse
 100 107 John 81 105 111 112 142
 Nathaniel 142 Willis 81 93 100 107
 121 161 179 181 186
CURRIE Washington 77
CURRIN Robert 171
CURRY David 1 George 191 Washington
 191
CURTIS Samuel 19 23 25 27
DAILY/DALEY/DALY R 72 76 David 23
DANIEL/DANNEL Allen/Allin 60 105
 106 125 131 191 192 James 56-58 60
 85 129 130 137 139 140 166 172 John
 60 80 103 Wm 19 24 25 Woodson 87
 92 94 118 119 166 172 174 176-178

DARBY Patrick 197
DAVENPORT Chauncy/Chancy 68 86 97
 164 -- 86
DAVEY James 68 John 44
DAVIDEL Elizabeth 30
DAVIDSON Elizabeth 129 George 67 91
 129 131 152 159 166 170 71 173
 Henry 103 128 John 97 Jonah 130
 Joseph 19 23 24 97 128 Josiah 33 34
 93 118 119 137 151 180 Levi 65
DAVIDSON COUNTY 31 80 109 145
 154
DAVIE J 99 James 62-64 66 77 82 87 92
 102 103 105 115 117 120 122 123 125
 155 160 167 174 185 194 196 197
 Winstead 117
DAVIS Isaac 144 147 148 James 72 142
 152 John 11 Joseph 76 86 165 Nathan
 65 Wiley 81 85 Willie 159 166 167
 168 169 170
DAVIS FERRY 60 142
DAVISON Josiah 60 184
DAWSON James 65 Willis 14 16 18 63
 67 69 98 188 192 Winnefd 69
DAY John 24
DEADRICK George 86
DEAN William 43 65
DEES Jesse 47 53 55 57 67 80 97 98
DELLIHAY Nathan 178
DELOACH Simon 128 136
DEVALL John 65
DEVANEYS BRANCH 167
DEVANPORT Chauncey 106 175 188
 197
DICKS John 120
DICKSON Adam 77 99 179 Alexr 4 6 7
 31 32 45 49-51 61 67-69 71 76 79 81-
 83 88 92 95 101 104 106 108-110 114
 115 121 124 125 128 131 136 152 157
 158 160 164 166-168 175 184 189
 Hugh 8 10 27 47 62 68 71 73 77-81 83
 84 87 88-90 93 95 99 100 117 136 151
 179 187 188 J 179 James 71 77 99 188
 Jane 99 John 23 24 26 77 84 90 91 99
 115 119 123 124 128 140 151 179
 Joseph 73 77 90 99 179 Mary 71 77 84
 99 117 165 187 188 Michael 21
 Molton 51 75 77 106 108-114 118 120
 121 126-129 133-135 137 141 144 146
 147 149 150 156 157 159 162 164
 166-171 177-181 183 185 186-188
 Polly 71 92 99 115 119 123 138 188

DICKSON (continued)
    Robert 73 90 99 123 179 Robertson 32
    33 109 Wallace 195
DILLEYHA/DILLIHAY &c Nathan 60 87
    92 94 131 136 145-148 166 189 190
DIXON Wallace 128 153 175 194
DODSON Elijah 53-55 69 76 77 92 103
    110 117 119 Elish 54 William 104 116
DONNELL James 53 55 57 58 John 65
    Wiley 52
DORTCH Isaac 32
DOUGLASS/DOUGHLASS James 1 27-
    30 45 50 60 64 80 86 147 148 163
    Washington 137
DOVER TN 90 136 142
DOZIER Peter 145
DRAINESS William 4
DRUMMOND Mark/Mack 57 64 72 74
    187 188 Thomas 92 93 99 101 Za-
    cheas/Zacheus 109 128 134 136 145-
    148 179
DUCARD Joseph 155
DUCK RIVER 4
DUDLEY/DUDLY Hudson/Hutson 59-61
    75 79 85 86 90 96 97 109-113 123 135
    141 144 146 147 149 150 157 165 196
    Nicholas 75 76 80 82 85 130 132 166
    174 175 194 Willis 68 75 80 123
DUKE Charlotte 135 John 32 Robert 54
    59 87 89 104 135 167
DUNAGAN/DUNIGAN/DUNGAN Alvin
    64 187 Benjamin 157 167 Charles 164
    179 Elizabeth 161 Henderson 178
    Hiram 65 161 167 168 197 James 164
    John 8 62 69 80 157 167 187 188
    Samuel 64 76 82 161 168 178 187
    Stanford 178 Thomas 8 110 William
    50 68 71 103 116 173
DUNEVANT Humphrey 104 Nacky 104
DUNING Jane/Jincey 15 John 15 59
    Robert 16
DUNLAP James 65 Robert 4 38
DUNNAGAN &c Hiram 52 160 John 10
    52 56 Samuel 52 83 William 56 58 66
DURAND Joseph 155
DURARD Joseph 168 169
EAKINS William 16
EARL William 125
EASLEY/EASLY Eliza 103 George 107
    James 103 John 103 Moses 76 103 122
    135 173 Robert 76 81 William 15 18
EASON Bethena 62 Calvin 21 38 40

EASON (continued)
    Captain 12 Carter 140 James 23-25 51
    52 58 59 61 79 86 87 90 98 101 103
    105 108 109 135 137 138 143 150 155
    178 196 Jane 59 Joseph 41 43 52 59 61
    62 80 87 98 105 110 140 141 172 177
    196 Mills 59 61 Savannah 59 William
    59
EATHERAGE Burwell 97 103 122 128
    Joseph 97 122 Kindrick 97 Nancy 67
    Nathan 67 Phillip 67
    Willoughby/Wiloby &c 67 69 71 73
    183 184 194 195
EDMOND (slave?) 103
EDWARD/EDWARDS Adonijah 29 44
    89 100 105 111 112 130 142 153 192
    Alfred 187 John 28 46 81 100 105 142
    181 Johnson 79 Joseph 81 87 89 90 97
    102 104 108 115 117 124 128 129 137
    183 Reuben 187 Sanford/Sandford 19
    27 32 37 159 166 167-170 187 Sel-
    mon/Sylman &c 57 58 60 83 87 93-95
    104 105 110-114 122 126 128 129 144
    152 173 197 198 Thomas 62 92 142
    153 William 2 23 24 26 29 46 55 56 64
    67 69 187 188
EGNUE Jesse 33
ELEAZER Stephen 122 190
ELIZA (slave) 169
ELLINGTON Edward 100
ELLIS Ephraim 51 61 80 115 Francis 1 2
    4-6 21 29 32 33 35 61 74 141 John 63
    72 Moses 119 126 Nancy 151 Ransom
    98 151 183 Thomas 6 36 69 105 144
    172
ENGLAND Anderson 19 51 56 99 167
    189 190 Washington 52 62-64 66 81
    87 89 121 125 178
EPPERSON James 52 55 69 81 87-89 144
    Jesse 8 10 19 22 61 144 152-154 156
    John 36 Thomas 91
ESTES Abraham 7 19 Jane 172 178 T 179
    Tharp 172 178
ETHERAGE/ETHEREDGE &c Acheus
    65 Willoughby/Willeby &c 19 22 61
    62 63 91
EVANS/EVENS John 14 20 32 34 George
    56 Richard 56 William 56
EVE (slave) 169
EVERLY George 114
EVINS Betsy 178 Elizabeth 86 158 172
    George 56 121 125 129 138 146 148

EVINS (continued)
178 179 195 196 Harriet &c 86 105
115 143 158 172 Hulda 158 Jacob 120
197 198 James 101 112 117 132 137
188 191 Jane 86 158 John 28-30 32 39
64 71 78 83 86 89 90 100 101 111 117
127 137 145 158 177 178 188-192 L
194 196 197 Lewis 80 85 86 104 105
115 150 178 Lorenzo 117 118 132 139
140 171 196 Mahulda 86 Margaret 85
104 Martha 172 Patsey 86 158 172
Polly 178 Richard 91 178 Turner 78
William 171
EZELL Timothy 63 70
FALKNER William 83
FANN Raleigh/Rolly 173 178
FARIS Edward 52 Eleanor 52
FARMBRO Agnes 112 Robert 112
FARMER Cyprian 44 Robert 46
FARMERS & MECHANICS/MERCHANTS BANK 37 43 44
FARRAR Field 42 47 51 54 63 82 94 98 112 117 120 123 128-131 145 150 152 154 159 162 169 172 181
FARRIS Edward 52 Eleanor 52
FENNER Richard 173
FENTRESS Absolom 127 131 134 145 John 85 98 128 130 137 178 William 143 144 153 155-157 165 -- 40
FERRELL/FERROLL &c James 52 122 166 174 175
FINDLEY/FENDLEY/FINLEY Elias 82 83 90 161 181 197
FLANNERY Eleanor 178 Isaac 111 John 92 99 101 178 Thomas 69 77 78 80 88 101 190
FLEET William 60
FLEMMING William 123 131 132 137 143 165
FLETCHER Aaron 5 6 9 11 12 16 21 24 26 31 34 John 11 16 28 Moses 9 11
FLOWERS Andrew 90 106
FLOYD William 48 153
FLUELLEN Shaderick 125
FLUMAN William 26
FLY Micajah 78
FORBES Thomas 119 126
FORBUSH Thomas 96
FORE Jacob 20
FORSEY Daniel 53-55 98 105 106 144 152-154 156

FORSYTHE John 113 118 145 169 180
Samuel 169
FORT -- 32
FOSTER Ephraim 87 Nathan 124 Robert 118 -- 87 88
FRANCE Matthew 75
FRANCIS Guidion 9 Matthew 108
FRANKLIN TN 122 172 178
FRASIER/FRAZIER David 68 75 76 80 82 83 117 125 166 174 175 George 68 John 75 103 108 Thomas 3 William 81
FREEMAN Howel 61 142 Jeremiah 20 William 20 21 49
FRENCH John 27 Thomas 9 12
FURGASON Rogal 16 21 30
FUSSELL Harrison 65 James 112 William 50 99 131 192 -- 164
GAFFORD Matilda 194 196 Michael 116 169 Thomas 94
GAINES William 76
GALLION George 8 43 87 92 117 136 151 160 161 165
GAMBLE Andrew 14-17 Edmond 65
GAMMEL/GAMMILL Andrew 11 27 59 123 Moses 47
GARNER James 116 John 117 143 Robert 116 Wilkinson 116
GARNERS CREEK 59 103 177
GARRETT Ephriam 130 137 145 169
GARRISON Jacob 3
GARTON John 69 87 143 Martin 136 143
GASTON John 92
GENTRY Anderson 157 161 173 Thomas 79 129 130 137 139 140 143 159 166-170 191 William 16 23 41 43 52 129 159
GEORGE Brinkley 62 68 80 92 Captain 61 86 Daniel 60 68 76 98 105
GERRALD -- 41
GIBBS John 91
GIBSON Elizabeth 32 33 Wm 96
GIFFIN/GIFFEN John 27 30 32 38-40 61 69 73 74 98 117 Wm 98
GILBERT (slave) 144
GILBERT Benjamin 41-44 81 87 89 Charles 31 85 91 143 Felix 178 Mabel 97 98 141 165 Maben 36 Nicy 165 Peter 8 9 William 14 16-18 26 47 64 92 99 101 160 161 165 Wilson 64
GILBREATH John 179
GILLIAM James 69
GILMORE James 104 117 118 128 129

GILMORE (continued)
132 139 140 172 192 193 197 John
129 M 129 Mathew 14 20 39 40 82 93
98 100 126 129 131 144 146 170 173
180 188 190 198 Mathias 188 Wm 129
GLASS James 48 49
GLOSTER Thomas 66
GOLD -- 32
GOODLOW Garret 57
GOODMAN Henry 64
GOODRICH Allis/Alice 72 162 Armstrong 164 Charlotte 72 162 Dorothy 72 88 101 114 162 175 184 George 116 123 130 171 Henry 51 63 87 92 94 115 143 150 164 172 177 187 188 James 30 33 59 72 88 101 109 114 116 158 162 167 176 184 John 56 60 72 162 181 Martha 72 162 ancy 116 Patsey 72 William 72 144 151 -- 188 189 197 198
GOODWIN Beal 168 172 Crafford 107 John 112 131 191-193 William 1 2 3 10 11
GORDAN William 16 -- 40
GORIN Gladdin 197
GOULD James 140 161 163 -- 148 50 162 180
GOWEN Samuel 61
GOWER Elisha 3 7 Jemima 3 7 Patsy 66
GRAHAM/GRAYHAM Lewis 66 Solomon/Soloman 41-44 64 109 110 181 187 188 191
GRAINGER John 65 68
GRAVEL William 85
GRAVES Thomas 68 166 174 175
GRAVIT Henry 116 122 Wm 81 85
GRAY Benjamin 62-64 66 77 93 158 174 189 190 193 196 197 David 85 97 I 183 Isaiah 83 J 183 John 11 65 Wm 122 136 177
GREEN James 151 169 173 Robert 28 38 Thomas 193 195 Sophronia 169 -- 48
GREENVILLE COUNTY VA 76
GREENWOOD Elisha 56
GREGER George 65
GREGHAM Louisa 30
GRIFFIN Ibby/Isbel 194 196
GRIFFITH John 198
GRIGORY/GRIGRY Stephen 152 159 162
GRIMES/GREYMES &c Captain 61 86 Catherine 68 Henry 68 74 106 115 130

GRIMES (continued)
141 Jacob 195 John 29 30 42 53 55-58 68 91 106 107 109 110 115 118 130 William 153 155 196
GRIMMET &c B 120 Benjamin 109 115 122 135 Captain 60 86 110 William 61 69 71 73 105 106 111 112 113 114 157
GRISHAM John 65
GRISSOM Thomas 34
GROCE Nancy 51 79 87 109 135 164
GROVE Isaac 179 181
GRYMES/GRIMES Jacob 98 150 173 John 47 117 118 120 121 144 166 168 Wm 138 139 140 167 194 197
GUM BRANCH 60 68 75 85
GUMMELL Andrew 110
GUMMIT Benjamin 80
GUNN Charles 21 42 Elisha 38-40 42 44 45 47 52 56 62 187 188 Elizabeth 191 James 42 56 109 142 155 156 160 167 174 175 180 181 196 197 John 98 117 125 174 Lawson 76 98 Neetly 174 Sally 174 William 8 41 43 68 77 148 156 196
HADDEN/HADDIN James 36 53 55-58 80 159 178 W 133 William 19 24 25 27 31 33 47 48 62 63 77 78 102 120 138 139 140 160 175 183 184 186 188-194 196 197
HAIL Nicholas 176 185
HAILY Widow 152
HALE Abraham 158 icholas 116 143 158
HALL Berryman 77 78 David 77 78 Elizabeth 29 Garrett 65 80 92 99 101 109 131 165 H 38 Henry 64 Jesse 55 62-64 70 74 77 78 82 83 89 92 93 99 101 102 111 112 116 151 188-191 John 6 10 11 30 38 52 62-64 70 74 77 78 82 87 88 93-96 110 112 122 124 151 157 158 181 187 189-191 Joseph 64 Joshua 115 130 Martha 29 Susannah 29 55 63 64 70 74 77 78 82 93 116 151 154 174 184 188-190 Wesley 124 -- 45
HALLIBURTON Humphries 52
HAMBRIC/HAMBRICK Jeremiah 146 147 180 Uriah 146 180 William 146 180 Yelverton 65 122
HAMBY Isaac 8 10
HAMILTON A 144 153 Alexander 82 99 120 188-190 192 194 Andrew 14 26-30 32 38-40 44 45 66 113 133 134 146

HAMILTON (continued)
  155 160 170 190 Henry 106 Joseph 1 3
  5 9 10 12 13 -- 32 191
HAMLIN William 94
HAND John 41 43 87 William 47 55 105
  111 112 142 178 187
HANDLIN/HANDLEN Joseph 118 119
  132 136 153 175 189 191-194 Stephen
  42 192 William 42 60 79 83 93 95 117
  132 189 192 193
HANDY Samuel 145 152 159 176 180
  182 Thomas 185
HANEY Joseph 92
HANKINS Harrison 112 120 William 33
  43
HARDEN Henry 4 143
HARDER Jacob 179
HARDON William 7
HARDY Nehemiah 1 39 52 53 61 62 75
  80 84 104 105 111-114 129 135 144
  152 153 154 156 172 188 William 10
  17 21 28 29
HARKINS/HARKIN Joshua 40 42
HARLEY John 58
HARMON John 102 113
HARPER Robert 173 Wm 69 167
HARPETH River 67 80 104 109 142 152
HARRIS Adum 165 Afred 19 Alby 1
  Alfred 20-27 31-35 37 40 41 Burgess
  165 Clabon/Claibourne 1 128 152 171
  176 177 Daniel 81 143 165 172 177
  178 Derely 61 Dillard 24 Donnell 114
  Dorrel 59 107 159 166 Dorsett 23
  Dowel 159 Everitt 165 Howel 188
  Jane 27 John 76 142 165 Mark 165
  Randolph 17 21 22 39 49 65 81 130
  159 Richard 177 178 Robert 59 68 130
  136 137 139 140 Sarah 178 Shaderick
  84 Silas 52 80 141 173 177 Stephen 23
  61 81 107 114 123 130 132 152 176
HARRISON Joseph 128 129 Mary 168
  Stephan 128
HARRISONS CREEK 4
HART Thomas 178
HARTLEY/HARTLY James 68 77 78 105
  116 178
HARVEY Oney 56 79 Thomas 128
HATCH Lemuel 66
HAWARD/HAWORD Joseph 155 161
HAWKINS Samuel 63 121 126 133 181
  182 191 192
HAY John 20 Thomas 7

HAYES Oliver 38
HAYNES Herbert 30 James 113 John 185
HAYS George 2 James 86 John 33 47 48
  81 104 106 108 123 135 157 158
  Oliver 8 Robert 48
HAYWOOD John 32 81
HAYWOOD COUNTY TN 187
HEATH Samuel 148 149
HEDGE Isaac 197 William 86 104 105
  115 143 146 156 157 158 172 177 178
  195 196
HENDERSON John 160 161 167 197
  Robert 9 William 26
HENDRICKS Andrew 79 Henry 74 John
  61 69 Wm 61 103 187 190
HENDRIX Elijah 143 Elizabeth 95 James
  143 William 55
HENSON/HINSON H 52 Henry 105 106
  112 113 132 146 147 191 192 John
  142
HERNDON William 40 46
HERREN William 11
HESLIP Joseph 26 -- 16 19
HICKERSON Armstrong 178 Daniel 23
  24 26 44 159 Ezekiel 38-40 Henry 173
  180 181 183 186 John 23 William 82
  113 136 138 139 144 149 150 189 192
  195
HICKISON Daniel 49 69 77 78
HICKMAN Thomas 20
HICKMAN COUNTY 15 25 35 60 67 80
  122 136 164
HICKS A 149 173 187 Arresus 148 E 84
  86 102 103 108 109 112 115 121 127
  128 134 145 152 Edward 51 63 84 104
  111 112 126 129 132 133 148 163 J
  111 James 19 68 96 137 196 W 128
  William 123 -- 83 100 118-121 125
  126 141 150 162 182 194
HICKSON Alexander 155
HIGGINBOTHAM Middleton 52 61 62
  112
HIGHLAND Captain 110 136 George 80
  109 110 116 117 119 Henry 79 85 109
  116 143 Joseph 98 105 106 109 110
  116-119 143 173
HIGHTOWER Captain 166 George 36 39
  40 52 53 55 58-62 67 69 71 74 75 77
  86 87 92-94 96-99 101-105 107 109
  115 116 122 123 130 132 138 144 159
  160 166 177-179 181 194 Henry 141
  James 52 92 99 128 183 198 Joseph

HIGHTOWER (continued)
  118 120 Martha 93 Mary 93 R 159 160
  Robert 52 122 174 178 180 William 19
  22 38-40 52 53 62 69 89 93 111 113
  115 118 122 130 166 180 185 198
HILL Isaac 60 76 82 83 85 116 166 178
  Francis 13 Thomas 12 13 17
HINSON Harriott 144 Henry 55 60 93 99
  106 134 138 139 155 185 186 188 190
  193 194 198 Herbert 60 169 170 James
  60 160 198 John 45 49 51 120 139 144
  153 154 M 99
HISLIP Joseph 22 23 37 44
HODGE/HODGES John 8 10 135 158 180
  William 80 98 130 150 178
HOGINS A 128 Abraham 128
HOGAN/HOGUN Archibald 80 David 1-
  3 31 43 123 James 102 Orrin/Orren 51
  59 87 93-95 97 115 117 125 143 150
  165 173 178-181 195 William 59 61
  75 84 86 90 91 108 181 187
HOGG John 138 Samuel 138
HOGINS William 63 97 102 109 110 128
  131 134 135 144 157 158 167 171 172
  177 178 179 188
HOGWOOD John 87 88 89
HOLL James 143
HOLLAND Benjamin 98 102 Green 23 24
  159
HOLLINGSWORTH/HOLLINSWORTH
  &c William 42 84 93 95 97 189 191
HOLLIWAY/HOLLOWAY &c John 79
  81 116 123 128 130 132 136 148 156
  157 Thomas 41 43 91 92 99 116 118
  124 129 133 141 148 149 154 155 156
  159 173 178 179 187 190 194 195 196
HOLLY Edward 52 136-138 142 Sophia
  198
HOLMES/HOLMS Robert 68 Simon 116
  125 Thomas 116
HOLT/HOTT Labon 62 124 143 151 176
HOOD Morgan 62 87 93-95 102 117 125
  128 187 188
HOOK Elisha 65
HOOPER William 51 81 116 163
HOPPER Mary Ann 135 158 180
HORNBARGER Philip 6 9 12
HORNER George 116
HOSLEY/HOSTLY &c Abraham 172
  Berryman 172 David 172 Stephen 38-
  40 71 94 100 126 131 132 192-195
  197 198

HOUSE/HOWSE Claibon/Claiborne 161
  168 -- 32
HOUSTON Edward 42 44 Harvey 52
  William 67 87 109 111 135 164 191
  192 193
HOWARD Allen 14-17 56 89 Chas 29 30
  Edmond 2 Elizabeth 89 Joseph 131
  132 140 141 159 166 170 171 192-194
  196 Richard 172 Stephen 26 William
  64 194
HOWELL Abner 34
HUDGINS Abner 168 169 Wm 136
HUDSON Baker 86 129 161 Benjn 32 33
  C 57 Charles 128 Christopher 97 165
  180 Cuthbert/Curthbird 27 79 97 143
  Lucy 57 97 104 Mrs 60 67 James 128
  152 Thomas 23 32 33 36 44 56 80 91
  Widow 80 William 13 19 31 43 69 77
  78 81 82 86 91 116 120 141
HUELING Frederick 26
HUEY Edward 23 24
HULING F 20 Fedrick 28 34
HUMPHREYS/HUMPHRIES Horatio 52
  64 137 138 185 187-90 John 4 9 23 61
  79 87 90 103 137 143 P 112
  Parry/Perry 13 14 20 27-29 31-33 41
  42 44-46 66 69 70 144 163 175 Stoke-
  ly 52 136 173 West 118 -- 127
HUMPHREYS COUNTY 15 18 33 35 60
  173
HUNNELS Captain 166
HUNT Daniel 92 John 90 Spencer 47 57
  89 92 97 128 158 160 161 173 180 190
HUNTER Alexander 105 138 Captn 60 86
  Isaac 92 James 49 John 6 2 137 Joseph
  88 L 57 Sally 187 192 Thomas 47 58
  150 Washington 53 55-57 67 76 104
  159 166 170 171 180 187 188 197 198
  Wm 188
HURLING Frederick 26
HURMAN William 78
HURRICANE CREEK 66 76 98 103 142
  165 167 173
HURT -- 20
HUSTON William 49
HUTCHINSON William 51
HUTCHISON Ambrose 125 C 69 70 John
  27 60-63 72 80 125 William 69 77 117
  123 125
HUTTON Francis 8
HYDE John 10 11
HYNES -- 184

HYRE Polly 25
IRWIN Cealy 198 David 42-44 47 48 79
  86 102 110 114 128 134 136 170
  Davis 133 James 111 120 144 Irwins
  old mill 127
IVY Elijah 61
JACK (slave) 123
JACKSON Barnwell/Burwell 76 82 181
  Epps 111 119 172 Mitchel 76 82 83 85
  128 Peter 51 122 133 163 166 174 175
  Richard 38-40 69 77 123 166 174 175
  Willis 19 20 21 27 28 29 30 53 58 190
JAMES Aaron 14 Alak 97 Amos 47 48 85
  97 Enoch 85 97 103 157 Enos 50 110
  179 Jane 97 John 58 82 Joshua 85 97
JARMON Richard 191 192 Robt 191
JEMMISON William 60
JENNING Dudly 33
JENNY (slave) 144
JERNAN Thomas 72
JERNIGAN Lewis 91 Thomas 69 70 71
  73 130
JERNS John 146
JERRALD/JERRALL Thomas 90 121 133
  187
JIMS John 146
JOE (slave) 147 180
JOHNSON Cave 30 36 52 64 79 101 108
  125 136 168 Henry 94 100 186
  Hudson 110 137 173 Isaac 6 10 12 13
  63 67 James 10 13 John 6 50 52 55 61
  67 69 70 72 81 84 86 87 90-93 96 97
  102 103 108-110 115 121 127 129-132
  134 135 157 171 173 177 179 181 183
  184 188 196 Mordecai 14-17 22 Richd
  75 79 Susannah 123 143 Thomas 3 5 6
  William 14 17 65 76 104 122 128 135
  144 152 157 173 Willie/Wilie 79 101
  108 112 121 151 178 Willis 173 174
  197 198 -- 83 100 162 Johnson Creek
  85
JOHNSTON John 55
JOLLY Young 178
JONAKIN Thomas 61
JONES Charles 118 119 Elijah 123 129
  136 Henry 7 James 53 116 142
  Jiles/Giles 6 9 53 54 58 76 80 83 85
  172 178 John 74 76 82 111 112 115
  157 181 198 R 68 Richard 68 80 93 97
  130 Rosetta 93 97 Samuel 70 Sion 194
  Thomas 10 12 13 144 William 68 78
  91 123 144 -- 40

JONES CREEK 4 66 85 89 98 103 122
  148 169 174 184
JORDAN George 75 80 81 John 75 80
  Mary 80 Robert 75 80 Seth 75 79 80
JOSLIN Benjamin 9 13 44 45 63 64 83
  Elizabeth 188-191 196 F 196 G 196
  Gabriel 105 111 112 132 140 145 160
  190-192 194 196 197 Henderson 196
  James 153 John 33 39 41 Lewis 18 21
  Rebecca 41 Samuel 39
JOURDAN/JOURDON John 4 6 15-17
JUDA (slave) 169
JURDEN/JURDIN John 15 142
JURNEGAN Lewis 92 Thomas 72-74 80
  129 135 144
JUSTICE John 48
KEAN Matthias 187
KEE John 187 Thomas 4
KELL Nathan 6
KELLET/KILLET James 15 16 17
KELLY Ebenezer 19 22 124 162 John 2
  23 24 25 26
KELTON Robert 164
KENEDA/KENNADY &c Alfred 92 136
  John 130 131 138 140 147 193 194
  195
KENTUCKY 10 12 46
KERCHEVILLE -- 53 55
KERNAN John 188
KEY John 62 Thomas 12 13 29
KILEBRO Mary 111
KILLET James 14
KIMBLE/KIMBELL James 91 Joseph 7
  10 12 13 17 19 21 26 28 29 36 41 43
  44 47 59 63 68 80 81 90 108 109 115
  117 124 128 129 135 136 139 141-143
  150-154 157 158 162 165 167 171-179
  181 197 198 Mr 76
KIMBRO Nathaniel 157
KIMES Michael 94
KING Benjamin 140 James 116 John 53-
  55 81 87 91 93-95 104 109 137 144
  165 Madison 185 Martha 137 Nathan-
  iel 80 Samuel 45 51 52 92 96 104 116
  122 128 129 136 145-148 159 167
  William 137 166 174 176 177
KINGSLEY Alpha 31
KIRCHEVILLE J 99 S 99
KIRK/KIRKE/KIERK James 23 29 40 63
  92 96 120 169 Jesse 18-21 23 40 47 50
  52 72 78 81 130 174 Mrs 116 122
  William 103 160 174

KISER John 69 70
KITTEL James 17
KNIGHT Thomas 33
KNOWLES -- 184
LAIN John 179
LAMPLEY Jacob 52 62 136 Joseph 52 62 117
LANCASTER John 170
LANDERS James 68
LANE Garret 145
LANIER Isaac 22 29 30 45 48 63 128 175 J 41 -- 23 24 36 40 42
LANKFORD Henry 68 123 136 159 John 69 77 Moses 85 110 117 119 Parish/Parrish 61 69 71 73 117 123 192
LANSELL Archibald 43
LARKINS James 49 51 56 63 92 115 118 127 130 137 139 140 183 187 189 190-193 John 4 21 92 105 113 115 137 138 161 170 173 190-193 Joseph 27-30 101 110 117 119 167 190-193 Robert 21 22 24 25 49 101 102 110 117-119 128 137 152 157 190-193 196
LATTIMORE Sylvanis 51
LAU John 145
LAUBER John 3
LAW John 179
LEACH/LEECH Daniel 2 21 47 49 52 62 79 104 105 111 112 121 123 130 132 138 139 159 166 170 171 173 180 181 183 186 Jacob 52 61 62 91 96 98 103 105 110 120 122 129 142 152 162 171 178 196 Joab 21 --118
LEATHERWOOD CREEK 66 76 100 130 136 182
LEE John 56
LEGGETT Henry 165
LEWIS A 94 Anderson 84 Andrew 52 75 76 82 100 131 188 189 190 George 153 174 187 194 195 John 70 129 Penelope 78 154 174 184 189 190 William 9 12 92 99 101
LIGHT George 12 15 42 45 47 Michael 47 49 76 102 104 109 134 142 165 173 180 181 183 186 Thomas 13 William 12 13 65 165
LILA (slave) 144
LILE Henry 13 Sally 127 192
LINCH John 69 77
LINDSEY/LINDSAY L 175 Levi 87 135 164 172

LINN Nathan 122
LITTLE Sally 25 Squire 25
LIVINGSTON Robert 47 51 55 57 97 102 116 127 130 137 138 145 147 169 173 174 182
LOCKER Samuel 70 129
LOCKHART Moses 32
LOFTES/LOFTIS Martin 140 156 158 172 196 Milton 140 Pheraby &c 156-158 William 68 69 75 77 81 156 157
LOGAN George 98 105 106
LOGAN COUNTY KY 10
LOMAX William 59 88 92 99 101 116 144 172
LONG Miles 103 William 89 183 184
LOVELADY Jane 126 Levi 59
LOW/LOWE John 145 Marvel 149 150
LOWEL/LOWELL Arrington 41 John 42 Nancy 41
LOWERY E 197 Elijah 175
LUCAS Edward 4 14 16 17 27 47 48 80 167 John 15 41 43 54 91 Nancy 91 Robert 10 11 52 91 William 8 9
LUCK Jacob 159
LUCKROY John 66
LUMENENAN James 58
LYLE Joseph 92 Robert 196
LYTLE Robert 98
MACK Robert 46-50
MADDIN Robert 94 95 188 190
MADLOCK James 14 21
MALLORY James 31 Wm 74
MALONE John 14 19 21
MALONEY William 92 99 101 102
MALUGIN/MALUGION &c J 92 James 93 95 104 117 124 125 189 193 Jonathan 52 87 94 130 137 139 140 Joseph 123 Thomas 117 125 128 William 165
MARABLE Ann 76 H 82 Henry 60 61 68 75 76 83 106-109 114 126 133 137 147 154 157 162 163 168 John 131 134 187 188
MARR Simon 77
MARSH Ann 91 Gilbert 91 Joel 14-18 52 68 69 75 76 82 83 91 120 124 158 178 John 21 52 54 64 72 88 187 Minor 117 124 125 158 165 Solomon/Salmon &c 68 81 87 89 110 124 129 147 152 159 160 161 173 181 183 184 186 196 197
MARTIN D 198 Daniel 122 123 131 136 144 152-154 156 167 193 194 195 197 198 J 153 James 69 77 78 105 111 112

MARTIN (continued)
  Jeremiah 153 167 173 180 182 Peter
  44 Robert 138 Samuel 92 William 82
MARY (slave) 147
MASON Edward 76 Robert 2
MASSEY/MASSIE Abijah/Abesah &c 81
  85 98 109 130 134 159 166-170 Captn
  61 86 David 130 137 139 140 Joel 57
  76 77 79 106 166 189 191 John 45
  Patsey 79
MATHEWS &c Dean 14 James 36 39 40
  76 81 82 116 136 172 Thomas 23 24
  26 31 51 55 68 76 81 100 142 William
  112 142
MATLOCK Benjamin 86 James 91 Little
  Berry 4 Luke 14 47 73
MAURY A 149 Daniel 149
MAURY COUNTY 25
MAXFIELD William 147
MAXWELL William 147 148 150 154
  162 163
MAY/MAYS Dempsey/Demsy 105 122
  165 179 Elizabeth 189 Jesse 2 15 16
  68 75 82 91 123 John 1-3 6 10 11 16
  19-21 50 51 61 69 71 73-75 77 81 92
  102 108-111 121 137 151 157 159 166
  170 171 173 189 192 Philip 122 Polly
  15 Sterling/Stirling 14 57 58 68 75 123
  188 189 Thomas 19 47 68 69 82 103
  104 117 123-126 157 159 166 170 171
  182 197
MAYSE Micajah 64
McADOO/MACADOO D 155 David 3
  14-17 24 32 63 72 87 89 97 98 100
  107 112 115 118 121 125-127 130
  134-137 144 152 155 155 156 166 175
  195 196 Eza/Ezor/Ezra 33 42 60 109
  132 133 160 167 John 2 20 60 67 69
  70 77 79 81 85 87 96 104 107-109 115
  118 119 127 135 142 144 145 152 153
  155 156 158 167 170 173 174 179 188
  194-196 Margret 81 William 27 33 64
  83 88 95 96 101-103 112 127 174 188
  189 190 192 193 194 196 197
McBRIDE John 65
McCALLISTER James 81 John 20
McCAMMON/McCAMMONS James 130
  132 155 156 181 193
McCARRELL John 32
McCASLEN Younger 88
McCAULEY/McCAULY James 8 10 39
  78 85 89 91 94 95 100 113 117 118

McCAULEY/McCAULY (continued)
  151 189 191 192 John 192
McCLELLAND Captain 135 166 Jane 110
  John 98 105 110 134 169 Malcom 111
  Nelson 47 48 98 105 110 136 142 145-
  148 150 173 186 Thomas 87-89 98 105
  106 110 131 132 138-140 144 William
  50 85 110 117 125
McCLURE A 32 Alexander 63 H 106
  Isabella 152 J 106 James 156 167
  Thomas 159 166 William 6 7 32 63
McCOLLUM James 191 Robert 92 131
  168 172 191 192 193
McCORD Elizabeth 194 James 68 80 117
  124 125 138 140 144 152 153 155 194
  196
McCORMACK &c Edward 53 106 125
  132 140 147 160 161 166 174 188 190
  191 John 159 166 170 171 173 180
  181 183 186 194
McCRACKIN Aquilla 4 -- 18
McCRARY William 56
McCREARY Joseph 196
McCRORY James 8 129 Jane 129 John
  120 Thomas 188
McCULLA John 110 142
McDANIEL James 11
McDANN Elizabeth 109
McDEARMAN Patrick 164 170 Sally 104
  116 164 170 Sarah 108 123 -- 197
McDONAL James 10
McDONNELL Duncan 65
McDOWELL Alexander 118
McDURMOND Letty 154 Patrick 154
McELYEA James 65
McFALL Samuel 132
McFARSON Ira 151
McGEE Michajah 132 Thomas 173 -- 107
McGUIRE Thomas 193 194
McKEE/McKEY Captn 86 James 4 19 33
  53 55-58 87 88 William 53 54
McKERNAN John 188
McLEOD Anguish 110
McMEANS J 20 James 13 14 19 26 28 34
McMILLAN &c Hugh 197 Robert 25 26
  27
McMINN Joseph 14
McMUNN George 152
McMURRAY/McMURRIE Robert 44 98
  Sally 129 136 152 Thomas 62 68 100
  114 115 130 136 142 155 173 192-195
  198 Washington 129 136 152 William

McMURRAY/McMURRIE (continued)
36 39 40 42 44 71 92 99-102 109 117
123 124 127-129 131 132 134-136 141
152 157 171 172 185 188-190 -- 136
McMURTRY James 6-8 19 Thomas 189
191
McNEELY Hugh 118 119 173 John 160
161 194 195 196 197
McNICHOL/McNICKLES &c William 65
82 88 136 145 154 159 163 189 190
191 192 193 194 195 196
McPHARSON Ira 87
McQUARLES Reuben 128
McRAE John 30 31 33 35 36 45 47 48 63
112 -- 23 24 40 42
McREARY Joseph 194
McSWAIN John 176
McVEY Reuben 146 153
MECK Ira 56
MEDLOCK/METLOCK James 22 64 79
103 117 125 153 159 166-170 Jno 123
172 Luke 15-18 61 69 71 112 Thomas
110 117 119
MEEK Ira 111 John 116
MEEKER Benjamin 92 169
MEIRS Simon 77
MELUGIN Joseph 60 62 151 159 162
Samuel 60
MEREDITH Samuel 169
MERICK Francis 184
MERRIT/MERIT &c C 52 Captn 135 166
H 78 84 136 187 188 191-193 195 197
198 Holloway/Holliway 49 52 57 62
64 72 74 75 78 83 89 95 101 105-107
113-115 119 120 123-126 130-132 138
140 142 155 168 183 185 189 192
Nancy 122 O 185 Or 122
Orsemus/Ansemus/Assemus 117 118
131 136 138 144 145 148 152-154 156
185 194 195 Thomas 13
METHENA/METHENY Peter 166 175
MICHEL George 9 Robert 9 -- 44
MICKLE James 142
MIERS Simon 69
MIGGS R 45
MILAM Ransom 80 142 159 Solomon 76
103 116 148 195
MILES Hardy 192
MILLER Edmond 87 Hosea 70 74 187
Isreal 45 Jacob 106 129 Jehu 64 87 88
160 161 164 188 196 John 187
Mathew 88 Sally 164 Thomas 113

MILLER (continued)
William 8 9 21 33 44 49 76 159
MILLS David 189 Gibson/Gipson 136 159
166 Peter 107 159 160 169
MISCOM Frank 82
MISSOURI/MISSOURA 111
MITCHEL George 60 67 85 110 117 129
John 1 Samuel 80 81 103 166 174 176
177 Thomas 1 60
MOCKBEE/MOCKBIE Howard 71 188
John 187 190 194 Resden 71 158 188
MOLTON Michael 6
MONDAY (slave) 17
MONTGOMERY John 14 57 67 76 95
111 120
MONTGOMERY COUNTY 20 33 43 44
60 64 66 130 142 177
MOODY Andrew 1 2 3 4
MOORE Daniel 92 98 99 101 103 107
128 144 166 174 176 177 Gully 125
Joseph 50 152 Robert 111
MORGAN James 179
MORRIS Edmond 98 Edwin 110 117 122
James 109 136 141 Joel 61 Joseph 41
43 54 59 61 67 69 86 87 91 94 104 108
109 110 135 136 176 197 198 Lucy
192 Newburn 92 99 101 136 William
61 69-74 98 102 116 136
MORRISETTE William 2 52
MORRISON Noble 113 118 186 William
71 81 82 104 123 128 130 136 151 157
173 179 187 188 197 198 -- 32
MORROW William 142
MOSLEY Jesse 105 153 William 123 128
144 152 172
MULHERIN/MULHERRIN James 25-27
MUNSEL Luke 174
MURFREE Edward 165 172
MURRELL Richard 19 80 87 92 94 145
156 164 175 Thomas 13 27 60 61 84
86 90 91 97 109-116 124 129 134 135
144 146 147 149 150 166 171 177-179
181 183 184 Wm 36 37 39 40
MURRY James 145 Wm 34 110
MYATT/MYATTE Alexander 61 69-74
Burwell 52 68 80 179 Kendrick/Kin-
dric 52 59 68 69 80 87 131 165 166
171 Matthew 68 Polly 179 R 68
Redick/Redic 61 69-74 80 130 137 144
149 150 173 181 183 184 186 Wilkie
51 Willie 129
MYERS Simon 96 115 129 152 159 162

MYER (continued)
198
MYRICK Francis 169 188 190 198
NALL Burgess 80 Daniel 59 80 86 130
  137 144 149 150 165 Nathan 4 6 7 17
  73 82 86 Oran/Orrin &c 80 81 87 89
  117 118 152-154 156 178 179 Richard
  10 12 13 191 William 175 186 197 198
NAPIER Charles 30 Col 98 179 E 146 147
  154 160 163 191 192 194 195 196 198
  Eli 190 Elias 1-3 5 10 11 13 17-19 23
  26 35 40 42 45 49 58 63 71 78 81 83
  89 90 100 107 111 125 132 145 147-
  149 153 154 159 164 175 176 179 183
  184 186-190 193 195 197 F 32 George
  2 12 13 15 18 19 52 62 63 80 144 145
  158 160 164 175 177 187 197 198 H
  64 194 Harry 13 Henry 2 13 45 53 68
  72-74 84 105 113 120 132 134 138-
  141 144 155 161 183 185 188 192 193
  196 198 J 61 67 98 108 156 164 167
  173 174 179 James 52 96 101 105 123
  157 190 John 15 16 23 24 36 37 39 45
  53 58 59-64 66 69 70 72 74 79 83 84
  86 90 96 99 101 103 104 106 107 109
  115 121 126 127 130-132 134 135 138
  144 150 157-159 161 162 166 168-171
  175 176 177 179-181 185-187 190 192
  198 Mary 177 R 57 67 78 87 109 135
  141 177 181 188-190 192 193 Richard
  2 4 9 10 17 19 28 30 34 38 40 41 44-
  46 49 61 63 66 71 73 84 99 125 136
  145 168 169 172 179 191 Susan 35
  Thomas 1 2 12 13 15 18 20 22 32
NASHVILLE TN 103 109 122 172
NATCHEZ TRACE 85
NEBLETT Jehu 20
NEEL Joseph 166
NEELY Elisha 169
NEILY Charles 80
NELSON Robert 17 22 William 107
NESBITT/NISBITT Andrew 147 154 198
  Captain 60 86 110 Eliza 158 James 63
  68 92 135-138 140 141 150 152 160
  161 166 173 174 180 182 Jeremiah 23
  82 109 110 152 167 168 170 176 179
  186 197 198 John 8 9 15 19 20 22 27
  49 51 70 71 79 87 102 107 108 189
  190 Joseph 44 69 72 77 78 197 Mar-
  grit/Margaret 188 189 Moses 51 158 N
  67 79 90 102 Nathan 50 53-55 57-61
  63 71 74 75 82-86 90 92-94 96 98 103

NESBITT/NISBITT (continued)
  108 111 112 123 128 130 147 154 176
  Robert 16 21 51 55 69 77 78 92 117
  124 125 127 130 131 134 136 137 144
  147 149 150 152 194 197 198 Samuel
  107 Thomas 8 9 36 39 40 69 81 87 89
  92 109 116 134 152 158 162 173
  William 158 -- 118
NEVIN David 193
NEW ORLEANS 45
NEWSOM Ellis 164 William 10 13
NIBLETT/NIBTELL John 12 15 20 21
  Sterling 21
NICHOL John 175
NIMMAS Allen 21
NIXON -- 32
NOLAND/NOLEN James 66 John 56 73
  104 Phillip 92 119 169 Thomas 55 73
  77
NOONER Gediah 105 111 112
NORMAN Nathan 6 54 65
NORRIS Alfred 80 82 166 Jane 60 Jesse
  82 88 169 Robert 76 142 Susannah 76
  142
NORSWORTHY Thomas 81 William 81
  98 105 117 124 125 155 158 173 181
  183 186 Willis 48 59 70 96 108 109
  116 128 129 151 152 156 158 159 162
  173 179 186 195 196
NORTH CAROLINA 10 107 139 140
NORTHERN/NORTHEN/NORTHREN
  John 10 14 16 32 62 Peter 169
NOTHERING/NOTHERN John 8 63
OGBURN J 186
OLIVER George 112 120 166 174 198
ORGAN Benjamin 21
ORMSBY Robert 188 189
OUTLAW William 20
OVERTON Elizabeth 91 Gabriel 80 124
  Moses 91 92 Rebecca 75 William 124
  158 178
OWEN David 187
OWENS Henry 145 154
OWINGS Daniel 34 41
PACK Benjamin 153 157 179 188 191
  196 198
PAIN David 171
PALMER Eliza 183 Henry 183 Thomas
  64 66 81 97 115 118 127 152 183

❖   ❖   ❖

PALMYRA road 151
PALSNER Thomas 159
PANNELL Thomas 8 10
PARKER Daniel 51 129 Edward 92 Esaph
  4 John 69 81 85 87 89 98 109 136
  Joseph 187 Moses 4 50 75 79 92 123
  William 1 2
PARMER Isham 8 Thomas 61
PARR John 192
PARREL John 143
PARRISH/PARISH Captain 60 86 110
  135 Eleanor 34 42 45 46 73 74 49 57
  72 76 78 89 93-95 99 100 102 108 110
  121 126 133 188 189-193 Elinor 165
  180 Eliza 180 Elkana 44 133 Ezekel
  180 Hasted 76 Hewel/Huel/Hughell 31
  32 44 87 97 106 115 123-125 128 131
  135 144 157 159 165 166 172 177-181
  Kendley 55-57 Jane 180 John 180
  Thomas 82 Wyatt 50 51 100 115 123
  165 178 180
PARROT John 23 24 25 104
PARTINS CREEK 152
PASCAL/PASCHAL Elisha 194 196
PASKEL Elizabeth 140
PASSMORE David 14 15 17 18 23-25 29
  30 57 112 113 130 131 135 158 191
  192 Passmore Creek 96
PATTERSON James 79 191 John 136 137
  151 173 Robt 128 130 Wm 81
PAXTON Thomas 129
PAYNE Joseph 85 166 174 175 193 194
  Pryor 59 87 108 135 158
PEACOCK Robert 196 Wm 11 12 17
PEARSALL Benjamin 23 24 69 Edward 6
  Jeremiah 1 4 6 7 23
PEARY John 68
PEDEER Jesse 85
PEELER Jacob 81
PENDERGRASS J 87 108 138 152-
  154 185 John 50 59-61 69 10 72 74 75 84
  86 96-98 103 105 106 109-111 115
  117 127 130 134 135 138 140 141 143
  144 156 157 159 160-162 165 167-171
  173 175 177 178 179 181 183 192 197
  198 Lucreacy 69 William 87 91 93-95
  101 111 136 138 144
PENNEL Thomas 63
PENRICE William 14 19
PEPPERS Daniel 84
PERKINS/PURKINS Daniel 20 31 136
  Eben 36 Edwd 36 123 136 Thos 11 30

PERRY John 115 136 159 173 Tel-
  man 91 122 William 178
PETERS Lemuel 32
PETERSON Robert 32 136
PETTY Ambrose 122 128 136 145-148
  Ebenezer 112 Gabriel 51 68 105 119
  128 177 James 92 122 128 Jane 165
  Jonathan 128 John 115 116 122
  Samuel 119 128 158 167 Solomon 128
  131 158 Thomas 81 87 88 89 91 105
  110 122 128
PHEREBY (slave) 69
PICKERING Charles 198
PICKETT Edward 8 9 74 Jacob 80 John
  47 49 52-55 62 90 103 115 131 133
  162 196 Peter 80
PIFFIN John 52 Polly 52
PINE RIVER 52 177
PINEGAR Leonard 158 167 179
PINER James 110
PINEY CREEK 66 167 180
PINSER William 21
PIPKINS Stewart 143
PLANT John 189 Williamson 104
PLUNKET Holden 65
POINIER James 116
PONDER/PONDERS Archibald 60 68 75
  85 194 196
POOL Joshua 178 William 98
POPE Burton 87
PORTER Beverly 121 125 148 149 Elijah
  120 156 163
POWELL Esther 48 George 1 8 9 31 53
  55-58 Richard 48
POWERS Barney 169 William 14 15 16
  18 47 116
PRATOR Brice 69
PRICE Drury 41-44 67 68 92 104
  108-110 123 124 128 135 James 116 141
  170 176 John 56 Jonathan 92 Joshua
  92 108 110 142 154 164 170 Thomas
  92 110 142 154 164 170 Willis 92 108
  110 142 154 164 170
PRIESTLY James 104 114 120 125 126
  134
PRINCE Bayless 14 27
PRYOR Benjamin 5
PUCKETT Jacob 76 82 83 85
PUGH -- 20
PULLEN/PULLIN Archibald 51 96
  101 102 136 144 149 150 158 165 166
  177 179 181

PURSLEY John 40 44 46 47 57
QUARLES Moses 49
QUINN Mathew 15 16 18
RAGAN Graves 117 118 173 H 82 Hosea
  91 98 116 Jesse 14 36 81 82 151 159
  162 Lewis 1 Nathan 50 61 69-74 166
  William 98
RAGAN BRANCH 142
RAMSEY -- 48
RAPE/RAPER Gustave/Gustavis 73 149
  192 195 Jacob 73 188
RAWORTH -- 5
RAY John 49
RAYBURN/RAIBOURN B 84 Benjamin
  49 78 Elizabeth 78
RAYMON Eleakun 58
RAYNOD Eliakim 59
READ David 100 107 James 10 11 29 32
  141 John 2 5 14 24 25 28 31 33 38 43
  45 57 62 84 91 99 190 Lemuel/Lamuel
  53 55 57 58 64 66 136 144 152-154
  156 182 189 190 William 62 -- 40
READDEN William 23
REDDING/REDING John 52 62-64 66 80
  92 Nancy 119
REEDER Levi 165 169
REFORD John 24
REYBOURN -- 94
REYNOLDS Captain 61 86 110 166
  Caroline 138 Catherine 197 Clinton
  138 142 Hanna 197 James 38 John 71
  72 98 105 130 136 138 142 167 176
  177 188 Mark 15-18 23-25 60 75 77-
  79 93 102 106 120 132 138 139 142
  146 155 176 177 180 185 188-191
  Melenton 160 161 S 60 Susannah 167
  176 177 197 198 Thomas 88 William
  52 57 60 82 94 95 110 116 122 128
  130 136 138-140 145-148 160 168-170
  173 176 177 187 189 190 191 193-195
  197 198
REYNOLDSBURGH 60 68 76 97 103
  142 149 172
RHEN John 138
RHUE John 47 138 139 140 157
RICE Green 154 175 Thomas 53 55-58 60
  136
RICHARDSON/RICHESON A 184
  Augustin/Austin 36 51 130 137 139
  140 159 Clinton 191 Frankey 87 Henry
  59 James 87 Jordan 76 83 128 136 L
  74 Lebius/Lebuour &c 31 60 87 101

RICHARDSON/RICHESON (cont)
  Lewis 155 196 197 Samuel 144 Seth
  76 83 Squire 116 122 134 165 Stith
  128 Thomas 61 66 69-74 80 124 127
  134 Wineford 190
RIGHT George 124 John 50 Nelly 135
  136 William 116
RILEY Samuel 81
RINER Charles 16 John 16 21 101
RIVERS Jones 111
ROACH Edward 64 112 158 187 191
ROBERTS A 142 Augustine 63 97 122
  123 130 147 160 190-192 David 138
  James 110 117-120 John 9
ROBERTSON Abraham 8 12 13 65 169 B
  179 Benjamin 168 185 C 25 49 53 104
  159 160 188 191 192 197 198 Christopher 1 5 13 26-32 36 40-43 45 47 48
  52 54 57 63 70-72 77 83 111 113 116
  119 132 137 145 148 155 168 170 171
  174 175 179 180 184 185 198 David
  172 192 193 Duncan 34 Henry 149
  162 James 4 6 7 47 John 65 M 24
  Michael 4 6 7 143 Peyton 111 Ryton
  91 Williamson 34 -- 45 Robertsons
  Hotell 14
ROBERTSON COUNTY 6 125
ROE Richard 158
ROGERS Callum 166 James 51 66
  76 91 104 Joel 115 John 191 192 Joseph
  173 Josiah 103 148 158 172 178 190
  Michael 130 137 139 140 Robert 51 68
  79 89 92 107 111 133 140 181 191
  Samuel 48 189 190 191 -- 102
ROLAND Willis 65
ROOK Daniel 30 John 174
ROSE Alexander 42 51 95 98 121 126 127
  164 Daniel 143 Mary 164
  Moran/Meran 157 159 Moreau 174
ROSS Daniel 144 185 George 22 83 129
  Hugh 106 James 12 53 55 64 68 71 74
  105 115 117 118 124 125 129 144 162
  166 174 176 177 179 180 183 186 191
  Jesse 5 52 Thomas 188 William 54
ROY Ephraim/Ephriam 59 60 118 119
  173 197 198 John 48 92 99 101 109
  147 148 William 116
RUE John 52 130
RUND William 101
RUSHING David 88 188 189 Jacob 29 36
  37 39 40
RUSSELL/RUSSEL James 7 Jesse 2 31

RUSSELL/RUSSEL(continued)
  42 45 61 69-74 Lemuel/Lamuel 47 85
  87 88 98 117 134 152 173 Samuel 110
  119 Tandy 5
RUTHERFORD James 32
RUTLEGE Ann 89 156 195
RYBURN Benjamin 140
RYE Benjamin 68 81 Joseph 42 43
  Solomon 33 Tristram &c 194-196
  William 19 51 53 54 96 103 113 116
  122 142 151 159-161 173 178 195-197
SAINSING Archibald 142 Harry 142
  Henry 169
SALMON James 81
SALMONS CREEK 66 73 74 129
SAMIL Archibald 81
SAMPSON Samuel 108
SANDERLIN Willson 151
SANDERS Benjamin 91 109 157 166 174
  176 177 John 131 132 158 Turner 24
  31 43
SANDERSON Jacob 76 129 152 159 162
  198
SANSELL/SANIEL Archibald 41 81
SANSOM/SANDSOM Barbary 187 D
  117 R 138 189 192 195 Richard 49 86
  89 90 99 101 102 112 113 119 120 122
  138 139 152 159 161 168 176 185
  187-190 William 18 21 86 116 135
  136 137 141 148 156 157 159 160 164
  169 176 177 181 182 184 185 186 187
SARA/SARAH (slave) 93 144
SAUL Joseph 40
SAUNDERS Benjamin 134 135
SAUNDERSON Jacob 69
SAWYERS Dampsey 66
SCHMIDT F 152 Frances 5
SCHMITTOE/SCHMITTON Francis 72
  95 102 Thomas 84
SCHNTTS Francis 7
SCOTT Alexander 129 J 111 James 55
  John 6 9 11 53 54 58 65 Mary 129 N
  111 195 Nehemiah 2 26 31 49 51 56
  66 69 77 87 92 94 101 102 110 113
  114 123 124 127-132 135 138 155 156
  158 166 170 173 195 Rosamond 65
SCROGGINS John 116
SEAL/SEALS James 104 126 Jesse 52 Jno
  60 137 Palatire/Palatina 58 104 126
  Peter 60 William 57
SEAMORE Alsey/Aulsey 53 55-58 68 80
SEARCY B 14 Bennett 4-8 Robt 15

SEARS Emsley/Emsly 60 136
SEISSILY (slave) 91
SELF Abraham 60 62 98 105 106 112 142
  181 191 198 Abram 54 187 James 116
  Peter 61 81 151 178 Samuel 52 61-63
  68 81 91 104 144 152-154 156
SELLAND John 151
SELLERS John 136 Saml 76 82 123
SEMORE Alsey 52
SETTLER Isaac 168
SEYARS Emsley 51
SHADDOCK John 169
SHAKEFORD Roger 78
SHARON Thomas 184
SHARP Maxwell 10
SHAW Thomas 106 -- 191
SHEARON T 198 Thomas 108 112 116
  129 133 135 137 144 145 155 158 163
  167 173 177 179 183 William 122
  177-179 -- 118-121 125 126 141 150
  162 182 194
SHELBY Wm 135-137 157 166 171
SHELBY COUNTY TN 81
SHELTON Archibald 14 61 69 Elisha 65
  Elizabeth 58 181 James 52 Robert 59
  87 William 10 11 51 116 174
SHEPHERD Simpson 180
SHIGOG William 131
SHIPMAN Jacob 88 90 117
SHOAT John 24
SHORE Reubin 11
SHOULDER STRAP CREEK 60 66
SHOUSE Joseph 136 143 144 149 150
SHROPSHIRE David 1 38 46 48
  130 171 Hudson/Hutson 52 62 87 89 92
  94 122 179
SHUTE John 148
SILVA (slave) 145
SIMMONS Elisha 6 Thomas 15 19 22 23
  45 51 67 86
SIMMS William 142
SIMPSON John 87 105 111-114 Nathaniel
  51 81 103 173 Samuel 158 193
  Thomas 2 17 18 22 William 50 51 81
  116 117 124 125 128 159 162 166
  167-169 178 181 183 193 197
SINGLETON James 111
SINKS Henry 103 Jesse 65 142 169 Powel
  60 110 115 178
SINSING John 156
SIZEMORE James 178
SKELTON Archibald 27 100 107 117 125

SKELTON (continued)
    136 144 John 123 Robert 109 135
SLADER/SLATEN William 62 179
SLAUGHTER Thomas 120
SLAYDEN/SLAYDON William 34 93
    116 128 173 180 184
SLY Jacob 145 Sarah 145
SMART John 72
SMELLY John 160 183
SMELTON Francis 71
SMITH Bartholomew 8 9 36 51 David 59-
    61 75 78 79 86 91 96 97 101 108 109
    127 130 131 132 135 157 158 171
    Drury 87 Eleazor 2 Elisha 60 68 75 80
    98 105 145 156 157 194 196 Francis
    33 George 91 94 111 115 118 126 134
    144 173 178 James 81 93 100 105
    Jesse 97 135 158 John 30 134 158 160
    165 166 Mrs 87 Mumford 47 86 104
    128 130-132 137 139 144 145 156 157
    158 160 172 Nancy 158 159 Rebecca
    158 159 Sally 168 170 186 197 198
    Samuel 20 32 56 89 91 191 Stephen
    144 Thomas 69 77 143 144 152 155-
    158 163 166 170 171 180 188
    Tryphence/Trefina 51 79 Washington
    116 William 173 -- 159
SMITTOE/SMITTON F 188 192-194
    Francis 71 75-78 84 93-95 100 113
    117 118 124 131 138 139 167 176 177
    185 189-192 197 198
SNEED Achilles 174
SOOTEN William 137
SOOTER Isabella 91 Wm 137 143
SOUTHERLAND/SUTHERLAND
    Alexander 53 55 57 58 103 128 Eli
    159 166 170 171 George 53 54 71 94
    98 105 Henry 157 Jane 63
    89
SOWELL Jno 44 51 81 91 101 Lewis 81
    91 143 Newby 81 Newton 51
SPARKS Samuel 2 41 43 99
SPEIGHT Albert 51 61 69 71 73 173
    Alsey 87 92 94 104 152 173 Jesse 160
    161 183 184 John 187 William 187
SPENCER Clark/Clarke 8 9 27 31 43 59
    85 109 110 137 184 Daniel 136 John
    10 11 20 21 24 29-31 43 78 100 188
    Samuel 11 William 110 184
SPICER Claiborne 23 Joseph 165
SQUIRES Francis 119 Robert 119
STACKER John 144

STAFFORD John 8 10 11 31 76 82
    102 116
STAILEY/STALEY William 82 92
STANDLEY John 10
STANDS William 3
STANFIELD Abraham 34
STEEL/STEELE Elizabeth 58 Robert 102
    141 180 -- 163 171 177
STEWART Andrew 53 59 61 75 82 87 88
    198 B 88 Elisha 53 54 Jehugh 3 Judith
    88 John 17 128 136 187 188 Robert 54
    Thomas 9 15 16
STEWART COUNTY 5 26
STINET John 136
STONE Hardeman 45 Henry 8 10 41-43
    John 31 44 51 69 81 110 143 164 175
    Marble 5 14 21 27 30 32 33 36 39 48
    63 66 William 11 12 17 52
STORY Henry 159 John 159 193-195
    Littleton 159 166 Samuel 8 9 27
STRANGE Rebeca 59 William 59
STRAUD Acles/Aculas 5 6 9 Jesse 5 6 11
STREET Moses 36 39 40 61 97 123 130
    137 144 149 150
STRICKLAN/STRICKLIN Duke 107
    Lodwick 100 107
STRINGER Edward 110 Joseph 11
STRONG C 33 96 196 197 Christopher 29
    38 42 50 68 80 81 123 171 -- 179
STROUD/STROWD/STROWND
    Acles/Aculas 1-3 12 Isaac 173 Jesse 3
    81 91
STUART Duncan 66 John 17 Thomas 8-
    10 14-18
STURDEVANT/STERDEVANT B 79
    188 Benjamin 51 60 61 67 68 72-74
    76-79 82-84 86 90 91 95 97 98 100
    106 110 111 114 133 164
SUGG Aquilla 54 Howel 54 Josiah 54
    Mary 54 Nancy 54 Noah 51 54 61 69
    71 73 Sally 54 William 54
SULLIVAN/SULLIVANT Daniel 129
    George 28 59 91 98 110 122 165 184
    197 198 Jeremiah 53 129 Jesse 20 32
    John 144 190 Orrin 92 111 112 Owen
    105 William 9 Williamson 193-195
SULPHER FORK 66 89 103 122 169
SUMMERVILLE John 34 37-39 41
SUMNER COUNTY 34 169
SWEANY Alexr 174 Bernard 174 Fanny
    174 Maria 174 Susanna 174 SWIFT
    Absalom 157 169 Susannah 103

SWEANY (continued)
    Thomas 61 69 72 103 104 142 143
TALLY David 40 46 John 11
TANNEHILL Wilkins 28 William 38
TANNER Samuel 61
TATE/TAIT James 68 151 152 160 196
    197 Larkin 172 Samuel 67 151 William 157 159
TATOM/TATUM Captain 110 135 166
    Delila 46 Eaton 106 153 George 81 86
    87 89 127 129 Green 164 James 41 43
    51 56 61 70 72-74 81 98 103 110 115
    117-120 138 143 164 172 178 188
    John 23-25 46 47 56 62 112 181 187
    188 Richard 41-44 53 54 86 110 115
    164 187 Sarah 13 Stephen 56 129 178
    Wilkins 64 66 138 153 155 170 William 2 10 11 14-17 19 21 55 57 61 68
    70-75 77 78 82 86 88 93 108 124 127
    130 134 135 137 142 144 146 149-151
    158 181
TAUGE William 52
TAYLOR/TALOR Claibourne 74 Daniel
    48 49 74 Drury 69 76 77 116 117 158
    165 173 Edward 175 186 George 158
    Gibson 142 173 Highram 67 Isaac 74
    James 74 Jesse 96 97 103 Lewis 74
    William 28 29 68 74 96
TEAGARDEN William 57 -- 40
TEAGUE/TEAUGE William 123 130 132
    158 160
TEAL Charles 1 29 Edward 5 7 28 29 41
    43 49 52 63 73 89 174 George 15-17
    23 24 26 29 174 John 128
TEAS Ellis 124
TEDFORD Captain 166 James 168
TERRELL Thomas 186
TERREN Charles 189
THARP Calvin 178
THEDFORD/THEADFORD Captain 60
    86 110 135 James 14-18 37 80 98
THOMAS Augustine 170 B 196 Benjamin
    11 14 18 21 148 183 195 196 James 32
    34 36 42 44 45 58 70 90 189 Jesse 179
    Lewis 195 Mary 173 Robert 69
    Samuel 72 88 188 Stephen 97 173 178
    Walker 154 165 171 194 William 20
    21 23 27 34 41 81 159 163 183 187
THOMASON -- 18
THOMPKINS Silas 59
THOMPSON Amos 52 74
    Augustin/Austin 111 138 144 154 164

THOMPSON (continued)
    173 181 186 Captn 135 C 197 Charles
    4 6 7 31 32 51 59 61 69 71 73 74 87 92
    108 135 155 164 175 189 197 D 59
    James 23-25 47 90 105 169 189 Jeremiah 166 John 163 197 Lewis 147 153
    160 161 195 196 Robert 3 Sally 196
    Sherrod/Shared 61 69-72 74
THORN/THORNE James 127 169 John
    73 74 81
THORNTON Easter 194 196 Josiah 140
    145 156-158 194 196 Mark 145 194
    Pheriba 196 Reuben 194 196
TIDFORD Captain 145
TICER Ellis 152
TIDWELL Aquilla 14-18 21 85 97 98
    Captain 60 86 110 135 166
    Edmond/Edmund 27 85 91 92 97 98
    123 143 Francis 68 98 111 136
    Isaiah/Isiah 67 98 103 178 James 27 57
    86 97 117 130 165 192 John 85 92 98
    99 101 136 152 165 Levi 50 97 104
    165 Nancy 59 87 Richard 27 Silas 143
TILLY George 159 166 170 171 184
TIMS John 153
TIPTON COUNTY TN 167
TODD Lucy 174 Thomas 174
TOLAND Jacob 105 Jonan 105 110
TOLAR/TOLER Daniel 48 132 176 192-
    194 196 John 42 58 71 106 113 116
    136 138 146 155 157 159 173 174 181
    183 184 186 189 191-194
TOMPKINS Isaac 19 105 111 112 123
    Silas 87 108 135 164
TOWN CREEK 86 130
TOWNSEND Thomas 10
TREBLE Alfred 61 Shadrack 61
TRIBBLE/TRIBLE Absolam 11-13 28 46
    48 51 52 92 98 105 106 109 116 118
    119 129 152 172 George 22 Jesse 11-
    13 27 28 37 44 46 48 66 181
TROUSDALE James 183
TUBB Elias 79 86 106 189 191 George 19
    22 29 32 42 44 47 52 61 62 104 105
    121 136 152 159 162 Isaac 28 36
    James 76 82 105 106 111 112 123 130
    132 189 190 John 189 Nathan 21 29 30
    33 47 62 63 80 85 91 104 109 121 123
    130 132 136 159 166 170 171 Samuel
    14-19
TUCK William 92
TUCKER Hansil 176 Henry 159 John 80

TUCKER (continued)
   116 173
TUNSTALL Peyton 57
TURKEY CREEK 131 167
TURLEY William 80
TURNBULL CREEK 3 66 122 169
TURNER/TERNER Captain 60 86
   Charles 164 Elisha 93 179 188 189
   Elizabeth 82 H 126 127 129 130 137
   138 141 142 153 157 166 193 197 198
   Howard 59 76 82 85 86 92 97 100 108
   109 110 115 121 123 126 129 135-138
   141 142 150 172 176 178 191 193 194
   John 23-25 59 69 75 77 81 91 95 96
   126 156 S 156 Samuel 15 16 18 39 59-
   63 74 77 79 86 90 91 95-99 101 102
   104 108 109 110 115 117 119 121-124
   126-128 134 135 137 140-142 150 151
   156 157 166 168 171 185 193 198
   Sumrel 52 William 4 26-28 30 42 50
   54 80 82 87 89 93-95 98 105 106 115
   117 124 125 137 144 145 166 172
   174-177 179 183 184 186
TYCER/TYSOR Ellis/Ellys 14 19 22 83
   159 162
UNDERHILL Daniel 105
UNDERWOOD Sally 198 Wiley 60
   William 60
VADEN Peterson 65
VALENTINE Benjamin 27 Hardy 6
VANCE Andrew 73 Samuel 2 42
VANHOOK A 133 Aaron 2 10 11 51 52
   61 68 69 74 94 133 157 Amonder 123
   Ashburn/Asburn 61 123 144 152 153
   156 Ashel 36 39 40 Lucy 68 157
   Robert 62 68 75 81 104 130 137 144
   149-151 159-161
VANLEER/VANLIER/VANLER A 54 58
   Anthony 22 26 37 38 39 40 44 78 119
   128 175 187 B 58 Bernard 54 Samuel
   137 144 W 161 -- 16 19 48
VANN Henry 100 107 Melisa 100 107
VARNAL William 189
VARNER Howard 90
VAUGHN James 66 Powell 43
VERNON TN 60 103 116 142 164
VICK Rowland 174
VICTOR Joseph 191
VINCENT James 62 63
VINEYARD/VINYARD George 46 50
   John 161 Patience 46 50
VINGOK -- 40

VIRGINIA (state) 76
VOORHEES/VOORHIES J 198 Jacob 66
   141 163 164 169 176 183 184 -- 148
   150 162 180
WADKINS James 178 John 19 22 Richard
   178
WAKE COUNTY NC 139
WALKER Berryman 142 Elijah 136 137
   144 149 150 Elizabeth 79 97 104 108
   124 150 155 158 G 142 George 68 79
   104 109 116 123 124 129 135 150 155
   157 158 Gorden 39 Isaac 16 64 116
   Jacob 65 79 104 108 116 150 155
   James 3 76 98 103 116 122 123 130
   137 142 143 145-148 John 16 27 32-34
   36 38-40 42 44 60 61 74 75 153 160
   167-169 Thomas 88 Willis 10 11 14 19
   53 55 56-58 117 125 -- 20 40
WALL Burgess/Burges 62 143 172
WALLACE/WALLICE Benjamin 21
   William 93 100 107
WALTON -- 32
WARD Jesse 50 193 194 William 3 6 31
   49 56 68 78 93 98 100 110 117 119
   130 159 161 188
WARDEN Francis 169 John 189
WARREN Caleb 100 107 John 107
WASHBURN Hiram 60
WATERS John 164
WATKINS John 92 99 101-103
WATSON James 8 65 151 155 164
   Matthew 180 Richard 169 Robert 78
   189 190 191 Thomas 7 70 77 157 163
   William 60
WATTS Edward 79
WAUGH Richard 51 61 63 123 133 144
   152 173 176 182
WEAKLEY/WEAKLY John 154 156
   Robert 1 3-6 9 10 12 14 86
WEAMS John 49
WEAVER Adam 122 Hartwell 92 123
WEBB James 167 Robert 65
WEBSTER Joseph 20 26 28
WEEKS William 20
WEEMS John 47 116 188
WELDON John 165
WELDRON John 151 158
WELLS Allen/Allin 128 153 155 Henry
   67 68 72 84 86 88-90 106 113 114 117
   164 169 175 176 197 John 120 121
   192 195 M 127 Morgan 76 82 106 114
   117 121 126 191 192 Rachel 1 2 5 12

WELLS (continued)
   13 Robt 128 Thomas 162 163 -- 86
WERT Henry 93 188
WEST Archibald 178 G 68 143 George 32
   46 48 55 86 90 115 124 137 144 157
   158 172 176-178 Henry 74 Isaac 51 53
   55 138 143 144 167 190 James 32-34
   38 43 47 82 124 137 144 151 157 158
   176-178 John 40 47 51 92 99 101 105
   110 111-114 132 136 Levina 137 Mary
   90 177 Napolian 170 Polly 55 68 115
   143 172 Robert 4 68 73 75 79 81 91 99
   102 106 108-110 115 117 119 124 130
   134 136 145 151 157 158 171 197 198
   Samuel 110 128 131 132 173 180 181
   183 186 Sarah 132 William 19 20 21
   79
WHARTON John 112
WHEATON Daniel 66 169
WHITE Charles 92 99 101 102 116 158
   James 117 124 125 John 158 Joshua 36
   39 40 110 123 136 Moses 103 117 124
   125 128 130 137 144 146 149 166 174
   176 177 William 10 20 61 75 77-79 82
   84 86-88 90 95-98 103 105-110 117
   138 140 141 144 160 162 165 166 171
   173 177 179 181 183
WHITEHEAD Ebenezer 50 75 104 Richard 49 104 132 192 193 Robert 110
   Samuel 81 Sidney 178 -- 151
WHITEWILL Robert 31
WHITINGTON William 142
WHITLEDGE Robert 49 52 124 137
WHITMILL Thomas 30 41-44 47
WHITWELL Robert 51 81 173
WICKHAM William 189 190
WIGGINS Cary 6 41-44 46 57 67 76
WIGHT A 120 121 148 163 Augustin 125
WILEY Azor 80 David 60 75 80 E 68
   Ebenezer 75 Joseph 81 Josiah 68 80
   William 60
WILKERSON John 60 65
WILKINS A 98 Alexander 8 9 60 64 92
   96 105 120 121 132 139 155 158 160
   163 169 Robert 123 132 Smith 121
WILKINSON/WILKISON William 9 11
WILLEY Ayer 61 Joseph 87 89 124 134
   John 8 10 44 William 10 11 91 111
   116 124 Willis 52 61 62 116 122
WILLIAMS Ailsey/Alsey 194 196 197
   Benjamin 1-3 27 116 143 178 Buckner
   17 18 Caleb 32 Charles 1-3 5 12 13 D

WILLIAMS (continued)
   50 51 53 59 61 62 64 67 74 78 79 81
   86 88 89 96 100 108 190 118 124 127
   135 137 141 150 152 154 157 167 168
   170 173 174 177 179-181 183 186-188
   193 197 Daniel 2 4 6 7 12 26 31 40 63
   66 69 84 90 94 95 101 107 113 114
   121 124 126 127 131 133-135 142 156
   162 164 171 173 179 181 183 184 186
   Edward 3 Elisha 83 127 Elsy 196
   Garland 118 H 178 J 69 198 James 33
   68 94 115 117 126 148 166 173 177
   180 193 195 John 40 122 174 176 177
   195-197 Jones 58 Joseph 2 48 64 68 92
   99 101 102 108 110 111 115 116 128
   152 155 156 157 159 162 166 195 196
   198 Major 142 Nathaniel 1-4 10 11 13
   Plummer 110 116-120 R 169 197
   Richard 35 39 48 68 76 115 142 152
   173 195 196 Robert 179 194 196 197
   Samuel 32 Sarah 111 T 109 Thomas
   68 98 103 110 115 142 145 151 188
   190 195 Tippo 116 William 21 -- 20
WILLIAMSON Burwell 34 George 23
   Thomas 99 190 Williamson Cr 152
WILLIAMSON COUNTY 20 178
WILLIS Jehu 68
WILLS Ann 177 Guilford 177 Martha 177
   Peter 107 Rachel 5
WILLEY/WILLY John 27-30 Joseph 108
   Thos 122 Willis 31 32 38-40
WILSON/WILLSON Adam 11 68 86 J
   88-90 James 11 88 117 122 125 130
   136 170 John 23 61 68 81 88 116 123
   143 169 Joseph 51 68 76 84 86 88-90
   98 102 104 108-110 128 135 154
   Robert 7 Thomas 58 73 74 79 85 143
WILSON COUNTY 34 96 138
WIM/WIMS John 32 42 80 81 102 187
   190
WINGATE Joseph 5
WINN/WINNES/WINNS John 39 44 45
   56 138
WINNEY (slave) 156
WINSTED/WINSTEAD Charles 15 16 18
   137 159
WINTERS Aaron 20
WISDOM Francis 52 81
WITLEY John 51
WOOD Mahlam/Malon 50 129 William
   130 137 144 149 150
WOODARD Edward 154 195

WOODFORD -- 32
WOODS James 163 -- 184
WOOLFOLK -- 41
WORD William 151
WORDEN John 188
WORLEY Elisha 136
WRIGHT John 103 116 142 166 172 Geo 142 151 158 Nelly 127 Richd 116

WRIGHT (continued)
   Wm 51 142 151 173 181 183 184 186
WYATT Benjamin 21 26
YELLOW CREEK 66 73-76 81 85 91 97 100 115 122 123 129 131 136 152
YOUNG Darryl 39 James 20 154 164 John 4 6 7 Parthina 146 154 Thomas 154 164 170 186

Heritage Books by Carol Wells:

Abstracts of Giles County, Tennessee: County Court Minutes, 1813–1816 and Circuit Court Minutes, 1810–1816

CD: Tennessee, Volume 1

Davidson County, Tennessee County Court Minutes, Volume 1, 1783–1792

Davidson County, Tennessee County Court Minutes, Volume 2, 1792–1799

Davidson County, Tennessee County Court Minutes, Volume 3, 1799–1803

Dickson County, Tennessee County and Circuit Court Minutes, 1816–1828 and Witness Docket

Edgefield County, South Carolina Probate Records, Boxes One through Three Packages 1–106

Edgefield County, South Carolina Probate Records, Boxes Four through Six Packages 107–218

Edgefield County, South Carolina: Deed Books 13, 14 and 15

Edgefield County, South Carolina: Deed Books 16, 17 and 18

Edgefield County, South Carolina: Deed Books 19, 20, 21 and 22

Edgefield County, South Carolina: Deed Books 23, 24, 25 and 26

Edgefield County, South Carolina: Deed Books 27, 28 and 29

Edgefield County, South Carolina: Deed Books 30 and 31

Edgefield County, South Carolina: Deed Books 32 and 33

Edgefield County, South Carolina: Deed Books 34 and 35

Edgefield County, South Carolina: Deed Books 36, 37 and 38

Edgefield County, South Carolina: Deed Books 39 and 40

Edgefield County, South Carolina: Deed Book 41

Edgefield County, South Carolina: Deed Books 42 and 43, 1826–1829

Genealogical Abstracts of Edgefield, South Carolina Equity Court Records

Natchez Postscripts, 1781–1798

Rhea County, Tennessee Circuit Court Minutes, September 1815–March 1836

Rhea County, Tennessee Tax Lists, 1832–1834, and County Court Minutes Volume D: 1829–1834

Robertson County, Tennessee Court Minutes, 1796–1807

Rutherford County, Tennessee Court Minutes, 1811–1815

Sumner County, Tennessee Court Minutes, 1787–1805 and 1808–1810

Williamson County, Tennessee County Court Minutes, July 1812–October 1815

Williamson County, Tennessee County Court Minutes, May 1806–April 1812

www.ingramcontent.com/pod-product-compliance
Lightning Source LLC
Chambersburg PA
CBHW062024220426
43662CB00010B/1459